Making History

Making History

Antiquaries in Britain
1707–2007

First published on the occasion of the exhibition 'Making History: Antiquaries in Britain, 1707–2007'

A joint exhibition organised by the Royal Academy of Arts and the Society of Antiquaries of London

Royal Academy of Arts, London
15 September – 2 December 2007

The Royal Academy of Arts is grateful to Her Majesty's Government for agreeing to indemnify this exhibition under the National Heritage Act 1980, and to The Museums, Libraries and Archives Council for its help in arranging the indemnity.

GUEST CURATOR
David Starkey

EXHIBITION CURATORS
Society of Antiquaries of London
David Gaimster
Bernard Nurse
Julia Steele

with the support of Prince Research Consultants
Eric Langham
Sarah McCarthy
Alex Patterson
David Prince

Royal Academy of Arts
Adrian Locke
Norman Rosenthal

EXHIBITION ORGANISATION
Royal Academy of Arts
Miranda Bennion

PHOTOGRAPHIC AND COPYRIGHT CO-ORDINATION
Royal Academy of Arts
Roberta Stansfield

CATALOGUE
Editors
David Gaimster
Sarah McCarthy (Managing Editor)
Bernard Nurse

Royal Academy Publications
David Breuer
Harry Burden
Claire Callow
Carola Krueger
Peter Sawbridge
Nick Tite

Copy-editing and proofreading: Rosalind Neely
Design: Esterson Associates
Printed in Belgium by Die Keure

Copyright © 2007 Royal Academy of Arts, London

Any copy of this book issued by the publisher as a paperback is sold subject to the condition that it shall not by way of trade or otherwise be lent, re-sold, hired out or otherwise circulated without the publisher's prior consent in any form of binding or cover other than that in which it is published and without a similar condition including these words being imposed on a subsequent purchaser.

All Rights Reserved. No part of this publication may be reproduced or transmitted in any form or by any means, electronic or mechanical, including photocopy, recording or any other information storage and retrieval system, without prior permission in writing from the publisher.

British Library Cataloguing-in-Publication Data
A catalogue record for this book is available from the British Library

ISBN 978-1-905711-04-8 (paperback)
ISBN 978-1-905711-03-1 (hardback)

Distributed outside the United States and Canada by Thames & Hudson Ltd, London

Distributed in the United States and Canada by Harry N. Abrams, Inc., New York

EDITORIAL NOTE
All measurements are given in centimetres, height before width before depth.

ILLUSTRATIONS
Page 2: detail of cat. 38
Pages 4–5: detail of cat. 114
Page 8: detail of cat. 17
Page 10: detail of cat. 93
Page 14: detail of cat. 5
Page 16: detail of cat. 1
Page 36: detail of cat. 19
Page 50: detail of cat. 27
Page 52: detail of cat. 39
Page 68: detail of cat. 41
Page 92: detail of cat. 74
Page 94: detail of cat. 56
Page 108: detail of cat. 77
Page 122: detail of cat. 92
Page 142: detail of cat. 113
Page 162: detail of cat. 118
Page 164: detail of cat. 126
Page 182: detail of cat. 139
Page 184: detail of cat. 135
Page 200: detail of cat. 140
Page 220: detail of cat. 153
Page 224: detail of cat. 155
Page 226: detail of cat. 156

CATALOGUE CONTRIBUTORS' INITIALS
SA   Sydney Anglo
SB   Sally Badham
DC   Derrick Chivers
JC   John Cherry
PC   Peter Cormack
SC   Stephen Calloway
CE   Christopher Evans
JF   Jill Franklin
DG   David Gaimster
TG   Tom Goskar
MH   Maria Hayward
SK   Simon Keynes
EL   Elizabeth Lewis
NM   Nicholas Mander
SMC Sarah McCarthy
BN   Bernard Nurse
AP   Ann Payne
ARP Alex Patterson
GP   Graham Parry
MP   Mike Pitts
PR   Paul Robinson
JS   Julia Steele
RS   Ray Sutcliffe
SS   Sam Smiles
TS   Tom Sharpe
PT-C Pamela Tudor-Craig
PW   Pamela Willetts
PJW Peter Woodward

ACKNOWLEDGEMENTS
Richard Abdy, Sydney Anglo, Cressida Annesley, Sally Badham, Jill Barnard, Peter Beal, Suzanne Bell, Nicholas Bennett, Claude Blair, Chris Brayne, David Brown, Stephen Calloway, Gill Cannell, Ian Carroll, Martin Carver, Wendy Cawthorne, John Cherry, Paul Childs, Derrick Chivers, Andrea Clarke, Peter Clayton, Philip Clarke, Melinda Corkery, Peter Cormack, Tim Darvill, Christopher de Hamel, Jane Ellis-Schön, Christopher Evans, Dai Morgan Evans, Jill Franklin, Andrew Fitzpatrick, Eric Fernie, Vince Gaffney, Helen Ganiaris, Graeme Gardiner, Joanna Gatcum, Tom Goskar, David Groundwater, John Hammond, Fiona Handley, Robert Harding, Maria Hayward, Ralph Jackson, Mick Jones, Simon Keynes, Stuart Laidlaw, Janet Larkin, Kevin Leahy, Sarah Lennox-Cook, Carenza Lewis, Elizabeth Lewis, Jack Lohman, Christine Longworth, Arthur MacGregor, Nicholas Mander, Barry Marsden, George McHardy, Ralph Montagu, Tim Murray, Stuart Needham, Graham Parry, Ann Payne, Melvyn Petterson, Mike Pitts, Anthony Pitt Rivers, Ian Potts, Mark Redknap, Julian Richards, Robin Richards, Paul Robinson, Tim Schadla-Hall, Tom Sharpe, Emma Shaw, Alan Slade, Sam Smiles, Lara Speroni, Michal Sofer-Frankel, the family of the late Alan Sorrell, Ray Sutcliffe, Rosemary Sweet, Chris Thomas, Pamela Tudor-Craig, Erica Utsi, Ken Walton, Jeremy Warren, Simon Wethered, Bill White, Romney Whitehead, Leslie Webster, Pamela Willetts, Thomas Woodcock, Peter Woodward.

Contents

Presidents' Foreword … 9

Making History
David Starkey … 11

The Discovery of Britain … 15
Mists of Time … 17
Graham Parry
Earliest Antiquaries … 37
Graham Parry

'To encourage the ingenious and curious' … 51
Founders and Fellows … 53
Rosemary Sweet
Collecting for Britain … 69
Bernard Nurse

Antiquaries in Action, 1707–1850 … 93
Opening the Tomb … 95
Barry M. Marsden and Bernard Nurse
Lost and Found … 109
Elizabeth Lewis
The Art of Recording … 123
Sam Smiles
Bringing Truth to Light … 143
Bernard Nurse

Antiquaries and the Arts … 163
Antiquaries and the Arts … 165
Stephen Calloway

From Antiquaries to Archaeologists, 1850–2007 … 183
The Birth of Modern Archaeology … 185
Christopher Evans
Rescuing the Past … 201
David Gaimster
Communicating the Past: From the Earth to the Airwaves … 215
Carenza Lewis
Face to Face with the Past … 221
Bill White

Stonehenge … 225
Stonehenge … 227
Mike Pitts

Endnotes … 254
Bibliography … 256
Lenders to the Exhibition … 263
Photographic Acknowledgements … 263
Index … 264

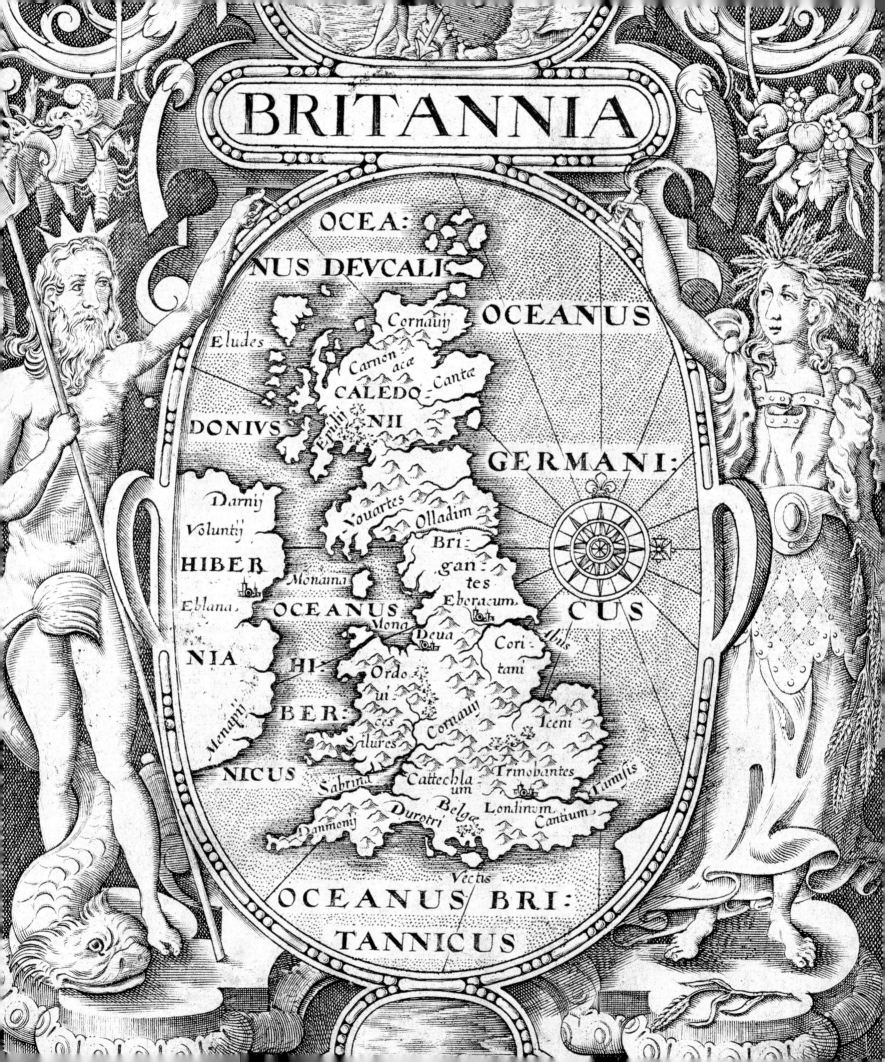

Presidents' Foreword

This spectacular exhibition, a public unveiling of the unique and historic collections of the Society of Antiquaries of London, is the focus for the tercentenary festivities of Britain's oldest learned society concerned with the study of the past. It celebrates the work and achievement of the Society's Fellowship from its foundation in the early eighteenth century to the present day.

From its earliest years, until the British Museum gradually began to assume the role in the middle of the nineteenth century, the Society was regarded as the repository for antiquities, historical documents and pictures. There is a long tradition of collecting among the Fellows, who have donated an astonishing variety of works. Today the collections contain antiquities of international importance, detailed records by notable artists commissioned by the Society of lost buildings and objects, historic royal portraits, and rare historical manuscripts. The Society has almost 2,500 Fellows around the world, working in the fields of archaeology, art and architectural history and related disciplines and serving in senior positions in public institutions as well as in private practice. In addition to its collections at Burlington House the Society owns Kelmscott Manor in Oxfordshire, the former home of William Morris, leader of the English Arts and Crafts movement.

The first public exhibition to explore the discovery, recording, interpretation, preservation and communication of Britain's past through its material footprint, 'Making History' contrasts beliefs that existed about the past before the Society was founded with new ideas, discoveries and technological breakthroughs that have transformed understanding of our island history over the past three hundred years. Through the collections of the Society, biographies of its Fellows and through key exhibits lent by museums in the regions and in London, with one important loan from the Bibliothèque Municipale at Douai, the visitor can trace each stage in the creation of Britain's historical narrative, from the first archaeological discoveries of the early modern age, through the rise of the professional historian and archaeologist in the twentieth century, to a view of how we might study the past in the future.

Many people have contributed to the realisation of this exhibition, not least its guest curator David Starkey, the celebrated historian of Britishness, who has been closely involved since the concept stage. That concept was first introduced by David Gaimster and Bernard Nurse, respectively General Secretary and Librarian of the Society, and has been developed by them in close collaboration with Norman Rosenthal and Adrian Locke of the Royal Academy of Arts. The Academy has also made available the advice of its curatorial, conservation, education, publishing, marketing and sponsorship teams. Content has been facilitated by Prince Research Consultants, notably Sarah McCarthy, Eric Langham, Alex Patterson and David Prince, while Julia Steele, the Society's Collections Officer, and Miranda Bennion of the Royal Academy have shouldered the burden of exhibition organisation and photographic co-ordination. Jayne Phenton of the Society has worked closely with Jennifer Francis of the Academy to promote the exhibition to the wider arts and heritage community and beyond. The beautiful design of the exhibition is due to Mike Stiff of Stiff and Trevillion and its installation to Dan Cowap and his team of art-handlers at the Royal Academy. We are indebted to the many Fellows and others who have assisted in the selection of works and to those who have contributed to this handsome catalogue.

No exhibition is possible without the generosity of sponsors. Grants towards conservation were received from the Leche Trust and private donations.

The Society and the Academy have long enjoyed close relations; indeed, the first individual to belong to both institutions was Sir Joshua Reynolds. The first major collaboration between one of the Burlington House learned societies and the Royal Academy, and the springboard of a programme of joint educational activities around the courtyard that will explore synergies between the arts, culture and the sciences by drawing on the combined knowledge of the learned societies' fellowships, this exhibition has converted that longstanding friendship into a real partnership.

Professor Geoffrey Wainwright MBE FSA
President, Society of Antiquaries of London

Sir Nicholas Grimshaw CBE PRA
President, Royal Academy of Arts

Making History

David Starkey

This exhibition celebrates the three-hundredth anniversary of the foundation of the Society of Antiquaries on 5 December 1707. The Society is the oldest extant antiquarian society in northern Europe. It was the first body dedicated to studying the history of Great Britain. And it has done more than any other institution to shape our view of the past, to conserve and record it, and, above all, to inspire people with passion for it.

For antiquaries do more than try to understand the past: they love it – which is one of the reasons that, like jealous lovers, they quarrel so much among themselves!

Nowadays, of course, history is central to our idea of ourselves and our society. It is an important subject in schools and universities. Museums and art galleries are arranged on historical principles, and historical books, journals and record sources fill the shelves of libraries. Family history is an absorbing hobby for millions. Millions more are regular visitors to historic houses, churches and castles. History programmes achieve high ratings on television and history books regularly top the bestseller charts.

But, at the beginning of the eighteenth century, little if any of this existed. There were no national libraries, museums or art galleries. The first university departments of history were not founded until the mid-nineteenth century, and archaeology only became a part of the university curriculum in the twentieth. This left the field pretty much open to the Society, and its extraordinary roll-call of scholars, pioneers and eccentrics.

We begin with the origins of the antiquarian movement. In one sense these are as old as humanity – the question 'where do I come from' has been asked since the beginning of recorded civilisation. But in England the question was largely answered by two major, if sharply contrasting, works. The first was Bede's *Ecclesiastical History of the English People*. This dealt with the history of the conquest of most of the former Roman province of Britain by the Anglo-Saxons and their subsequent conversion to Christianity. Using a wide range of oral, written and physical evidence, Bede constructed a clear narrative and rooted it in an accurate chronology.

This is history as it should be written. At the opposite pole was Geoffrey of Monmouth's *History of the Kings of Britain*. Written a generation or two after the Anglo-Saxons had in turn been conquered by the Normans, Geoffrey set himself to fill in the gaps left by Bede. Who had been in Britain before the Romans? And what had happened in the dark days between the fall of the Roman province and the establishment of the first Anglo-Saxon kingdoms? Actually no one knew. But that did not stop Geoffrey, who made up in imagination for what he lacked in fact. The result was a glorious tale, which began with the occupation of Britain by Trojan refugees fleeing from the sack of their native city and ended with Arthur's heroic resistance to the Anglo-Saxon foe.

It was all nonsense and was denounced as such by sharp contemporaries. But it was *compelling* nonsense, with the result that it was almost universally accepted as fact for the following four centuries *because people wanted to believe it*.

Many other European countries had similar foundation legends, though none was such powerful fiction. But most gave way before the first wave of Renaissance scholarship in the fifteenth and sixteenth centuries. In England, however, Geoffrey proved harder to dislodge. This was partly because of dynastic accident. Henry Tudor, who seized the throne in 1485, claimed descent from Geoffrey's line of British kings; he fought under Cadwallader's banner at Bosworth and even named his eldest son Arthur. More important were the peculiar circumstances of the English Reformation. Carried out by Henry's second son, Henry VIII, who succeeded him after Arthur's premature death, it marked a rupture in our history almost as profound as the Anglo-Saxon and Norman Conquests. They had overthrown peoples; this overthrew the Church. Six hundred monasteries were dissolved. A handful continued as churches, but the rest were stripped of their lead roofs and treasures and left to rot. Service books and images were mutilated, and libraries dispersed in an orgy of vandalistic desecration.

One man, John Leland (see cat. 15), tried to save something from the wreckage. In so doing, he laid the foundations of the modern antiquarian movement. He toured much of the kingdom as the cataclysm got underway and noted down what he saw; he tried to rescue important monastic books and lodge them in the King's Library, which he hoped to turn into a national research collection. And he had ambitions to do much more. He wanted to produce a catalogue of British writers, a complete peerage, county histories and topographies, collections of laws and so on. It was a programme for whole academies of scholars and entire centuries. Trying to do it all himself in a single lifetime, Leland went mad. But his hopes lived on, to set an agenda for his successors.

There is a final paradox in Leland's career. Appalled though he was at its destructive consequences for scholarship, he was a staunch supporter of Henry VIII's religious Reformation. And, as Henry found Arthur and the rest of Geoffrey's 'British history' useful for his claim for the independence of the English Church from Rome, Leland defended these too – indefensible though they were according to his own scholarly criteria. Indeed, it was not for another fifty years or more that English scholars abandoned Arthur and began instead to defend the antiquity and autonomy of the English Church on the securer ground of Bede and the Anglo-Saxons. This in turn left them free to catch up with their continental colleagues; it also opened the way to the establishment of the first, short-lived Elizabethan society of antiquaries. Its members met regularly to read papers and increasingly focused their activities round Sir Robert Cotton's magnificent library.

But all this was shipwrecked by another dispute about origins: not of the Church this time but of Parliament. It proved every bit as divisive and dangerous to the authorities, however, and the society was closed down and Cotton's library sealed up.

A century later, in 1707, comparable political upheaval formed the background to the re-establishment of the Augustan Society of Antiquaries. Seven months previously, on 1 May, Union had been proclaimed and the separate and often warring kingdoms of England and Scotland had become the new state of the United Kingdom of Great Britain. The United Kingdom was to have a new ruling dynasty from 1714, the Hanoverians, a new commitment to Protestantism and a new imperial Parliament that met with new regularity. Great Britain also enjoyed a new status in the world, having just defeated the hitherto invincible armies of Louis XIV's France at Blenheim. There were new fashions in dress, architecture and literature, and a new financial system, centring on the Bank of England. Above all, there were the new intellectual horizons opened up by Newton's physics and Locke's political theories.

This new world offered both a sense of distance from the old, and new means of understanding it. It also, for those that way inclined, lent it enchantment. And it was, I think, out of this mixture of nostalgia and a quest for knowledge that the new Society of Antiquaries of London was born. At first, it looked as though it might go the same way as the old and, for much the same reason as its hoped-for political patron Robert Harley, fell under a cloud. But the Society hung on and regular meetings resumed in 1717. They have continued ever since. In 1751 the Society was given its Royal Charter and thirty years later a fine suite of rooms at Somerset House, alongside its senior learned partner, the Royal Society, and its junior, the Royal Academy of Arts. By 1875 all three had moved again to still larger accommodation in Burlington House, Piccadilly, where the Society and the Academy still remain and where this exhibition is being held.

But, even though the Society has gone up in the world, it has also stuck to the principles of its founders. At their second weekly meeting, on 12 December 1707, they agreed that 'The Business of this Society shall be limited to the subject of Antiquities; and more particularly, to such *things* as may Illustrate and Relate to the History of Great Britain'. They then went on to gloss some of what they meant by 'things': these included 'Antient Coins, books, sepulchres or other Remains of Antient Workmanship'.

And it is this 'thinginess', above and beyond mere book-learning, which has given the Society its peculiar flavour and accounts for its unique contribution to our understanding of the past. It even shaped its meetings. Until the 1920s, the Society's principal meeting room was arranged, not like a lecture room, but like an anatomy theatre: seats were ranged around a huge table on which the 'Remains of Antient Workmanship' were placed to be discussed and anatomised like medical or scientific specimens.

Everything else, really, stems from this.

From examining antiquities, it was a short and natural step to collecting them and, from its earliest days, the Society began to acquire objects. Indeed, in default of any other art galleries or museums, it became a sort of collector of last resort. It bought or was given early royal portraits, like Hans Eworth's splendid painting of Mary I (cat. 53), that would later be the preserve of the National Portrait Gallery. It built up collections of medieval and prehistoric artefacts (like cats 83, 71) that the British Museum, then snobbishly focused on the Classical world, rejected as uninteresting for the first century of its existence. It painstakingly recorded buildings, tombs and paintings, like an early National Monuments Record, and published the results in a magnificent series of engravings and lithographs (like cats 112–16).

It is these early collections of the Society, rarely seen in public and filled with treasures, that form the basis of the present exhibition. But the exhibition is also about our idea of the past and how it was formed. Here again the Society was central.

Fundamental is our ability to visualise the past. From the beginning, as we have seen, the Society was interested in recording the things its members studied. And to do so it employed the services of a notable series of engravers and painters, including George Vertue, James Basire and the great J. M. W. Turner himself. A special size of paper, still known as 'Antiquarian', was milled to accommodate the huge, detailed prints the Society commissioned. Many of these reproductions are things of extraordinary beauty in themselves. But their importance goes beyond the merely aesthetic. The images the Society selected – the Field of Cloth of Gold (cat. 112) or the Coronation Procession of Edward VI (cat. 114) – by their very frequency of reproduction have helped to shape our image of the past. Many, too, record things which have vanished: like the ring of Mary, Queen of Scots (cat. 86); or the wall-painting on which much of our knowledge of the sinking of the *Mary Rose* depends (cat. 113); or the wall-decorations of St Stephen's Chapel and the Painted Chamber in the Palace of Westminster (cat. 106). These had been progressively damaged after Parliament's post-Reformation takeover of the Palace and were destroyed utterly in the great fire that consumed the rambling complex of buildings in 1834. They are among the most glorious works of art of medieval England. But they would have vanished without trace had the Society not recorded them.

As indeed would much more of the Middle Ages. For the Society's Fellows were pioneers in appreciating the medieval at a time when most refined taste regarded it merely as a barbarous interlude between the Classical world and the revival of Antiquity in the Renaissance. Members of the Society produced detailed measured drawings of the great cathedrals; studied their architecture and classified it into the stylistic periods we still use: Norman, Early English, Decorated and Perpendicular; and campaigned to protect their fabric from over-zealous and destructive 'restoration'. The result culminated in a revolution of taste, in which the gothic became the new rage and the preferred style for the great buildings of the nineteenth-century age of steam, from the rebuilt Palace of Westminster itself to railway stations, schools and hospitals – to say nothing of the innumerable new churches of the Victorian religious revival.

At it most thorough-going, all this went beyond an architectural revival to an attempt to relive the Middle Ages, in which life was seen as saner and more just, with a proper relationship between God and Man and a better balance between life and work and rich and poor. Most extreme in this respect was William Morris, who became a fellow of the Society in 1894. He tried to revive not only medieval designs, but also the medieval craft-skills that had been used to make them. And, unlike many prophets, he lived as he preached, building, restoring and furnishing a series of notable houses in town and country. The most complete and perfect, Kelmscott Manor in Oxfordshire, is now owned by the Society and preserved as a monument to Morris and his ideals.

This is doubly appropriate since arguably Morris's (and indeed the Society's) greatest contribution is the conservation movement. The Society and its Fellows had always been pioneers in preservation. But, confronted with the forces of 'progress' in the vast infrastructure projects of Victorian England and its relentless urban sprawl, the results were haphazard and patchy at best. In 1877, however, Morris founded the Society for the Preservation of Ancient (that word again!) Buildings. This gave the forces of conservation fresh heart, organisation and political clout and helped to make the battle against the Philistines the rather more even one that it has become in the twentieth century.

But the greatest single triumph of 'thinginess' is archaeology itself, the science of understanding past societies through their physical remains in the more or less complete absence of written evidence. The Society was the natural pioneer of archaeology and played the key role in its perfection. Its Fellows turned excavation from random treasure-hunting to systematic exploration and recording. They developed, in close association with geology, the technique of stratification, on which archaeological dating primarily depends. They classified the results and coined the language in which we describe the different periods of human culture: Palaeolithic, Mesolithic and Neolithic; Bronze Age and Iron Age. Finally, with a fellowship always rich in characters, the Society supplied the personalities, like Mortimer Wheeler, who helped to popularise the new subject and win it a devoted mass following.

There are times indeed when archaeology has seemed poised to take over the Society. But it has never quite done so. Because, despite its 'thinginess', the Society is also about the written word. Following the establishment of the main national museums and galleries by the middle decades of the nineteenth century, the Society even stopped collecting objects and concentrated its resources and accommodation, both of which have always been in short supply, on developing its library into the present magnificent collection on the history of material culture. But 'books' too were included in the original list of 'antiquities'. And, from the beginning, the Society has collected manuscripts and transcribed and printed them. Some were conventional historical texts. But a bias soon developed away from conventional political history and towards the history of culture, dress and food, of families and communities, and everyday life and death. A particular sort of high academic used to refer, contemptuously, to such topics as 'antiquarian'. But now the boot is rather on the other foot as political history struggles for its place in the popular sun.

For what is striking is the correlation between the original antiquarian agenda and the leading fields of popular history now: family history and local history; collecting and collectibles; antiques and 'how people lived'. It is the antiquarian agenda democratised, of course. We are more interested in the family of the dustman than the duke, in downstairs rather than upstairs, and in the back-to-back instead of the royal household. But although the focus has changed, the underlying spirit remains the same.

All this raises an awkward question of its own. With so much of the antiquarian agenda accomplished and vindicated, what is left for the future of the Society? The concern is understandable but misplaced, I think. First, with its desire to see the life of past times in the whole and in the round, the antiquarian agenda is capable of continual self-refreshment. It has shown this repeatedly in the past, as it has spun off new disciplines. And there is every reason to think it will continue to do so in the future. Next, there is the fact that the Society is, in fact as well as in name, a fellowship. We are introduced to it by individuals and fertilised, as I was, by their very different insights and concerns. Finally, the key antiquarian motive, the love of the past and the sense of wonder at it, will never die, so long as human memory and human society endure.

As Mike Pitts points out in his essay on Stonehenge, the first antiquaries, starting with that old romancer, Geoffrey of Monmouth himself, wondered at Stonehenge. We, with the benefit of almost two hundred years of scientific archaeology, understand it infinitely better than they. But when we see it in the half-light of a summer dawn, we are struck, not by the smug satisfaction of knowledge, but by a sense of ancient, atavistic wonder.

Which is the proper antiquarian response.

The Discovery of Britain

Before the seventeenth century people in Britain had a limited understanding of their past, and were strongly influenced by pagan or Christian beliefs and ancestral myths. Calculations based on the Bible suggested that all human activity had been confined to a few thousand years and that all the earth's earliest inhabitants, except Noah and his family, had been wiped out by a worldwide flood. There was little sense of distinguishing periods in the past and little expertise in identifying its material remains. People knew nothing of the rural and urban landscape beyond their own localities; early maps did not show roads or distances, and images of places and buildings were rare.

The first antiquaries began to challenge previously held views of Britain's past. Concerned by the destruction of British antiquities caused by the dissolution of the monasteries, and by the Civil War, they studied and recorded historic monuments in the landscape, as well as manuscript sources relating to family property rights, heraldry and genealogy. They were determined not to be 'strangers in their own country', as William Camden called those without knowledge of history. Some antiquaries formed small groups, such as the College of Antiquaries, which met in the reigns of Elizabeth I and James I, but these were short-lived.

nonos qui Britanniā expugnauerūt s3 postea recesserūt
& Scotos qui g[ue]rre eam bellis [pro]uauerūt nec obtinuerūt
p[er] Anglicos qui eam debellauerūt et optinuerūt Quarto p[er]
... qui eam bello optinuerūt s3 postea dep[er]ierūt Quintū p[er]
... ios qui eam sub duce Willmo ...... Anglos Anglia[m]
... hodie possidentes

...to mortuo ist[i] 3
... et regnū Britannie
...uerūt vn[de] Locrin[us]
... possedit media[m]
... q[ue] ex n[omi]e suo Lo-
...ellabat q[ue] n[un]c d[icitu]r
... Cambri v[el] p[ar]te
... ult[ra] Sabrinā
... q[ue] ex n[omi]e suo Cam-
...ellat q[ue] n[un]c Wallia
... et Albanact minor
... patria q[ue] lingua ut[...]
...pib[us] Scotie appellat q[ue] ex n[om]ie
... banua p[ri]mo uocabat[ur]

Brut[us] co[n]questor gi-
gantium.

Angl[ia]

Mists of Time

Graham Parry

Until quite late in the sixteenth century, educated Englishmen showed remarkably little curiosity about the remote past of their own country, and, in any case, the obstacles to a proper understanding of the past were considerable. For a start, the imaginable timescale of human history was very short. As the Bible was accepted as the one true record of the early world, chronologers such as Archbishop Ussher (cat. 2) could deduce from the generations of the Old Testament that some 1,500 years had elapsed from the Creation to the Flood, and 2,500 from the Flood to the birth of Christ. So, all human activity had to be crammed into the space of a few thousand years. When people thought about the history of Britain, their understanding was coloured by the ancestral myths that had accumulated during the Middle Ages, and still prevailed in Stuart times (fig. 1). The broadly accepted view – commonly known as 'The British History' – was that Britain had been settled by the Trojan prince Brutus and his followers, wanderers since the destruction of Troy. (*The Cronycle of Englonde* [cat. 3] is characteristic of this outlook.) Brutus named his new home after himself; hence Britain, and his companions became Britons. These foundation myths were put into circulation by the twelfth-century chronicler Geoffrey of Monmouth, whose 'History of the Kings of Britain' also paraded a line of sturdy British kings and heroes that included Lud, Lear and Cymbeline, and concluded with Arthur and Merlin.

Other medieval myths told how the British Isles were originally inhabited by a race of giants. They had built Stonehenge, and their great bones were sometimes found deep in the earth. Britain had to be linked to the biblical record in some way, so there were stories of tribes who were the descendants of Noah's son Japhet making their way there. John Dee (cat. 4) even tried using magic to find out the secrets of that early world. Some later writers, including Aylett Sammes (cat. 13), speculated about a Phoenician settlement of Britain. When combined, the rich ingredients of these various fantasies furnished an eminent antiquity for Britain that few scholars were disposed to question (fig. 2). They were much more agreeable and flattering than the surviving eyewitness accounts of Britain given by Caesar and Tacitus, which described a primitive tribal society, almost entirely lacking in civility. The myths gave Britain a pre-history that went back to the beginnings of the world, and, besides, there was nothing else with which to fill in the featureless blank of early times, before the Roman invasion. Only when printed editions of classical editions became widely available did doubts arise, for these Roman writers made no mention of the flourishing civilisation of early Britain that had been praised in the medieval chronicles. The first book to express a critical opinion of these old legends, the *Anglica Historia* (1534) by the Italian scholar Polydore Vergil (who lived in England), was coldly received by English readers as a work designed by an envious foreigner to diminish the glorious antiquity of Britain.

In Italy, the recovery of the Roman past was well under way by the second half of the fifteenth century, as scholars, artists and architects and prominent churchmen encouraged excavation, sought manuscripts of ancient texts, collected and studied coins and gems, admired and copied antique sculpture, and began to understand the principles of classical architecture. The ubiquitous and impressive remains of the Roman world were an obvious stimulus to this process, and the rewards of research in such rich

FIGURE 1
'King James I Enthroned', from the
Lyte Pedigree
Thomas Lyte
c. 1605
Vellum roll
British Library, London, Add. MS 48343

This roll charts the descent of King James from the Trojan prince Brutus. The legendary hero was thought to have been the first prince to rule over all of Britain, and James, who reunited the kingdoms of Scotland and England after many centuries of separation, was hailed as a second Brutus.

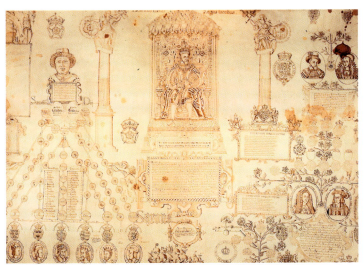

terrain were immediate and abundant. It was very different in England, where the material remains of the different pasts of Britain – the Ancient British, Roman and Saxon – were not so eye-catching, where there was little relevant literature and where the necessary spirit of curiosity was not so evident. It takes a great deal of effort to form a culture of scholarly enquiry and painstaking research, and to accumulate knowledge in a subject that has previously attracted no serious attention. Antiquarian studies were very slow to emerge in England. Those who were in a position to undertake them, clerics and educated laymen, were accustomed to working with manuscripts and books, and the traditions of learning persisting from the Middle Ages stressed respect for written authority; an independent critical faculty was not easy to develop. Looking at evidence in an objective way, having a notion of probability that took chronology and related activities in other places and societies into account, forming ideas of categories of objects with common features that could be studied comparatively: these habits of mind were rarely seen in early Tudor England.

Not only was there no sense of different periods in the past, with identifiable features, there was also an inability to look at objects or remains with a discriminating eye. No vocabulary existed to describe the remains of the past. It was even difficult to distinguish between natural and cultural objects. Fossils were often considered to be the products of human craft; stone implements, such as the Gray's Inn axe (cat. 14), were sometimes seen as the products of nature. In the seventeenth century, the cabinets of curiosities assembled by gentlemen who had a taste for antiquity promiscuously mingled genuine antiquities with oddities of the natural world and interesting and unusual items. John Bargrave's cabinet (cat. 7) is a good example of these miscellaneous collections without definition or categories. After the foundation of the Royal Society in London in 1660, there was a shift towards the systematic ordering of knowledge along lines set out by the lawyer and philosopher Sir Francis Bacon in the early part of the seventeenth century; he had demonstrated the necessity of methodical research and verifiable information. The Royal Society, however, directed its research principally towards the phenomena of the natural world, and had little interest in antiquities.

Just as the depth of the past was not understood, so the varied topography of Britain was not appreciated. Most people did not travel far beyond their own locality, and did not know what different parts of the country looked like. The appearance of major towns or important buildings was unfamiliar to the great majority of Englishmen. Not until William Camden attempted to trace the routes of the Roman roads in his *Britannia* of 1586 (cat. 17) was there a comprehensive topographical view of the country, but very few scholars tried to develop Camden's interest in the relationship of landscape to antiquities until the middle of the seventeenth century. When maps of the country (such as those by John Speed [cat. 6]) began to appear towards the end of Elizabeth's reign, they did not show any roads; rivers were the defining features of the land (fig. 3). The rivers ran between geography and mythology, as they did in poetry. The illustrations to Michael Drayton's *Poly-Olbion* (cat. 5) show that their banks are full of nymphs and river gods; there was a happy coexistence of the natural and the mythological that few wished to disturb.

FIGURE 2
A Pictish Warrior
John White
c. 1588
Watercolour touched with white over graphite, with pen and brown ink
British Museum, London, Department of Prints and Drawings, 1906,0509.1.24

This fanciful watercolour of a Pictish warrior is based on classical sources. On the Virginia expedition of 1585, John White had noted similarities between the natives of Virginia and the Ancient Britons as described by classical historians.

FIGURE 3
'Hertfordshire' from *An Atlas of England and Wales*
Christopher Saxton (*c.* 1542–*c.* 1610)
1579
Coloured engraving on paper
Society of Antiquaries of London

Christopher Saxton published the first county maps in 1579, thereby enabling Englishmen to envisage in detail the land in which they lived.

Myths and legends are hard to dislodge, particularly when they are flattering to national identity. Trojan origins and legends such as those telling of Joseph of Arimathea's coming to Britain after the Crucifixion with the Holy Grail and spreading the Christian gospel here had a remarkably long currency, and got in the way of objective enquiry. The material remains of the past attracted little attention: there was no expertise in identifying or interpreting such remains, nor were they thought to be of much significance. How could one identify anything in the wreckage of the past? What did a Roman urn look like? How could one recognise a Saxon arch? How did one begin to make sense of what was often called the 'rubbish' of the past, and put it into a coherent historical context? Thomas Browne's *Hydriotaphia, Urne-Buriall* (cat. 16) was an early attempt to interpret the anonymous objects that came out of the earth.

The first person publicly to declare himself 'Antiquarius' or an antiquary was John Leland (*c.* 1505–1552) whose activities well exemplify the limitations of outlook in one who aspired to review the historical remains of England. He was a court-scholar and priest who received a licence from King Henry VIII to search the monasteries and colleges throughout the country for rare and important manuscripts that could be removed to the King's own libraries. Thereafter he formed the ambition to travel the kingdom in order to give a comprehensive description of Britain, and made a 'Laboryouse Journey & Serche … for Englandes Antiquitees' (cat. 15). The results – which he never published – were disappointing. His voluminous notes give only the barest accounts of towns and villages. The prominent medieval structures are recorded, but of genuine antiquities there is scarcely a trace. The Saxon world did not exist for Leland, and he largely ignored the Roman presence underlying everything. His work is nonetheless valued because it is the only survey of its kind before the time of Elizabeth I, and Leland remains an honoured name in antiquarian circles.

The prospects for an effective advancement of antiquarian learning in England depended on a number of requirements: detailed knowledge of the Greek and Latin texts that referred to Britain; an ability to understand the Anglo-Saxon language; and an acquaintance, at least, with the methods that continental scholars were using to explore their own national pasts. These methods included philology, etymology, numismatics, comparison (both of texts and objects), linking written sources with material remains and publication of results. In addition, it was desirable to define certain subjects that could become the focus of organised investigation. As antiquarian activity increased in Elizabeth's reign, it became clear that these would include the origins of the early inhabitants of Britain, the languages spoken here, the planting and growth of Christianity in the British Isles, the modes of government in post-Roman society, the evolution of the laws of England, and the origins of institutions and offices of Church and state, including that most sensitive subject, the nature and powers of Parliament. It is worth noting that investigation of ancient sites – archaeology – was not a concern of early antiquaries.

1

Roll Chronicle
Mid-fifteenth century with additions of c. 1665
Illumination with coloured inks and tint on vellum rolls, 1245 × 58 cm; 192.5 × 58 cm
Society of Antiquaries of London, MS 501
Selected references: Brown and Harriss 1999; Willetts 2000, p. 240

This genealogical roll charts the descent of Charles II from Adam and Eve, via Noah and the Dukes of Normandy. Such fanciful descents were not uncommon in medieval attempts to see backwards through the mists of time. Since the Bible provided the links from Adam down to Christ, the difficult sections, those for which ingenuity and imagination were required, lay in the first thousand years of the Christian era.

Rolls such as these illustrate the desire of the nobility of all European nations to associate themselves with the famous figures of the remote past, and although such compilations are notoriously imaginative, the curiosity about the past they excited helped to develop serious research into antiquarian matters. Comparable genealogies exist showing the descent of James I from the Trojan prince Brutus.

The dedication to Henry VI and other references suggests that the earlier roll was one of a group dating from c. 1455 that were constructed to show his rightful title to the throne after he had been defeated by the Yorkists at the Battle of St Albans (1455). The author was reputed to be Roger Alban, a Carmelite monk living in London, and it is possible that this copy is in his hand, and is the one presented to Henry VI. The fine illuminations in the roundels have been attributed to William Abell (d. 1474), who was outstanding in this line of work.

A second roll carries the genealogical tree forward to the reign of Charles II, who was also concerned to establish his claim to the English throne. However, by then, genealogies of this kind had come to seem rather far-fetched because so many of the claims made in them had been discredited by antiquarian research. GP/PW

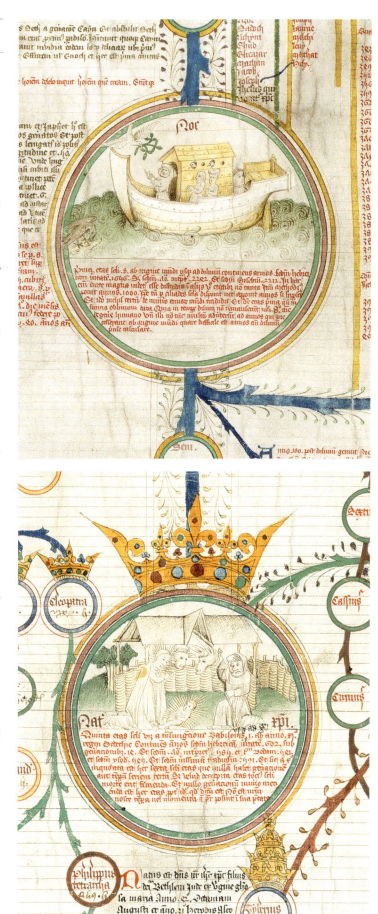

Mists of Time | 21

2

The Annals of the World
James Ussher (1581–1656)
1658
Printed book, 35 × 46.5 cm
Society of Antiquaries of London,
Frontispiece
Selected references: Trevor-Roper 1987, pp. 120–65; Parry 1995, pp. 130–56

The compilation of a universal chronology was one of the great ambitions of antiquarian scholarship in the Renaissance. Such a work would correlate the histories of the nations of antiquity, and make it possible to understand the relative position of events in different nations. The greatest exponent of chronology in Britain was the Irishman James Ussher, Archbishop of Armagh from 1625, and a scholar famous for his prodigious knowledge of early Christianity. He devised a complete dating system based on the Old Testament, which gave the generations of the patriarchs and rulers of Israel from the Creation down to the time of the prophets. But how could one give dates to these figures, and what was the date of Creation? By the laborious study of the biblical genealogies, with a fine understanding of the different dating systems used in antiquity and with a sure knowledge of the work of previous chronologers, Ussher carefully assigned dates to Old Testament events, and calculated that the Creation itself took place in 4004 BC. He was even able to declare that Creation began on the evening of the 22 October, which was a Saturday. So convincing was Ussher's scheme that it became accepted as definitive in Britain, and his dates were printed in the margins of Bibles until well into the nineteenth century.

Ussher's chronology was broadly in line with estimates of the age of the world made by European scholars. The limited timescale of these chronologies, which allowed four thousand years for all the activities of humankind before the time of Christ, had a detrimental effect on antiquarian attempts to form a credible idea of the prehistoric past. GP

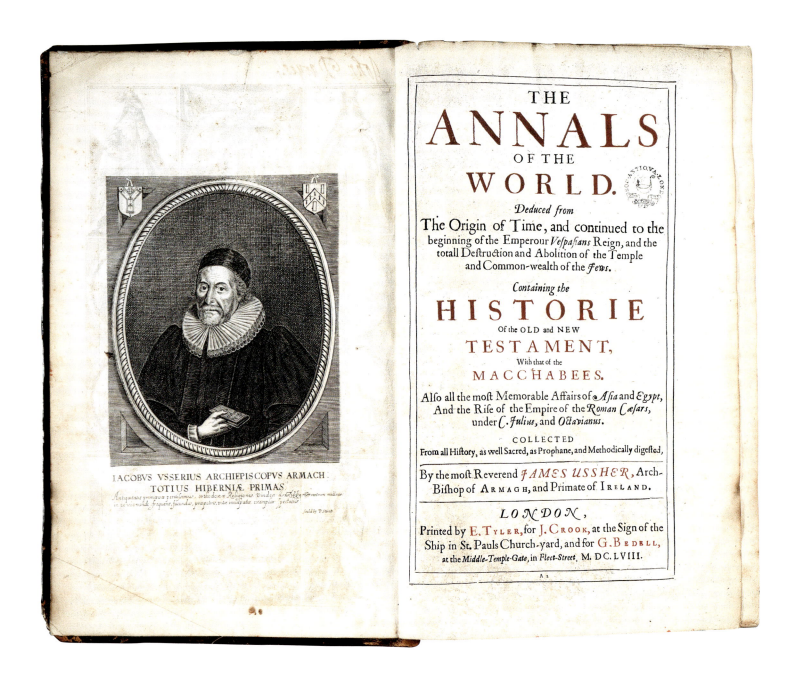

3

The Cronycle of Englonde and the Descrypcyon of Englonde
Wynkyn de Worde (d. 1534/35) after William Caxton (1415–1492)
1502
Printed book, 26.8 × 34 cm
Society of Antiquaries of London, Frontispiece
Selected references: London 1976, p. 46; Hay 1977, pp. 63–86; Matheson 1998

One of the innumerable consequences of the advent of printing was that the history of Britain, as it was understood in the fifteenth century, became widely disseminated. History writing ceased to be the domain of monks and began to attract the attention of secular scholars. Chronicles up to the sixteenth century tended to repeat material from existing compilations, and consisted largely of accounts of events, without much commentary or interpretation. The writing of history along lines we might recognise as modern, in which evidence is weighed and evaluated, sources are recognised to have grades of reliability and commentary plays a significant role, began with Polydore Vergil in the 1530s.

The chronicle under discussion was originally printed by William Caxton in 1480. It is a composite affair translated from French chronicle sources, mainly the *Brut d'Angleterre*, which in turn derived from Geoffrey of Monmouth, with various updates. It begins with the settlement of Britain by the Trojan prince Brutus, grandson of Aeneas, and his followers, which provided Britain with a foundation myth comparable to that of Rome. It is accompanied by a geographical description of Britain taken from Ranulph Higden's *Polychronicon*, a mid-fourteenth-century account of Britain and its history, which had been translated into English by John de Trevisa in 1387. Both men were Benedictine monks at Chester.

This edition was printed in 1502 by Wynkyn de Worde, who was left Caxton's business on his death, which included the types of woodcut. The book retains the device of William Caxton as the original printer and publisher of the chronicle. The woodcut for the frontispiece may show a fictionalised English landscape with towns, although it is more likely to have been borrowed from a Germanic source. GP

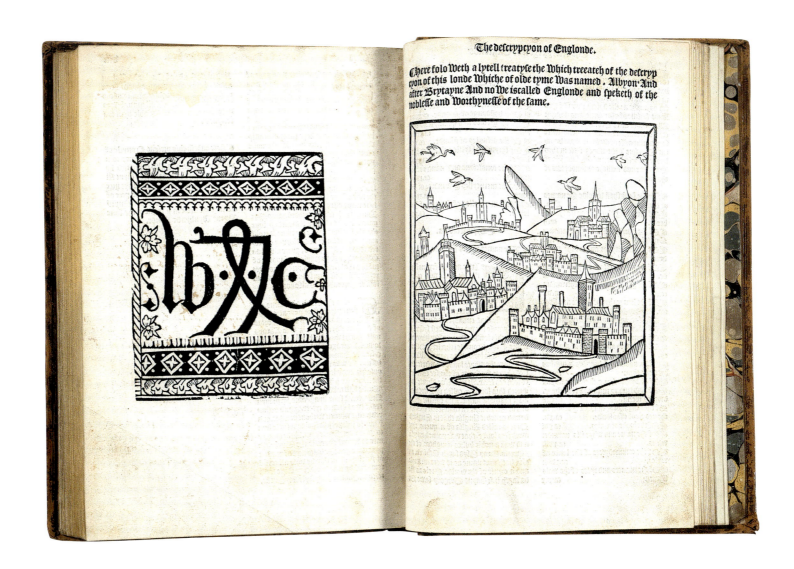

Mists of Time | 23

4

(opposite)
John Dee's *Holy Table*
Late seventeenth century
Carved marble, 60 × 46.3 cm
Museum of the History of Science, Oxford
Selected references: Dee 1659; Deacon 1968, pp. 138–56; French 1972, pp. 188–207; Bennett 1999, pp. 4–5

Magic and antiquarianism coexisted in the mind of the Elizabethan polymath, alchemist and magus John Dee (1527–1608). Primarily a mathematician, the idiosyncratic Dee had a universal curiosity that encompassed both the physical and the spiritual world. His desire to understand the secrets of the natural world and his ambition to know the future course of events led him to attempt to communicate with spirits. He believed that angels had a perfect knowledge of all things, given by God, just as Adam had. Yet Adam had fallen, and the knowledge of his descendants was distorted and erroneous.

In order to gain access to this angelic knowledge, Dee used his associate Edward Kelly as a medium. Kelly conjured up the angel Uriel, and spiritual conversations ensued. The angel instructed Dee to make this 'holy table', with characters written in the original language of Eden, which was also the language of angels. The angels' communications were spelt out in these characters by Kelly, who then translated them. Dee's crystal ball and magic mirror (an Aztec obsidian disc) are displayed in the Enlightenment Gallery of the British Museum in London.

Dee also had strong antiquarian interests, and was a friend of the Flemish cartographer Abraham Ortelius, the antiquary William Camden and the London historian John Stow. He was a believer in Geoffrey of Monmouth's 'British History', and wrote in favour of the authenticity of the Trojan Brutus and King Arthur. Dee undertook an antiquarian journey in Wales in 1574, noting historic places and curiosities in the manner of Leland, and searching for traces of Arthur. He collected manuscripts, gathered information about family pedigrees and heraldry, and shared Camden's interest in the relations between topography and local history. This eagerness to know allied him to the Elizabethan antiquaries, but his view of the British past was essentially medieval, while his spiritualism and alchemy were promising Renaissance experiments that led nowhere.

The table is a late seventeenth-century copy in marble of the original wooden table, which was last recorded in the library of the notable Elizabethan antiquary, Sir Robert Cotton. The copy formerly belonged to Richard Rawlinson (1690–1755), who was a Vice-President of the Society. GP

The HOLY TABLE

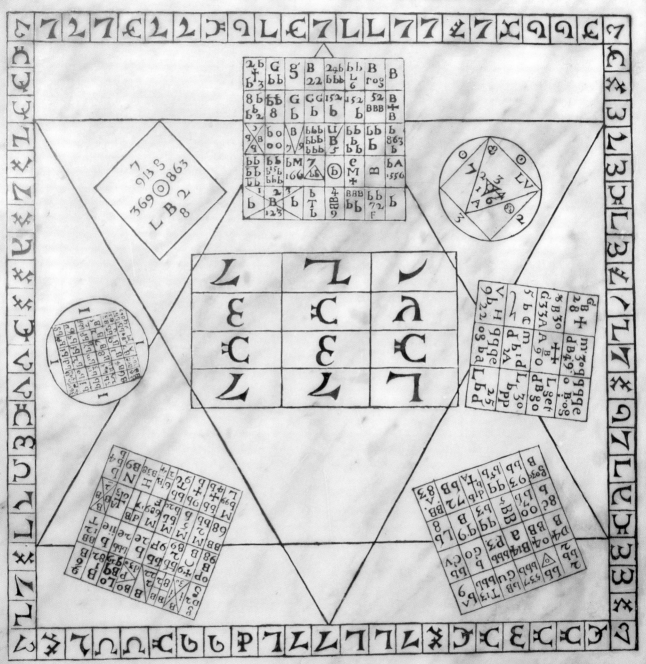

5

'River Severn' from *Poly-Olbion*
Michael Drayton (1563–1631)
1613
Printed book, 28 × 49 cm
Society of Antiquaries of London,
opp. p. 5
Selected references: Helgerson 1992,
pp. 105–48; Parry 1995, pp. 108–12;
Barbour 2003, pp. 59–117

Poly-Olbion is in some ways a versification of William Camden's *Britannia*. Its subtitle reads 'a Chorographicall Description of Tracts, Rivers, Mountains, Forests ... of Great Britain'. The title is a Greek confection meaning something like 'the Variety of Britain'. Drayton was a Warwickshire poet who produced a great deal of verse on pastoral themes and on English historical subjects. In *Poly-Olbion* he celebrated the beauties of the land of Albion and the historical and legendary scenes enacted there. Like Camden, he followed the course of the rivers of each county, and among the pleasures of his book are the illustrations by William Hole showing river nymphs disporting themselves in a variety of engaging poses on the county maps. In Glamorganshire, the nymphs of England and Wales are engaged in a musical contest across the Severn. A notable feature of the 1613 volume was the learned annotation by Drayton's friend John Selden, who brought a much more advanced view of antiquity to the book. Drayton was committed to 'The British History' as told by Geoffrey of Monmouth, and used the stories of the Trojan Brutus as the legendary background for his poem. Selden was sceptical about these stories, and took the opportunity to denounce the whole Trojan charade as an intolerable imposition on the modern reader. He did, however, provide interesting discourses on Druids and bards and the character of Ancient British society in his notes. Drayton did not invite him to comment on the second part of his poem, published in 1622. GP

6

'Surrey' from the *Theatre of the Empire of Great Britain*
John Speed (1551/52–1629)
1676
Printed book, 44 × 63 cm
Society of Antiquaries of London, pp. 11–12
Selected reference: Nicolson and Hawkyard 1995

John Speed, like the historian John Stow, was a tailor turned antiquary, who, in the small and cliquish world of Jacobean London, managed to join part of the circle around William Camden. He became a historian and cartographer. His *Theatre ... of Great Britain*, first published in 1611, was essentially an atlas, containing 67 maps, mostly of the English and Welsh counties, with a few of Scotland and Ireland. Many of the maps are by Christopher Saxton, the most accomplished of English Renaissance cartographers; others are by Jodocus Hondius and by Speed himself. They are notable for their flamboyance, and for the important plans of the chief towns – the first such collection to appear in print. The coats of arms of the principal families in a particular county are visible in the margins of the county maps. No roads are shown on the maps, a sign that they were not fit to be used; rivers were the most reliable thoroughfares.

The map of Surrey shows the lost royal palaces of Richmond and Nonsuch. These images are among the most important contemporary records of these important buildings, which no longer exist. GP

28 | Making History

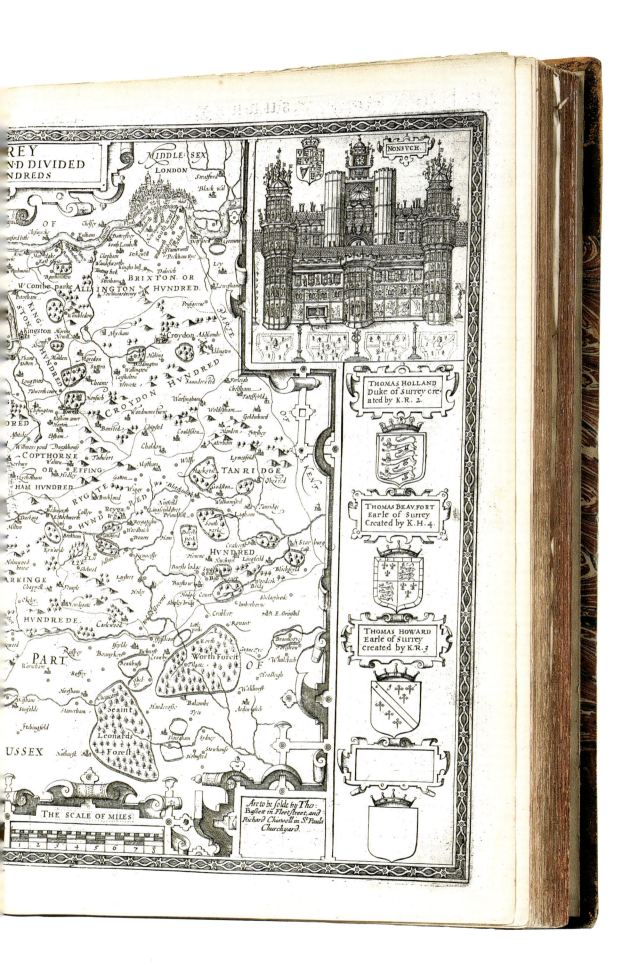

John Bargrave's Cabinet of Curiosities
CATALOGUE NUMBERS 7–12

This cabinet belonged to John Bargrave, a canon of Canterbury Cathedral, and contains the miscellaneous collections he made in the course of his travels in Europe and North Africa from 1646 to 1660. Such cabinets of curiosity were not uncommon among gentlemen with antiquarian leanings in the seventeenth century, but this is a rare survival, with its contents almost complete. GP

7

Cabinet of Curiosities
Late seventeenth century
Mahogany, 52 × 46.5 (max.) × 28.7 cm
Canterbury Cathedral Archives, Dean and Chapter of Canterbury
Selected references: Sturdy and Henig 1983; MacGregor and Impey 1985, pp. 153–4; Bann 1994; Swann 2001

The courtier and philosopher Sir Francis Bacon described the scope of such cabinets at the beginning of the century: 'Whatsoever the hand of man by exquisite art or engine has made rare in stuff, form or motion; whatsoever singularity, chance and the shuffle of things hath produced; whatsoever Nature has wrought in things that want life and may be kept.' The favoured objects for such collections were coins, medals, mineral specimens, fossils and unusual examples of natural history. They were tiny personal museums, and the habit of collecting that created them eventually led to the formation of substantial repositories such as that at the Royal Society in London and the Ashmolean Museum, Oxford. An early exemplar for these collections was that made by John Tradescant in Lambeth.

Bargrave's cabinet was typical: it contained antique engraved gems, bronze figurines, Roman items, such as lamps and glass vials, and an assortment of Roman coins and modern medals. There were also anthropological items, including native dress from Hudson's Bay, Canada, given by a merchant whom Bargrave helped to ransom from captivity in North Africa. Many of the objects in his collection have genuine antiquarian value, while others are from the realm of curiosity; there was no attempt to distinguish between these categories or between genuine and fake, or to assign dates or offer interpretations of the objects. By the mid-eighteenth century the idea of such collections had become unfashionable. GP

8

Ring
1650
Gold, with garnet jewel inset, 2 × 1.2 cm
Canterbury Cathedral Archives,
Dean and Chapter of Canterbury

Bargrave had this ring made in Rome in 1650 to hold the engraved garnet that Philip, Lord Stanhope, gave him. Bargrave thought it was Greek, with the head of Aristotle, but it is now considered to be Roman, with the head of Jupiter. GP

9

Stylus
Date unknown
Bronze, 11 cm (length)
Canterbury Cathedral Archives,
Dean and Chapter of Canterbury

One end is pointed for writing on a wax tablet, the other flat for erasing letters. Bargrave's note says it all: 'Stylus Romanus. The antiquarian that sold it me avowed it to be truly ancient, but thousands may daily be made.' GP

10

Plaquette
Seventeenth century
Bronze, 8.8 × 4.8 × 3 cm
Canterbury Cathedral Archives,
Dean and Chapter of Canterbury

According to Bargrave's note, this is 'a flat brass piece, of several Cupidons scaring one another with a vizard; being a bachanalia piece, dugg out of the Temple of Bacchus'. The modern view inclines to the belief that it is a seventeenth-century copy or forgery. There was a flourishing trade in fake antiquities in Italy in the seventeenth century. GP

11

'Finger of a Frenchman'
Date unknown
Preserved human remains,
8.7 × 2.2 cm
Canterbury Cathedral Archives,
Dean and Chapter of Canterbury

Bargrave bought this relic from Franciscan friars in Toulouse, after they had shown him the preserved corpses in their vaults. They also offered him a mummified baby. This is a curiosity, not an antiquity, and an unusual piece to include in a cabinet of curiosities. GP

12

Box of stone fragments
Date unknown
Painted wood, oval, 7.6 × 4.4 × 3.9 cm
Canterbury Cathedral Archives,
Dean and Chapter of Canterbury

John Bargrave used to chip off bits of stone from historic monuments as souvenirs, as many tourists have done. This box contains fragments from the Colosseum, the Arch of Constantine, the Arch of Titus and the Arch of Septimius Severus – all in Rome – a stone from the grotto of the Cumean Sybil, near Naples, and some pieces of mosaic from St Mark's, Venice, all wrapped in their original labels. On the lid of the box is a faded painting of a female figure. GP

13

The 'Wicker' image from *Britannia Antiqua Illustrata*
Aylett Sammes (c. 1636–c. 1679)
1676
Printed book, 37.2 × 49 cm
Society of Antiquaries of London, p. 105
Selected reference: Parry 1995, pp. 308–25

Aylett Sammes, a maverick among the antiquaries of the seventeenth century, produced one of the most bizarre books of the age. Educated at Christ's College, Cambridge, and associated with the Inner Temple, one of the Inns of Court, London, he turned to antiquarian studies, which he pursued seemingly in isolation. His thesis was that Britain had been first settled by the Phoenicians, a proposition that had respectable antecedents, for a number of writers had suggested that the Phoenicians may have been the earliest visitors to the British Isles, to trade for tin. Yet Sammes overplays his hand: he evokes a flourishing Phoenician civilisation, and claims that the original language of Britain was Phoenician, which he represents as a variant of Hebrew. The language, he maintained, survives in Welsh, for, in the seventeenth century, the Welsh were commonly regarded as the survivors of the Ancient Britons, who retreated into their mountainous terrain after their defeat by the Saxons. The Phoenicians naturally brought their gods with them, and Sammes's book has a number of disconcerting illustrations showing their monstrous deities and strange rituals. Their principal cult was that of the Phoenician Hercules, with Stonehenge as its headquarters. Much of Sammes's argument was carried on by means of ingenious etymologies, but there is no presentation of material evidence at all. Sammes's imaginary picture of a wicker image represented the giant statue, which, according to classical sources, Druids filled with live men and set on fire. They were said to believe in human sacrifice as a means of saving others from desperate sickness or danger of war. GP

14

The Gray's Inn Axe
Lower Palaeolithic, *c.* 350,000 BP
Worked flint, 17 × 10 × 5 cm
British Museum, London, PEE SL. 246
Selected references: Bagford 1715, pp. lxiii–lxv; Cook 2003, p. 183

This flint handaxe was discovered by the London apothecary and antiquary John Conyers in the 1690s, at a building site in Gray's Inn Road, London. It lay in river gravel, close to the bones of what was probably either a mammoth or the straight-tusked elephant (*E. antiquus*), both long extinct.

In the Middle Ages, such implements had been interpreted as 'thunderbolts from the gods'. By the Restoration period they were beginning to be recognised as extremely ancient man-made objects, but the conventional estimate of the age of the earth – some 5,600 years by the seventeenth century – made it difficult to assign a date of any significant time to such items. The first antiquary to draw attention to flint axes was William Dugdale, in *The Antiquities of Warwickshire* (1656). He illustrated a specimen, which he attributed to 'the ancient Britans' before they 'attained to the knowledge of working iron or brass'.

In their attempts to understand the Gray's Inn axe, contemporaries suggested that the gravel could have been the result of Noah's Flood, but they struggled to find an explanation for the elephant. In 1715 John Bagford, one of the founder members of the Society of Antiquaries, proposed that the Romans had brought the elephant with them at the time of the invasion in AD 43, and it had been killed by an ancient Briton using the stone axe. Modern scholarship dates this axe to the Lower Palaeolithic period (500,000–70,000 BP, before present), making it about 350,000 years old. The axe passed to the British Museum at the time of its foundation in 1753 as part of the collections of Sir Hans Sloane. GP/BN

Mists of Time | 33

15

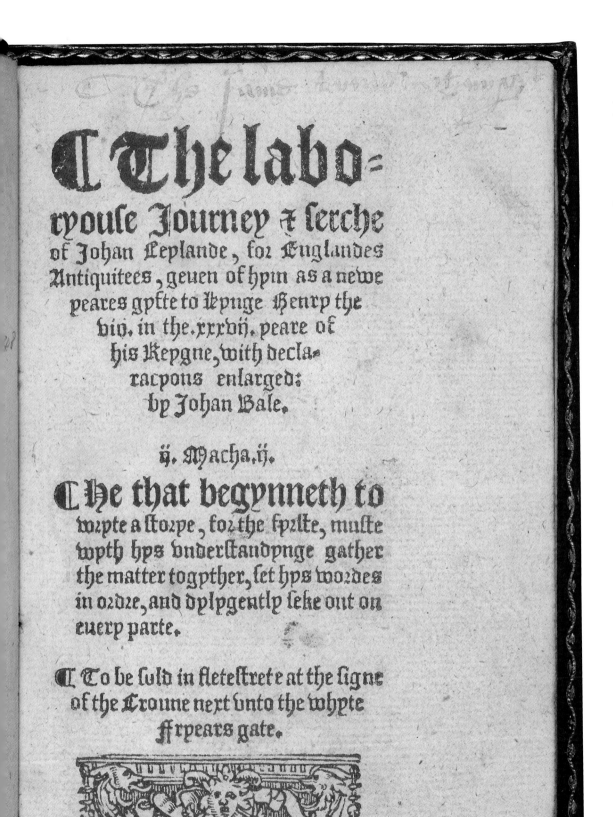

*The Laboryouse Journey & Serche …
for Englandes Antiquitees*
John Leland (*c*. 1505–1552)
1549
Printed book, 15 × 19.5 cm
British Library, London, BL G.2931
Selected references: Smith 1907–10;
Kendrick 1950; Chandler 1993

John Leland was the proto-antiquary of England, the first scholar to attempt to give a topographical account of the antiquities of England and Wales. The product of a humanist education at St Paul's School, London, and the University of Cambridge, he became the keeper of Henry VIII's libraries, and in 1533 received a commission from the King to search for books by ancient writers in the monasteries and colleges of the realm. He diversified his numerous bibliographic journeys by taking copious notes of the places he visited, recording the most notable features of towns, abbeys and ancient sites. In 1546, in a letter to Henry VIII known as 'The New-Years Gift', he gave an account of his activities, explaining how he hoped to produce a book to be known as 'De Antiquitate Britannica', and also a catalogue of all British writers, 'begynning at the Druides'. He completed the catalogue, but not the greater work. Leland's notes were brief and lacking in detail. He listed castles, churches, gates and bridges, and gave a simple description of the countryside, whether it was fertile or not. He noted certain tombs and their inscriptions. Occasionally he would suggest that a castle or chapel was built in a certain king's reign. However, he was unable to give coherence to the material he had collected, and a contemporary report indicates that he became deranged.

His papers later came into the hands of the historian John Stow, who transcribed many of them; the Leicestershire antiquary William Burton also owned many of his manuscripts, and through him they came to the Bodleian Library at Oxford. The 'Itinerary', as Leland's survey is known, was first published in nine volumes from 1710 to 1712 by the antiquary Thomas Hearne, but his manuscripts were frequently consulted by antiquaries before they went into print. GP

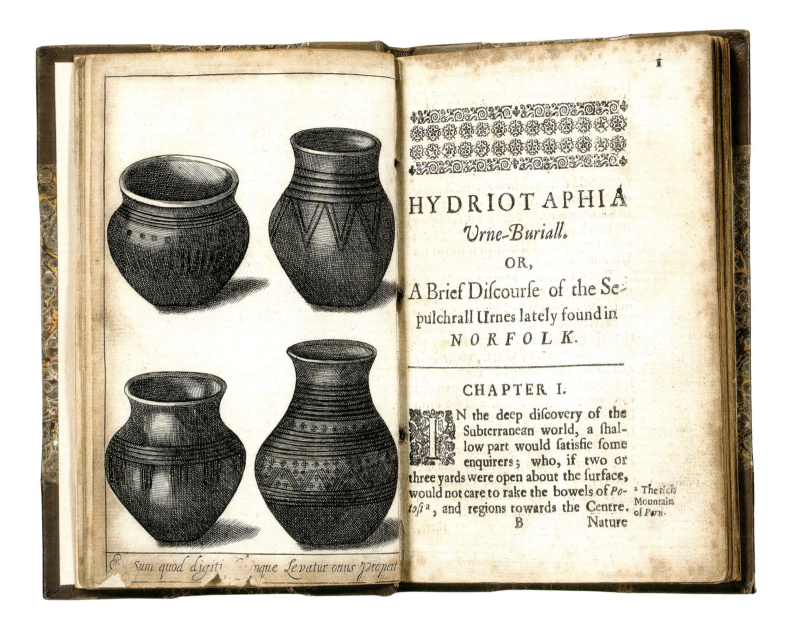

16

Hydriotaphia, Urne-Buriall or, A Brief Discourse of the Sepulchrall Urnes lately found in Norfolk
Thomas Browne (1605–1682)
1658
Printed book, 16.8 × 20 cm
Society of Antiquaries of London, p. 1
Selected references: Piggott 1989, pp. 257–69; Parry 1995, pp. 249–60

Urne-Buriall professes to be a treatise on the discovery of some sepulchral urns in Norfolk, but it is, in fact, part excavation report and part meditation on the vanity of humankind's desire to assert its identity against the power of oblivion. It is also a brief discourse on the funeral customs of the nations of antiquity. The author, Sir Thomas Browne, was a Norwich physician famous for his polymathic learning, who maintained a lifelong interest in antiquities.

Browne assumed his urns to be Roman, whereas the illustration indicates Saxon origins. It did occur to him that the urns might be British or Saxon, but he had no means of knowing. He understood, however, that careful excavation, record-keeping, location, illustration and comparison would be the way to greater knowledge. His medical skills enabled him to declare that bones in one urn were female. 'But who were the proprietaries of these bones, or what bodies these ashes made up, were a question above Antiquarism.' Browne described the urns as 'sad and sepulchral Pitchers, which have no joyful voices; silently espressing the old mortality, the ruins of forgotten time'.

This, the most celebrated antiquarian discourse of the seventeenth century, is memorable more for the exceptional eloquence of Browne's prose than for its archaeological content. GP

Earliest Antiquaries

Graham Parry

FIGURE 4
William Dugdale
Etched by Wenceslaus Hollar for the frontispiece to William Dugdale's *The Antiquities of Warwickshire*, 1656
Society of Antiquaries of London

The industrious antiquary (1605–1686) is shown in his study, warmly dressed and alert. Out of the confusion of his manuscripts and documents, Dugdale produced an impressive range of works over a span of fifty years.

By the 1570s, the intellectual climate had become more propitious for antiquarian research. The recovery of the Anglo-Saxon language was being accomplished by the circle of scholars around the Archbishop of Canterbury, Matthew Parker, who were making great progress in understanding the forgotten language by studying bilingual texts in Latin and Saxon that had survived in monastic libraries. There was a strong interest, encouraged by Parker and by William Cecil, Lord Burghley, Elizabeth I's chief minister, in elaborating a history of Saxon Christianity that would reveal a native church untainted by interference from Rome. The cultivation of humanist scholarship in the universities was beginning to produce men equipped to undertake an intelligent study of antiquities. From this background came William Camden (cat. 18), the master-antiquary who has always commanded the respect of his successors. With the support initially of the courtier Sir Philip Sidney, and later of Lord Burghley, he began the ambitious project that was eventually published as *Britannia* in 1586 (cat. 17). The impetus to compile this innovative work came from the Flemish cartographer Abraham Ortelius, who urged Camden to give the world an account of Roman Britain that would be as detailed as modern scholarship would permit. Camden accepted the challenge. He determined to describe the configuration of the Roman settlements in Britain, a plan that required him to give an account of the native British tribes that the Romans had overcome and ruled. After that he started to enquire into the origins of the peoples who had occupied the land before the Romans came, and into their language and customs – customs that could be credibly reconstructed from a wide range of classical accounts then in print. Camden made a number of journeys around the country to inspect towns and ancient sites, and decided to structure his book as a county-by-county perambulation in which history and topography would be combined, and all phases of human activity recorded. He fulfilled his main aim admirably, in giving a thorough account of Roman Britain and its remains. Most creditably, he came to recognise that the Saxons had exercised a far more formative influence on the country than the Romans. His blind spot was his inability to identify pre-Roman remains; although he wrote much about the Ancient Britons, he seemed unaware that any physical traces of their presence had survived.

Britannia was written in Latin, and went through six editions before being translated into English in 1610. Its success made Camden an intellectual hero, and provoked much antiquarian activity in England. About the time of its publication, a group of Camden's friends and associates formed themselves into a society of antiquaries, meeting regularly to discuss matters relating to the institutions, offices and customs of England. Most members, including Sir John Dodderidge (cat. 24), were lawyers or heralds, who had a professional interest in such subjects. One who is still remembered today was John Stow, the historian whose invaluable *Survey of London* was first published in 1598. This Elizabethan society of antiquaries ceased to meet about 1607. An attempt to revive it in 1614 met with James I's displeasure; he believed it would give rise to undesirable enquiries into such sensitive subjects as royal prerogative and the rights of Parliament. A few years later the herald and historian Edmund Bolton petitioned the King to establish an academy that would promote antiquarian research (cat. 23), among other subjects, but this project also foundered.

Sir Robert Cotton, a close friend of Camden, has always been associated with the remarkable library he built up at his house in London and made available to all who were intent on antiquarian research. Consisting predominantly of Saxon and medieval manuscripts, mostly rescued from monastic libraries, the library became the archive for, and meeting-place of, Jacobean antiquaries. Those who benefited from its resources, and became in consequence lifelong friends of Cotton, included the polymath John Selden, and the church antiquaries Archbishop James Ussher, Sir Henry Spelman and John Weever. Selden's expertise stretched from ancient Hebraic law and customs to modern maritime rights. In a long career, he wrote discourses on the ancient Syrian gods, on Greek statuary and inscriptions, on Byzantine historians and Norman chroniclers, on the origins of the law in England, on tithes, titles of honour and on British topography (cat. 5). Ussher documented the complex history of Christianity in Britain and Ireland and compiled a universal chronology (cat. 2). Spelman clarified the legal rights of the Church, gave a history of Church councils and elucidated the legal terminology of Saxon and medieval England. Weever studied comparative funerary customs and made vast collections of epitaphs, with commentaries. Cotton's library was closed in 1629 on the orders of Charles I, who thought it was being used for seditious purposes by Parliamentarians opposed to his royal prerogative. Its closure seems to have hastened the death of its owner: Cotton pined for his books, and went into a fatal decline. By the time of the Civil War, however, the library was available to scholars once more.

Antiquaries depend on fellowship and the assistance of their peers. Many were based in London, where the great repositories of national records lay, yet a considerable number flourished in the provinces. A network of correspondence held them together, and intermittent meetings fortified their common interests. Older men helped younger, while proficient linguists helped less able friends. The vast scale of many antiquarian enterprises required cooperation, which, for the most part, was willingly given, out of friendship and in the interest of English scholarship. The activities of William Dugdale (later Sir) (fig. 4) illustrate this point. His incomparable survey of his home county, *The Antiquities of Warwickshire* (1656), was compiled over twenty-five years with the assistance of numerous members of the local gentry and custodians of records in London. In the mid-1630s, Dugdale joined up with Sir Christopher Hatton, Sir Thomas Shirley and Sir Edward Dering in an attempt to form an antiquarian society, 'Antiquitas Rediviva', but it did not thrive (cats 21, 22). Dugdale had helped the Yorkshire antiquary Roger Dodsworth with the immense task of recovering the charters and deeds of the monasteries of England, and then took over this project when Dodsworth died, producing the three seminal volumes of monastic studies, entitled *Monasticon Anglicanum*, in 1655, 1661 and 1673 (fig. 5). His later works, on the history of St Paul's Cathedral and on the baronage of England, all benefited from the contributions of others. Dugdale in turn helped to launch the career of the Oxford antiquary Anthony Wood, and so the chain went on.

Archaeological activity, in the sense of inspecting and excavating ancient sites, and interpreting finds, was slow to develop. In 1600 Camden and Cotton made an expedition to Hadrian's Wall, where they noted inscriptions and collected some small altars and pieces

FIGURE 5
The Ruins of Osney Abbey
Etched by Wenceslaus Hollar for William Dugdale's *Monasticon Anglicanum*, vol. 2, 1661
Society of Antiquaries of London

At the Dissolution of the Monasteries, Osney Abbey was made the cathedral of Oxford, but in 1546 the seat of the bishop was moved to Christ Church, and Osney fell into decay. In 1643, John Aubrey had some drawings made of the ruins. By the time this view was published, the abbey had been demolished, and this etching is the only record of the vanished building.

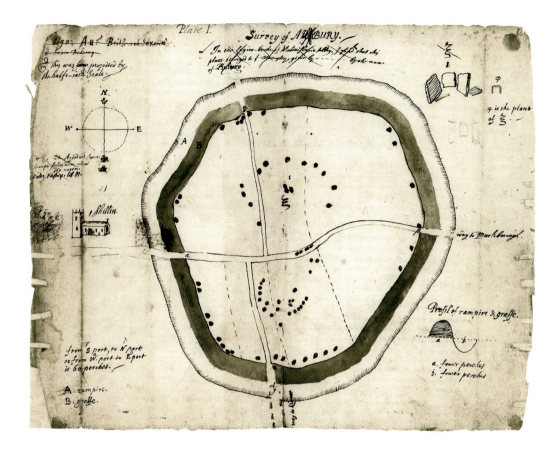

FIGURE 6
'Plan of Avebury' from *Monumenta Britannica*
John Aubrey (1626–1697)
1663
Pen and ink with graphite
Bodleian Library, Oxford, MS.
Top gen c.24, fols 39v–40r

John Aubrey discovered the great prehistoric monument at Avebury in 1649 in the course of a hunt. He drew this plan of the site for inclusion in his treatise *Monumenta Britannica*, on the ancient stone structures of Britain, which he began in 1663 but never brought to publication.

of statuary, which were transported to Cotton's house in Cambridgeshire. In 1620 James I, puzzled by Stonehenge, asked his surveyor, the architect Inigo Jones, to carry out some excavations and draw up a report of his views on the monument's origin and purpose. Jones dug and measured, but his unexpected conclusions – that it was a Roman temple – were not published until 1655, after his death. Urns were frequently dug up, mosaic pavements uncovered, hoards of coins unearthed, but no proper record was made of them and they disappeared into private collections or were dispersed and lost.

Not until the Wiltshire antiquary John Aubrey became fascinated by ancient stone monuments did any systematic recording begin. In 1649, Aubrey found himself in the Avebury stone circle during a hunt, and lingered to inspect it. He soon recognised that it was a complex of circles, and not a random collection of stones, as was commonly thought. In repeated visits, he measured the site, identified the great avenue, and plotted the scheme of the monument (fig. 6). He saw affinities with Stonehenge, and understood how features of Avebury helped to clarify the layout of Stonehenge. The rudeness of the stones convinced him that these were works of the Ancient Britons, made long before the Romans came. Both Aubrey and his friend Walter Charleton made presentations about Avebury to the Royal Society in 1663 (cat. 25). Aubrey was exceptional in that he had a vigorous imagination that was fired by places rich in historical associations. He imagined these stone circles as ceremonial sites, as temples, and attempted to envisage what kind of society had made and used them. Excited by his discovery of a new field of study, he began to write a book about the stone monuments of Britain, gathering information by direct observation and by correspondence with people in the remoter parts of the country. The result of his enquiries was *Monumenta Britannica*, the first credible archaeological treatise in English. It remained in manuscript form until the twentieth century, however, although it was known and used by antiquaries concerned with prehistoric Britain.

Aubrey became a member of the Royal Society in 1663, and his work with antiquities properly belonged to the Baconian ethos of the new institution, with its emphasis on collecting and interpreting data. Measurement, comparison and verification were methods he employed, and in his county surveys of Wiltshire and Surrey he paid attention to natural history and local phenomena in ways that the Royal Society approved. In general, however, antiquarian matters did not fit into the Royal Society's programme and during the Restoration period few outstanding developments occurred. However, by this time antiquarian interests had become widespread among the gentry of England, and it was no longer unusual to be well informed about local history, to make small collections of coins and urns and other *curiosa*, or to read works of antiquarian scholarship. When Edmund Gibson of The Queen's College, Oxford, undertook to produce a vastly enlarged edition of Camden's *Britannia* at the end of the century, he found a large pool of contributors willing to revise each county, and a gratifyingly large readership.

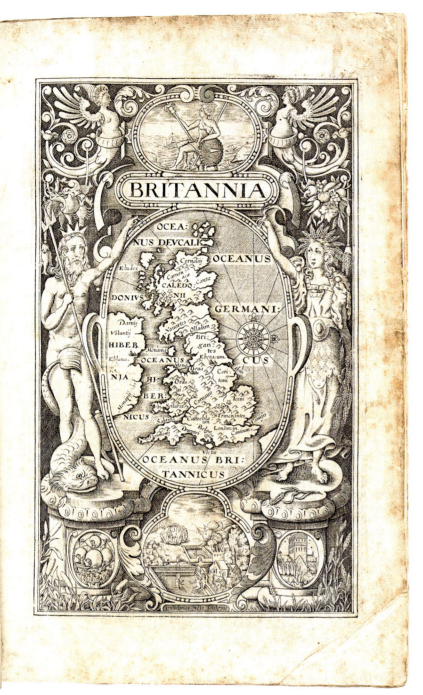

17

Britannia
William Camden (1551–1623)
1610
Printed book, 34 × 48 cm
Society of Antiquaries of London,
Frontispiece
Selected references: Kendrick 1950;
Piggott 1976, pp. 33–54; Parry 1995,
pp. 22–48

This book, the seminal work of antiquarian studies, first published in England in 1586, put Britain on the map of European humanist scholarship. Camden's early interests in the history and antiquities of his country were given focus by the Flemish cartographer Abraham Ortelius, who suggested in 1577 that he should give an account of Roman Britain to the scholars of continental Europe. Initially, Camden had wanted to identify and comment on the places mentioned in the lists of military stations that had survived from antiquity. However, the project soon grew to become a perambulation of the land with a description of the peoples who had inhabited it, their languages and customs, and a county-by-county survey that reviewed the geography, history, ancient remains and towns of each region.

Camden made many journeys through Britain to gather information and see the sites at first hand. By observation, attention to local knowledge, use of documents and study of classical histories and medieval chronicles, he produced a work of unprecedented originality and authority. Successive editions of *Britannia* up until 1607 contained new material, much of it emphasising the contribution of the Saxons to the shaping of the nation that became England. Translated into English in 1610 by Philemon Holland, *Britannia* inspired a large number of county surveys and several topographical poems. Much of the antiquarian writing of the seventeenth century had its genesis in *Britannia*. GP

18

(opposite)
William Camden
By or after Marcus Gheeraerts
the Younger (1561/62–1636)
1609
Oil on panel, 56.5 × 41.9 cm
National Portrait Gallery, London,
NPG 528
Selected reference: Strong 1969,
vol. 1, pp. 35–7

William Camden (1551–1623) was the pre-eminent antiquary of his day, and the father of antiquarian studies in Britain. Educated in London at Christ's Hospital and St Paul's School, and then at the University of Oxford, he showed an early interest in antiquities; he was encouraged at Oxford by Sir Philip Sidney, and later by Lord Burghley. He became a master at Westminster School, then headmaster from 1593 to 1597. His scheme for a book on Roman Britain eventually became a celebration of the nation through the many phases of its history and the diversity of its topography. Associated with the Latin *Britannia* was a smaller work in English, *Remains Concerning Britain*, a miscellaneous collection of essays on topics of cultural and social history, which has always had strong popular appeal. As a humanist scholar, Camden formed a network of learned friends and associates on the Continent that was quite exceptional for an Englishman of his time.

His other important work was a history of the reign of Elizabeth I, undertaken with the encouragement of Lord Burghley; this was first published in Latin in 1615, then in English in 1625. Camden's eminence as a scholar was recognised by his appointment as a herald (Clarenceux King of Arms) in 1597. He is buried in Westminster Abbey. This portrait was originally in the possession of his friend Sir Robert Cotton. GP

19

Diptych of *Old St Paul's*
John Gipkyn (fl. 1594–1629)
1616
Oil on two panels, each panel
127 × 101.6 cm
Society of Antiquaries of London,
LDSAL 304
Selected references: Scharf 1865, no. 43,
pp. 32–8; Tudor-Craig et al. 2004

This diptych was made for a London scrivener or legal clerk, Henry Farley, as part of his campaign for the restoration of St Paul's Cathedral from 1615 until 1622. A freeman of the City, Farley felt that the dilapidated condition of the church was a civic disgrace. He attempted through pamphlets and poems to prompt the Mayor, the Bishop of London and finally James I to attend to the repair of the fabric, which had been badly damaged by lightning in 1561, when the spire was destroyed and the roof burnt. Farley's poem *The Complaint of Paules*, published in 1616, presents the cathedral lamenting her fallen state, and concludes with a dream in which the author imagines her newly restored. Farley seems to have commissioned this painting as a private record of his hopes. It is possibly the first oil-painting of a historic monument in English art.

The diptych (a work consisting of two painted panels that are hinged together) should be read from the outside first: one panel has a painting on both sides, and the second panel could be fixed to a wall. The outer painting (above left), which is visible when the diptych is closed, depicts ships sailing up the English Channel, and a procession of civic and religious figures, headed by the King and the royal family, moving across London Bridge to the City. When opened, the first inner panel (opposite) shows their destination, Paul's Cross, the preaching place where they assemble to hear a sermon that urges the rebuilding of the cathedral. The third and final panel (above right) offers a vision of the restored church, with a new cupola, with images of the royal family, and angels rejoicing in the wonderful work of restoration.

An inscription states that the diptych was made by John Gipkyn, a painter extensively employed in the Lord Mayor's pageants between 1604 and 1618. The picture was probably in the possession of the poet John Donne (1572–1631) when he was Dean of St Paul's from 1621 to 1631. GP/PT-C

42 | Making History

Earliest Antiquaries | 43

20

'The Tomb of John Donne' from the *Book of Monuments*
Drawing by William Sedgwick
(fl. 1638–1641); book compiled by
William Dugdale (1605–1686)
1640–41
Pen, ink and watercolour, 42 × 27 cm
British Library, London, ADD MS 71474, fol. 164
Selected references: Hamper 1827, p. 14; Parry 1995, pp. 221, 236–40

One of the greatest of the seventeenth-century antiquaries was the Warwickshire gentleman William Dugdale, whose first major enterprise was an account of the antiquities of his own county. For this project he collected vast amounts of information on church monuments and their inscriptions. Around 1640, concerned that the worsening political climate might lead to attacks on cathedrals, the seats of the widely disliked bishops, and prompted by Sir Christopher Hatton, he undertook a preservationist mission to major churches to record their monuments and inscriptions for posterity.

Accompanied by William Sedgwick, 'a skyllfull Armes-paynter', he went first to St Paul's Cathedral, where he made 'exact draughts of all the Monuments' and copied the epitaphs. His foresight was accurate, for, during the Civil War, St Paul's was grievously damaged. Dugdale was able to make use of his notes and Sedgwick's drawings when he came to write *The History of St Paul's Cathedral* (1658), a book that recorded the appearance of the medieval cathedral with its Norman nave. Many of the drawings were etched by the famous Bohemian topographic artist Wenceslaus (Wenzel) Hollar. After the Great Fire of London in 1666, when St Paul's Cathedral was destroyed, Dugdale's book and Sedgwick's drawings remained as an invaluable record of what had been lost. The only monument to survive the fire intact was the one shown here, that of John Donne (1572–1631), the poet and Dean of St Paul's, which was carved by Nicholas Stone, and depicts the shrouded Donne rising from his urn – or is he about to descend into it? GP

44 | Making History

21

Heraldic shields, from the Hatton-Dugdale *Book of Arms*
Compiled by Sir Christopher Hatton (bap. 1605–1670) and William Dugdale (later Sir) (1605–1686)
Late 1630s
Pen, ink and watercolour on vellum, 47 × 72.5 cm
Society of Antiquaries of London, MS 664/1 fol. 15v/16r
Selected references: Maclagan 1956, pp. 31–48; Willetts 2000, pp. 284–6

Heraldry and genealogy were subjects of the highest interest to Elizabethan and early Stuart antiquaries, for the history of noble and gentry families was central to national and local history, and besides, many antiquaries were heralds. William Camden was a herald, as was Sir William Dethick, Garter King of Arms (the senior of the three English Kings of Arms) at the end of the sixteenth century, who enabled the Elizabethan society of antiquaries to meet in the Office of Heralds at Derby House, London. William Dugdale rose through the ranks of heralds to become Garter in 1677, the year in which he was also knighted. Dugdale's patron was Sir Christopher Hatton; with Sir Thomas Shirley and Sir Edward Dering, they formed a short-lived group called 'Antiquitas Rediviva' in the late 1630s, and this book of arms is a product of their collaboration. It records the coats of arms copied from 26 medieval and sixteenth-century rolls. The illuminator was probably William Sedgwick, the arms painter who did a good deal of work for Dugdale. Associated productions from this phase of antiquarian activity are the *Book of Monuments* (cat. 20), and the *Book of Seals* in the Northampton Record Office. Dugdale consummated his interest in heraldry with his vast *Baronage of England* published from 1675 to 1676.

Displayed are pages from the copy of Charles's Roll, named after Nicholas Charles, who owned it in 1605. The Society of Antiquaries has the earliest known manuscript of this roll, which was originally compiled around 1300. It has 486 coloured shields of those entitled to bear arms. GP

22

Church notes and drawings relating to Kent
Sir Edward Dering (1598–1644)
1628–34
Pen and ink, 35 × 45 cm
Society of Antiquaries of London, MS 497A, pp. 12–13
Selected references: Belcher 1888, vol. 1, plates 8, 9; Evans 1956, pp. 21–4; Bertram 1971, p. 39, figs 12–13; Willetts 2000, p. 238

Along with Sir Christopher Hatton, William Dugdale and Sir Thomas Shirley, Sir Edward Dering tried to establish an antiquarian society with the title 'Antiquitas Rediviva' in 1638, but the enterprise did not prosper.

Dering set himself to record the church monuments and inscriptions of his home county of Kent, because these were invaluable records of family descents and alliances. These accurate drawings of monuments and brasses are among the earliest of their type. The notes cover 32 parishes in Kent, including Maidstone, Sittingbourne, Ashford and Cranbrook. This preservationist concern on the part of Dering and other early Stuart antiquaries was well founded, because the Civil War, beginning in 1642, resulted in the destruction of many memorials.

The pages displayed illustrate memorials from St Mary's, Ashford, which were recorded by Dering on 20 July 1628. They have since suffered considerable damage, and without this antiquarian record it would be difficult to envisage the original state of these monumental brasses.

The monument to Sir John Fogge (d. 1490), on the right, survives in its original position beneath the arch dividing the North Chapel from the Chancel. However, all that remains in the slab is Fogge's head resting on his impressive helmet with a crest depicting a unicorn, together with the unusual wreath enclosing an angel holding the inscription on the side of the tomb chest.

In the mid-1630s, Dering handsomely furnished the family chapel in his church at Pluckley in Kent, and had a number of mock-medieval brasses made to commemorate older members of his family – an early case of Gothic revivalism. GP/DC

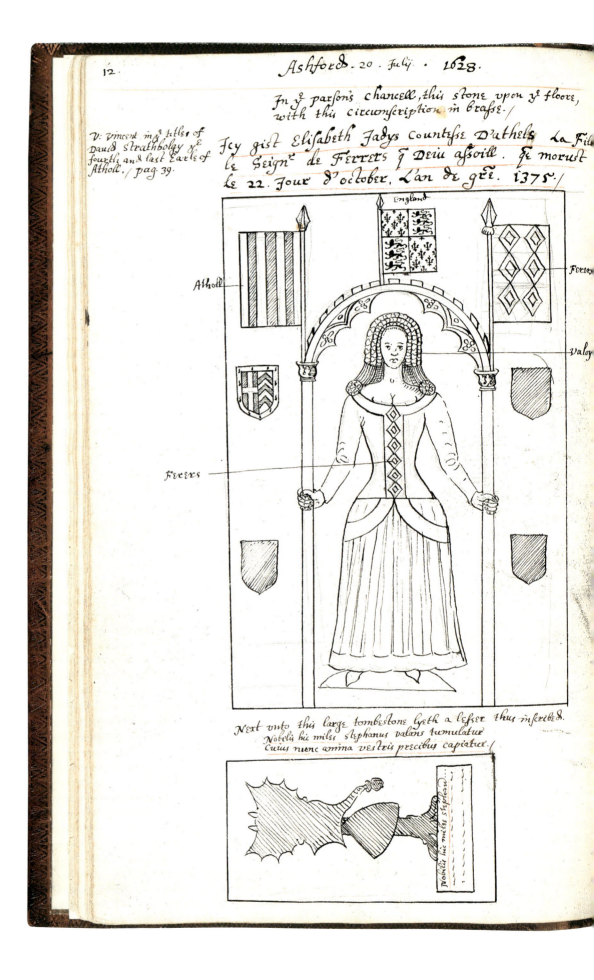

46 | Making History

Ashford.

Betweene ye chancell and Fogges Chappell, now belonging to ye Ld Tufton, this monument thus circumscribed upon ye edge thereof.

Edwardi quarti Regis specialis Amator

Semper Catholicus, Populi vulgaris amicus, et sic decedens a mundo mente.

These three escocheons are placed on ye farther side of this monument.

Plenius hic sequitur qd fecerat iste Johannes
sumptibus ex proprijs ecclam renovavit,
Cum Campanili qd funditus ædificavit.
Pluribus atq; libris chorus hic p eu veneratur.
Ac ornamentis altare Dei decoratur.
Vestibulum ditans, ac plura iocalia donans.
Ut patet intuitu pro posteris memorandum.
Ad laudem domini, cui laus sit nunc et in ævu.
Amen.

48

Most deare, and most dread Soue=
reign.

May it please yor sacred Ma:^{tie}

For the vniuersal embetterment of your
people in their manners; for the more
aduantage of your kingly prerogatiue;
certainly, for your Ma:^{ties} greater comfort,
and the euerlasting fresher
glorie of your name
among vs.

This most humblie submitted work,
doth reason for a Corporation voial, to bee
founded vnder the tytle of Kinge
James his Academ, or
College of Honor.

SIR,

Moses heard Jethro, and old Rome
Hermodorus for composing her twelue
tables. The matter makes the author.
But yor humblest loial Subiect speaks
nothing herein, but yor own most princelie
thoughts & wishes ouer. Many yeres medita-
tions shipt into one half howrs reading.
May it please yor roial goodnesse to vouchsafe it.

23

Petition to King James I for a
Royal Academy
Edmund Bolton (1575–1633)
1619
Manuscript, 30.4 × 32.5 cm
Society of Antiquaries of London,
MS 103
Selected references: Evans 1956,
pp. 16–19; Willetts 2000, pp. 47–8

Edmund Bolton was a Catholic lawyer, herald and historian who enjoyed the protection and patronage of the Duke of Buckingham. He spent a number of years promoting a scheme for an academy of scholars who would devote their energies to a broad patriotic celebration of the achievements of secular Englishmen, translating and writing histories of subjects relevant to the greatness and antiquity of the nation, and keeping a detailed record of contemporary events in England. Bolton looked back to the Elizabethan society of antiquaries as a possible model for what he called his 'Academ Roial', and several members of that group – including Cotton, Selden and Spelman – appeared in the lists of suitable candidates he compiled for his academical senate. In 1617 he addressed a petition to Buckingham to realise his scheme, and then two petitions to James I, in 1619 and 1620. The King was favourably disposed, and a charter was promised, but no progress was made, and with the King's death in 1625, Bolton's project faded. GP

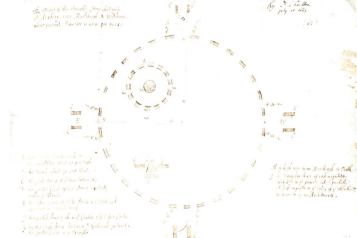

24

Sir John Dodderidge
Artist unknown
c. 1612
Oil on panel, 69 × 59 cm
Society of Antiquaries of London,
Scharf 79
Selected references: Hearne 1773, vol. 2, pp. 432–3; Ibbetson 2004, pp. 402–3

Shown in his robes as a judge of the King's Bench, Sir John Dodderidge (1555–1628) was a member of the Elizabethan society of antiquaries that congregated around William Camden. By his profession and his interests, Dodderidge was typical of those men who undertook research into British antiquities in Elizabeth's reign.

A man of broad learning, he contributed a number of papers to the society, including one on the origin and duties of heralds, and one on the antiquity of Parliament. Shortly before Elizabeth's death, he drew up a petition to the Queen with Sir Robert Cotton and James Lee for the establishment for 'an Academy for the Study of Antiquity and History', a plea that failed. His history of Wales, Cornwall and Chester was published in 1630. Dodderidge was a Devon man, and there is a fine monument to him and his wife in the Lady Chapel of Exeter Cathedral. GP

25

Plan of Avebury
Walter Charleton (1620–1707)
1663
Pen and ink on paper, 24 × 35.5 cm
By permission of the President and Council of the Royal Society, London, MS CL.P XVI.18, fols 101v/102r
Selected references: Hunter 1975, pp. 184–7; Ucko et al. 1991, pp. 17–21; Parry 1995, pp. 283–300

Walter Charleton was a London physician with a strong interest in antiquities. In 1663, he published *Chorea Gigantum*, a rebuttal of the architect Inigo Jones's proposition that Stonehenge was a Roman temple, claiming instead that it was a monument built by the Danes, as a ceremonial centre and as a place where their kings were elected. While discussing Stonehenge with Charles II, Charleton mentioned his friend John Aubrey's 'discovery' of the monumental complex at Avebury, 'which did as much excell Stonehenge as a Cathedrall does a Parish Church'. Aubrey was summoned to give an account of Avebury to the King.

In July 1663, both Charleton and Aubrey presented papers on Avebury to the Royal Society, and this plan is Charleton's measured drawing made for the occasion, the first time that an antiquarian subject had been discussed at the Society. Charleton maintained that the monument was raised by the Danes, and drew all his evidence from books; Aubrey, however (who also produced a measured plan – see fig. 6), discussed the monument in relation to other stone monuments, made deductions from the structure, and did not force preconceptions onto the interpretation of the monument. The Society requested that excavations take place, but they were not carried out. GP

Earliest Antiquaries | 49

'To encourage the ingenious and curious'

The idea of Britain as a nation was promoted following the Act of Union with Scotland in 1707. This was accompanied by a growing curiosity about, and a greater appreciation of, Britain's history. On 5 December 1707 Humfrey Wanley, John Talman and John Bagford, brought together by their common interest in British history, met in a London tavern. By 1718 this informal group had grown in number, and the Society of Antiquaries of London was established with the aim of encouraging 'the ingenious and curious' in the subject of 'Bryttish antiquitys'. A Royal Charter was granted in 1751, and further status came with the Society's move to new premises in Somerset House in 1781, which were shared with the Royal Academy of Arts and the Royal Society. The Society of Antiquaries of London became increasingly fashionable, attracting members of the aristocracy to its Fellowship.

An astonishing variety of items was displayed at the Society's meetings so that others could study them; historical objects, documents and pictures were presented, and often donated. In the period before 1850 the Society was one of the few institutions collecting British antiquities.

Founders and Fellows

Rosemary Sweet

FIGURE 7
Martin Folkes
Jonathan Richardson (1667–1745)
1718
Oil on canvas
Society of Antiquaries of London

Martin Folkes was President of the Society of Antiquaries when it was granted its Royal Charter in 1751.

The late seventeenth century saw considerable amounts of antiquarian research but no attempt to revive the Elizabethan society of antiquaries. The leading forum for the discussion of antiquarian and literary matters, as well as scientific subjects, was the Royal Society, founded in 1660. Such broad-mindedness, however, was discouraged from 1703 under the presidency of Sir Isaac Newton, who favoured a more rigorously scientific approach. There was clearly now a need for a separate society for the study of antiquities. On 5 December 1707, a group of three men, Humfrey Wanley, John Talman and John Bagford (cats 27, 29), gathered together at a London tavern to discuss matters of antiquity. This meeting was to prove the genesis of the Society of Antiquaries of London (cat. 26). A few weeks later, however, the career of Wanley's patron, Robert Harley, 1st Earl of Oxford, as Secretary of State was abruptly ended with accusations of sedition. The turbulence of eighteenth-century politics meant that the early flush of antiquarian enthusiasm was not immediately consolidated. Even so, the group met informally for ten years. Other antiquaries, such as the herald Peter Le Neve (cat. 28), gradually joined the group.

By 1717 a decision had been taken to establish a properly constituted society: thus the formal minutes of the Society of Antiquaries begin on 1 January 1718, where we find the names of 23 founder members.[1] The Society was one of many such associations which were springing up across the country from the late seventeenth century, a period often depicted as a golden age of clubs and societies, when coffee houses and taverns were the settings for a lively ferment of ideas, information exchange and conviviality.[2]

The articles of association proclaimed the study of antiquities to be a 'considerable part of Good Literature' and 'no less curious than useful'. The aims of the Society were 'to encourage the ingenious and curious', to render a knowledge of antiquities more universal, to communicate private knowledge and to collect and print accounts of any monument that might illustrate the history of 'Bryttish antiquitys'. The founder members were well aware that similar bodies for the study of national antiquities already existed in France, Sweden and Italy. Today, the Society of Antiquaries of London is the only one of these bodies that has continued to exist without interruption. The recent passage of the Act of Union in 1707 and the Hanoverian succession gave added impetus to the study of a common British past as a means of consolidating political stability: collaboration, free communication and a common spirit of patriotism constituted the Society's essential rationale. The emphasis on domestic antiquities was also a response to the fashionable lure of classical antiquity in Italy, and a reflection of the interests of members such as the First Secretary, William Stukeley (who joined in 1717), who, at the time, was surveying the sites of Stonehenge and Avebury, believing them to be products of a Druidical civilisation that could match that of Ancient Rome for intellectual and technological sophistication.[3]

Up until the mid-eighteenth century the Society continued as a small, ad hoc gathering with few resources. Its membership was capped at 100 (this was increased to 120 in 1746). Election to the Society depended upon personal recommendation: it was never a matter of political or religious affiliation. At a time when society was still deeply divided along political and religious lines, the Society of Antiquaries of London – and other comparable bodies – explicitly set out to transcend such divisions and to create a space for rational discussion: early members included Catholics (such as the first director, John Talman) and supporters of the exiled Stuarts, as well as staunch Hanoverians. Most, but not all, of the members came from the gentry and the professional classes, with a strong component of clergymen, heralds (including the first president, Peter Le Neve) and lawyers. Yet, of the 23 members in 1718, John Bagford was a shoemaker, George Vertue an engraver, and Humfrey Wanley the son of a draper.

In later years the Society became much more socially exclusive (the London archaeologist Charles Roach Smith [see pp. 201–13]) was initially blackballed for membership in 1836 when it became known that he was 'in business'.[4] Although a few noblemen, such as Lord Coleraine, were active members, the Society lacked the kind of aristocratic or royal patronage that might have subsidised its activities, and its financial resources were limited to membership fees and fines for non-attendance. Throughout the early eighteenth century it kept a low profile, occasionally publishing prints in the series *Vetusta Monumenta*, most of which were engraved by Vertue. It had no permanent meeting-place and attendance was often patchy. It was a struggle to keep going and the Society might easily have faded away, as so many other similar bodies did.

A bequest of drawings and engravings from Lord Coleraine in 1749, however, prompted an important change. Because the Society was not incorporated, it could not legally hold property, meaning that this and any future bequests were invalid. To overcome this problem, under the Presidency of Martin Folkes (fig. 7) a charter of incorporation was obtained in 1751 that established the Society on a sounder and more permanent footing, allowing it to own property, as the Royal Society did, and putting it in a better position to promote the causes for which it had been established (fig. 8). Coleraine's bequest was eventually received in 1754.[5]

In the second half of the eighteenth century the Society of Antiquaries of London can be seen to be taking its national role more seriously: incorporation seems to have created a sense of public responsibility among the new Fellowship. Thus, during the 1760s, it was closely involved in the printing of a facsimile edition of the Domesday Book; in 1770 it began publishing its proceedings, *Archaeologia*, under the direction of Richard Gough, and continued with its publication of historical prints (begun with *Vetusta Monumenta*), which became highly regarded as collectors' items. Its European role was enhanced by the election of honorary fellows from across Europe (particularly in Italy where so many Englishmen travelled on the Grand Tour) and the exchange of publications with continental bodies. Despite these European connections, the emphasis at meetings and in its publications continued to be on domestic antiquities, with a clear and growing concern with the medieval past. Fellows such as Richard Gough and the engraver John Carter urged the Society to do more to preserve the nation's architectural heritage.[6] As early as 1721 William Stukeley had made an eloquent plea for the preservation of the Waltham Cross, which was the subject of one of the earliest prints to be published in *Vetusta Monumenta* (cat. 31).[7] The publication of prints continued: they not only constitute an important documentary record of buildings and antiquities, but they also show a growing awareness of the importance of preservation in the late eighteenth century.

The Society had long felt the need for permanent (and affordable) accommodation. In 1775, when the government announced plans to pull down old Somerset House and erect public offices, which would house the Royal Academy and the Royal Society, members of the Society of Antiquaries saw the opportunity to find a more permanent home, and petitioned the King accordingly. The move to chambers in the newly built Somerset House in 1781 was a visible statement of the Society's national standing and status as a learned body. It also allowed those Fellows who belonged to both the Royal Society and the Society

FIGURE 8
The Royal Charter
1751
Pen and ink on vellum
Society of Antiquaries of London

The decorated initial encloses an engraved portrait of George II, and his great seal is attached.

of Antiquaries to move easily from one meeting to the next; for convenience these meetings were held consecutively on the same evening (fig. 9).

The move also brought with it considerable financial outlay and this was one of the reasons for lifting the bar on membership, which now expanded rapidly. In 1780 it had stood at 180, by 1807 there were 849 Fellows, drawn from all over the country, outstripping the Royal Society by nearly 300.[8] The names of candidates for election were displayed at four consecutive meetings on a certificate signed by their supporters. They were then balloted before they could be admitted to the Society in a formal ceremony. Although many provincial members never attended a meeting, they received the publications and reports of meetings, to which they often sent in contributions to be read out by the Secretary. The social composition continued to be dominated by the gentry and professional classes, but the Society was also becoming increasingly attractive to artists, literary figures, politicians and even minor royalty. Despite this fashionable patina, the public reputation of the Society of Antiquaries as a body tended to the ridiculous, as contemporary cartoons and satires suggest (cats 38, 39). Contemporary taste admired the aesthetic qualities of classical antiquities and architecture, rather than the 'ruder' specimens of domestic antiquity collected by the Society. Antiquaries were regarded as myopic, pedantic and gullible individuals. They were depicted as being easily taken in by forgeries, and lacking the taste or discernment to distinguish art from artifice.[9]

During the first half of the nineteenth century little changed in terms of the Society's sphere of activity or in its own view of its public role. *Archaeologia* and *Vetusta Monumenta* continued to appear at regular intervals with articles of scholarly importance, accompanied by high-quality engravings. The Society also undertook the publication of Anglo-Saxon texts and other historical documents, although they proved prohibitively expensive.[10] The collections of antiquities, books and manuscripts continued to grow. Membership, however, proved less buoyant: from a peak in 1807 numbers declined to 592 in 1846 (with serious implications for the Society's finances), while Fellows continued to be recruited principally from the gentry and professional classes. The Society also had to face new challenges, as it no longer exercised the same dominance over the study of antiquities and the past: new bodies for the study of archaeology and antiquities were being established at both a national and a local level, such as the British Archaeological Association and numerous county archaeological and historical societies, which were more inclusive and less elitist in their membership.[11] The intellectual climate had changed too: disciplinary boundaries were being drawn more tightly and specialist societies, such as the Geological Society of London, were established.[12] The polymathic approach of the eighteenth century, when many Fellows combined interests in science and antiquities, was no longer reflected in the meetings or the membership of the nineteenth century, although in the long term the advances made in the study of geology were to have a significant influence upon the interests of the Society and its Fellowship. Lord Aberdeen, the Society's president from 1812 to 1846, provided desirable aristocratic credentials, but he rarely attended meetings and failed to provide the necessary dynamic leadership.[13] From the 1840s a period of reform and retrenchment began, with the publication of the *Proceedings*, internal administrative changes and the election of new and more energetic Secretaries and officers, laying the foundation upon which reinvigoration and recovery could take place in the second half of the century.

FIGURE 9
Meeting of the Society of Antiquaries at Somerset House
Engraved by H. S. Melville from the drawing by F. W. Fairholt; published as plate 42 in *London Interiors*
March 1844
Society of Antiquaries of London

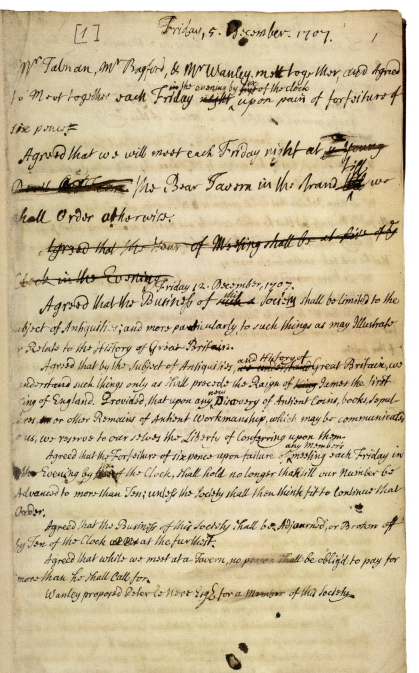

26

Minutes of the first meeting of the Society of Antiquaries
1707
Manuscript on paper, 30 × 18 cm
British Library, London, Harleian
MS 7055, fol. 1
Selected reference: Evans 1956, pp. 36–9

The present Society of Antiquaries of London can trace its origins to the meeting of three friends with an interest in history, Humfrey Wanley, John Talman and John Bagford, in a London tavern on 5 December 1707. They agreed to form themselves into a society that would meet regularly, every Friday night, at the Bear Tavern in the Strand. The following week, they decided that their business should be limited to the subject of antiquities especially relating to British history. Other members were proposed at later meetings and by 9 January 1708 they had moved to the Young Devil Tavern, Fleet Street. Wanley took the minutes of the first meetings and those for 5 December 1707 to 20 February 1708 survive among his papers.

After this time, and perhaps because of the fall from power of Wanley's patron, the Secretary of State Robert Harley, 1st Earl of Oxford, only informal meetings appear to have been held until 1717. In July of that year 23 antiquaries, including six from the 1707 society, met in the Mitre Tavern, Fleet Street. In the following months they decided on a title – the Society of Antiquaries, London (later, of London) – articles of association and a procedure for electing members and officers. These were agreed at a meeting on 1 January 1718, the date when the Society can be said to have been formally constituted. A continuous sequence of handwritten minutes from then until the present day exists. BN

27

(opposite)
Humfrey Wanley
Thomas Hill (c. 1661–1734?)
1711
Oil on canvas, 122 × 102 cm
Society of Antiquaries of London,
LDSAL 309
Selected references: Scharf 1865, no. 51, pp. 44–5; Evans 1956, pp. 33–8; Wright and Wright 1966; Keynes 1996

Humfrey Wanley (1672–1726) was one of the three founding members of the Society of Antiquaries of London in 1707. He took the minutes at their first meetings and on 12 December 1707 recorded that: 'Agreed that the Business of this Society shall be limited to the subject of Antiquities; and more particularly, to such things as may Illustrate and Relate to the History of Great Britain.'

Wanley was a pioneer in the study of palaeography and Anglo-Saxon. He advised Robert Harley, 1st Earl of Oxford, on the purchase of books and manuscripts for his library and later became his librarian. In this capacity Wanley would have met and dealt with John Bagford, a book dealer and another founding member of the Society (cat. 29).

This portrait shows Wanley seated at a desk surrounded by items of antiquarian interest. In particular he holds open a book showing a cruciform text in Greek from St Matthew's Gospel. It was originally identified as the *Covel Gospel* (BL MS HARLEY 5598), a treasured manuscript from the library of Dr John Covel, Master of Christ's College, Cambridge. Wanley had just received promise of the library's sale to Robert Harley. However, the book is now recognised as Wanley's own facsimile of the work in his *Book of Specimens*, a skilled compilation of copied scripts from ancient manuscripts.

The portrait was commissioned by Wanley himself and was probably intended as a gesture of goodwill to his employers. It was purchased at the sale of the Harley collection and later presented to the Society by George Vertue in 1755. JS/SK

28

(opposite)
Peter Le Neve, Norroy King of Arms
Attributed to George Vertue
(1684–1756)
Date unknown
Oil on canvas, 76.2 × 63.5 cm
College of Arms, London
Selected references: Evans 1956; Wagner 1987, pp. 346–7; Sweet 2004, p. 48; Woodcock 2004

Peter Le Neve (1661–1729) was proposed as a member to the fledgling Society by Humfrey Wanley on 12 December 1707 and was chosen as its first Chairman in 1708. By 1717, he was one of only six members left of the original Society and was elected the first President from 1718 to 1724. Like many early members, he was also a freemason; unlike most, he kept a mistress (known as Durham Dolly) during his first marriage and was described as an infidel when buried.

Le Neve exemplified the strong links between antiquaries and heralds. He took an early interest in genealogy and was appointed Rouge Croix Pursuivant (junior officer of arms) at the College of Arms in 1690. He succeeded as Norroy King of Arms in 1704 and the portrait shows him in Norroy's robes. Le Neve was a collector rather than a writer, purchasing sources, especially on the history of Norfolk and Suffolk, many of which formed the basis of Francis Blomefield's five-volume history of Norfolk (1739–75). Prior to his death in 1729, Le Neve expressed the desire that these collections be deposited at a public building in Norwich, such as the cathedral, for 'the use of curious persons'. Most are now in local record offices, but his other collections are widely dispersed. ARP/BN

29

John Bagford
George Vertue (1684–1756), after Hugh Howard (1675–1738)
1728
Engraving, 20.1 × 13.3 cm
Society of Antiquaries of London
Selected references: Evans 1956; Gatch 1986, pp. 150–71; Harmsen 2000, pp. 122–5; Harmsen 2004; Sweet 2004

John Bagford (1650/51–1716) was one of the three original founder members of the Society who met on 5 December 1707. A shoemaker by trade, he was interested in books and collecting ballads. Little is known of his early life but it would appear that he had no formal education; his contemporaries often described him as a remarkable, self-educated man.

By 1686, and until his death, Bagford was at the centre of the London book trade, supplying antiquaries with the resources they required for study. He also acted as a library agent and was instrumental in supplying several major collections, including those of Robert Harley, 1st Earl of Oxford, and Sir Hans Sloane. Both collections were later bought by the government and, together with the earlier collection of Robert Cotton, formed the basis of the British Museum established in 1753. It would have been in this position that Bagford got to know Humfrey Wanley, who was an adviser to Harley on library matters.

Bagford's interest in books and prints led him to research and write the history of printing, including the lives of early English printers. The preliminary results were published; one of them was co-authored with Wanley in the Royal Society's *Philosophical Transactions* of 1707–08. Bagford also wrote an important essay on antiquities that had been found in London, including the Gray's Inn axe (cat. 14). The original painting by Hugh Howard was purchased by Harley, who allowed George Vertue to engrave it. ARP

Founders and Fellows | 59

30

George Vertue
Thomas Gibson (*c.* 1680–1751)
1723
Oil on canvas, 73.5 × 50.8 cm
Society of Antiquaries of London,
LDSAL 314
Selected references: Society of
Antiquaries of London 1773; Scharf
1865, no. 57, pp. 44–5; Vertue 1929–30,
pp. x–xiii, 1–21; London 1987b, no. 30;
Myrone 2007

George Vertue (1684–1756) is shown in informal clothes, working on a copperplate. Vertue was the Society's official engraver from 1717 until a few months before his death. During these years he was also employed by the University of Oxford and continued to take private commissions from Fellows of the Society and others.

A draughtsman noted for his exactness, Vertue drew carefully in pen, ink and watercolour many of the objects and historic monuments that he subsequently engraved for the Society. He was also celebrated as an art historian, and his notebooks on the history of British art have remained a major source of information for scholars.

The artist Thomas Gibson was director of the short-lived academy established in London from 1711 to 1720 for drawing and painting that was governed by the court painter Sir Godfrey Kneller, and which Vertue had attended. After Vertue's death, his widow presented this portrait to the Society in 1773. Some of Vertue's copperplates remain in possession of the Society. JS/PT-C

60 | Making History

31

Waltham Cross from the Swans Inn Looking towards London
Jacob Schnebbelie (1760–1792)
1789
Watercolour with pen and ink on wire-laid paper, 48.9 × 37.3 cm
Society of Antiquaries of London, *Hertfordshire Red Portfolio*, fol. 14
Selected references: Vetusta Monumenta 1796, vol. 3, pls 16, 17; Evans 1956, pp. 72, 121; London 1987A, pp. 361–3; Sweet 2004, p. 302

Waltham Cross, in the High Street of the village of Waltham Cross in Hertfordshire, is one of twelve monuments that marked the resting place of the funeral cortège of Queen Eleanor, wife of Edward I, during its journey back to London from Lincolnshire in 1290. The London crosses at Charing and Cheapside were destroyed during the 1640s, and the preservation of the cross at Waltham Cross became a matter of concern to the Society.

In 1721, at the instigation of William Stukeley (cat. 33), the Society paid ten shillings for the erection of two oak bollards to prevent the Cross being damaged by passing carts. This was probably the first time that payment had been made to protect a historic monument by anyone other than the owner. The Antiquaries also published Stukeley's drawings of the Cross. When he visited the site in later years, Stukeley found that the Turnpike Commission had removed the bollards and dug the ground away from the Cross. He persuaded the local squire to reinstate the oak bollards and to construct a wall around the base of the steps. Stukeley presented a paper in 1757 to the Society on the events surrounding the Cross, noting an increase in similar incidents of damage at other historical monuments. In 1789 it was agreed by the Society that Jacob Schnebbelie, draughtsman of the Society, was to make drawings of the surviving Crosses at Northampton, Geddington and Waltham. Schnebbelie's depiction of the Cross shows the oak bollards and low wall protecting the base of the monument. This is one of many contributions made by Schnebbelie to the Society's large-format published series *Vetusta Monumenta* (see pp. 143–4). ARP

32

Lamp of Knowledge
Fourteenth century
Bronze, 13 × 16.2 cm
Society of Antiquaries of London, LDSAL 56
Selected references: Richmond 1950; Piggott 1951, p. 74; Emanuel 2000

This lamp was adopted by the Society as its emblem in 1770. It is depicted on the Society's publications and represented in brass on the floor of its entrance hall at Burlington House, London. It is often accompanied by a Latin inscription *non extinguetur*, translated as 'shall not be extinguished', drawing an analogy between the lamp and the belief in knowledge and discovery that lies at the heart of the Society's activities.

The lamp was presented to the Society in 1736 by Sir Hans Sloane, an eminent physician and collector, whose later bequest to the nation helped to form the basis of the British Museum. It was the subject of the first engraving issued to members in 1718, the original drawings for which were executed by the Society's director John Talman. The base is not original to the lamp, but was added before the first drawings were made, when it was believed to be a table lamp.

At first the lamp was presumed to be Roman; it was found at St Leonard's Hill, Windsor, in 1717 together with various Roman remains, and closely resembles oil lamps discovered at Pompeii and Herculaneum. However, it is now known to be medieval and recent research suggests it may be Jewish; lamps similar to this were lit every Friday evening in preparation for the Sabbath day of rest. Originally designed to be suspended, the lamp would have had a drip-pan hanging below the burners to collect leaking oil. JS

Founders and Fellows | 61

33

William Stukeley
Attributed to Richard Collins
(fl. 1726–1732)
c. 1726–29
Oil on canvas, 234 × 147.5 cm
Society of Antiquaries of London,
LDSAL 315
Selected references: Scharf 1865, no. 58, pp. 45–6; Piggott 1985, pp. 36–7, 42–3; Scoones 1999, pp. 158–65; Haycock 2002, pp. 49–51

William Stukeley (1687–1765), antiquary and natural philosopher, was a founder member of the re-established Society of Antiquaries of London in 1717 and became its first Secretary. He is remembered for his antiquarian excursions, especially to Avebury and Stonehenge, his researches on prehistoric and Roman sites, and for his interest in Druidism. His illustrated publications include *Itinerarium Curiosum, OR, An Account of the Antiquitys and Remarkable Curiositys in Nature or Art, Observ'd in Travels thro' Great Brittan* (1724), *Stonehenge* (1740) and *Abury* (1743). The last two, in particular, were the result of comprehensive fieldwork and include sketches, detailed drawings and accurate measurements of the monuments; they helped to earn Stukeley the epithet 'the father of British field archaeology'.

Stukeley had many prominent friends, including the mathematician Sir Isaac Newton, and his scientific interests gained him election to the Council of the Royal Society. He practised medicine for a few years before becoming a clergyman in 1729. He took a great interest in gardening and this portrait probably shows him standing in his garden at Grantham, where he lived from 1726 to 1729. His garden featured a 'Temple of the Druids' and other antiquarian artefacts. Bought by the Society for £5 in 1829, the portrait is its largest painting. JS/PT-C

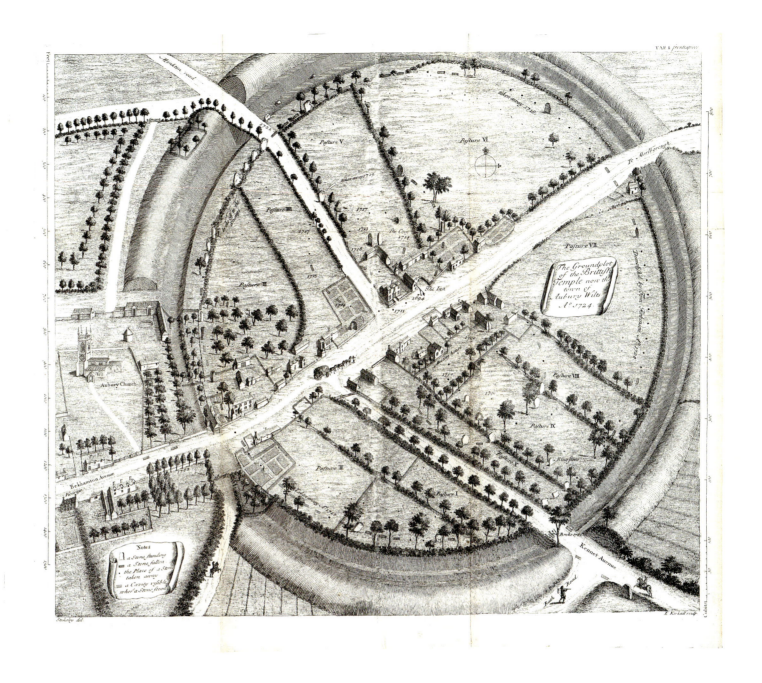

34

Ground Plot of Avebury
William Stukeley (1687–1765)
1724
Engraving, 34.4 × 50 cm
Society of Antiquaries of London
Selected references: Ucko et al. 1991, pp. 48–53; Haycock 2004; Sweet 2004, pp. 128–30

The Avebury henge complex is one of the most impressive in Britain. William Stukeley first visited the site in 1719, his interest aroused by reading John Aubrey's suggestion that the Ancient Britons were responsible for building the stone circles. Stukeley was also concerned about the site's destruction by local landowners, who saw the stones merely as a source of building material.

Between 1719 and 1724 Stukeley undertook a series of well-documented visits, when he carried out some of the earliest extensive systematic surveys of a historical monument by an antiquary. He used a theodolite, a measuring instrument fitted with a telescope that is used to determine the level of the land, and the latest survey techniques to draw an exact geometrical representation of the layout and orientation of the monuments. This allowed him to calculate the original number of stones. Combining his results with previous research, he was able to show where standing stones had been removed in previous decades, as well as providing dates of those losses. The outcome of this work was a comprehensive plan of Avebury in its landscape before further losses. He showed not only the ancient monument but also field boundaries and the contemporary village and roads. The results were published in *Abury, a temple of the British Druids, with some others described* (1743), in which his interpretation was coloured by his ideas of Druidic ceremonies. The ground plot shown here formed the frontispiece for the publication. ARP

Founders and Fellows | 63

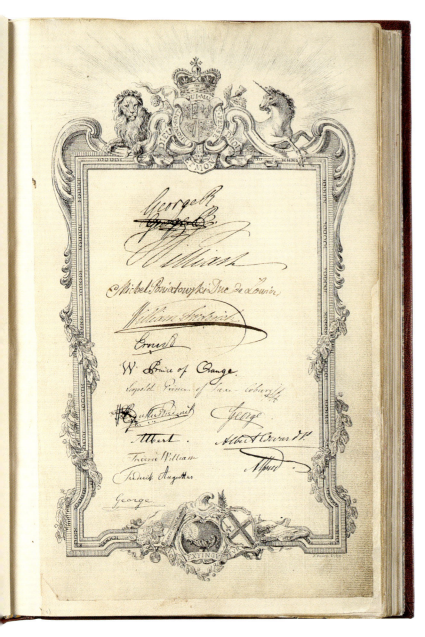

35

Register of Admissions
1752–2001
Manuscript, 42 × 54 cm
Society of Antiquaries of London
Selected references: Bruce-Mitford 1951;
Evans 1956, pp. 130–1

The Royal Charter granted to the Society in November 1751 stipulated that a register should be kept of members. Under the Statutes those elected were required to sign an obligation 'to promote the honour and interest of the Society'. Members were entitled to call themselves Fellows and this register contains the signatures of all those admitted to the Society between 1752 and 2001, when a new register was acquired.

Displayed here is one of two pages added to the beginning of the volume for the signatures of Patrons and Royal Fellows. George II was the first Patron and the Society's Council could propose members of the royal families of Britain and other countries to be elected as Royal Fellows. The ornamental frame was drawn by James Basire, the Society's engraver from 1759 to 1802. The Society's arms displaying the cross of St George with the royal crown in the centre were assumed in 1770, so the page was decorated after this date. The lower part incorporates the Society's lamp emblem, its motto, arms, charter and seal.

The signatures begin with those of George III (who signed in 1761), George IV and William IV and include Prince Albert, Albert Edward (later Edward VII), finishing with George, Duke of York (later George V). A second page was added at the end of the nineteenth century for later signatures. BN

36

(below)
Ballot box
Eighteenth century
Mahogany with brass handles and ivory labels, 36 × 24 × 32 cm
Society of Antiquaries of London
Selected references: Evans 1956;
Society of Antiquaries of London, 2004

This ballot box is an early example of those still used at Society elections, and is likely to be the one ordered by the new President, Edward King, in 1784. Balloting for new members first took place in 1718: 'It was Ordered by the Society yt all Members to be Admitted into the same be Balloted for and that a Balloting Box be Prepar'd for the Purpose.' To be elected, a person shall be 'excelling in the knowledge of the antiquities and history of this and other nations' and be 'desirous to promote the honour, business and emoluments of the Society'.

The Royal Charter granted to the Society by George II in 1751 permitted members to be called Fellows of the Society of Antiquaries (FSA). The number of Fellows was then limited to 150; it currently stands at over 2,400. Proposals for membership can come only from existing Fellows; a candidate must have at least five and up to twelve nominations. The candidate's name is then included in the next available secret ballot, of which there are now routinely seven a year. Originally Fellows could only vote in person but today they also have the choice of casting their vote by post or online.

Through the circular opening of the box voters insert their hand in order to drop a cork ball into either side of the 'yea' or 'no' partition. The Society uses 25 such boxes at meetings today. To be successful, a candidate needs to achieve a ratio of four 'yea' votes for every no or 'blackball'. Failure to be elected is known as being 'blackballed'. JS

37

The Reception of a New Member in the Society of Antiquarians
Thomas Rowlandson (1757–1827)
1782
Pen and ink and watercolour over pencil, 37.4 × 23.5 cm
Society of Antiquaries of London
Selected references: Pfungst 1911–12, p. 6; Oppé 1923, p. 9, pl. 14; London 1934, no. 798, pl. 162; Bury 1949, p. 82, pl. 18; Bruce-Mitford 1951, p. 71, pl. 22; Evans 1956, p. 180, pl. 19

Rowlandson's watercolour shows Dr Jeremiah Milles, the small and corpulent Dean of Exeter, President of the Society from 1769 to 1784, admitting a new member to the Society soon after the move into Somerset House. Although he makes little attempt to record the meeting room accurately, Rowlandson does capture the President's likeness. Dean Milles had suffered a stroke in 1780 that left him without the use of his right arm. He therefore shook hands with his left. In the picture it is the new member who appears to adopt the curious practice of shaking hands with his left hand, while Milles uses his right; in a print this arrangement of hands would be reversed; Rowlandson may have planned an eventual engraving. The new member may also be intended as a portrait of a real person, although he remains unidentified. Tall, aristocratic and something of a dandy with his blue-striped coat and newfangled umbrella, he stands out from Rowlandson's more conventional portrayal of the other antiquaries, who are unlikely to represent more than types.

Although not an Academician, Rowlandson was well connected with the RA and would have had access to its rooms. A connecting door between the rooms occupied by the Society of Antiquaries in Somerset House and those of the Academy made it perfectly possible that the artist had glimpsed the Society's activities. He had perhaps a particular interest. At the end of 1781 Dean Milles had been gullible enough to sponsor a second edition of the poems of Thomas Rowley, the entirely fictitious fifteenth-century poet of Thomas Chatterton's celebrated deception. Thomas Rowlandson – 'Rowly' to his friends – may well have taken considerable teasing during the controversy through the coincidence of the shared names; he must have found Dean Milles, Thomas Rowley's champion, something of a curiosity. AP

38

An Antiquarian
Thomas Rowlandson (1757–1827)
1789
Hand-coloured etching, 36.2 × 25.6 cm
Private collection
Selected references: Falk 1949, opp.
p. 101; Sotheby's 1994, lot 23;
Knox 2003

Antiquaries did not escape the satirical wit of the artist and caricaturist Thomas Rowlandson. Much of what Rowlandson found comic reflected the view, widespread at the time, of an antiquary as a man obsessed with the long-dead past. Here an elderly and desiccated antiquary peers agape through his scissor-glasses at an Egyptian mummy and other relics of antiquity. The use of a mummy or mummy-case to illustrate the morbid preoccupations of the antiquary occurs in a number of Rowlandson's drawings – for example, a roughly sketched mummified figure can be seen in the background to *The Reception of a New Member in the Society of Antiquaries* (cat. 37). In later caricatures, with the mania of the Napoleonic era for all things Egyptian sweeping the country, his depiction of mummies became more convincing.

The Egyptian mummy in this caricature has traditionally been identified as one sent back to England in 1738 by Dr Richard Pococke, an early British traveller to the Near East. The mummy was subsequently displayed among the collections of the Duke of Richmond in his gallery at Whitehall, where Rowlandson drew as an art student. It later belonged to Sir John Soane and is still in his museum at Lincoln's Inn Fields in London.

Although hardly flattering, Rowlandson's lampoon of 'An Antiquarian' is relatively mild. He reserved his more savage satires for the medical profession, rich clergymen and lawyers. AP

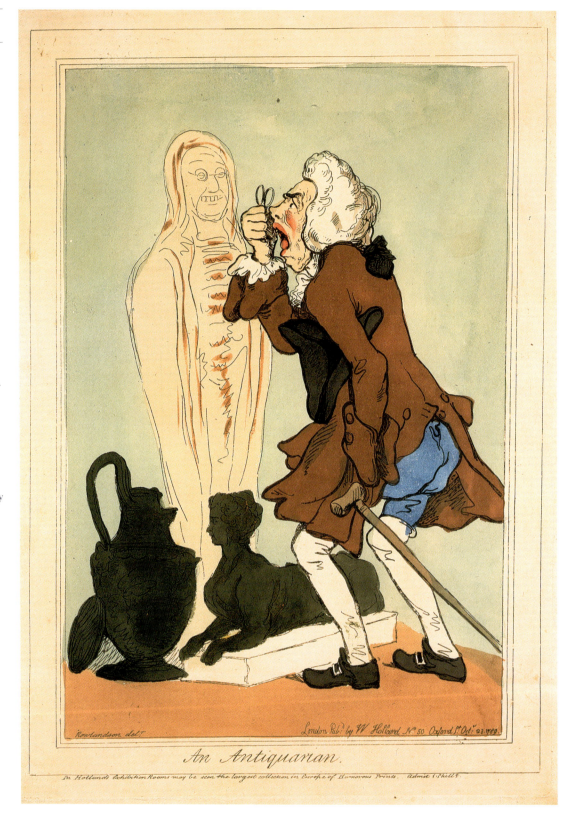

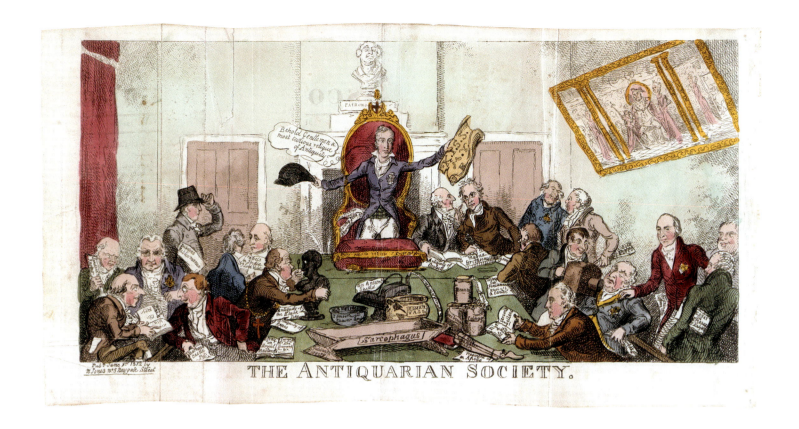

39

The Antiquarian Society
George Cruikshank (1792–1878)
1812
Coloured engraving, 20.5 × 39.5 cm
Derrick Chivers
Selected references: Cruikshank 1812, pp. 431, 450–5; George 1949, pp. 171–2; Nurse 2000, pp. 316–20

Cruikshank's satirical print of an imaginary meeting of the Society was published in the issue for 1 June 1812 of the radical monthly magazine *The Scourge* (1811–16). Cruikshank was one of the most original, productive and skilful caricaturists of the day. A controversial election for president of the Society had taken place five weeks previously and Cruikshank had evidently been informed of the proceedings by a person clearly hostile to the winning faction of the newly elected president and future Prime Minister, Lord Aberdeen, who is shown holding a scroll inscribed as on a monument 'K.I.S.S.M.Y.R.'. In the print nobody listens to him, and the Duke of Norfolk, on the right, is fast asleep. Aberdeen's Catholic opponent for the presidency, Sir Henry Englefield, who had contributed more to antiquarian scholarship, examines a bust presumably meant to represent his former Jamaican mistress. The table is shown strewn with such everyday objects as a coal skuttle (labelled 'Ancient Shield'), jars of pickled cabbage and gooseberries ('Funerial Urns'), a pigswill trough ('Roman Sarcophagus') and a chamber pot masquerading as a 'Roman Vase'.

Although a caricature, Cruikshank's print is one of the earliest images of a Society meeting. The room at Somerset House, now used by the Courtauld Institute of Art Gallery, is accurately depicted. The Society still has the same President's chair, the bust of George III. The painting of the family of Henry VIII depicted on the right was then on loan from the King. The seating in Somerset House, and in Burlington House until the 1920s, was arranged parliamentary fashion, facing across a long table, so that objects could be examined and discussed. BN/EL

facere ñ plegiū ipsius debitoris distingant̄ s’mdm ip-
tionem debiti. Et si capitalis debitor defecit: in solu-
uǁ reddit noliit cum possit. plegii respondeant de deb-
debitoris quousq; eis sit satisfcm de debito qd ante p
strauerit se inde ee quietū uersus eosdem plegios.

Ciuitas lond’ hat omnes antiquas libtates & oms
Preica uolum’ & concedim’ qd’ oms alie ciuitates & bur-
tubz & omnes portus hant oms libtates & libas cōsue
nullus distingat̄ ad faciendū mai’ seruitiū de feodo

Communia placita non sequntur curiam nram s; t
recognitones de noua deseisina & de morte antecesso
Nos uǁ si ext’ regnū fuim’: capital’ iustic’ nr’ mittem’
semel in anno qui cū militibz comitatuū capiant in
in illo aduentu suo in comitatu p iustic p̄dictos ad d
nari non possūt p eosdem terminent̄ alibi in itiner
cultate aliquo$_{r}$ articulo$_{r}$ terminari non possūt refer
terminent̄. Assise de ultima p̄sntatoē semp capiant̄
Liber homo n’ amciet̄ p puo delicto n’ scdm modū d
magno delicto scdm magnitudinē delicti. saluo cont-
ua mercandisa sua z uillan’ alt’^{s} ī nr’ eodem n’ ã

Collecting for Britain

Bernard Nurse

FIGURE 10
Four Scenes from the Life of St Etheldreda, Abbess of Ely in the Seventh Century
Robert Pygot
c. 1455
Oil on oak panel
Society of Antiquaries of London,
Scharf 11

The panels were bequeathed to the Society in 1828 by Thomas Kerrich, who had found them being used as cupboard doors in a cottage in Ely.

The unique nature of the collections of the Society of Antiquaries of London arises from the continuous support of its members over 300 years. They have been generous in their gifts and far-sighted in their acquisitions; the result is a resource of extraordinary richness and diversity. For the first half of the eighteenth century space was restricted to a room generally in a tavern where regular meetings were held, and without corporate status the Society was unable to receive bequests. Nevertheless, by 1751, a small collection of topographical prints and drawings, a few portraits, manuscripts, antiquities and some books had been acquired. The situation improved in that year with the grant of a Royal Charter giving the Society the clear objective of encouraging the study of the past of Britain and other countries, and the power to enjoy in perpetuity any antiquities, manuscripts, goods and chattels. The move to Robin's Coffee House, Chancery Lane, in 1753 provided the Society with exclusive use of sizeable premises for the first time. Some notable gifts followed and the collections started to grow.[1]

Prints and Drawings
Prints and drawings formed the most distinctive element in the Society's collections in the eighteenth century. In 1708 Humfrey Wanley drew up a list of activities that should be promoted that included 'to take the prospects of Ancient fortifications, Castles, Churches, Houses etc. To take drafts of Tombs, Inscriptions, Epitaphs, Figures in painted Glass etc'.[2] After the Society was formally constituted in 1718, drawings were commissioned for record and publication (see pp. 123–8 and 143–61). Even more were acquired by purchase or gift (fig. 11); and the first substantial collection bought was that of the Director of the Society, John Talman, in 1727 (fig. 19).

By 1850, the Society possessed an extensive collection of illustrations. It had employed the best draughtsmen of the period, such as George Vertue, John Carter, Charles Stothard and Richard and Robert Smirke. Other well-known artists, such as Thomas Girtin, Richard Cosway and William Blake, are also represented by drawings made early in their careers. The illustrations formed two main subject groups: portable antiquities and (mostly British) topography. With the historic brass rubbings acquired later, the extent, quality and early date of this material have resulted in collections of outstanding national importance.[3]

Manuscripts
Before the bequest of Charles Lyttelton, President from 1765 to 1768 and Bishop of Carlisle, was received in 1769, the Society owned about a dozen manuscripts, the most important being letters to Oliver Cromwell formerly in the care of John Milton and donated in 1746. Lyttelton added another thirty, including the Lindsey Psalter (cat. 42) and the contemporary copy of the *Magna Carta* (cat. 41). He also left papers on Worcestershire history, establishing the Society as a place of deposit for manuscripts on antiquarian and historical subjects long before the creation of county record offices. Several other important county collections followed.

Towards the end of the eighteenth century the Society was active in purchasing manuscripts regarded as significant sources for British history. One of the earliest acquisitions was the Bolton petition for a Royal Academy of 1619, which was purchased in

FIGURE 11
'Caerlaverock Castle' from *Antiquities and Topography of Nithsdale*
Robert Riddell
1787
Watercolour
Society of Antiquaries of London,
MS 117 fol. 61

This watercolour of the thirteenth-century Scottish castle from a collection of drawings and notes by Robert Riddell, a friend of the Scottish poet Robert Burns, was presented to the Society by Riddell in 1793.

1770 (cat. 23); the twelfth-century *Winton Domesday* (cat. 40) and the *Inventory of Henry VIII* of 1550 (cat. 54) were acquired at the same auction in 1790. Documents as well as artefacts and monuments were judged important by antiquaries for studying the past; inventories and accounts combined an interest in all three aspects and would make potentially valuable publications.[4] Heraldry was another subject of study, not just because of the number of heralds who were Fellows, but also for its use in dating monuments. In 1796, Joseph Jekyll MP, gave some early heraldic manuscripts, including the fourteenth-century roll of arms that became known as the Antiquaries Roll, and the curious jousting cheque for a contest at the Field of Cloth of Gold (cat. 44). The collection of heraldic manuscripts developed considerably at the end of the nineteenth century with further important deposits. By 1816, when the first catalogue was published, there were 216 manuscripts and 34 rolls and charters ably listed by the Society's Secretary, Sir Henry Ellis, who was also Keeper of Manuscripts at the British Museum. The latest catalogue published in 2000 has over 1,000 entries, ranging from single to multi-volume acquisitions.[5]

Pictures and Antiquities
The history of the British monarchy was a long-standing area of interest to members. The first items purchased by the Society for its collections were three royal portraits acquired in 1718 (Henry V, Edward IV and Elizabeth of York). A portrait of Henry VII was added in 1753. The bequest of the Revd Thomas Kerrich received in 1828 made the collection an outstanding one. He gave 26 fifteenth- and sixteenth-century paintings (fig. 10), including two of the earliest portraits of Edward IV (cat. 48) and Richard III (cat. 49), and one of the best-known images of Mary I (cat. 53). The National Portrait Gallery, London, had not then been established, and the Society had fine rooms for displaying pictures at Somerset House, where Kerrich had often attended meetings. The bequest was timely as the Society had just been asked to return several large historical paintings that had been loaned by George III in 1804.

Purchases were rare, but included two large paintings: the 1616 diptych of Old St Paul's, acquired around 1781 (cat. 19) and the full-length portrait of the first Secretary, William Stukeley (cat. 33). Portraits of Fellows such as Humfrey Wanley (cat. 27) and George Vertue (cat. 30) were generally donated. The opportunity to rehang the framed pictures in chronological order was taken after the Royal Society's former meeting room in Somerset House was taken over by the Antiquaries in 1858. Soon afterwards George Scharf, Director of the National Portrait Gallery, wrote a descriptive catalogue of the 68 pictures then in the collection.[6]

Whereas wall space to hang a limited number of paintings could be found, finding room to display historic artefacts adequately presented more serious difficulties. They were never purchased and sometimes had to be given away because of their size. A large model of the Temple of the Sybil at Tivoli, which had occupied much of the space in the library, went to the United Services Museum in London in 1846. The Society's meetings were often occupied by discussion of new discoveries of portable antiquities and the Society was seen by Fellows as a natural place for depositing smaller items. One of the first to be discussed was the lamp found at Windsor, which achieved a special significance as an emblem of 'the light of learning'. It eventually became the Society's

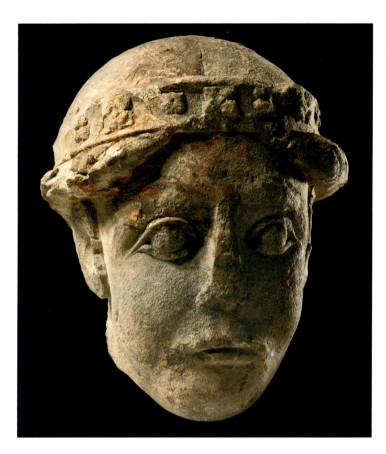

FIGURE 12
The Merton Head
Fifteenth century
Stone with traces of gilt
Society of Antiquaries of London,
LDSAL 148

This stone head with coronet was found on the site of Merton Priory in Surrey in 1797. The landowner made the find known to the diplomat and collector Sir William Hamilton, who presented the head to the Society on his behalf in 1802.

device and was donated (cat. 32). In 1754 Henry Baker, one of the leading scientists of the day, presented two urns 'to be lodged in some future museum of the Society'.[7] Sir William Hamilton presented the medieval stone head found at Merton (fig. 12) and the Becket casket (cat. 43). Other gifts donated to the Society included an early model of a prehistoric monument (cat. 87) and the prehistoric axes from Hoxne in 1795 (cat. 128). Although the result of accumulation rather than design, an extraordinary variety of objects was always present in the rooms for Fellows to see and handle, providing a distinctive element to the Society's character.

Before the 1850s, the Society was one of the few national organisations collecting British antiquities and, in 1828, John Markland, the Director of the Society, attempted to promote the establishment of a museum of national antiquities based on the Society's collections. The Trustees of the British Museum were hostile at the time towards the idea of actively collecting British material themselves, but the government would not provide the Society with any more space. About 400 objects or groups of objects from a wide variety of periods and places were in the collection when Albert Way, the Director, compiled the first catalogue, published in 1847.[8] After the objects had been rearranged in cabinets in 1863, Lord Stanhope, the Society's President, commented in his anniversary address, 'A museum in the proper sense of the word, we have neither the space nor the inclination to keep up. We content ourselves with the humbler object of decorating our meeting room with a few typical specimens of antiquities, classical or medieval.'[9] By then, the British Museum had been persuaded, after considerable pressure from Fellows, to develop its own British collections (see pp. 201–13).

Printed Books
The holdings of printed material were slow to develop. When the first catalogue of printed books was published in 1816, it listed only about 3,000 titles, less than many country-house libraries, and contained few books published before 1700. The main strengths were in British topography and the rare early broadsides, such as that of the Virginia Company Lottery (cat. 45), and proclamations.[10] The chief period of growth came in the second half of the nineteenth century with the rapid increase in archaeological journals and historical publications, a concerted effort to improve the library from the 1840s, and the provision of far more space for books at Burlington House. Fellows were encouraged to donate books, the Society set aside regular sums for new acquisitions and an active exchange programme was pursued with related institutions. At the end of the nineteenth century, therefore, the historic special collections of manuscripts, drawings, pictures and artefacts were expanding less than the collections of printed books and journals. By then all the collections complemented each other to create the leading specialist library for research into the physical evidence of the human past in Britain, a position that the Society's library still holds today. Although developed as a private resource by its Fellows, the Society has made all its collections increasingly accessible to others, and they are widely used by scholars.

Collecting for Britain | 71

40

Winton Domesday
Twelfth century
Brown calf leather covers, manuscript on vellum leaves, each 25.3 × 18 cm
Society of Antiquaries of London, MS 154
Selected references: Biddle 1976; Willetts 2000, p. 72

The Domesday Survey ordered by William the Conqueror did not include London or Winchester. However, the royal properties in Winchester were recorded around 1110 and the whole city was surveyed for Bishop Henry of Blois in 1148. These two manuscripts, written in Latin, survive in a single volume, bound about 1150, and are known as the *Winton Domesday* because of the amount of information they provide about the inhabitants; Winton is the Latin name for Winchester. They form the earliest and most detailed descriptions of any European town of the early Middle Ages, and were carried out at a time when Winchester was at the height of its prosperity.

The volume passed down through the family of a former Dean of Winchester and was exhibited at one of the Society's meetings in 1756. Recognising its value as source material for British history, the Society's Treasurer, John Topham, purchased the volume at an auction in 1790 for five guineas.

The brown tanned-leather covers of the original binding are exceptionally well preserved and have been mounted on a later calf binding. Blind impressions made with ten different tools depict such figures as birds with human heads, dragons, running deer and feeding animals. None of these subjects is Christian, and it has been suggested that Jewish craftsmen were responsible, as the Jewish community in Winchester was the wealthiest and most important in the country at the time. The survey was first published by the Record Commission in 1816. BN

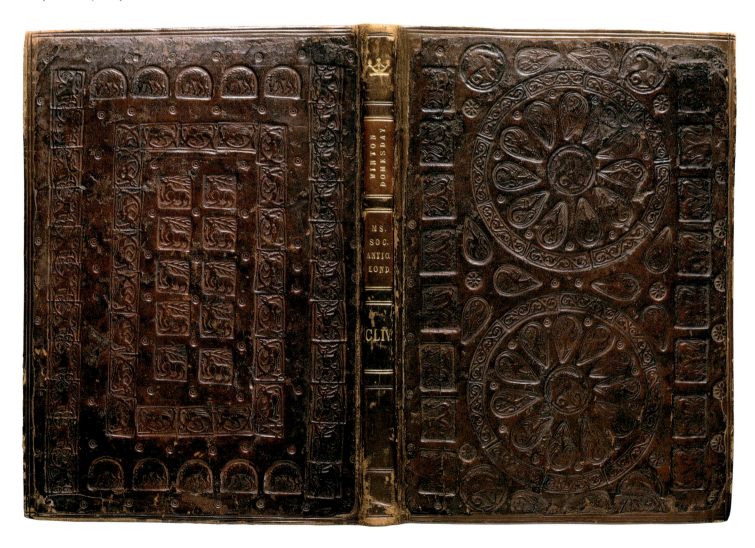

72 | Making History

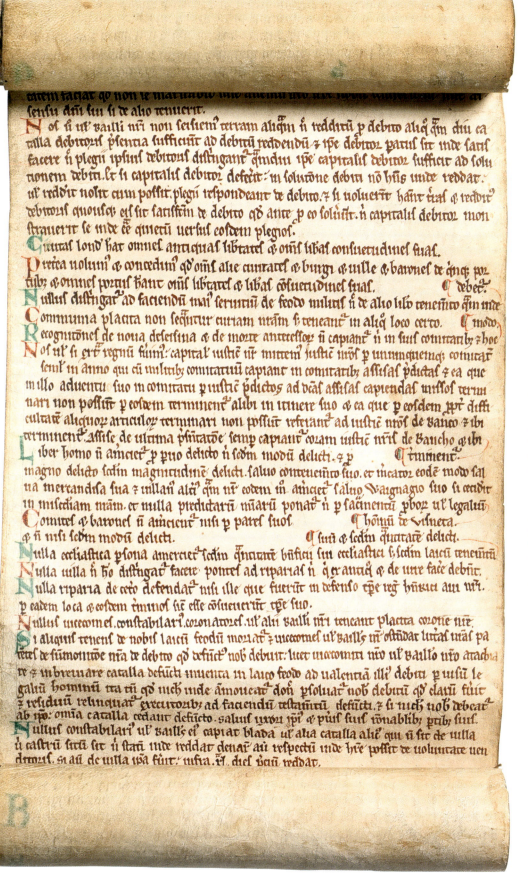

41

Magna Carta
After 1225
Manuscript with illuminated capitals on three membranes of joined parchment, 170 × 20.4 cm
Society of Antiquaries of London, MS 544
Selected references: Blackstone 1759; Holt 1969; Davis 1977; Willetts 2000, p. 251

Magna Carta, the Great Charter of English liberties, was first issued by King John in 1215 and then annulled by Pope Innocent III. This is a contemporary copy of the text of the third revision issued by Henry III in 1225, when still a minor, and it represents the final form as later confirmed and enshrined in English law with 47 clauses instead of the original 63. Since then it has been regarded by all who have adopted English laws as the chief constitutional defence against arbitrary rule. Written in Latin, the most famous clause (no. 29) starting 'Nullus liber homo' translates as 'No free man shall be … imprisoned, or stripped of his rights or possessions … except by the lawful judgement of his equals or by the law of the land.'

The Society's copy is believed to have belonged to Halesowen Abbey, Worcestershire. It was owned by Bishop Charles Lyttelton, the Society's President from 1765 to 1768, and was exhibited by him at meetings in 1749 and 1761. In the eighteenth century, members of the Society were concerned to investigate all aspects of British history and the most eminent legal historian of the time, William Blackstone, studied this copy. It was donated by Thomas Pitt, Lyttelton's nephew and executor in 1771, with other records of Halesowen Abbey. BN

Collecting for Britain | 73

42

Lindsey Psalter
Before 1222
Illumination on vellum, 25 × 35 cm
Society of Antiquaries of London,
MS 59
Selected references: Morgan 1982,
no. 47; London 1987A; no. 254;
Willetts 2000, p. 28

This illuminated book of psalms in Latin from the Old Testament of the Bible with a calendar and various prayers was owned by Robert de Lindesey, the Benedictine Abbot of Peterborough from 1214 to 1222. It is one of the few prayer books from the thirteenth century that can be connected to a named individual and, therefore, closely dated. The manuscript includes two full-page miniatures of the Crucifixion and Christ in Majesty and one full-page ornamented initial, all attributed to the same artist. These, with other decorated initials, are regarded as prime examples of the early Gothic style in English painting. The initial B on folio 38v shown here is at the beginning of Psalm 1 starting 'Beatus …' or 'Blessed is the man …' The illumination is filled with concentric coils inhabited by lions, squirrels and rabbits. Seated figures of Old Testament prophets, King David playing a harp and other musicians occupy medallions in the frame.

The psalter was bequeathed in 1768 by Charles Lyttelton, Bishop of Carlisle and President from 1765 to 1768, who had acquired it from another Fellow, Smart Lethieullier. Lyttelton's substantial bequest of manuscripts and books greatly enhanced the Society's collections a few years after the Royal Charter had been granted. The psalter is one of the Society's greatest treasures.
BN

43

(opposite)
St Thomas Becket Casket
1195–1200
Enamel on copper, 15.5 × 21 × 9.3 cm
Society of Antiquaries of London,
LDSAL 110
Selected references: Bruce-Mitford 1951, p. 40, pl. 21; Evans 1956, p. 218; Caudron 1975, p. 67; Limoges 1999, pp. 100–1, no. 15

This ornate reliquary was designed to hold remains of St Thomas Becket, Archbishop of Canterbury, who was murdered in Canterbury Cathedral in 1170. He had been in conflict for many years with Henry II after changing his allegiance from the Crown to the Pope and the Church. Four knights allegedly overheard the King's rage and took seriously his shouts to rid him of the priest. Thomas Becket's dramatic martyrdom was allegedly followed three days later by a series of miracles. He was canonised within three years of his death.

The casket was purchased by Sir William Hamilton in Naples, when he was British Ambassador in the city, and presented to the Society in 1801. Hamilton originally believed it to be Russian or modern Greek. Similar reliquaries had previously been exhibited to the Society, one by William Stukeley in 1748.

The casket is one of at least forty designed to distribute the saint's relics throughout Europe, reflecting his popularity in the late twelfth century. It is made of copper alloy decorated in champlevé enamel, a technique developed and exploited at Limoges in France. It would originally have had four legs and been lined with wood. This is one of the few caskets to depict all four knights. One side represents St Thomas's martyrdom, the lid shows his entombment, and the two end panels each depict a standing saint. A tapestry based on this design is on display in the Hall of the Worshipful Company of Mercers in London. JS

44

Jousting cheque for a contest at the Field of Cloth of Gold
1520
Manuscript with bodycolour on vellum, 36.5 × 27.3 cm
Society of Antiquaries of London,
MS 136/2
Selected references: Anglo 1961, pp. 153–62; Willetts 2000, p. 61

A jousting cheque is a document on which a herald noted the scores achieved by knights competing in mounted lance combats. Sixteenth-century tournaments generally comprised three types of contest: two opposing knights jousting across a barrier (the tilt); groups of knights, separated by a barrier, fighting on foot with spears or swords (the barriers); or groups of mounted knights fighting with swords (the tourney). A series of tilting contests, augmented by tourneying and barriers, constituted the principal entertainment during the meeting of Henry VIII and François I, King of France, at the Field of Cloth of Gold in 1520 (see cat. 112).

This cheque is a hybrid document. It is evidently the beginning of an armorial roll of those attending the meeting and on the top left displays François's shield of arms within the collar of the Order of St Michael; on the top right, Henry's within that of the Garter; and below, seven further shields of arms. But squeezed into the spaces beside the royal arms are the scores for nine pairs of knights, each of whom ran eight courses as prescribed in the articles of challenge. However, it is impossible to assign the contest to a particular day.

Apart from a small collection at the College of Arms, few jousting cheques survive. This example was presented to the Society in 1796 with a fourteenth-century roll of arms known as the Antiquaries Roll by Joseph Jekyll MP at a time of a revival of interest in heraldry. SA

45

Virginia Company Lottery
Felix Kyngston for William Welby
1615
Printed broadside with woodcuts,
36.2 × 30 cm
Society of Antiquaries of London
Selected references: Lemon 1866,
no. 151; Johnson 1966

The Virginia Company was created by Royal Charter in 1606 to promote the settlement of Jamestown. In 1612, the Company was given permission to hold lotteries in order to raise money for the plantation; the Lord Mayor supported the work as removing 'many Idle and Vagrant persons' to America. However, the administrators were accused of taking money from those who could not afford to gamble, and the licence was suspended in 1621. James I opposed the smoking of tobacco, the Company's main export, and in 1624, Virginia became a royal colony under the direct rule of a governor.

Of the fifteen broadsides, printed on one side of a sheet of paper like a poster, known to have been issued by the Company, the Society holds five, including this one, which are unique. It has been suggested that the pictures of Indians were taken from life as they show authentic details of dress not found on other contemporary images, and name the subjects. They provide the earliest printed illustrations of Native Americans from what is now Virginia. Although the date of the lottery was fixed for June, the draw did not take place until November 1615, to allow more tickets to be sold.

Twelve volumes of broadsides and proclamations printed in Britain were bought by Thomas Hollis, who generously presented them to the Society in 1757, although he was not then a Fellow. As a result, with its later additions, the Society now holds one of the largest and most important collections of these historic printed documents. BN

46

Banner of 'St Martin and the Beggar'
Artist unknown
c. 1440
Distemper or oil on linen, 43 × 28.5 cm
Society of Antiquaries of London,
LDSAL 501
Selected references: Scharf 1865, no. 10, pp. 11–12; Baring-Gould 1914, pp. 241–61; Cross 1961; Wilson 1968

St Martin (d. 397) is depicted, on both sides of the cloth, dressed as a civilian and sharing his cloak with a beggar. Perhaps the earliest sizeable fragment of an English painted cloth in existence, it was probably used as a church's processional banner or as a pennon attached to a processional cross. Recent research suggests that it might have been the banner of the Worshipful Company of Drapers in London, and may even have been painted by John Ruddock, who carried out other work for the guild.

Although he lived in France, St Martin has been popular in England for many years and is celebrated by the Western church on 11 November. He is remembered for sharing his cloak with a disabled beggar outside Amiens, while stationed there with the Roman army. He left the army in 356 on the grounds that he was Christ's soldier and was therefore not allowed to fight. He was later elected Bishop of Tours, where he is especially venerated.

The painted cloth was presented to the Society in 1855 by James Wallis Pycroft, an eccentric Fellow who specialised in ecclesiastical legalities and was later expelled from the Society. Pycroft left no record of provenance, but the letter accompanying his gift notes its uniqueness and remarks on the characters portrayed; the beggar wears more clothing in this representation than is usual in medieval depictions, and, unlike in many other images, St Martin is not riding a horse. The execution of one side is inferior to the other, suggesting that it was copied from the original by an assistant. JS, NM, PT-C

Collecting for Britain | 79

47.1–2

Saxon Kings
Artist unknown
Early sixteenth century
Two framents from mural frieze.
Oil on oak panels: Athelstan 165 × 83 cm, unknown king 150 × 84 cm
Society of Antiquaries of London, LDSAL 509
Selected references: Kempe 1830, pp. 497–502; Society of Antiquaries of London 1830; Society of Antiquaries of London 1880, pp. 381–3; London 2007, no. 5

These are the two largest sections from possibly the earliest cycle of paintings of the Saxon Kings of England. The Society holds six of these painted fragments altogether. They were discovered in 1813 by Alfred John Kempe at Baston House in Keston, Kent. He describes how they were 'sadly mutilated to form the wainscot of a small closet'. Kempe published his discovery in the *Gentleman's Magazine* in 1830, illustrated with engravings by his close friend the antiquarian draughtsman Charles Stothard. He exhibited a selection of the panels to the Society in the same year.

The seated king (right) can be identified from the inscription as Athelstan (who reigned between 925 and 939), the first monarch who could be called king of all England. The text is taken from the Brut chronicle in Latin, in which Athelstan is described as achieving English supremacy over the Welsh and Scots in 937. The second portrait (opposite) depicts an unknown Saxon ruler of the English. Attempts to identify this king remain unsuccessful. A mural representing the unification of Britain would have been a fitting subject: Henry VII, in whose reign the cycle was probably painted, tried to project an image of himself as the king who brought stability after the Wars of the Roses.

The whole composition, which would have been unified by the brocade curtain painted in the background, must have been of a considerable size and would have demanded a large room for display. It is possible that the paintings were first hung in Eltham Palace, which was used by Henry VII and had a hall sufficiently large for them.

The six panels were given to the Society in 1880 by Canon Jackson on behalf of his cousin, Elizabeth Branson, heiress of Baston House. JS, PT-C

80 | Making History

Kerrich Collection of Royal Portraits
CATALOGUE NUMBERS 48–53

In 1828, the Reverend Thomas Kerrich (1748–1828) bequeathed his remarkable collection of fifteenth- and early sixteenth-century English and European paintings to the Society, of which he was a Fellow. Librarian to the University of Cambridge, Kerrich was also an artist and antiquary. He took great interest in the infant discipline of art history, attended meetings and published articles in the Society's journal *Archaeologia*. Given the Society's interest in British history, its rooms adjacent to those of the Royal Academy then in Somerset House were a particularly appropriate place to hang his historical portraits at a time before the foundation of the National Portrait Gallery. JS, PT-C, JF

Selected references: Tudor-Craig 2004

48

(previous page left; and below left)
Edward IV
Artist unknown, probably English
Probably soon after 1510
Oil on oak panel, 40.5 × 27.5 cm (integral frame)
Society of Antiquaries of London, LDSAL 320
Selected references: Scharf 1865, no. 18, pp. 17–18; London 1977, pp. 93–4; Hepburn 1986, pp. 54–70, pl. 53; London 2003B

49

(previous page right; and below right)
Richard III
Artist unknown
Probably soon after 1510
Oil on oak panel, 40 × 28 cm (integral frame)
Society of Antiquaries of London, LDSAL 321
Selected references: Scharf 1865, no. 20, pp. 18–19; London 1977, p. 92, pl. 42; Hepburn 1986, pp. 71–89, pl. 55

Edward IV (1442–1483) ruled England from 1461 to 1470 and from 1471 to 1483, the interruption to his reign due to a brief restoration of Henry VI. The Society's portrait of him is perhaps the finest to have survived. It is a copy of a lost original, which itself may have been painted from life. The prototype of this, with one of his wife, might well have been painted on Edward's return to England from exile in 1471.

The portrait of Edward's brother Richard III (1452–1485) is probably the earliest surviving version of a prototype made during the King's lifetime. All other portraits of Richard show him with very uneven shoulders, as in the other picture of the King held by the Society (cat. 50). The disfigurement was ascribed to Richard only after his death and was seized upon by Tudor critics as the physical manifestation of his inherently villainous nature. A slight unevenness is apparent here, but the absence of deformity suggests that this image follows an original painted during the sitter's reign, between 1482 and 1485.

Examination of both panels has revealed that their wood came from the same tree. Tree-ring analysis has indicated that the tree was felled after 1510 and probably came from the eastern Baltic region. It is likely that both were produced in a single workshop for the same client, although they eventually reached Kerrich from two different sources.

Edward wears a splendid gold robe, lined with fur, similar to that worn by his brother in the companion portrait. Garments such as these would have been made from expensive and prestigious imported cloth-of-gold.

The portrait also gives a good account of Edward's jewels. They include trefoil pendants in the centre of the loops of pearls, which may refer to the Trinity; the flanking rose and quatrefoil pendants recall the Yorkist badge; and his jewelled hat badge appears to represent the *rose en soleil*, the sunburst version of the Yorkist motif with which Edward is especially associated. Aptly enough, he also holds a white rose.

The only image of the monarch to do so, Richard's portrait shows him toying with a ring on the third finger of his left hand, possibly a sign of his readiness to remarry after the death in March 1485 of his wife Anne. The convention of wearing a ring on this particular finger as a token of love and faithfulness was well established by Richard's day. In the standard portrait type in the Royal Collection, with more than twenty versions, he looks in the other direction, and holds a ring on the little finger of his other hand. JS, PT-C, JF

50

Richard III with a Broken Sword
Artist unknown
Probably soon after 1523
Oil on oak panel, 48.5 × 35.5 cm
Society of Antiquaries of London,
LDSAL 331
Selected references: Scharf 1865,
no. 21, p. 19; London 1977, pp. 90–1,
pl. 40; Hepburn 1986, pp. 71–89,
pl. 60

This portrait of Richard III (1452–1485) was acquired by Kerrich from a lumber shop in 1783. Tree-ring analysis of the wood reveals that it came from an oak tree felled in the eastern Baltic region after 1550.

Richard III's reputation has fluctuated since his reign (1482–85), as this portrait reveals. The broken sword in his hand indicates broken kingship. Most existing images also show the King with some measure of deformity; for his posthumous Tudor detractors, deformity spelt villainy. John Rous (*c.* 1420–1492), the contemporary chronicler, turning his coat a year after the Battle of Bosworth in 1485, mentioned a raised *right* shoulder, as shown in the portrait in the Royal Collection and subsequent versions. However, Thomas More's unfinished *History of King Richard III* of 1513 described his withered *left* arm, which is how the King is painted here. X-ray photography has shown later overpainting, probably in the eighteenth century, to reduce his deformity, reflecting a revival of his reputation.

The Society's other portrait of Richard III (cat. 49) shows him without such deformity. JS, PT-C, JF

Collecting for Britain | 85

51

Henry VI
Artist unknown
Probably *c.* 1520
Oil on oak panel, 32 × 25 cm
Society of Antiquaries of London,
LDSAL 330
Selected references: Scharf 1865, no. 16, pp. 16–17; Starkey 1999

This is a standard portrait type of Henry VI (1421–1471), several versions of which have survived. It seems to show the King in his younger, less turbulent days, perhaps in the 1450s. It came to Thomas Kerrich with a companion portrait, now lost, of Richard III. The pair were probably made posthumously for one of the many portrait sets of English monarchs that were produced for royal and noble patrons from the time of Henry VIII.

Henry VI reigned between 1429 and 1461 (with a Regent until 1437) and was then reinstated briefly from 1470 to 1471, interrupting Edward IV's reign. The two kings belonged to opposing branches of the Plantagenet royal house, Henry representing the House of Lancaster and Edward the House of York. Both reigns were marked by a succession of civil wars, continuing beyond Edward's reign and now remembered as the Wars of the Roses. Henry's Lancastrian allegiance is symbolised by the gilded S-shaped motifs of gems and pearls on his collar. Similar symbols are seen in many portraits of Henry and other Lancastrian adherents, but the use of gems and pairs of the letter 'S' set back-to-back make this version unique.

JS, PT-C, JF

86 | Making History

52

Henry VII
Artist unknown
c. 1501
Oil on oak panel, 46 × 33 cm (integral frame)
Society of Antiquaries of London, LDSAL 329
Selected references: Scharf 1865, no. 22, pp. 19–20; Strong 1969, pp. 149–52

This portrait of Henry Tudor (1457–1509) is likely to be a replica of the portrait made to celebrate the marriage treaty between Henry's heir, Prince Arthur, and Catherine of Aragon. Henry had been negotiating the match since Arthur was one year old and it was the keystone of his dynastic ambition. The marriage took place in 1501. This seems to be the first occasion on which Henry sat for a formal portrait since claiming the throne on the eve of the Battle of Bosworth in 1485. It was at this battle that Richard III and the Yorkist opposition were defeated, concluding the Wars of the Roses and leading to the foundation of the Tudor dynasty. Henry holds a red rose, symbol of the House of Lancaster.

It is possible that this painting and another in the Society's collection that closely resembles it stem from the workshop of Maynard Vewicke, the court artist. Recent infrared examination indicates that the portrait may have been produced by means of 'pouncing', a copying process by which the artist reproduced an image from a cartoon by pricking through the outline onto the surface beneath. The other portrait of Henry VII in the Kerrich bequest also displays signs of this technique. The panel for the portrait was cut from the same tree as two others bearing portraits of Henry's sons, Arthur and Henry, in other collections. Recent conservation has revealed the original and striking 'barber pole' decoration painted on this contemporary frame.
JS, PT-C, JF

Collecting for Britain | 87

53

Mary I
Hans Eworth (*c*. 1520–1574)
1554
Oil on oak panels, 104 × 78 cm
Society of Antiquaries of London,
LDSAL 336
Selected references: Scharf 1865,
no. 37, pp. 28–9; Bruce-Mitford 1951,
p. 56, pl. 15; Strong 1995–98, pp. 135–7,
143, pl. 107

This portrait of Mary I (1516–1558), Queen of England from 1553 to 1558, was painted around her thirty-eighth birthday. The picture secured for Eworth, recently arrived from Antwerp, a position of eminence in England while Mary lived. He is now recognised as the most distinguished foreign painter in Tudor England after Hans Holbein. Mary is wearing her winter apparel and shows off two diamond rings on the ring finger of her left hand, but no plain loop wedding ring. The painting was therefore started in the last months of 1553 and finished before she was married in July 1554 to the Catholic Philip (later Philip II) of Spain.

Three conspicuous items of jewellery match those depicted in other portraits of Mary as Queen: she wears a Tau, or 'headless' cross, at her neck; at her breast an ouche (brooch), with a table diamond in an elaborate setting, and a large pearl pendant; and from her waist hangs a reliquary of the four Evangelists.

During Mary's short reign she attempted to reverse the Reformation in England that had been initiated by her father Henry VIII. She managed to achieve reconciliation with the Roman Catholic Church, but her marriage and the policy of burning heretics made her very unpopular with her English subjects. She died without heir and the crown passed to her half-sister Elizabeth I. JS/PT-C/JF

Collecting for Britain | 89

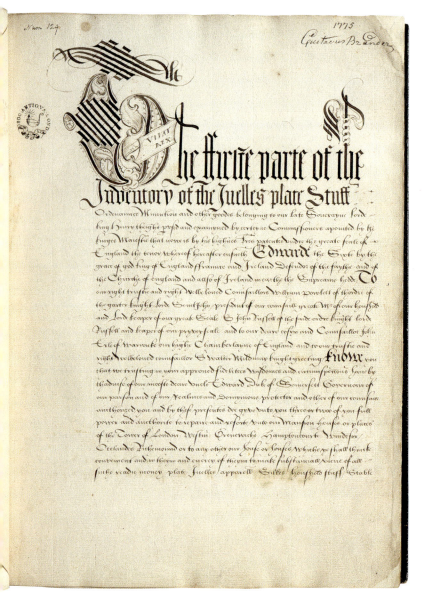

54

Inventory of Henry VIII
1550–51
Manuscript, ink on paper,
38.4 × 29.7 cm
Society of Antiquaries of London,
MS 129A
Selected references: Starkey 1998; Willetts 2000, pp. 58–9; Starkey et al. in prep.

When Henry VIII (1491–1547) died at the age of 55 in his bedchamber at the Palace of Whitehall on 28 January 1547, he left his nine-year-old son Edward to inherit the English throne. As part of the arrangements for Edward VI's minority, his late father's moveable goods were inventoried. The resulting document had 17,810 entries covering a wide variety of items, from ships and their ordnance to musical instruments, paintings, maps and furnishings. The manuscript was compiled between 1550 and 1551 and its great size meant that the text was bound in two volumes. It appears to have been kept at the Tower of London until the first half was purchased in the eighteenth century by one of the Society's Fellows, Gustavus Brander. After his death it was sold at auction in 1790 to the Society's Treasurer, John Topham, who bought the *Winton Domesday* (cat. 40) at the same sale. The second half of the Inventory was acquired by Robert Harley, Earl of Oxford, and is now in the British Library, along with a contemporary annotated copy of the first volume.

When it was first compiled, the Inventory was a functional, administrative document that allowed the keepers of the King's possessions to keep track of the objects placed in their charge. However, over time it has become a manuscript in a library and a very significant source for historians who wish to analyse the material culture of Henry VIII's court. Highly visible within the text is the spectrum of goods considered essential for a Renaissance prince, including clothes, furs, jewels, furnishings, chapel goods and horse harness. Hidden within the document is information about how the King's apartments were laid out at the lost palaces of Whitehall and Greenwich, how household ordinances were implemented, how the liturgical year was observed, and how Henry passed the contents of the queen's jewel coffer from one wife to the next. Equally it is possible to piece together how the King's collection was acquired, displayed and dispersed. For example, a blue cloth of estate kept at Greenwich which 'did serue at the burial of king henry the viijth' was given to the grooms of the privy chamber as a perquisite, or 'perk'.

The Inventory also provides information about the King's private, everyday existence by recording the objects that he kept in his removing coffers. Like his predecessors, Henry VIII was an itinerant king, and his glasses, medicines, reading matter and keys travelled with him. His group of 21 removing coffers, or chests, which were identified using letters of the alphabet, contained a vast array of items including a copy of the King's own book, *Assertio septem sacramentorum*. The level of detail about the King helps to perpetuate our enduring interest in the Tudors.

The Inventory was purchased by John Topham 'with the avowed intention of publication'. However, nothing came of the purchase until over 200 years later, when a transcript of both parts with a full index was issued. A scholarly analysis of the objects in the Inventory by type, echoing the way in which they were recorded, has also been undertaken and the essays will be published in three volumes from 2008 to 2009. Ready access to the text of the Inventory and the essays will undoubtedly inspire future research.
MH

55

Henry VIII
Artist unknown
Late 1530s
Oil on oak panel, 48 × 35 cm
Society of Antiquaries of London,
LDSAL 333
Selected references: Scharf 1865,
no. 35. p. 27; Evans 1956; Strong 1969;
Hayward 1996

Although identification of the subject of this portrait has not always been agreed, it is now widely accepted as Henry VIII, King of England from 1509 to 1547. Kerrich records that he acquired it in 1799 from the grandson of Dr Samuel Knight, an early member of the Society.

This is one of two paintings of Henry VIII bequeathed to the Society by Kerrich, both based on a portrait type pre-dating Holbein's more famous image of the King. This picture may have been produced within Henry's lifetime, although not from a live sitting. His appearance – square-shouldered, bearded and with his hair worn short – is consistent with the image of him that emerges from written and pictorial sources around 1535. Tree-ring analysis of the oak panel confirms this date; it shows that the tree was grown in the south-east of England and felled between 1507 and 1543.

Note the fictive shadows on the background, painted as if cast by the picture frame and by the sitter's head and hat. This visual device can be found in a number of sixteenth-century portraits, often accompanied by individual brush strokes for such details as hair and fur, clearly visible here. Henry's costume in this portrait is restrained by comparison with more familiar, later images of him. Although the official view was to disapprove of conspicuous luxury for ordinary citizens in early Tudor England, it was considered essential for the monarch to present a distinctive and magnificent public image. JS, PT-C, JF

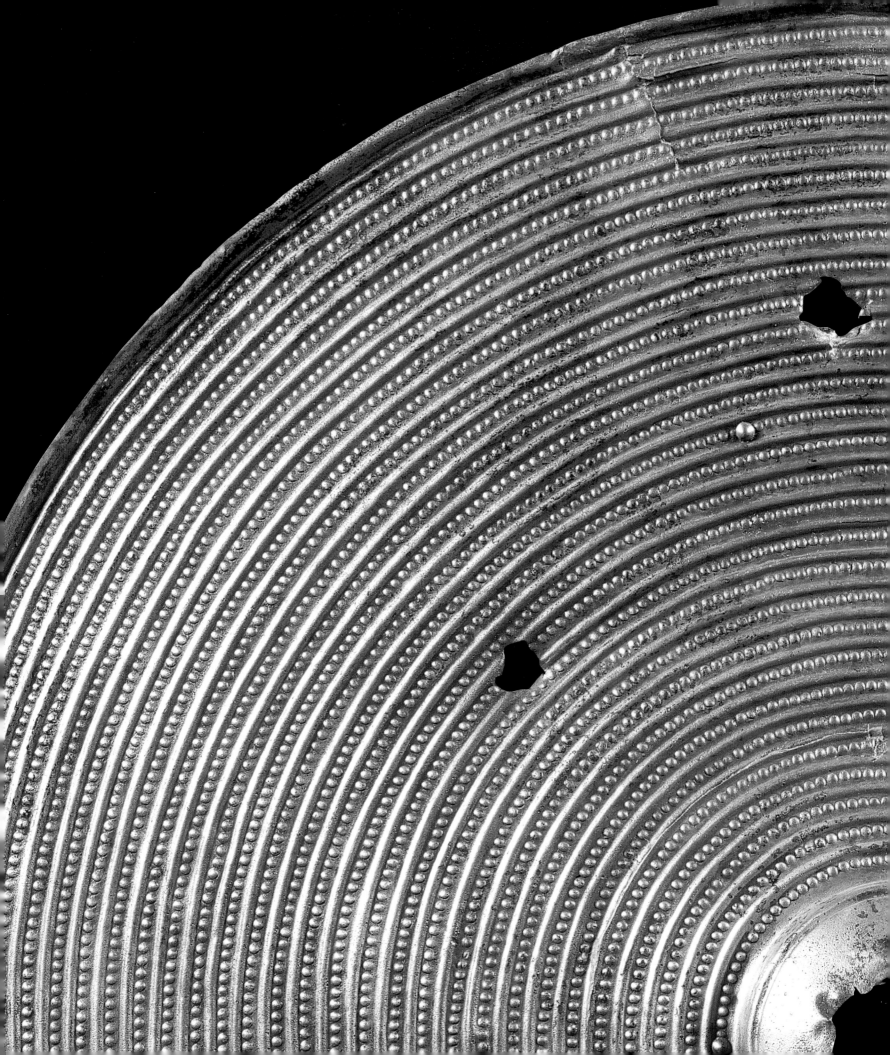

Antiquaries in Action, 1707–1850

From the outset, the Fellows of the Society were active in making archaeological discoveries, recording historic buildings and publishing the results in elaborately produced volumes. Many early antiquaries were curious about features in the landscape that were obviously man-made, and these 'barrow-diggers' enthusiastically opened burial sites to recover what they hoped would be their rich contents. Others, intrigued by royalty, opened the church tombs of famous kings and queens.

The impact of the Industrial Revolution, the intensification of agriculture and the expansion of transport infrastructure generated abundant chance discoveries of historical artefacts, some of outstanding importance, such as the Ribchester helmet. This was in the age before photography, and accurate drawings were regarded as essential for identification and comparison. Artists, among them J. M. W. Turner and Thomas Girtin, were commissioned to record historic buildings, monuments and objects for Fellows' collections and publications.

Detailed drawings were made of items exhibited at Society meetings, and to illustrate its publications. These now provide the best records of major finds, such as the Witham bowl, now lost, and historic buildings, such as the medieval Palace of Westminster, now destroyed.

In the eighteenth and nineteenth centuries, the Society embarked on several major projects to publish large engravings, which brought its recording work to a wider audience. These activities were to prove highly influential in the development of an understanding of medieval architecture.

Opening the Tomb

Barry M. Marsden and Bernard Nurse

FIGURE 13
'Skeleton Surrounded by Its Grave Goods' from *Nenia Britannica* 1786–93
James Douglas
1786
Aquatint
Society of Antiquaries of London

This Anglo-Saxon burial was found in 1779, when a mound near Rochester was opened during the repair of some military defences around Chatham.

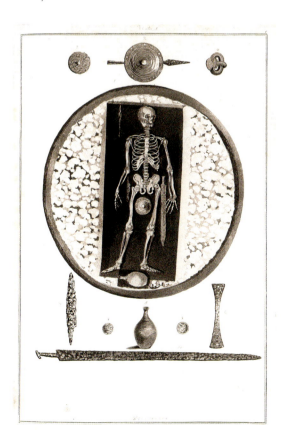

Barrows had been investigated in England from medieval times, but the interest of the early investigators was stimulated either by financial motives (a search for illusory treasure) or idle curiosity. The first explorer to dig into burial mounds for the purpose of providing information on the past was William Stukeley, sometime doctor, cleric and first secretary of the Society of Antiquaries of London. Beset by wild imaginings (mainly relatng to Druidism and primitive religions), he carried out the first objective delvings into barrows in Wessex, proving that they predated the Roman period, and commenting on their diverse shapes and composition. He produced one sketch of a section through a mound near Stonehenge, and was the first antiquary to record his presence by the deposition of tokens in the form of coins.

The two most influential barrow diggers of the eighteenth century were the Revd Bryan Faussett (1720–1776) and the Revd James Douglas (1753–1819). Both concerned themselves with opening large numbers of pagan Anglo-Saxon tumuli in Kent and elsewhere. Faussett explored over 700 examples, and, as his field diaries (cat. 61) show, provided a wealth of detail and illustration that was exemplary for the times, though his digging was often hasty, and he failed to date the period of his discoveries accurately. He referred to those buried within the barrows as 'Britons Romanised', though he did realise that they did not represent battle casualties, but were simply 'the peaceable inhabitants' of nearby settlements. Faussett's great collection of Anglo-Saxon material from Kent was sold in the 1850s and is now housed at the World Museum Liverpool. In 1856 his diaries were published as *Inventorium Sepulchrale*, some 80 years after his death (cat. 61).

James Douglas was a soldier who first came across barrow clusters when, as a military engineer, he helped to remodel the defensive earthworks protecting the Medway and Chatham Docks in Kent. Many barrows were disturbed during these operations, and from them Douglas amassed a collection of Saxon relics, which he carefully recorded. He produced perhaps the earliest ground plan of an excavated tumulus known to English archaeology (fig. 13). He later took holy orders, and in the 1780s began a general illustrated history of the 'Ancient Britons', *Nenia Britannica* (1793), based mainly on the results of his own excavations. Sadly, this work was not well received at the time. It was only after his death that its pioneering importance was recognised (cat. 60).

In the early nineteenth century, people gradually began to take more interest in barrows and their contents, probably because of the influence of the Romantic movement. In the case of Sir Richard Colt Hoare (1758–1838), a wealthy Wiltshire baronet, when Continental wars prevented him from travelling abroad to study the ancient monuments on Classical Europe, he decided to concentrate on the landscape antiquities of his own county. He employed William Cunnington (1754–1810), an 'ingenious tradesman', to conduct the searches and scrutiny of local field monuments, organised as seasonal military campaigns, with a corps of diggers to accompany him (fig. 14). The eventual idea was to publish a survey and analysis of the ancient antiquities of Wiltshire, using the carefully (for the times) recorded results of their plunderings. In the first decade of the nineteenth century, Colt Hoare's workforce dug over 400 burial mounds, mainly dating from the prehistoric period.

Colt Hoare's two landmark volumes, *The History of Ancient Wiltshire* (1812–19), were pioneering by any standards. Replete with

FIGURE 14
Bronze Age Barrow at Upton Lovell
Philip Crocker
1802–06
Watercolour with pen and ink
Society of Antiquaries of London,
Primeval Antiquities, 52.3

This drawing shows a view of a barrow as described by William Cunnington when it was opened in June 1802. One of the two figures is thought to be Cunnington.

illustrations, particularly of artefacts, they detailed barrows by shape and form, and benefited from the inclusion of large-scale maps and plans of barrow groups. However, they lacked any indication of how the barrows were constructed and failed to separate primary from subsequent deposits, thus ignoring sequence. Indeed, the tumuli were usually opened by sinking a central shaft, to preserve the outer shape of the tumulus, which left many secondary interments undiscovered. In addition, Cunnington's men totally neglected human skeletal remains, which were simply left where they were found. Indeed, later nineteenth-century diggers, such as John Thurnam, reopened a number of Colt Hoare's barrows to salvage the interments he had described but left *in situ*. All the relics exhumed from the tumuli remained in Cunnington's possession until after his death, when Colt Hoare purchased them. In 1878 they were loaned to the Wiltshire Archaeological Museum in Devizes, which bought them outright five years later. They remain a vital part of its collection of material from the culture of pre-Roman Wessex, derived primarily from rich Bronze Age burials of southern England.

The field of barrow study remained fallow for over twenty years after Hoare's operations ceased, apart from isolated digs that led to literary curiosities such as William Miles's *A Description of the Deverel Barrow* (1826) and Charles Woolls's *The Barrow Diggers* (1839), both dealing with single openings of individual barrows.

In fact, the first glimmerings of any sort of scientific approach to the pursuit were provided by the Derbyshire collector and antiquary Thomas Bateman (1821–1861), who, inspired by Colt Hoare's works, commenced barrow-digging in his native county of Derbyshire and in north Staffordshire in 1843. During his short lifetime he personally opened some 200 burial mounds. Bateman's work is important in many respects. He drew the first consistent plans and sections of the mounds he opened, revealing their make-up, and scrupulously collected every relic, which was duly enshrined in his purpose-built museum at his mansion, Lomberdale House. He was the first antiquary to study skeletal remains, especially skulls and long bones, and was the first of his breed to note the differences between the dolichocephalic crania (long-headed) from the long barrows, and the brachycephalic (round-headed) examples from the later, round ones. He was usually careful to isolate primary burials from later intrusions, and was the first barrow student to attempt a classification of the pottery he disinterred. He also commented on the variety of animal bones and mineral substances he unearthed in the cairns of the Derbyshire Peak District. He even exhibited grave finds in individual groupings, and illustrated every item found in his excavations in a series of journals. He also ensured fairly swift publication of his researches in his *Vestiges of the Antiquities of Derbyshire* (1848) and *Ten Years' Diggings in Celtic and Saxon Grave Hills* (1861).

Although Bateman's great collection was dispersed at the end of the nineteenth century, his archaeological items were purchased by Sheffield City Museum and remain an important part of its collection. Though the work of these early activists was surpassed by those who followed them, they remain pioneers; whatever their motives, they were forerunners and adventurers who opened up a whole new area of archaeological study.

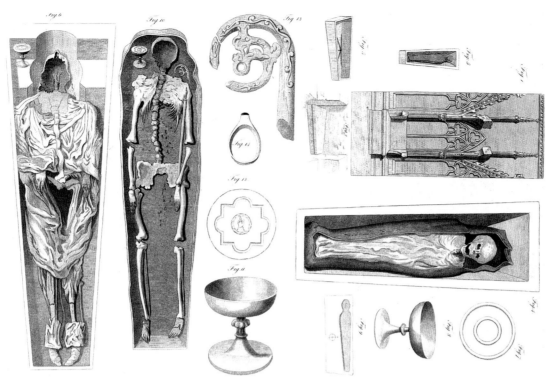

FIGURE 15
'Contents of Bishop Gravesend's Tomb, Lincolnshire' from *Sepulchral Monuments in Great Britain* 1786–96
Richard Gough
Society of Antiquaries of London

The skeleton and skull of Little St Hugh and the skeleton and grave goods of Bishop Gravesend were found when their tombs were opened in August 1791.

While antiquaries with an interest in the prehistory of the British Isles were exploring the countryside in search of burial mounds, others with an interest in the medieval period were looking at churches, especially tombs and monuments. From the sixteenth century, antiquaries regarded memorials as a source of information about family history. Richard Gough (1735–1809), Director of the Society of Antiquaries from 1771 to 1797, took a particular and active interest in researching funeral monuments as a way of finding out more about the manners and customs of earlier times; he was keen to open tombs where possible. His series of folio volumes entitled *Sepulchral Monuments in Great Britain*, published between 1786 and 1796, contains a large number of invaluable illustrations. The date of artefacts interred with the deceased could be gleaned from the date of burial, and burial practices could be observed. In particular, there was the potential with royal burials for significant finds to be made. Permission was given in 1774 to open the tomb of Edward I (d. 1307) at Westminster Abbey, revealing the body in a good state of preservation, accompanied by royal sceptres and vestments (cat. 70). The tomb of Edward IV (d. 1483) at St George's Chapel, Windsor, was opened in 1789 and some of the contents removed (cats 71, 72). King John's body was discovered at Worcester Cathedral in 1797, and Charles I's at Windsor in 1813.[1]

Bishops were also of interest because of the church plate that was often buried with them. Richard Kaye, when Dean of Lincoln, and Richard Gough were able to open several tombs and remove silver plate found when the paving was being relaid at Lincoln Cathedral in 1791 (fig. 15). Members of the Royal Society were interested in the science of how the bodies were preserved. At the opening of the tomb of Bishop Grosseteste at Lincoln in 1782, Sir Joseph Banks, President of the Royal Society and an influential member of the Society of Antiquaries, was present and took a sample of liquid found in the coffin for chemical analysis. He was not able to interpret the results and no scientific analysis could be carried out on skeletons at this time. It was only later, in the nineteenth century, as with the tomb of Archbishop Walter, that care was taken to preserve fragile clothing (see pp. 203 and 209), and later, in the twentieth century, that forensic archaeology developed (see pp. 221–3).

Early antiquaries seemed to devote more attention to burials than settlements. In the period around 1800 when Romanticism was flourishing, contemporaries had mixed reactions to their activities, vividly demonstrated in Rowlandson's celebrated print *Death and the Antiquaries* (cat. 69). Whereas Rowlandson depicts the figure of Death striking at antiquaries for disturbing his victims, William Combe, the author of the accompanying poem, is more sympathetic. He recognised perhaps that antiquaries were Romantics at heart; they could be commended for resisting Death's sway and attempting to draw deeper understanding of humanity from decay and ruins.[2]

The Kingston Barrow
CATALOGUE NUMBERS 56–59

The Revd Bryan Faussett was one of the most prolific barrow explorers of the eighteenth century. Over a sixteen-year period, Faussett was responsible for opening roughly 750 ancient burial mounds and graves. The Kingston Down range was among a group of barrow sites that Faussett examined close to his Canterbury home.

The material featured comes from Grave 205 of the Kingston Barrow group and includes some of the finest examples of Anglo-Saxon art. The impressive Kingston brooch (cat. 56), with its fine zoomorphic filigree, narrow bead and twisted-wire rim decoration, was recovered by Faussett's son Henry in August 1771, while the Revd Faussett sat in his carriage suffering from a severe attack of gout. Other pieces include the pair of silver bow brooches (cat. 57), with incised decoration along the shaft which is coiled to form a spring; the sheet-gold pendant (cat. 58) with a central repoussé boss surrounded by concentric zones of stamped circles; and the complete glass palm cup (cat. 59).

The grave goods were found with a skeleton, which Faussett identified as female because of the associated finds. While he held a vague idea that the graves were Anglo-Saxon, he had no way of proving his theory. It was not until James Douglas produced his *Nenia Britannica* in 1793, allowing comparison with other similar material from different sites, that Faussett's ideas were proven. Unfortunately, Faussett did not live to see this acceptance of his views.

By the time Faussett died, his collection numbered more than 400 items of jewellery alone. The artefacts were kept within his family for a time, until they were put on sale in 1853. The Trustees of the British Museum refused to purchase the material, maintaining that it held no aesthetic value. Eventually the complete collection was bought by a Fellow, Joseph Mayer, who left it to the City of Liverpool along with his other collections.

About a third of the objects were destroyed during the Second World War. However, as a result of a recent research project at the University of Oxford, a database has been compiled providing information and images of all Faussett's finds as well as some later excavations of Anglo-Saxon burials in Kent. Called the *Novum Inventorium Sepulchrale*, this is available on the internet. ARP/BN

Selected references: Smith 1856; Hawkes 1990, pp. 1–24; London 1991, pp. 50–1; Marsden 1999, pp. 13–16; Ramsay 2004

56

(below left)
The Kingston Brooch
Seventh century AD
Gold, inlaid with blue glass, white shell and flat-cut garnets, 8.5 cm diameter
National Museums Liverpool (World Museum Liverpool), M6226

57

(top)
Pair of bow brooches
Seventh century AD
Silver, 0.7 × 3.7 × 0.1 cm
National Museums Liverpool (World Museum Liverpool), M6235

58

(middle)
Pendant
Seventh century AD
Gold, 2.7 cm diameter
National Museums Liverpool (World Museum Liverpool), M6231

59

(bottom)
Palm cup
Seventh century AD
Glass, 7 × 9.5 cm
National Museums Liverpool (World Museum Liverpool), M6228

60

Nenia Britannica: or, a Sepulchral History of Great Britain, from the Earliest Period to its General Conversion to Christianity
James Douglas (1753–1819)
c. 1793
Watercolour, 52 × 66 cm
British Library, London, G6863
Selected references: Jessup 1975; Piggott 1978; Marsden 1999

James Douglas's *Nenia Britannica* was the first publication in Britain in which artefacts discovered through excavation were systematically illustrated and given precedence over the narrative. The range of sites included, and the approach to their illustration, allowed the reader to compare the associated artefacts. Douglas used aquatint, executing the plates himself, as he felt it was the best medium to illustrate the objects. Initially *Nenia Britannica* was rejected by Douglas's contemporaries as too scientific in its approach, but it is now seen as the first successful attempt in Britain at systematic recording of archaeological material. It includes the first-known scale recording of a human skeleton *in situ*, and also the first sections and plan of a grave in British field archaeology.

Douglas intended *Nenia* (meaning 'dirge') to be a general history of funerary customs, ranging from those of the 'native British' to the Romans and Anglo-Saxons. The history primarily consists of archaeological reports taken from his own work in Kent, as well as from other contemporary antiquaries, including the Revd Bryan Faussett. The plate featured shows the grave goods found in Grave 205 at Kingston Down, which had been excavated by Faussett. Prior to excavations at Sutton Hoo in the late 1930s, the site was regarded as the finest source of Anglo-Saxon grave goods in England.

Nenia Britannica was originally published in parts between 1786 and 1793. This is the author's copy with original hand-coloured drawings. The objects that Douglas discovered were sold by his widow to Sir Richard Colt Hoare who presented them to the Ashmolean Museum, Oxford. ARP

Opening the Tomb | 99

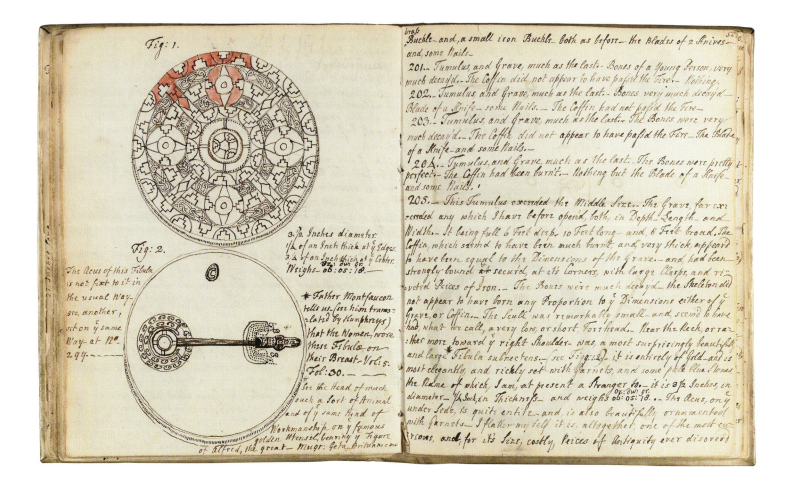

61

Field diaries
Bryan Faussett (1720–1776)
c. 1770
Pen and ink on paper, 20.7 × 33 cm
National Museums Liverpool (World Museum Liverpool), vol. 3, pp. 51–2
Selected references: Smith 1856; Hawkes 1990, pp. 1–24; Marsden 1999, pp. 13–16; Ramsay 2004

The Revd Bryan Faussett's field diaries illustrate his remarkable knowledge of human anatomy – attributed to his studies of the subject at Oxford – and include highly detailed descriptions of the type of barrows excavated and their contents. After his death, James Douglas used Faussett's detailed notes and drawings to reproduce sites for his publication *Nenia Britannica*. Although Douglas had to go and take exact measurements of the actual mounds, all the other information was accurate. From this Douglas was able to confirm Faussett's belief that he was working on Anglo-Saxon material, by comparing it with finds from other sites on which he had worked. The page shown illustrates the Kingston brooch (cat. 56) and Faussett's detailed notes.

This is the third volume of Bryan Faussett's diary of work. There were six in total, written in leather-bound books. Even though he opened a vast quantity of barrows during his sixteen-year excavating career, Faussett was exceptional for the period in terms of the quality of his recording.

Eighty years after Faussett's death, his diaries were edited by Charles Roach Smith (1806–1890) (see pp. 201–13) and published in 1856 under the title *Inventorium Sepulchrale*, thanks to the support of Joseph Mayer, who had bought the Faussett collection. Faussett's literary and scientific skills meant that Smith found he had little editing to do; each diary was almost ready for publication. ARP/BN

62

The Barrow Diggers
James Douglas (1753–1819)
c. 1787
Pen and ink wash on paper,
41 × 34 cm
Society of Antiquaries of London
Selected references: Jessup 1975;
Marsden 1999; Nurse 2001

This picture, one of the earliest-known depictions of barrow digging, presents a light-hearted view of the activity. It is attributed to James Douglas on the basis of the inscription found below the painting:

An Antiquarian & a Soldier Bred
I Damn'd the living & dig'd up the dead
As Parson now [my steps I here] retread
I bless the living & Inter the dead

Initially a soldier, Douglas had a reputation as a skilled draughtsman that earned him a commission with the newly formed Corps of Engineers in the British Army, which was remodelling earthworks forming the Chatham Lines, protecting the Medway estuary and Chatham Docks in Kent. During the remodelling, many Roman and Saxon artefacts were uncovered, reawakening Douglas's interest in antiquities, which had first been aroused during earlier service in Flanders. He later resigned his position in the army and was ordained in 1787.

However, Douglas continued to dig barrows and wrote that on one occasion he was joined on Wimbledon Common by a Quaker. 'Not content with the mere digging [his companion] … insisted on the necessity of procuring a sieve to explore the contents of a grave with more accuracy; this is true enthusiasm.' It is possible that the drawing records this scene and Douglas has depicted himself with a pickaxe.
ARP/BN

Opening the Tomb | 101

The 'Golden Barrow', Upton Lovell
CATALOGUE NUMBERS 63–68

William Cunnington and Sir Richard Colt Hoare investigated 465 barrows in the county of Wiltshire between 1803 and Cunnington's death in 1810. One of the more spectacular opened by Cunnington was the 'Golden Barrow' near Upton Lovell. First investigated in 1803, he initially discovered two cremation burials with accompanying grave goods, including thirteen gold beads (cat. 64), a decorated gold wristguard (cat. 65), a shale button and its gold cover (cat. 66) and two small gold ornamental fittings (cat. 67). Adjacent to these spectacular finds were over 1,000 amber beads (cat. 63). His finds and the accompanying drawing (cat. 68) were first published by the Society in *Archaeologia* with an account by William Cunnington. Not completely satisfied with the original work, Cunnington and Colt Hoare returned to the barrow in 1807. Under the position of the previous cremations found in 1803 they discovered further artefacts, including decorated pottery and a bronze awl. Intent on digging down to the original floor of the barrow, they uncovered an earlier burial, a simple interment of burnt bones in an oblong grave.

Dating these items was generally approached with caution, due to the limited chronology then available and the dominating influence of the Roman occupation: Colt Hoare labelled many finds as 'Ancient British', while Cunnington, attempting to be more precise, speculated that the 'Golden Barrow' was intended for a chief buried near the time of Caesar's invasion of Britain in 55 BC. These finds were dated to the Bronze Age only in the late nineteenth century in the light of an improved prehistoric chronology.
ARP/BN

Selected references: Cunnington 1806, pp. 122–9; Hoare 1812; Annable and Simpson 1964; Beck and Shennan 1991; Marsden 1999, pp. 20–39; Barber 2003, pp. 31, 33; Taylor 2005, pp. 316–26

63

Bead necklace
Early Bronze Age, *c.* 1800 BC
Amber, 27.5 cm diameter
Wiltshire Heritage Museum, Devizes

These amber beads came from the principal deposition of finds in the upper level of the barrow and were associated with the two cremation burials. This was a necklace of exceptional size, originally upwards of 1,000 amber beads of differing dimensions. The reconstruction of the necklace is conjectural and is based on the premise that the beads had belonged to one necklace.

The source of the amber has been traced to the Baltic, an area rich in this highly valued raw material. Appearances of this precious material in Bronze Age burials in England highlight the importance of the person buried, and also reveal the widespread trade network that developed between the area of southern Britain and the Baltic.
PR/ARP

64

(below top)
Cylindrical beads
Gold, each bead 0.7 × 1 cm
Wiltshire Heritage Museum, Devizes

Usually assumed to form part of a necklace, these beads might have adorned the fringe of a garment such as a cap, part of a dress or another object. Each bead is formed of three sections: the cylindrical body, which has two perforated holes, and two end caps. These are decorated with a groove design, enhanced by impressed dots. This feature is one of the trademarks of the 'Wessex master goldsmith', to whom several important items of Early Bronze Age goldwork in southern Britain are attributed. PR/ARP

65

(below bottom left)
Wristguard
Gold, 14.4 cm (length), 6.8 cm (width), 2 cm (height)
Wiltshire Heritage Museum, Devizes

This rectangular plaque with grooved decoration is made of very thin sheet gold and was originally attached through perforations at the corners to a backplate, presumably made of wood or thick leather. The design indicates that it is also the work of the 'Wessex master goldsmith'. It has been suggested that this object was a ceremonial archer's wristguard of exaggerated size. PR/ARP

66

(below middle)
Button with cover
Shale and gold, 3.5 × 4.7 × 4.7 cm (shale), 3.7 × 4.7 × 4.7 cm (gold)
Wiltshire Heritage Museum, Devizes

The button cover is made in two parts. The conical cap is decorated with three bands, each composed of three impressed lines. Between the lower bands is an impressed zigzag that is characteristic of the celebrated work attributed to the 'Wessex master goldsmith'. The convex base is decorated with a double-cross motif and is pierced by two irregular perforations. The grooved ornament on the gold cover is repeated on the shale core. PR/ARP

67

(below bottom right)
Ornamental fittings
Gold, each 2 × 2.5 cm
Wiltshire Heritage Museum, Devizes

Two of these fittings were found and originally identified by Cunnington as the terminals of 'two staves'. He was overruled by Hoare, who considered them to be the lids and bases of two boxes; they have been displayed as such ever since. Cunnington's interpretation is, however, the most likely, as two parts were found some distance apart and there is no means of closing them as a box. A similar pair of gold terminals was found in an Early Bronze Age burial at Little Cressingham, Norfolk. PR/ARP

68

(below right)
Articles of gold found in a barrow at Upton Lovell Wilts
Attributed to Philip Crocker (1780–1840)
1803–05
Pen and ink wash on paper, 18 × 22 cm
Society of Antiquaries of London, *Primeval Antiquities*, 43.5

The illustration of finds from the 'Golden Barrow' was drawn to accompany William Cunnington's account published in the Society's journal *Archaeologia*. From 1802 to 1804 he had written four letters to Aylmer Lambert, who was also a Fellow of the Society and had estates in Wiltshire, giving details of barrows he had opened at his own expense and one which Lambert had paid for. Because of the importance of the finds, Lambert sent the letters to the Society to be read out during meetings and it was decided to publish them. The drawings are undated and unsigned but were probably drawn by Philip Crocker, Sir Richard Colt Hoare's artist and surveyor, who is acknowledged in one of the letters. BN

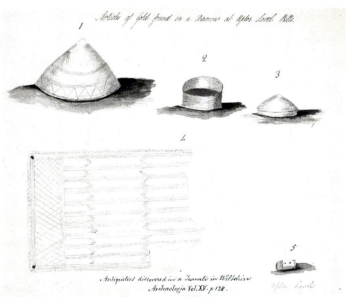

69

Death and the Antiquaries
Thomas Rowlandson (1757–1827)
1816
Aquatint, 14 × 24 cm
Private collection of Derrick Chivers
Selected references: Combe 1814–16;
Wark 1975, p. 95, figs 324–5; Peltz
and Myrone 1999, pp. 115–34; Scalia
2005, pp. 1–13; Sutton et al. 2005,
pp. 122–4, fig. 21

This satire of antiquaries investigating a tomb forms one of the illustrations by Thomas Rowlandson for *The English Dance of Death*, published from 1814 to 1816 with a verse text by William Combe. The series follows a long graphic tradition – most famously expounded by Hans Holbein in the sixteenth century – designed to show Death as the fate shared by all ranks of society. Rowlandson chose also to satirise the behaviour and attributes of assorted figures in English contemporary life, antiquaries among them. The plate shows a clutch of antiquaries peering at the body of a crowned king in a newly opened coffin. Death stands on a nearby tomb, his arrow poised to strike. Rowlandson's first design for this scene set his antiquaries in a ruined church with the expressed aim of highlighting how buildings too had their own mortality.

For this published version, Combe asked Rowlandson to shift the setting to Westminster Abbey and have one of the antiquaries pull a finger off the corpse while stealing a ring. Complying with Combe's request, Rowlandson economically copied the background of architecture and monuments straight from an engraving by A. C. Pugin in Combe's *The History of the Abbey Church of St Peter's, Westminster* (1812).

What Combe had in mind in these changes was the involvement of the Society of Antiquaries in the opening of royal tombs (with occasional disturbing rumours of trafficking in relics and mementoes):

A curious wish their fancies tickled
To know how Royal Folk were pickled.

In particular, the present scene recalls the opening of Edward I's coffin in Westminster Abbey and the subsequent widespread rumour of the attempted theft of a finger (see cat. 70).

According to Rowlandson's drawing, Death's dart is aimed at one of the antiquaries guilty of the 'burglarious entry'. Combe's verse is more indulgent. Mindful of their 'useful Labours' in the pursuit of knowledge, and because, in this instance at least, they returned the body and relics unharmed to the royal grave, he allows the antiquaries to escape death. AP

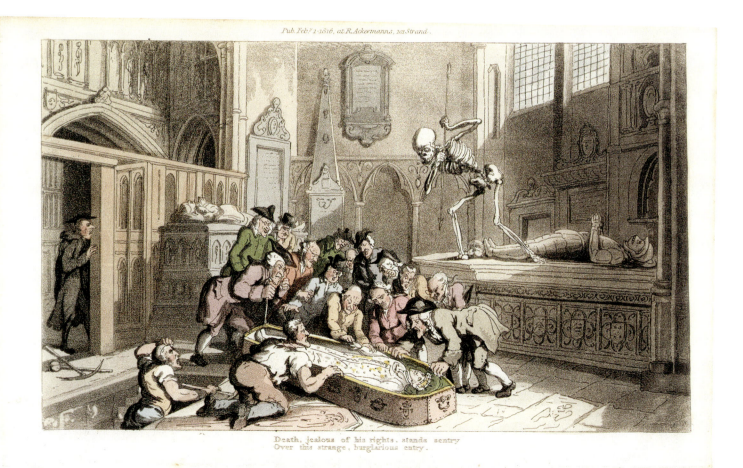

104 | Making History

70

The Opening of the Tomb of Edward I
Attributed to William Blake
(1757–1827)
1774
Pen and ink with wash, 23.5 × 45.5 cm
Society of Antiquaries of London
Selected references: Ayloffe 1775,
pp. 376–413; Gough 1786, vol. 1, part 1,
pp. lv–lvi; Grose 1792, pp. 176–7;
Evans 1956, pp. 154, 158; Butlin 1981,
vol. 1, p. 2; London 1987A, pp. 368–9,
no. 383; Dodson 2004, pp. 64–7

The Society's interest in tombs in the late eighteenth century was most actively pursued by Richard Gough, the director of the Society at that time, who was collecting material for his book on medieval sepulchral monuments. The opening of Edward I's tomb in Westminster Abbey took place on 2 May 1774. Under the watchful eye of John Thomas, Dean of Westminster, a select group of antiquaries, including Sir Joseph Ayloffe and Richard Gough, were invited to examine the contents of the tomb.

The body was found to be well preserved, with the lips and chin still recognisable. In the drawing, below the shrouded body, is shown one of the sceptres, while below the body in the other view, which is covered by vestments, is the second sceptre, the gilt brooch and a detail of the pearl-encrusted stole. It was alleged afterwards that Gough tried to remove part of a finger and was told to return it to the coffin, the Dean insisting that no remains be taken away.

The investigation threw much light on the nature of royal burials and was widely reported. A detailed account was read to the Society by Ayloffe and published the following year. No official artist was present, but Gough made sketches that may have been later worked up for possible engraving. William Blake has been suggested as the artist on grounds of style and because he was apprenticed to the Society's engraver, James Basire, at the time. The drawings were never published, but forty years later Rowlandson caricatured the scene in *Death and the Antiquaries* (cat. 69). ARP/BN

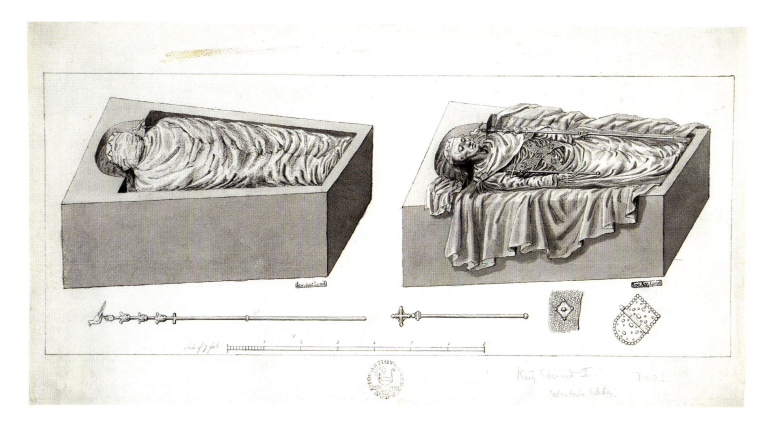

Opening the Tomb | 105

71

The Tomb of Edward IV at St George's Chapel, Windsor
Henry Emlyn (1728/9–1815)
1789
Watercolour on paper, 50.6 × 43.3 cm
Society of Antiquaries of London, RP
Berks, fol. 22
Selected references: Vetusta
Monumenta 1796, vol. 3, pl. 7,
pp. 1–4; Sutton et al. 2005

72

(below)
Lock of hair of Edward IV
1483
6 cm
Society of Antiquaries of London,
LDSAL 122

Edward IV's tomb was discovered in March 1789 during the restoration of St George's Chapel, Windsor. He had been buried there in 1483. The architect Henry Emlyn superintended the restoration, and his diagram of the excavated tomb is shown here.

An ineffective attempt to find the entrance to the tomb in 1788 had damaged one of the stones, marked here on Emlyn's drawing. The tomb was subsequently discovered during work in the north aisle when stones closing the entrance to the vault fell out. Inside the lead coffin was the King's skeleton, and Emlyn records, 'Some long brown hair lay near the skull; and some of the same colour, but shorter, was on the neck of the skeleton. There was in the bottom of the coffin a liquid, which at the feet was about three inches deep.' Emlyn's drawing shows the skeleton with long hair, and feet immersed in the dark liquid.

An analysis of this liquid was carried out by James Lind MD, physician at Windsor, who concluded that it came from the dissolution of the body. After the discovery of the tomb, many relics were removed, including locks of the King's hair. A small phial containing some of the liquid, a lock of Edward's hair and wood from the adjacent Queen's coffin were presented to the Society by John Douglas, Dean of Windsor and Bishop of Carlisle, in 1790. Emlyn's diagram and the accompanying account were published by the Society in 1790. The phial and its contents no longer survive. JS

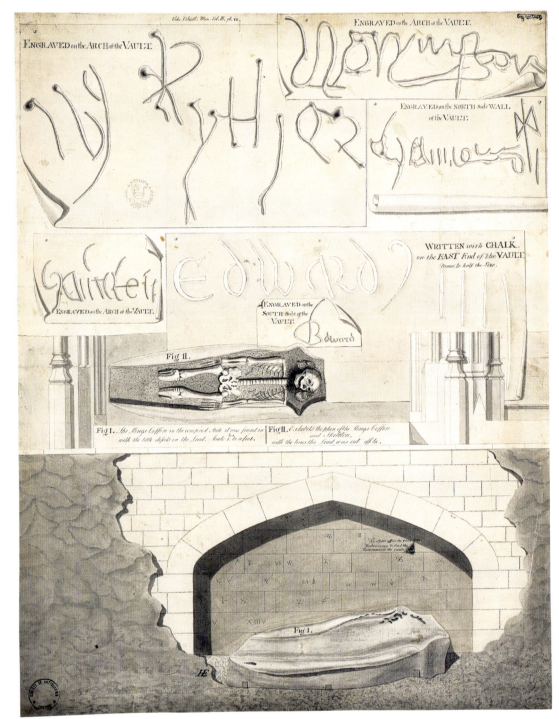

106 | Making History

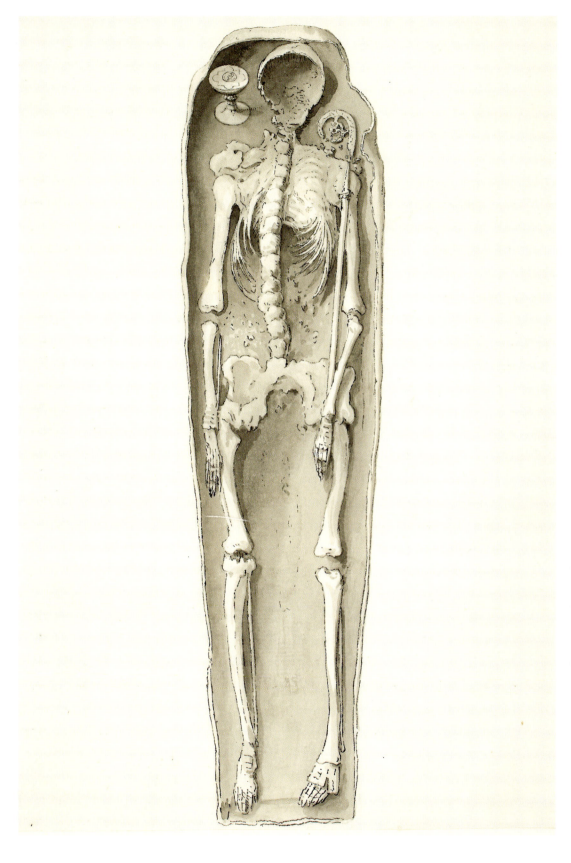

73

Skeleton of Bishop Gravesend in Lincoln Cathedral
Samuel Hieronymous Grimm
(c. 1733–1794)
1791
Ink and wash on paper, 18.2 × 26.9 cm
British Library, London, Add. MS 15541, fol. 88v
Selected references: Gough 1786, vol. 1, part 1, pp. 47–8; Gough 1796, vol. 2, part 1, pp. lxviii–lxxvii, pl. 2

Within a two-day period, 25 and 26 August 1791, three coffins were opened in the south transept and south aisle of the choir of Lincoln Cathedral. They had been uncovered during paving works. The discoveries were recorded by S. H. Grimm, the artist-friend of the Dean, Sir Richard Kaye. Richard Gough, the Society's director, witnessed the scene. The skeleton and skull of Little Saint Hugh, the boy alleged to have been murdered by Jews in 1255, was found on 25 August. The next day, the skeleton and grave goods of Richard of Gravesend were uncovered and recorded.

Richard of Gravesend was a former Dean and Bishop of Lincoln. He died in 1279 at about the time when the magnificent 'angel' choir of the cathedral was nearing completion. In his coffin were found a silver-gilt chalice, the head of a gilded ivory crozier, a 'much corroded' ornament to fix the head of the crozier onto its staff and a gold ring. It was carefully noted that a piece of wood, 'apparently modern', had come into the grave accidentally. All the skeletons as well as the finds were carefully drawn and Gough published them in his *Sepulchral Monuments in Great Britain* together with an account of the opening in 1782 of another tomb in Lincoln Cathedral (fig. 15).

Gravesend's chalice and paten are today on display at Lincoln Cathedral Treasury; the other grave goods have since disappeared. BN

Lost and Found

Elizabeth Lewis

FIGURE 16
Sketch of Bathhouse at Benwell
Robert Shafto
c. 1751
Pen and ink wash on paper
Society of Antiquaries of London,
Britannia Romana 89.4

This hypocaust was discovered near the Roman fort at Benwell (Condercum) when the Newcastle to Carlisle road was being built. It was surveyed and drawn by the landowner.

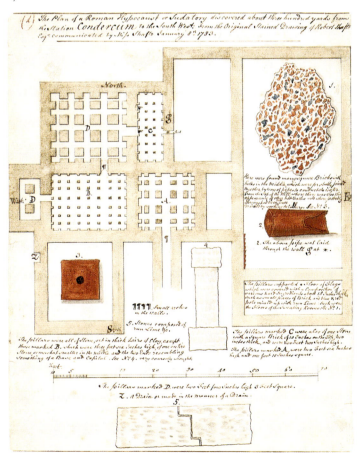

In the eighteenth and nineteenth centuries, a number of significant changes in the physical quality of the British landscape took place as a result of the enclosure movement, the building of infrastructure for a transport network and increasing industrialisation. The Enclosure Acts, the majority of which were passed between 1750 and 1860, effectively privatised large tracts of what had hitherto been common land. Landlords saw financial incentive in making agricultural improvements such as land drainage, hedgerow plantation, fence construction, peat and marl extraction, and the removal of trees and old boundaries. The intensification of agriculture was further driven by the need to provide for mushrooming populations in the industrial urban centres. Railway building, canal digging and river dredging, in addition to the widening of existing routeways, brought about landscape restructuring on a grand scale. One of the results was to make large parts of the countryside accessible for the first time. The long years of the Napoleonic wars made the Continent inaccessible to gentlemen wishing to undertake the Grand Tour, and instead they turned their attention to their own, domestic antiquities. Touring was undertaken in the summer months, with visits to ancient sites and private collections, and active enquiries were made into local finds.

One of the consequences of agricultural or mineral exploitation was the frequent, if random, discovery of archaeological structures and objects. Peat extraction accounted for the discovery of the Bronze Age shield in Ayrshire, Scotland, which was found in a deposit with five or six others around 1779 (cat. 74). Quarrying for sand and gravel revealed rich grave deposits at Ash in Kent, which became a focus of early archaeological activity from the 1750s, and the source of important Anglo-Saxon artefacts; Bryan Faussett, James Douglas and the late C. Roach Smith all excavated here.[1] The construction of canals, dredging of rivers and other excavation works in hitherto marshy land led to discoveries of well-preserved organic items, besides spectacular finds of weapons of bronze and iron of all periods. Some of these chance finds went to furnish local antiquarian collections, including that of the Society of Antiquaries of London, but many made of precious metals were sold for bullion.

The Society received numerous communications about newly found antiquities from the landed gentry, some of whom made careful observations of the situation in which finds were made on their estates. Philip Rashleigh noted of the Trewhiddle hoard, found during tin-working on his brother's estate, that 'the quantity of earth and stone which had accumulated over the cup since it was deposited in the stream works shows it had remained there a number of years'.[2]

Robert Shafto surveyed the Roman fort near his house at Benwell on Hadrian's Wall during the construction of the Newcastle to Carlisle road from 1751 to 1752, in the course of which some fine altars were discovered (cat. 76). Shafto also made a detailed study of the bathhouse uncovered just outside the fort (fig. 16). Urban developments, such as the laying of sewers, led to such discoveries as the Roman pavement and pottery finds at Lombard Street in London in 1786.[3] The construction of the Basingstoke canal basin yielded the medieval bronze aeolipile (fig. 18), which was rescued from a scrap-metal merchant and presented to the Society by the typesetter Edmund Fry in 1799.[4]

Lost and Found | 109

The Society had always promoted the exhibition and discussion of antiquities, including those recently discovered and others in private collections. Through the growing network of antiquaries and supporting local correspondents, newly discovered objects were regularly made available to the Society at their weekly meetings. William Stukeley, the Society's first Secretary, looking back through the minutes of meetings for a report of 1762, emphasised how important this role was to the Society, and remarked on the wide variety of exhibits that were 'worthy to be produced' at the round table at the Mitre Tavern (one of the Society's earliest meeting-places), 'whereby every person present had a proper opportunity of viewing, considering and speaking upon each particular'.[5] In this manner, by discussion and appraisal, a consensus was reached on the function and dating of artefacts. Stukeley also saw the importance of noting the objects brought in, and the pages of the first Minute Book (1718–24) and 'the great Folio drawing book' are filled with his drawings of antiquities (fig. 17). However, it was not until 26 February 1784 that the president recognised the need for a more formal and detailed record, intended for publication; he brought in a motion to appoint a draughtsman to attend meetings to draw the objects exhibited.[6] A succession of draughtsmen, professional artists in their own right, were responsible for bringing to public attention some of the most outstanding archaeological discoveries of the age, published in the pages of *Archaeologia* or *Vetusta Monumenta*, such as the Ribchester helmet (cats 77, 78), the Bronze Age Mold Cape and the early medieval Lewis chessmen, all now in the British Museum in London.

After drawing and publication, some objects were presented to the Society, such as the Anglo-Saxon brooch found when a ditch was dug at Rothley Temple from 1784 to 1785, which was given by Thomas Babington and the Viking silver torc and penannular brooch from Orton Scar, discovered in 1847 (cat. 81). Today they form a significant part of the Society's collections. Other objects in private hands eventually found their way, by gift or later purchase, to the British Museum and other institutions. The Trewhiddle hoard of ninth-century silver fragments (cat. 79), exhibited first in 1788, remained in the possession of the Rashleigh family until they presented it to the British Museum in 1880 in appreciation of the work of Sir Augustus Wollaston Franks in forming the national collection there.[7] In 1870 Franks, Keeper of the Department of British and Medieval Antiquities and Ethnography at the British Museum and, for a time, Director of the Society of Antiquaries, exhibited an Iron Age sword in its scabbard, which had been picked up on the moors near Cotterdale, North Yorkshire; it was donated to the Society by Lord Wharncliffe. Franks's account in *Archaeologia*, the Society's journal, united all other examples then 'brought down to our present state of knowledge' for comparison and dating, and noted the similarity between the handle and that of a Roman sword in the British Museum. The Society later deposited the sword in the British Museum on loan (cat. 75).[8] The lack of information about the discovery of chance finds made it difficult to identify them and to compare them with other objects. Provenance was generally poorly recorded, if at all, and there was a lack of reliable dating methods and appreciation of the importance of context. Antiquities were, in the main, unearthed by unsupervised labourers, and associated groups of objects, especially valuable ones such as coins (on which dating heavily depended), were often dispersed before

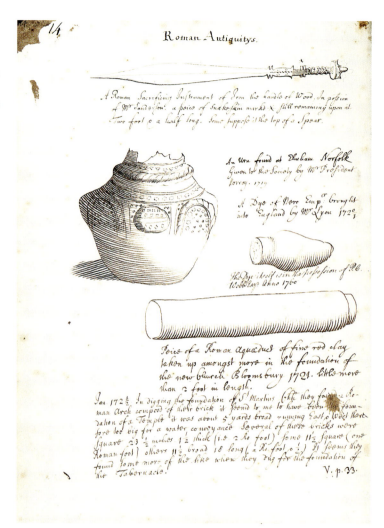

FIGURE 17
Roman Antiquitys
William Stukeley
1718–24
Society of Antiquaries of London,
MS 265, fol. 1v

William Stukeley, the Society's first Secretary, recorded discoveries exhibited at meetings in this 'drawing book' by subject; some of these finds are now known to date from other periods. The 'Roman' urn was, in fact, Anglo-Saxon.

they could be adequately recorded. The association of coins with otherwise undatable objects such as the Trewhiddle silver added greatly to the study both of archaeology and numismatics.

Even after discovery and recording, objects were often subject to damage or loss; Jacob Schnebbelie's drawing of the Trewhiddle hoard (cat. 80), and the sketch in the Minutes include some objects, notably the gold pendant, which had disappeared before the hoard came into the possession of the British Museum. The Society's drawings may thus be the only surviving records of many pieces that have since been lost or melted down. Some important objects have not been seen since their appearance at meetings, and the Society's written and drawn records have been the only sources for later scholars to assess their significance. The drawings of the ninth-century silver bowl found in the River Witham (cat. 84), made perhaps at the time of its exhibition in London in 1850 or in Leeds in 1868, but not recognised or published until 1941, are the only surviving record of this extraordinary treasure, which has in its base the tiny figure of a sea-monster.[9]

In some cases the recorded context cast a whole new light on an object, especially where a link could be made with historical sources. In 1810 the Earl of Mansfield sent a drawing of a gold and enamel ring which, he said, had been presented to one of his ancestors by Mary, Queen of Scots (cat. 86); the similarity of the Darnley badge to the winged heart depicted inside the little compartment on the ring tends to support his case, but the ring itself has long since been lost. Finds from known battlefield sites acquired a special aura; the late medieval processional cross (cat. 83) found on Bosworth Field was associated with Richard III, while the silver-gilt spur found at the battlefield at Towton contributed to the development of the chronology of arms and armour, primarily based on tombs, which were always of interest to the Society.

Towards the end of the eighteenth century the number of casual finds being reported increased, stimulated by the publication of comparable discoveries in *Archaeologia*, and, by extension, of a web of active county members with good contacts, such as the local clergy. Governor Pownall and Dr Pococke in Ireland and Robert Riddell on the Scottish Borders sent detailed accounts with sketches of discoveries of interest. As the interest in British antiquities grew, so too did the number of organisations and events, both local and national, concerned with their study. The Archaeological Institute and the British Archaeological Association, both of which had members in common with each other and the Society from which they sprang, held (and reported on) annual congresses in county towns from 1844 onwards, with successful exhibitions of local antiquities. They acted as a stimulus to local interest that gave rise to the foundation of county archaeological societies and local museums.

In London the antiquary Charles Roach Smith, a chemist with a pharmacy business in the City from 1834, became a most active and vociferous investigator and recorder of finds made during building works in the capital. He fully recognised that chance discoveries were important in building up a body of reference and could lead to a more intensive investigation or excavation of a site (see pp. 202– 03). During the nineteenth century the principles of stratigraphy were better appreciated as an aid to developing chronological frameworks for artefacts, instead of relying on stylistic comparisons. Along with the advancement in techniques of investigation and recording, this knowledge led to a fuller understanding of the unstratified objects in existing collections.

The interest and debate that has attended, and continues to illuminate, the discovery of antiquities affirms Frederick Ouvry's 1852 vision of the Society as 'the best, as it is the proper channel through which Antiquarian discoveries are brought forward for discussion and investigation, through which the results of these discussions and of that learning may be communicated to the public through the pages of *Archaeologia* and otherwise'.[10]

FIGURE 18
Aeolipile
Late medieval period
Bronze
Society of Antiquaries of London,
LDSAL 105

This rare example of a hearth-blower was found during the digging of the Basingstoke Canal, and presented to the Society in 1799. When it was filled with water and heated, steam came from the mouth of the figure, noisily fanning the flames.

74

Late Bronze Age shield from Beith, Ayrshire
c. 1300–1100 BC
Bronze, 67.7 cm diameter
Society of Antiquaries of London, LDSAL 80
Selected references: Society of Antiquaries of London 1791, p. 147; Evans 1881, pp. 348–9; Coles 1962, pp. 165–8; Needham 1979, pp. 111–34

A chance find in an Ayrshire bog yielded this impressive shield, along with five or six others. The discovery was made during peat extraction on Luggtonrigge Farm in the parish of Beith around 1779. The shields were found under six to seven feet (1.8 to 2.1 metres) of peat and 'were observed to have been regularly placed in a ring'.

The thinness of the bronze, combined with the arrangement of the shields, gives weight to the theory that they might well have had a ceremonial function. The shield shown here would have offered little defence from an attack by bronze swords and may even have been designed deliberately for deposition. It is not known when the punctures in its surface were made, and it is impossible to tell what damage has resulted from decay and handling since it has been discovered, but it is feasible that the shield might have been deliberately damaged or 'killed' before it was deposited in its final spot.

The shield was presented to the Society in 1791 by a Dr Ferris, who had himself acquired it from the estate's owner, Baillie John Storie. The remaining shields had already been dispersed by the labourers who found them and nothing more is known of their fate.

This decorated Bronze Age shield has been classified as one of the Yetholm type after the location of the first find in Roxburghshire, Scotland. About twenty of this style have been discovered in Britain and Ireland. JS/EL

75

Iron Age sword and scabbard from Cotterdale, Yorkshire
c. AD 45–125
Iron and bronze, 76.2 cm (sword length); 56.8 cm (scabbard length)
Society of Antiquaries of London, LDSAL 700
Selected references: Society of Antiquaries of London 1870; Franks 1880; Piggott 1950, pp. 17–20, 27; Stead and Lang 2006, pp. 192–3, no. 204, fig. 100

Among the finest examples of an Iron Age sword with its scabbard in Britain, they were discovered together on the moors of Cotterdale in North Yorkshire. No further details of their provenance survive, but it is known that they had been lying about one foot (30 cm) underground.

The find was exhibited to the Society through Lord Wharncliffe in 1870. Ten years later the significance of the find (its good condition and distinctive design) was recognised in a paper by A. W. Franks. He noted that a considerable part of the handle remained, something that was often missing, and remarked on the rarity of the find. Other discoveries from this period share the same general characteristics, but vary in detail from the Cotterdale find. However, there is a strong similarity between this scabbard and another from Mortonhall, Edinburgh. These two are distinguishable from the rest by their decoration and the centrally placed strap-loop.

Wharncliffe was himself not a Fellow, but it was common for local correspondents to alert the Society of notable finds. The Society also holds a drawing of the sword and scabbard, made between 1870 and 1880. JS/EL

76

Roman altar from Benwell, Northumberland
1ST/2ND AD
Sandstone, 80.5 × 40.6 × 32.4 cm
Society of Antiquaries of London, LDSAL 964
Selected references: Brand 1789, p. 607; Society of Antiquaries of Newcastle upon Tyne 1816, p. 8; Bruce 1875, pp. 28–9; Hodgson 1913

The building of the Newcastle to Carlisle road, now the A69, through Benwell fort from 1751 to 1752 led to many exciting discoveries, including a hypocaust system (fig. 16) (which can be taken as evidence of a bathhouse) and this altar. Benwell, its Roman name Condercum, sits on high ground just over two miles from Newcastle along Hadrian's Wall.

The altar was found over three feet (one metre) underground on the north side of the turnpike road at Benwell. The inscription, 'LAMIIS TRIBUS', means 'to the three witches'. This is a unique dedication, although grouping gods and goddesses into threes was a common practice in the so-called 'Celtic' provinces. It is believed to represent an instance of Roman soldiers adopting local religious beliefs and combining these with their own rituals, a custom widely practised in many provinces throughout the Roman Empire.

Several Roman altars were found at Benwell and elsewhere during the construction of the road in the 1750s; some were presented to the Society in 1759 by one of its Fellows, the judge Heneage Legge. This altar may have been given later. It was chosen by the Society of Antiquaries of Newcastle upon Tyne to feature on their seal from their foundation in 1813. All of the altars are currently on loan to the Museum of Antiquities, Newcastle upon Tyne. JS/EL/ARP

Roman Cavalry Parade Helmet
from Ribchester, Lancashire
CATALOGUE NUMBERS 77–78

77

(below)
The Ribchester Helmet
Late first or early second century AD
Brass, two-piece face mask visor helmet,
30 × 30 × 30 cm
British Museum, London, PEE
1814.7-5.1

78

(opposite)
Drawing of the Ribchester helmet
Attributed to Thomas Underwood
(1772–1835)
1798
Watercolour on paper, 41 × 34 cm
Society of Antiquaries of London,
Britannia Romana, 78
Selected references: Vetusta
Monumenta 1815; Brailsford 1958, p. 67,
fig. 4, pl. 26; Edwards 1992; Jackson and
Craddock 1995, pp. 75–102; Stephenson
and Dixon 2003, pp. 20–2; Smiles 2007;
Lewis 2007 forthcoming

This remains one of the finest examples of a cavalry parade helmet from Roman Britain, it would have been worn by an élite trooper at a sports event when both men and horses were elaborately equipped. Part of a hoard of Roman military equipment, made chiefly of bronze, it was discovered accidentally in 1796 by the son of a clog-maker, who was playing in a hollow on some waste land at Ribchester, Lancashire. The helmet, which was buried in red sand about nine feet (2.7 metres) below ground level, was the first item to be noticed. The majority of the hoard was purchased by the antiquary Charles Townley in December 1797 and later acquired by the British Museum.

The helmet consists of two parts – an ornate headpiece and a face mask with detailed human features and a diadem. The headpiece is decorated with a scene depicting a skirmish between infantry and cavalry. The decoration is low- and high-relief embossing with incised and punched details. A leather strap would have held the two pieces together and a crest-box and pair of 'manes' would have been attached to the headpiece.

The helmet and drawings are reunited here for the first time since the eighteenth century, when the helmet was exhibited at the Society. Comparison of the two highlights the achievement of the artist in recording the fine decorative detail of the ancient artefact. The drawing shows the helmet 'as found', complete with corrosion, and affords an interesting comparison with the cleaned and conserved helmet. Although the drawing is inscribed 'J Basire', the artist is more likely to have been Thomas Underwood, the Society's draughtsman, who was commissioned by Charles Townley in 1798 to draw the helmet. Underwood's drawings were not published, as others by James Basire, the Society's engraver, were thought more suitable for engraving. JS/ARP/EL

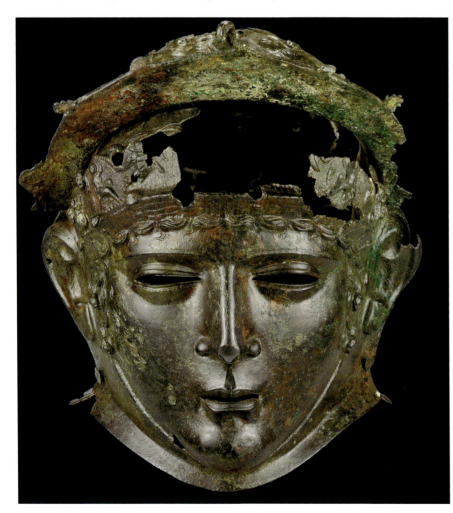

Antique Helmet of Bronze, of the same Size, found at Ribchester, in the Possession of Charles Townley Esq.
Vetust. Mon. Vol. IV. pl. 1.

J. Basire delt.

Anglo-Saxon Hoard from
Trewhiddle, Cornwall
CATALOGUE NUMBERS 79–80

79

(below)
Scourge from the Trewhiddle hoard
c. AD 875
Silver; 57 cm (length), 2.1 cm (width)
British Museum, London

80

(opposite)
Drawing of the Anglo-Saxon hoard
from Trewhiddle, Cornwall
Jacob Schnebbelie (1760–1792)
1788
Pen and ink wash, 48.6 × 32 cm
Society of Antiquaries of London,
Early Medieval Antiquities 67.1
Selected references: Society of
Antiquaries of London 1788; Rashleigh
1789, pp. 187–8, pl. 8; Rashleigh 1808,
pp. 83–4, pl. 7; Rogers 1867; Wilson
and Blunt 1961, pp. 75–122; Wilson
1964, pp. 2, 59, 181, no. 91, pl. 35

Schnebbelie's drawing records a hoard of ninth-century silver and gold objects, discovered in 1774 by Cornish miners near St Austell. They made the find while prospecting for tin; the hoard was found at a depth of seventeen feet (5.2 metres) in an old mine working. It has since been known as the Trewhiddle hoard after the location of its discovery, and is recognised as one of the most important finds of Late Saxon ornamental metalwork from Britain, giving its name to a particular Anglo-Saxon art style.

The hoard has been dated to *c.* 875 on the evidence of several coins found with it. Besides the scourge, there were parts of a silver chalice, decorative mounts, which were perhaps from drinking horns, strap-ends, a pin with a decorative head, finger rings and a gold pendant. It is possible that the hoard comprised the entire portable treasure of a church, perhaps hidden during a Viking raid and never recovered. The ornate scourge (cat. 79) is the only object of its kind known from Early Christian Europe. It is made from lengths of plaited silver and decorated with a bead of blue glass with white veining. Although it is similar to scourges used in acts of religious mortification and penance, the high degree of decoration suggests that the Trewhiddle example was more symbolic than functional.

The site of the find in Cornwall belonged to John Rashleigh, brother of the mineralogist and collector Philip Rashleigh. Philip exhibited the hoard to the Society in 1788, the year he was elected a Fellow. The Society's draughtsman Jacob Schnebbelie was commissioned to illustrate Rashleigh's account, which was published in *Archaeologia* (1789). Schnebbelie's drawing of the cup fragments shows his misunderstanding of its assembly and construction. The cup was republished by Rashleigh with an illustration of its assembly in the correct order in a later volume of *Archaeologia* (1808). The drawing is also of interest because it shows objects such as the gold pendant, which had already been lost by 1880, when the collection was donated to the British Museum. JS/EL

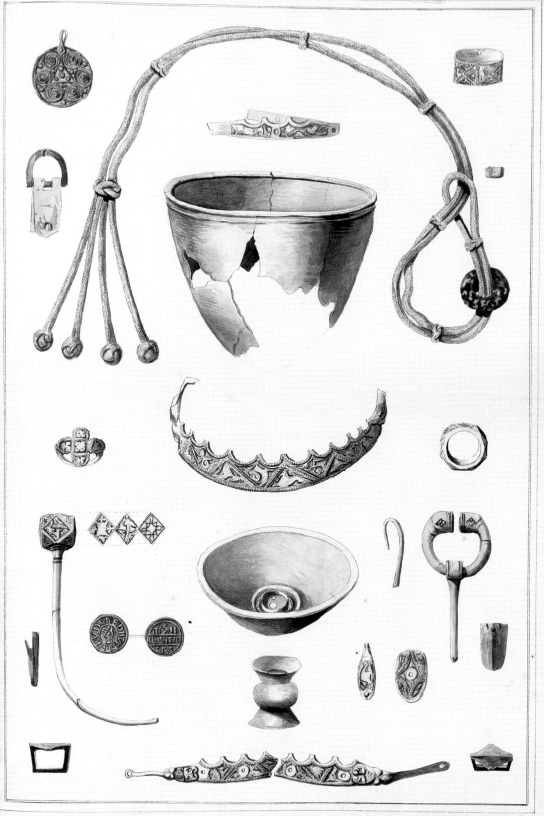

Found in searching for Tin in a streamwork near St Austell Cornwall 1774. Vide Archæol. Vol. IX. p. 186.

81

Viking torque and brooch found at Orton Scar, Westmorland
Ninth–tenth centuries AD
Silver; torque diameter 14.7 cm, brooch 28.2 × 12.6 cm
Society of Antiquaries of London, LDSAL 366
Selected references: Society of Antiquaries of London 1851; Reveley 1852, p. 446, pl. 38; Birley 1964; Graham-Campbell 1975; Graham-Campbell 1992, pp. 109–10, fig. 9.2; Hinton 2005, pp. 120–1, fig. 4.6

Discovered together deep in a rock crevice at Orton Scar, now in Cumbria, the torque and brooch were a chance find in 1847 by a labourer quarrying stone for gateposts. He sold them on to Thomas Reveley, a local lawyer and antiquary, who in turn presented them to the Society in 1851. Reveley believed the finds to be Roman and provided evidence for the line of the Roman road from Overborough. They are now understood to be largely of Viking origin because of the typical twisting of the torque and the stamped pattern on the pin of the brooch. The decoration featured on the body of the brooch is thought to be earlier, ninth-century Irish work, while the Norse pin is a later replacement.

The torque, formed from silver wire twisted 79 times, is generally regarded as a neck-ring, although its small diameter suggests it would have been worn more comfortably as an armlet. The brooch was probably intended to fasten clothing, as suggested by the signs of wear on its underside. However, it is still not known how these treasures were used when they were abandoned: were they being worn as ornaments or being carried specifically for use as portable bullion? Contemporary hoards of Viking treasure frequently comprise of hack-silver (fragments cut from ornaments such as these) and often displaying nicks where they had been tested for value. JS

82

Medieval spur from the site of the Battle of Towton
First half of the fifteenth century
Gilded copper alloy,
4.1 × 10 × 13.9 cm
Society of Antiquaries of London, LDSAL 127
Selected references: Society of Antiquaries 1792; Anon. 1794, p. 433, pl. 20; Gravett 2003

The spur was exhibited at the Society in November 1792 by the Revd John Brand, the Society's resident Secretary. He records that it was found on Towton field, the site of the Battle of Towton in Yorkshire. The battle took place on Palm Sunday (29 March) 1461 when Edward, Duke of York met his Lancastrian foes in what is reputedly the bloodiest clash of the Wars of the Roses. These were a series of civil wars fought in medieval England from 1455 to 1485 between the Houses of Lancaster and York. Edward's victory at Towton led to his coronation in June as Edward IV. The spur has been dated to the first half of the fifteenth century so it could well have been worn, and lost, during the conflict.

The shank carrying to the rowel is ornately engraved and is inscribed on the outer edge with a motto in French: *en loial amour tout mon coer*, which means 'you have all my heart with loyal love'. Spurs with inscriptions are unusual. In this context it may perhaps be read as a pledge of loyalty rather than (as on the more common posy rings of the period) of love. JS/JC

83

Medieval processional cross from the site of the Battle of Bosworth
Fifteenth century, before 1485
Bronze gilt, 58.4 × 27.9 cm
Society of Antiquaries of London, LDSAL 446
Selected references: Nichols 1811, vol. 4, part 2, p. 557, pl. 91; Comerford 1881, p. 541; London 1977, no. 209, pls 4, 67; Ashdown-Hill 2004; Hourihane 2005, p. 99, plates 70, 71

The Bosworth cross is named after the place of its discovery in Leicestershire around 1778. An account of its discovery was published by the historian John Nichols in 1811; quoting a Mr Sharp of Coventry, he described it among other finds ploughed up on the Field of Bosworth. The Battle of Bosworth, which brought the Wars of the Roses to a conclusion, took place on 22 August 1485 and was fought between the House of York, led by Richard III, and the House of Lancaster, under Henry Tudor. The outcome of the battle was the defeat and death of Richard and the coronation of Henry Tudor as Henry VII.

The cross (or crucifix) is one of a number of English late medieval processional crosses of similar design. They all have a socket by which they could be mounted on a base when the crucifix was placed on the altar, or on a shaft for carrying in procession. They were used on such a regular basis in liturgical contexts that they came to be known as 'dallye crosses'. Nichols's account of the discovery noted that the cross had been found with the decaying remains of a wooden staff bearing traces of paint and gilding. This suggests that it was lost in its processional mode, and might indeed have been abandoned on the field of battle.

The roundels at the four ends of the cross carry the symbols of the four Evangelists: the eagle of St John, the winged man of St Matthew, the winged lion of St Mark and the winged ox of St Luke. On the reverse of these are incised sunburst symbols, a Yorkist motif known on two further examples of English processional crosses of this type. It is possible that the cross was carried by Richard's supporters at the battle; an association that would explain the considerable interest that surrounded the publication of the cross in the early nineteenth century. The cross was presented to the Society in 1881.
JS/EL/PT-C

Lost and Found | 119

84

Drawing of an Anglo-Saxon silver hanging bowl
Attributed to Robert T. Stothard (fl. 1821–1865)
c. 1850
Pen, ink and watercolour on paper, 32.5 × 50 cm
Society of Antiquaries of London, *Early Medieval Antiquities*, 61.1
Selected references: Graham-Campbell 2004, pp. 358–71; Bruce-Mitford and Raven 2005, no. 58, pp. 208–12

The bowl represented was one of a number of objects discovered in April 1816 during improvement works on the River Witham near Washingborough in Lincolnshire. The *Stamford Mercury* reported: 'The object of greatest value is the beautiful cup or basin, richly ornamented with wild animals etc. and having in the centre a small statue: this is now in the possession of a gentleman in the neighbourhood.'

The bowl was exhibited in London in 1850, when the drawing may have been made, perhaps by the Society's draughtsman, Robert Stothard. The bowl itself, last publicly shown at the Leeds exhibition of ornamental art in 1868, has since disappeared. The drawing, rediscovered while the Society's collection was being packed prior to its evacuation during the Second World War, was published for the first time in 1941. The bowl, which has been hailed as 'the most remarkable piece of pre-Conquest plate ever found in England', has been the subject of much discussion.

The drawing comprises four very detailed views of the bowl, which is shown life size. The decoration is of raised silver filigree with semi-precious stones studding the interior, and panels of millefiore decorating the four escutcheons supporting suspension hooks. In the centre is a quadruped (perhaps a sea-creature) with a long neck, which would have peered above the liquid filling the bowl. It has been suggested that such hanging bowls held water for liturgical purposes, or were used as ceremonial serving vessels in high-status households. On the basis of comparative analysis the Witham bowl has been dated to the end of the eighth or the early ninth centuries. ARP/EL

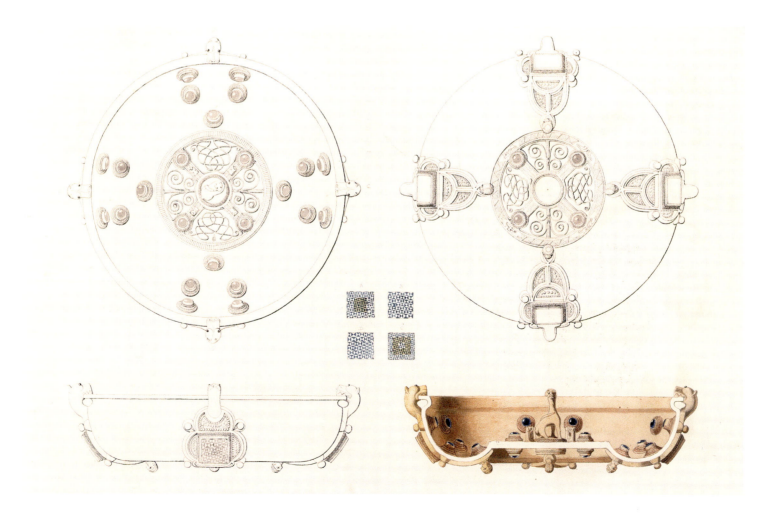

85

Drawing of a Viking gold armlet from Ireland
Richard Smirke (1778–1815)
c. 1812–13
Pen, ink and wash on paper, 24 × 31 cm
Society of Antiquaries of London, *Primeval Antiquities*, 28.1
Selected references: Vetusta Monumenta 1819, 5, pl. 30; Graham-Campbell 1974, pp. 269–72; Graham-Campbell 1980, p. 63

In 1802 two Viking Age gold and silver hoards were found on Hare Island in the River Shannon in Ireland. One consisted of ten armrings of gold, dating from the late ninth to the early tenth centuries AD. Charles Vallancey, an antiquary and military surveyor who was also founder of the Royal Irish Academy, recorded the hoards in his *Collectanea de Rebus Hibernicis* (1804). He listed the contents as 'ten gold bracelets, and a number of silver anklets, with some ingots of silver' and illustrated four of the arm rings from the gold hoard. The total weight of the gold hoard was believed to be about 5 kilos (11 lbs), making it the largest known from the Viking period. The fate of the silver is unknown, but the gold was subsequently seen in 1804 in Dublin, and was purchased by the Marquess of Lansdowne.

After his death the gold hoard passed into the possession of the silversmiths Rundel and Bridge in London, who exhibited it to the Society on 26 November 1812. One of the Society's Fellows, Francis Douce, who had seen it earlier, urged the Society to commission drawings before the hoard was melted down for bullion. These drawings, showing several views of one of the gold arm rings, were made by the Society's draughtsman Richard Smirke and published in *Vetusta Monumenta* in 1819. All pieces are presumed to have been destroyed shortly afterwards. ARP/EL

86

Drawing of the ring of Mary, Queen of Scots
Unknown artist
c. 1810
Watercolour on paper, 25.5 × 19.2 cm
Society of Antiquaries of London, *Personal Ornaments*, 8.1
Selected references: Anon. 1810, p. 372; Way 1858, pp. 253–66; Jury 2007

This drawing was presented as a gift to the Society in 1810 by the 3rd Earl of Mansfield with a letter explaining how his family came to own it. The letter claims that the ring was given by Mary, Queen of Scots, to a relative who lived close to Falkland Palace where Mary 'for some time resided, but I do not know to which of my family it was given nor on what occasion'.

Mary is now known to have visited Falkland twice. The second occasion was in January 1565, when she was on her way to meet for the first time her handsome first cousin Henry Stuart, Lord Darnley, whom she was to marry that July as her second husband. There was considerable opposition to their union, presumably on the grounds of Darnley's Catholicism. It has been speculated that Mary may have given her ring as a bribe to the Mansfields, one of the most important Scottish aristocratic families, to gain their support.

The drawing shows different views of an extremely elaborate sixteenth-century ring made of gold and enamel. The bezel, where the gem is attached, is supported by two caryatids, or sculpted female forms, and bears a gem on the lid of a compartment that opens to reveal a winged heart in the lid and clasped hands in the base. This emblem links the ring to Mary's second husband, who was murdered by the Earl of Bothwell, Mary's third husband. The Darnley badge with its winged and crowned heart can be seen on the Lennox jewel in the Royal Collection.

The ring is now missing. It was presumably kept at Scone Palace, where the Earls of Mansfield resided, and may have been lost during a fire there in the 1940s when much of the collection was evacuated. ARP/SMC

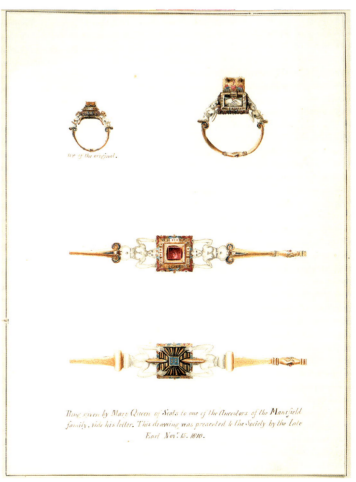

The Art of Recording

Sam Smiles

FIGURE 19
Shrine of St Edward the Confessor
Westminster Abbey
Engraved by George Vertue (1684–1756)
after John Talman (1677–1726)
1724
Engraving with contemporary colouring
Society of Antiquaries of London

The shrine was recognised as a major example of medieval art, and in 1722 the Society's engraver, George Vertue, was requested to print a drawing of the shrine by John Talman, the Society's Director. This example has been hand coloured.

The art of recording was always poised between two imperatives: it involved not only professional competence (with the accent on *art*) but also the discipline required to delineate antiquities exactly (with the accent on *recording*).

From its inception the Society of Antiquaries of London understood how visual records of relics of the past would benefit scholarship. As early as the 1710s the need to disseminate antiquarian research via high-quality images was acknowledged by John Talman (fig. 19), William Stukeley and others, and, on its re-establishment in 1718, the Society's articles specified the importance of producing engravings of antiquities.[1] In much the same way as the Royal Society prioritised the collecting of accurate empirical data from which valid scientific inferences could be drawn, so the Society of Antiquaries undertook to illustrate scrupulously the objects and monuments within its remit. Stukeley, the Society's first Secretary, wrote that 'without drawing and designing the study of Antiquities … is lame and imperfect.'[2] Likewise, in 1768, the Director of the Society, Richard Gough, declared, that 'the pencil is as essential as the pen to illustrate antiquities'.[3]

These opinions were widely shared and the Society accumulated drawings as part of its investigations. From 1721 drawings deposited by members were kept in portfolios, of which about twenty existed by the 1750s. After the move to Chancery Lane in 1753 safe storage in the library on a permanent basis was at last possible for these records.[4] The visual data contained in them allowed scholars to put together what history and geography had scattered across Britain and thus to comprehend the legacy of the past more systematically than before. Moreover, at a time of social and economic change, with many sites vulnerable to 'improvement' or demolition, the visual record of a monument or a building helped to preserve something of its existence for the future.

Most antiquaries possessed some ability as draughtsmen and some, for example William Stukeley, William Borlase and James Douglas, were capable designers, but the proficiency in drawing needed to record antiquities to the most exacting standards could be found only in those who had undertaken some sort of artistic training. From the 1780s, therefore, the Society employed its own draughtsmen to record and disseminate its findings. This activity extended from drawing items presented at the Society's meetings to making highly wrought and detailed visual surveys of cathedrals and facsimile copies of wall paintings and tapestries. The policy was instituted in 1784 with the appointment of John Carter (1748–1817; figs 21, 24). He soon developed his own antiquarian reputation (he was elected a Fellow in 1795) and worked only intermittently as a draughtsman for the Society after 1785, so much of this work was undertaken by Jacob Schnebbelie (1760–1792) and then by Thomas Underwood (1772–1835), who was appointed Draughtsman-in-Ordinary in 1792. After Carter, the most significant artist-antiquary associated with the Society was Charles Alfred Stothard (1786–1821), who began publishing his *Monumental Effigies of Great Britain* in 1811. He made facsimile drawings of the Bayeux Tapestry for the Society in 1816 (cats 109, 110) and was elected a Fellow in 1819, when he made a notable series of drawings of the Painted Chamber at Westminster (cat. 107).[5]

These images, and the engravings derived from some of them, cannot be seen in isolation, however, for the Society had to battle against two aesthetic prejudices: first, that its primary orientation to

British antiquity associated it with works of art and architecture that were necessarily inferior to their classical equivalents; second, that its reproductions were inescapably dull and prosaic by virtue of their obligation to visual accuracy. With respect to the first of these difficulties the Society could do little, except to proselytise for a better-informed understanding of British antiquity that would overcome classical bias. Here the production of expertly engraved prints, showing the historic legacy in all its splendour and variety, could demonstrate that Britain's early history and, especially, its medieval culture were not as barbarous or uncultivated as the ignorant suggested.

The second prejudice was more difficult to overcome. The Society viewed the recording of monuments as essentially a research enterprise, where accuracy of depiction was the paramount virtue if scholarship was to be advanced. John Carter talked of good antiquarian drawing as calculated 'to give information and instruction' and singled out for disapproval 'picturesque appearances produced by the skill of the Artist … tending more to accredit the modern delineator than the antient Architect'.[6] James Douglas referred to the aquatinted plates in his *Nenia Britannica* (cat. 60) as 'the facts here established'.[7] 'Correct data' was the phrase used by Richard Tongue when presenting a collection of his paintings and models to the British Museum in 1838.[8]

From a connoisseur's point of view, however, accurate depiction was essentially hack-work, for the artist had to forswear the creative and individual touches that dignified his calling. William Gilpin, the theorist of the Picturesque, described George Vertue as 'an excellent antiquarian, but no artist. He copied with painful exactness; in a dry, disagreeable manner, without force, or freedom'.[9] Written in the year that the Royal Academy was founded (1768), Gilpin's observation reminds us that the increased prominence of the visual arts in England tended to elevate the imaginative and the ideal over the prosaic and the real. Twenty years later Richard Gough noted ruefully: 'The walk of fame for modern artists is not sufficiently enlarged. Emulous of succeeding in History, Portrait, or Landscape, they overlook the unprofitable, though not the less tasteful, walk of Antiquity, or, in Grecian and Roman forget Gothic and more domestic monuments.'[10]

Gough himself was a victim of this situation. Although he employed Jacob Schnebbelie, Samuel Hieronymous Grimm and others to provide the illustrations for his topographical publications – for example *Sepulchral Monuments in Great Britain* (1786) – the drawings from which they worked were inadequate, particularly when judged by the more exacting standards of the next generation of draughtsmen. As Charles Stothard noted of these early and pioneering efforts:

the delineating part is so extremely incorrect and full of errors, that at a future period, when the originals no longer exist, it will be impossible to form any correct idea of what they really were … Had Mr Gough been draughtsman sufficient to have executed his own drawings, he might have avoided the innumerable mistakes which, from circumstances, and the nature of the subject, must unavoidably have arisen. He could not transfer that enthusiasm which he himself felt to the persons he employed, to enable them to overcome such difficulties.[11]

By the 1790s, however, it was at last possible to recruit technical proficiency that matched the antiquarian's demands. James Moore,

FIGURE 20
A Bronze Age Palstave and a Roman Bow Brooch
Thomas Girtin
c. 1796
Watercolour on paper
Society of Antiquaries of London, *Primeval Antiquities*, 6.4

This remarkable image shows Girtin's developing and revolutionary style in which he used strong colours and shadows to record objects. The drawing was exhibited to the Society in 1796.

for example, published *Monastic Remains and Ancient Castles in England and Wales* in 1791, including aquatint engravings after his own designs by Schnebbelie. Moore also employed the watercolour artist Edward Dayes to collaborate with him in producing drawings of British antiquities after his original sketches of cathedral and monastic remains. From this contact Moore moved on, from 1792 to 1795, to collaborate with Dayes's apprentice, Thomas Girtin (fig. 20), paying him six shillings a day.[12]

Sir Richard Colt Hoare, owner of Stourhead, was one of Turner's most important early patrons, commissioning from him an extensive series of watercolour drawings of Salisbury Cathedral and its environs (cat. 96); Turner worked on them from *c.* 1795 to 1806. Indeed, by the winter of 1798–99 Colt Hoare was alone responsible for nearly half the commissioned watercolours Turner then had in hand.[13] At the turn of the century Turner also worked for the Revd Thomas Dunham Whitaker, providing illustrations for his *History of … Whalley* (1800–01) and three subsequent topographical publications. Although most of these watercolours were of natural landscapes, religious buildings and country seats, in the *History of … Whalley* Turner also made detailed drawings of ancient cross shafts, misericords and seals that are unique in his work (cat. 100).[14]

Sir Henry Englefield, a Vice-President of the Society, met the young John Sell Cotman around 1803 and was later described by Cotman as one of his most loyal friends.[15] Cotman dedicated his *Miscellaneous Etchings* of 1811 to him, and Englefield, for his part, was clearly interested in supporting Cotman's interest in medieval architecture.[16] On his departure for Normandy in 1817, Cotman was presented by Englefield with a drawing instrument that would facilitate the accuracy of his notation. It was a form of camera lucida, the so-called Graphic Telescope, designed by another of Englefield's artist contacts, Cornelius Varley.[17]

But the work of Turner, Girtin and Cotman should not be allowed to eclipse the work of less well-known draughtsmen. Looking at these images today, it is clear that the Society's stress on empirical data has allowed much to be preserved that the aesthetic prejudice of the time would have discarded. We are thus able to see details of excavations, as well as the objects found in them, some of which have now disappeared completely. In addition, for all the desire to use images as databanks there is an aesthetic quality to even purely documentary records. The draughtsmen's resoluteness of approach, diligence in research and commitment to accuracy have together produced a distinctive vision of British antiquity.

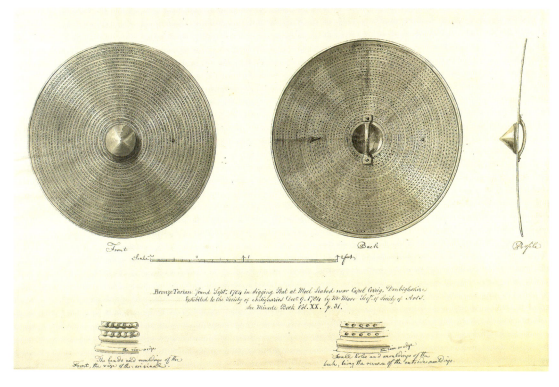

FIGURE 21
A Bronze Age Shield from Capel Curig, Conwy
John Carter (1748–1817)
1784
Pen and ink wash
Society of Antiquaries of London, *Primeval Antiquities*, 82.1

Found while digging peat, the shield was exhibited to the Society in 1784, where it was drawn by John Carter, who had just been appointed the Society's draughtsman.

87

Model of a passage-grave from Jersey
1787
Painted wood with vellum label,
10.4 × 40.5 × 35.8 cm
Society of Antiquaries of London,
LDSAL 57
Selected references: Molesworth 1787, pp. 384–5; Society of Antiquaries of London 1787; Hibbs 1985, pl. 2; Evans 2000, pp. 363–5, fig. 5; Evans 2004, pp. 111–13

One of the earliest surviving models of a British ancient monument, this replica depicts the passage-grave found at Mont St Helier in Jersey. The stones were discovered under an earthen mound in 1785, following an order from the Colonel of the Militia to level the land in preparation for an exercise ground at a time of French hostilities. When first revealed, the monument was thought to be a Druidic temple and became known as 'Little Master Stonehenge'. It is now believed to be a Neolithic tomb, consisting of a passageway and a burial chamber.

The Jersey Assembly presented the unearthed stones to the retiring governor of the island, General (later Field-Marshal) Conway, and had them shipped to England and re-erected at his estate, Park Place in Henley-on-Thames. They remain there today, although the current stone arrangement differs slightly from the original layout as represented in the model.

The model – on a scale of three feet to one inch – was commissioned by Conway before the monument was removed and is an accurate record of its original configuration. In 1787, Conway donated the model to the Society, along with a description and a drawing of the site.

Conway was elected a Fellow of the Society and invited the Society's Council to visit. However, on learning that the monument had been moved from its original site, Council showed an early concern for the historical importance of ancient ruins in situ and declined on the grounds that 'its principal value was lost, and ... Posterity might erroneously believe that Park Place was a resort to the Philosophic Priests of the Ancient Britons'. JS/BN

126 | Making History

88

Excavation of a Hypocaust at Lincoln
George Vertue (1684–1756)
1740
Pen, ink and watercolour on paper,
33.4 × 48.5 cm
Society of Antiquaries of London
Selected references: Sympson 1739–41,
pp. 855–60; Vetusta Monumenta 1740,
pl. 57; Wood 2004, pp. 73–4

One of the earliest measured drawings of an archaeological excavation in Britain was occasioned by a chance find in Lincoln. Interest in Roman remains in Britain was developing in the eighteenth century, when they were seen as a tangible link between the growing British Empire and that of the Romans. Drawings of Roman mosaics, ruins and finds were well known, but, unusually for the time, these Lincoln drawings show the remains as they were discovered, in context, carefully measured and in considerable detail.

Around 1740, workmen found a Roman hypocaust while digging a cellar at the Precentory, to the south of Exchequergate and to the west of Lincoln Cathedral. Thomas Sympson, who had been informed as Clerk of the Fabric, told his friend Browne Willis, an active member of the Society. Sympson was astonished to find ancient remains 13 feet (4 metres) below ground level. He took detailed measurements with the help of a young man who crawled between the low columns and sent Willis a full description. Willis noted the similarity with the hypocaust found at Bath in 1727 and sent Sympson's letters to be read out at meetings of the Society of Antiquaries. The Royal Society published the letters in their *Philosophical Transactions* with illustrations based on Sympson's sketches. George Vertue, the engraver of the Society of Antiquaries, made a new drawing showing the hypocaust in perspective, added the plan and pillars according to scale, and engraved it for members.

The hypocaust still remains beneath the subdeanery and forms a model example of an underfloor heating system commonly used in Roman buildings in Britain. BN

Paintings by Richard Tongue
(fl. 1835–1838)
CATALOGUE NUMBERS 89–90

Selected references: Piggott 1978, p. 33; Michell 1982; Evans 1994, figs 1, 2

89

Chamber Tomb of Pentre Ifan near Newport, Pembrokeshire
1835
Oil on canvas, 51 × 71 cm
Society of Antiquaries of London, LDSAL 344

90

(opposite)
The Tolmen at Constantine, Cornwall
1835
Oil on canvas, 51 × 71 cm
Society of Antiquaries of London, LDSAL 344

Richard Tongue of Bath advertised himself as 'a painter and modeller of megaliths', an unusual specialism for his day. In a letter to the British Museum he emphasised the importance of recording ancient monuments, pointing out that his work preserved information at risk from decay and increased the awareness of those who would have no opportunity of visiting the sites; thus, he concluded, the public might be induced to respect and preserve such monuments.

This pair of paintings was presented to the Society by Tongue in 1835. Their similar composition suggests that they were intended to be hung together with the impression of a continuous background. The tomb at Pentre Ifan, which still stands, is the largest Neolithic burial chamber in Wales. The Tolmen, a natural phenomenon no longer in existence, was once believed to have had Druidic connections. It used to stand in the parish of Constantine above a valuable granite quarry. The huge stone was dislodged by workers in 1869 and rolled into the 40-foot (12-metre) quarry below. The public outcry that ensued led the Ethnological Society to appoint a committee to investigate prehistoric monuments in Britain, and contributed to the campaign that led to the passing of the Ancient Monuments Protection Act of 1882.

Tongue made a second painting of this subject, since lost, which, along with a painting of a burial chamber at Plas Newydd and one of Stonehenge (cat. 167), was donated to the British Museum. JS/PT-C/CE

Woodchester Roman Villa, Gloucestershire
CATALOGUE NUMBERS 91–92

91

The Excavation of Woodchester Roman Villa
Samuel Lysons (1763–1819) or Robert Smirke (1753–1845)
1793
Pencil, pen, ink and wash, 45 × 59 cm
Society of Antiquaries of London

92

(opposite)
The Great Pavement (the 'Orpheus Mosaic') at Woodchester Roman Villa
Engraved by unknown artist after Samuel Lysons (1763–1819) and Robert Smirke (1753–1845),
1797
Hand-coloured engraving,
47.4 × 46.8 cm
Society of Antiquaries of London
Selected references: Lysons 1797, pl. 10; Neal 1981, pp. 115–22; Clarke 1982, pp. 197–228

One of the most extensive Roman villas to have been discovered in Britain, Woodchester, near Stroud in Gloucestershire, lies partly beneath an old churchyard. The grandest mosaic depicts Orpheus, the ancient Greek musician who could subdue wild animals with his playing. At 39 feet (12 metres) square, it is the largest discovered north of the Alps and was first recorded in the 1695 edition of Camden's *Britannia*. It was continually damaged by digging for new graves and in 1793, when the mosaic was again disturbed, Samuel Lysons, the Gloucestershire antiquary and later director of the Society, took an interest in the site. He was the first to uncover it in its entirety, and no further burials were placed over it. Lysons was able to excavate much of the surrounding villa in succeeding years.

The drawing shows workmen digging in room ten, one of several important rooms on the western range of the inner courtyard. A compressed version of this view without the workmen was engraved for the frontispiece of Lysons's *Account … of Woodchester*, published in 1797. Despite some errors of detail, the scholarly accuracy of Lysons's reconstruction of the villa's layout has been confirmed by more recent excavations. He was assisted by Robert Smirke, who carefully showed conjectured areas on the reconstruction drawing of the Orpheus mosaic with dotted outlines, although the identification of some of the animals is now disputed.

George III was interested in the discovery and was shown the drawings; the folio volume was a highly extravagant publication with only fifty copies printed at considerable expense. BN

93

The Entrance to the Prison Chamber at Lincoln Cathedral
Samuel Hieronymous Grimm
(c. 1733–1794)
c. 1784
Ink and wash on paper, 27.4 × 18.5 cm
British Library, London, Add. MS 15541, fol. 79
Selected references: Clay 1941; Dolman 2003

Samuel Hieronymous Grimm was a Swiss artist who moved to England in 1768 and exhibited frequently at the Royal Academy. His eye for the picturesque and the 'vein of humour', noted by the naturalist Gilbert White, can be seen in this simple drawing of the entrance to the prison chamber under the north-west tower of Lincoln Cathedral. One man is shown holding the ladder steady while others, possibly adventurous antiquaries, cautiously climb up and in through the narrow entrance to explore the chamber. Prisoners were held there before making public atonement in the porch of the cathedral's Galilee Chapel.

This is one of over 2,600 drawings that Grimm made for Sir Richard Kaye, a Fellow of the Society of Antiquaries and of the Royal Society. Kaye was a career churchman who was appointed Dean of Lincoln in 1783. Over a period of 21 years he commissioned Grimm to tour the country, recording the history and antiquities of England and depicting 'everything curious'. Grimm spent from July to October 1784 in Lincoln, mostly drawing views of the cathedral, and returned later for occasional visits. It was during one of these that he drew Bishop Gravesend's tomb (cat. 73). Kaye left his drawings and notebooks to the British Museum at his death in 1809.

Another antiquary, Sir William Burrell, commissioned nearly 900 drawings of Sussex antiquities from Grimm, and he was also employed by the Society of Antiquaries to copy the wall painting at Cowdray House depicting the coronation procession of Edward VI (cat. 114). BN

94

Ely Cathedral from the South-East
Thomas Girtin (1775–1802)
c. 1794
Watercolour over pencil,
39.1 × 47.8 cm
Ashmolean Museum, Oxford
Selected references: Girtin and Loshak 1954; Manchester 1975; Morris 1986; London 2002

This watercolour was commissioned by the antiquary James Moore, who became Girtin's patron in about 1792. Moore had recently published *Monastic Remains and Ancient Castles in England and Wales* (1791) with plates 'finished and etched' by Jacob Schnebbelie (the Society's official draughtsman) and aquatinted by George Isham Parkyns. However, Schnebbelie died in 1792, aged only thirty-two, and it was perhaps because he had lost his designer that Moore now employed Girtin to work up his sketches into finished views.

Girtin produced a large number of such works for Moore from 1792 to 1795. This view was produced on a bigger scale than most of them and was the first work Girtin showed at the Royal Academy, making his début in the 1794 exhibition.

Moore's own sketch of the cathedral was made in 1790. Ely would have been of particular interest to Moore because it had been the subject of a recent antiquarian investigation. James Bentham's *History of the Conventual and Cathedral Church of Ely* (1771) was one of the first attempts to examine the stylistic sequences marking the development of medieval architecture. ss

The Art of Recording | 133

95

Tintern Abbey, the Transept
J. M. W. Turner (1775–1851)
c. 1794
Watercolour over pencil, with pen and ink, 35.5 × 26 cm
Ashmolean Museum, Oxford
Selected references: Gage 1965, pp. 16–25; Wilton 1979; Llandudno 1984

The rise of picturesque tourism in the 1790s was conditioned by the fact that foreign travel was made more difficult by the war with France, which broke out in 1793 and continued until 1815, with the exception of the short-lived Treaty of Amiens (1802–03). The educated public now toured the United Kingdom rather than abroad. As a result, the Society's long-standing championing of Britain's medieval legacy was vindicated in a new and widespread appreciation of the Middle Ages.

In the 1790s Turner produced numerous watercolours of cathedrals, abbeys and castles, in tune with the contemporary taste for picturesque views. Through attention to detail, careful selection of viewpoint and control of light and shade, Turner invested these sites with a dignity and monumentality that was lost in most topographical treatments.

Perhaps influenced by Gilpin, who had picked out Tintern for special praise as a site of picturesque beauty in his *Observations on the River Wye* (1782), Turner visited the abbey in 1792 and painted five finished watercolours from about 1794 to 1795. This watercolour belonged to James Moore and was purchased by him in 1795, after its exhibition at the Royal Academy. Although his patronage of Girtin was to continue, Moore commissioned no work from Turner. ss

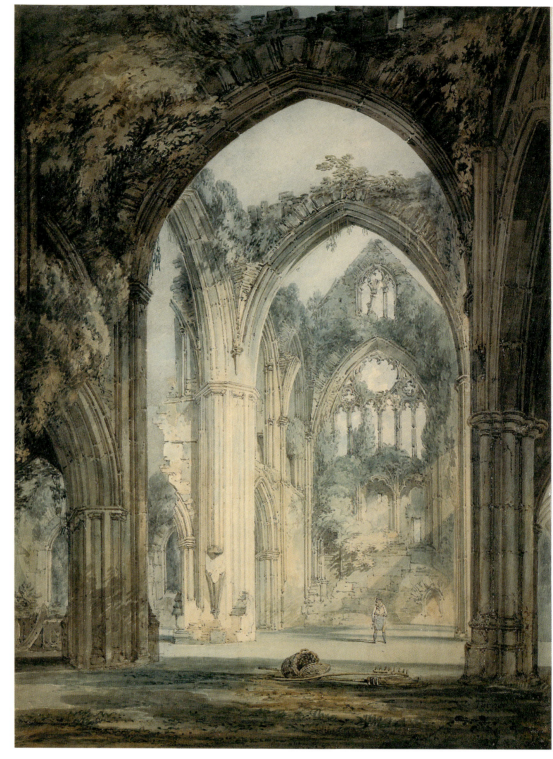

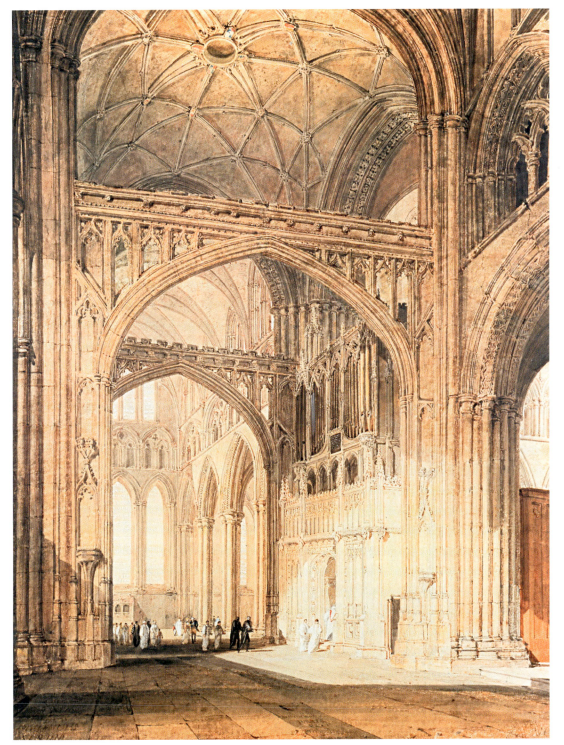

96

The Interior of Salisbury Cathedral, looking towards the North Transept
J. M. W. Turner (1775–1851)
c. 1802–05
Pencil and watercolour, 66 × 50.8 cm
Salisbury and South Wiltshire Museum
Selected references: Whittingham 1973; Wilton 1979

This drawing was commissioned by the antiquary Sir Richard Colt Hoare, the owner of Stourhead in Wiltshire. Colt Hoare's researches led to the publication of his magisterial *History of Ancient Wiltshire* (1812–19). He was also planning a modern history of the county, for which he commissioned Turner to make twenty watercolours divided into two categories: ten large drawings of Salisbury Cathedral and ten smaller drawings of buildings in and around Salisbury. Unfortunately, they were never published.

Even in his twenties, Turner was developing a considerable reputation for his ability to capture the intricacies of Gothic architecture. His early training as an architectural draughtsman was combined with a technical control of watercolour rivalled only by Thomas Girtin.

Turner's Isle of Wight sketchbook of 1795 includes the first orders from Colt Hoare. The following year he began making drawings for him, continuing with the project until about 1806, by which time seventeen drawings had been completed. From 1796 to 1797 Colt Hoare also bought two watercolours of Ely Cathedral from Turner and made further purchases of pictures in 1806 and 1815. ss

The Art of Recording | 135

Seal of Elizabeth I and Casts of Seals
CATALOGUE NUMBERS 97–100

Wax seals, whose fragile nature rendered them liable both to decay and to damage on the raised parts of the impression, were initially recorded with drawings, and these were sometimes issued as engravings. From the late seventeenth century onwards, however, the technique of casting provides us with a valuable record of seals, some of which have since been lost. Metal and plaster were used for casting in the eighteenth century. To these were added sulphide and gutta percha (a rubber solution derived from a tree) in the nineteenth century. Seals were of particular interest to antiquaries because of their usefulness in dating documents, as well as showing contemporary images. The Society of Antiquaries has one of the most important collections of casts of seals. The cast of the seal of Henry de Lacy (cat. 99) is similar to the seal that appears in the bottom left corner of the fine drawing by J. M. W. Turner (cat 100). JC

97

Elizabeth I, second Great Seal
Nicholas Hilliard (1547–1619) and Derrick Anthony (c. 1522–1599)
1586–1603
Wax, 14.5 cm diameter
Society of Antiquaries of London, MS 1008/A9

98.1–2

Casts of Elizabeth I's second Great Seal and counterseal
Nineteenth century
Green sulphide, 15 cm diameter
Society of Antiquaries of London, A27 (2)
Selected references: Wyon 1887, pp. 77–8; London 2003A, cat. 38, p. 49

Elizabeth I's second Great Seal was designed by Nicholas Hilliard, the celebrated miniaturist, in 1584, but not introduced until 1586. Hilliard worked with Derrick Anthony, chief engraver of the Mint, to produce a new seal matrix in silver from which wax impressions could be made. The images on both sides were approved by the Queen. The detailed representations of her costume, regalia, badges and heraldry and, on the reverse, of her costume, horse and badges testify to Hilliard's great skill as a designer. The legend around the edge of the seal reads ELIZABETHA DEI GRACIA ANGLIE FRANCIE ET HIBERNIE REGINA FIDEI DEFENSOR (Elizabeth, by the Grace of God, Queen of England, France and Ireland). It is not known from which document this wax impression was taken. JC

99

Cast of seal of Henry de Lacy, Earl of Lincoln (c. 1250–1311)
Nineteenth century
Green sulphide, 7 cm diameter
Society of Antiquaries of London, F25

Nobles were portrayed on their seals as warriors on horseback. This cast was taken from a seal of the son of Edmund de Lacy (d. 1258) whose seal was drawn by J. M. W. Turner (cat. 100). JC

136 | Making History

100

Studies of seals from Whalley Abbey
J. M. W. Turner (1775–1851)
c. 1799–1800
Watercolour, with pencil and ink,
26.7 × 19.4 cm
Fitzwilliam Museum, Cambridge
Selected references: Cormack 1975;
Wilton 1979; Burnley 1982; Smiles 2000

Turner was commissioned to produce this watercolour by the antiquary Thomas Dunham Whitaker, whose topographical work *History of … Whalley* was published from 1800 to 1801 with nine engravings after Turner by James Basire.

Turner stayed at Whitaker's house in Cliviger, near Burnley, in the autumn of 1799, touring the surrounding countryside to sketch country houses and religious buildings, the kinds of subject on which he had built his early reputation. However, Whitaker also asked him to provide watercolours of seals, stone crosses and misericords, two of which survive.

The seals in this image comprise those of church dignitaries associated with Whalley Abbey, as well as seals of the de Lacy family, Lords of the Honor of Clitheroe and religious benefactors in the area in the Middle Ages.

These documentary records are extremely unusual in Turner's *oeuvre* and when John Ruskin gave this watercolour to the Fitzwilliam Museum in 1861, he described it merely as an example of 'what simple work [Turner] would undertake' early in his career.

The seals were engraved by Basire in different plates of Whitaker's book: seven of them in Plate 3 ('The Seals of Whalley Abbey') and seven in Plate 10 ('The Seals of the Lords of Blackburnshire'). ss

The Art of Recording | 137

101

Rubbing of a lost brass at Ingham commemorating Ela Brews (d. 1456)
The Revd Thomas Sugden Talbot (1778–1832)
1793–94
Graphite, 157 × 51 cm
Society of Antiquaries of London
Selected references: Cotman 1819, p. xxix, pl. 20; Badham and Fiske 2002, pp. 505–8; Badham 2006, pp. 20–2

The Society of Antiquaries holds the most complete collection of rubbings of monumental brasses in Britain, including many which have since been lost or damaged. Among the earliest examples are 79 graphite rubbings of Norfolk brasses made by Thomas Talbot from 1793 to 1794, when he was still a schoolboy. In 1813 Talbot gave his collection to John Sell Cotman for his planned volumes on East Anglian brasses. Cotman drew a pencilled grid over each rubbing in order to produce a scaled drawing from which he prepared the etching, later published in *Engravings of the Most Remarkable of the Sepulchral Brasses in Norfolk* (1819).

Among the rubbings that Cotman was most delighted to receive was a series taken from the brasses of the Stapleton family of Ingham, which were famed as the finest in the county. He had visited the church in the company of his patron, Dawson Turner, a few weeks before meeting Talbot, only to discover that the brasses had been sold for the value of the metal in 1799. This rubbing has only a shield to help identify the person commemorated. Cotman wrongly attributed it to Ela, wife of Sir Miles II (d. after 1419), but antiquarian notes recording other lost shields enable the widow to be identified as the couple's daughter, Ela. She died in 1456, but the brass was probably made shortly after the death of her husband, Sir Robert Brews of Salle, in 1424. No other rubbing of this brass survives. SB

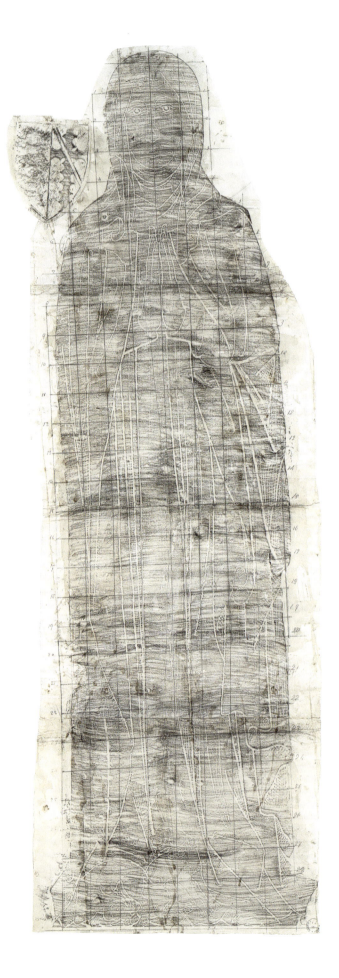

102

Drawing of a brass at Ketteringham, Norfolk, commemorating Thomas Hevynyngham Esq. (d. 1499) and his wife, Anne Yerde
John Sell Cotman (1782–1842)
c. 1816
Pencil, pen and ink and watercolour, 22 × 30.5 cm
Department of Prints and Drawings, Victoria and Albert Museum, London, H.7.BD.1527-1889
Selected references: Cotman 1819, p. xxxv, pl. 44; Fiske 2000, pp. 133–4; Badham and Fiske 2002, pp. 505–8

Although now famed as the most gifted watercolourist of the Norwich School, a nineteenth-century group of landscape painters who met fortnightly in Norwich, Cotman enjoyed little success in his own lifetime. With a growing family to support, he devoted much time from 1810 to 1822 to producing etchings for commercial publication, even applying in 1821 for the post of Historical Draughtsman to the Society of Antiquaries. The etchings he made for his *Engravings of the Most Remarkable of the Sepulchral Brasses in Norfolk* perhaps indicate why he was judged unsuitable; instead of reproducing the brasses with archaeological accuracy, he viewed them with an artist's eye, often 'improving' the original compositions.

The Hevynyngham brass at Ketteringham, set into the back wall of an altar tomb that might have served as an Easter sepulchre, is gilded and silvered, and retains original polychromy in the shields and heraldic dress. Unlike the published etching, Cotman's drawing is coloured, albeit inaccurately. On the lady's figure, he muddled the tinctures of the arms of Hevynyngham (which are erroneously shown counter-changed on the brass) and Yerde, and also those of Scott on the associated shield. There are many minor discrepancies in his drawing and hence the published etching. More seriously, Cotman showed the shields between the figures, although they are actually positioned under the scrolls, and he drew one more daughter than appears on the brass. SB

103

Drawings of a top view and details of the effigy commemorating Sir Oliver de Ingham (d. 1344) from his tomb in Ingham Church, Norfolk
Charles Alfred Stothard (1786–1821)
1812
Pen and grey ink, variously with grey wash and watercolour, 25 × 8.2 cm (566), 25.1 × 7.6 cm (567), 25.1 × 3 cm (568)
British Museum, London, Prints and Drawings, 1883.0714.566-8
Selected references: Stothard 1817–32, pl. 66; Lankester 2004, pp. 6–7; Badham 2007 forthcoming

These drawings of the effigy from Sir Oliver de Ingham's tomb at Ingham epitomise the careful recording process of Charles Stothard, who was appointed Historical Draughtsman to the Society of Antiquaries on 18 July 1815 and elected a Fellow in 1819. The tomb is one of the most important and unusual surviving examples of mid-fourteenth-century monumental sculpture. Lord Ingham is shown in the act of rising from a bed of stones with his gaze transfixed by the mural that formerly adorned the back wall of the tomb, as if his action were a response to a religious vision.

The coloured vignettes are of particular value because, since the mid-nineteenth century, the tomb has been covered by multiple layers of limewash that has delaminated the surface of the stone, removing significant areas of polychromy. Recent analysis of paint traces shows that the original decoration was both complex and sophisticated, as is exemplified by the use of expensive pigments such as red lake, as well as gold and silver leaf, the layering of pigments and the use of pastiglia (a form of raised decoration). In only a few areas can the decorative scheme still be seen; the belt-end is one such area and comparison shows that it was faithfully depicted by Stothard. In only one minor respect can Stothard's colour reconstruction of the effigy be faulted; the sword and the arm- and leg-plate defences are shown as black, but were actually silver leaf, which, having lost its protective translucent covering glaze, had become tarnished.

These drawings are the originals of plate 66 in Stothard's *Monumental Effigies of Great Britain*. SB

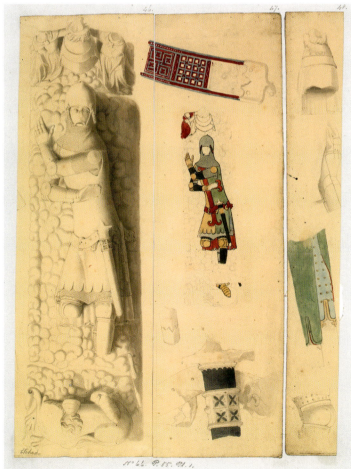

104

Stained-Glass Window from New Hall, Essex
Daniel Chandler (fl. 1737)
1737
Pen, ink and watercolour on paper,
45 × 36.7 cm
Society of Antiquaries of London
Selected references: Vetusta
Monumenta 1768, pl. 26; Vetusta
Monumenta 1789, plates 41, 42;
Wayment 1981, pp. 292–301; Colvin
1982, pp. 172–5

New Hall near Chelmsford in Essex was built on a lavish scale by Henry VIII soon after his acquisition of the property in 1516. A large stained-glass window dating from *c.* 1515 to 1527 that commemorated his marriage to Catherine of Aragon (from 1509 to 1533) was installed in the chapel. The figures kneeling at the bottom of the two side panels represent Henry VIII and his consort. The window may have been moved there from Waltham Abbey when New Hall was occupied by their daughter, Princess Mary, before she became Queen. In 1737, the abandoned and derelict house was sold to John Olmius, 1st Lord Waltham, who proceeded to demolish most of it; the glass was eventually purchased in 1758 for St Margaret's, Westminster. It was set up in the rebuilt east wall of the church and is acknowledged as some of the finest pre-Reformation Flemish glass in London.

The Society's engraver, George Vertue, was directed in 1737 'to employ a proper person to make a drawing and measure of the painted window in the Chappel of New Hall in Essex illuminated with its proper colours and also to take an elevation of the said house'. The person sent, Daniel Chandler, may have been Vertue's brother-in-law. His drawings include the only elevations known of the lost Tudor palace. The one representing the window is important because it shows how much was altered before installation in the new location. An engraving depicting the new state was published by the Society in 1768. BN

Bringing Truth to Light

Bernard Nurse

FIGURE 22
Monogram from the Book of Kells, fol. 34r
from *Vetusta Monumenta* VI, 1868
Society of Antiquaries of London

This chromolithograph after a drawing by Margaret Stokes (1832–1900) shows probably the best-known page from the *Book of Kells* (Trinity College, Dublin, MS 58), completed in about 800 AD. The illumination represents the shortened Greek form of the name of Christ, XPI.

In 1784, the Society's retiring President Edward King declared that one of the principal aims of the Society should be 'to bring *truth* to light' and develop the true history of mankind.[1] At the end of the eighteenth century, the Society's publications of illustrations were among the most ambitious and innovative of the period. They comprised three main large-format series: *Vetusta Monumenta*, which ran from 1718 to 1906; the historical prints, issued between 1775 and 1788; and the Cathedral Series, from 1795 to 1810. At the same time, the Society was publishing its regular journal *Archaeologia*, major monographs such as William Roy's *The Military Antiquities of the Romans in Great Britain* (1793), and transcripts of source material for British history.[2]

The origins of these publications can be traced back to the early days of the Society when the office of Director was established in 1718 to superintend all works of printing, drawing and engraving. The publication of prints was said to have been instigated by John Talman, the first Director, who was a talented draughtsman as well as a wealthy collector and patron.[3] He drew the subject of the first engraving, the lamp found at Windsor that became the Society's emblem (cat. 32), and also Edward the Confessor's shrine in Westminster Abbey (fig. 19). The Society's first Secretary, William Stukeley, was a strong advocate of the importance of accurate drawings and the value of engravings to convey understanding of historical monuments and antiquities. The Society was also fortunate in being able to employ one of the country's leading engravers, George Vertue, who was responsible for almost every print issued by the Society until his death in 1756 (cat. 88, fig. 19).[4] After a few years he was succeeded by another skilled engraver, James Basire, whose son and grandson, both also called James, continued to serve the Society.[5] Among the apprentices of the first James was the artist and poet William Blake, who is known to have worked on drawings and copperplates for the Society while serving his apprenticeship from 1772 to 1779 (cat. 105).

Vetusta Monumenta
Almost 350 prints were issued in the series that was known as *Vetusta Monumenta* from 1747 but which began with the first print of the lamp issued in 1718. All were printed on imperial-folio size paper (21½ × 14½ in.; 54.6 × 36 cm). Most were published before 1842, although the series continued intermittently until 1906, and all but three related to Great Britain. The title page, issued in 1747, followed Stukeley in outlining the purpose of the series as the preservation of the memory of British things.[6] The Society was thinking of future generations; concerned by the number of losses of historic monuments, it included drawings discovered of buildings previously demolished that were 'thus transmitted to posterity'.[7]

The 70 engravings in the first volume were accompanied by no more than brief descriptive captions, but gradually more text was added, which developed into substantial articles. There was a great diversity of subjects and any survivals from the past were seen as suitable: coins, seals, documents, historic buildings, wall paintings and mosaics were all featured. By producing representations of ordinary objects, the Society extended the idea of what would be acceptable for publication, and some of the first illustrations showing archaeological excavations in Britain were included (cat. 88). Although drawings were often prepared in watercolour, such as those attributed to William Blake of monuments in Westminster

FIGURE 23
The Embarkation of Henry VIII at Dover
1520
Samuel Hieronymus Grimm
1779
Watercolour
Society of Antiquaries of London

This is a copy of the painting in the Royal Collection at Hampton Court. An engraving was published in 1781 in the series Historical Prints as a companion piece to *The Field of Cloth of Gold*.

Abbey (cat. 105), they were reproduced in black and white. Colour plates were first published in 1803, but not again until 1821–23, when Charles Stothard's recording of the Bayeux Tapestry resulted in its first complete reproduction in colour (cat. 109). Stothard's fine watercolours of the thirteenth-century wall paintings in the Painted Chamber of the Palace of Westminster (cat. 107), recorded in 1819, were not published until 1842, and hand-colouring of prints was offered at extra cost. Later in the century, the Society went on to publish high-quality chromolithographic facsimiles of illuminated manuscripts, commissioning copies from accomplished women artists such as Rosa Wallis and Margaret Stokes (fig. 22).[8] When *Vetusta Monumenta* was briefly revived at the end of the nineteenth century, William St John Hope, the Society's Assistant Secretary, used it to publish his research on the vestments of Hubert Walter, Archbishop of Canterbury (1193–1205), found at Canterbury Cathedral; the size of the page and use of colour allowed him to reproduce the illustrations (cat. 148) better than in the smaller format *Archaeologia*.

Historical Prints
The engravings published in *Vetusta Monumenta* had their critics among the Fellows. Sir Joseph Ayloffe, a barrister employed in the State Paper Office, wrote in 1778 that the common run was taken from originals 'of little consequence and less amusement'.[9] He credited Philip Yorke, 2nd Earl of Hardwicke, with the idea of engraving historical paintings that commemorated remarkable events in Britain's national history. At a time of imperial and domestic crisis, the proposal gained strong support in the Society as contributing towards a sense of patriotism and national identity; and it complemented the vogue for history painting within the Royal Academy. Most of the subjects chosen concerned Henry VIII's fluctuating relations with France, which paralleled the changing attitudes of George III's governments. By 1769, Ayloffe was telling Lord Hardwicke that the painting of *The Field of Cloth of Gold* in the Royal Collection was 'indisputably the most capital antiquarian picture now extant' and would pursue the attempt to have it engraved.[10] The following year he read a paper to the Society describing some of the important works of art showing major events in British history, from the Bayeux Tapestry to sixteenth-century wall paintings at Cowdray House in Sussex, to help members consider suitable subjects for reproduction.

Between 1770 and 1780, the Society concentrated on this new series of historical prints and no engravings were published in *Vetusta Monumenta*. Seven prints were engraved by James Basire and published between 1775 and 1788. Two of these reproduced twelve-foot-long paintings in the Royal Collection at Windsor, painted in the mid-sixteenth century of events that had taken place in 1520, *The Field of Cloth of Gold* (Le Champ de Drap d'Or) (cat. 112), and the *Embarkation of Henry VIII at Dover* (fig. 23). Five prints reproduced wall paintings from Cowdray showing scenes from the war with France from 1544 to 1545 (cat. 113) and the coronation procession of Edward VI of 1547 (cat. 114). A new large size of paper, 'Antiquarian', had to be devised on which to print *The Field of Cloth of Gold*, and the effort and expense of producing detailed and reliable reproductions of such large-scale originals was so great that the last three paintings from Cowdray were copied and engraved in outline only.

The Society never recovered its costs despite financial support from Lord Hardwicke. Four hundred copies of each subject were printed, of which about 230 were given to Fellows as part of their subscription for the year and the rest were sold to the public at varying prices over a long period of time. Restrikes have been made from the copperplates according to demand, and three of the plates still survive, two in remarkably good condition (cat. 112).[11] However, the publication of historical prints was a triumph in terms of raising the Society's profile at a crucial time when it was campaigning to obtain apartments in the new Somerset House with the Royal Society and the Royal Academy. The copies commissioned by the Society of the Cowdray wall paintings provide the only record of their appearance, as the interior of the house was destroyed by fire shortly afterwards. Thus two of the best-known images from the mid-sixteenth century – the City of London at the time of Edward VI's coronation and Portsmouth at the time of the sinking of the *Mary Rose* – have been preserved.

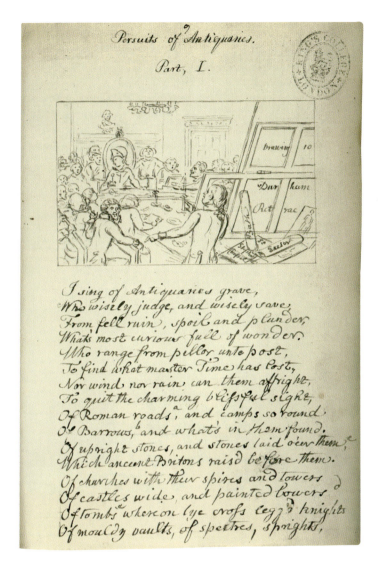

FIGURE 24
'John Carter Exhibiting His Drawings of Durham Cathedral to the Society' from *Persuits of Antiquaries during the years 1791–1799*
John Carter
1800
Pencil, pen and ink on paper
Kings College, London, Archives
Leathes 7/5

John Carter drew the scene in a notebook, signing his name Retrac (Carter backwards) and adding a humorous poem. The event depicted probably occurred abuot 1795.

The Cathedral Series

The historical prints did not find favour with the Society's Director, Richard Gough, who complained about their cost and their neglect of the medieval period.[12] Ironically, the next series, which he supported, proved even more expensive. Sir William Chambers, the architect of Somerset House, urged that the Society of Antiquaries 'undertake a correct publication of our own Cathedrals ... before they totally fall into ruin, it would be of real service to the Arts of Design'.[13] The idea was taken up with vigour by Sir Henry Englefield and his fellow member of the Society of Dilettanti, Sir Joseph Windham. The Dilettanti were publishing a lavish series of architectural surveys of Greece in the *Antiquities of Ionia* (1769–97), and, in 1792, Englefield proposed that the Society should commission artists to make architectural drawings of British cathedrals and religious houses. They found an outstanding draughtsman in John Carter, who had previously been employed by Richard Gough and the Society. The following year Carter submitted drawings that he had begun in 1790 of St Stephen's Chapel at the Palace of Westminster, and it was decided that they should be engraved. Over a five-year period, from 1794 to 1798, Carter was employed to survey Exeter, Bath, Wells, Durham and Gloucester, and the Society appointed Englefield and Windham to form 'The Committee for superintending the publication of drawings of the ancient ecclesiastical buildings of this country'. They acted with considerable efficiency, publishing Carter's drawings of St Stephen's Chapel in 1795, Exeter Cathedral in 1797, Bath Abbey in 1798 and Durham Cathedral (cat. 115) in 1801.

The series was the first to attempt accurate, detailed and measured drawings of the religious houses of England. Carter was responsible for nearly 70 drawings and the accompanying text of five of the sets. He has been acclaimed as 'the principal creator of a series which in detail and scholarship was unique in Europe ... in range, scale and consistency of purpose there was nothing in its generation to match Carter's Cathedrals'.[14] He was elected a Fellow in 1795 (fig. 24) but made many enemies with his outspoken remarks on the destruction of medieval features in the name of restoration. Englefield and Windham managed to secure the publication of the Durham drawings but those of Wells (cat. 116) were never engraved and remained unpublished until 2006.[15] Carter was refused entry into St Stephen's Chapel to carry out drawings of the wall paintings uncovered in 1800 and the Society sent Richard Smirke in his place (cat. 106).

The format, at atlas size, was smaller than the historical prints, and the plates were issued folded into volumes similar in size to *Vetusta Monumenta*. As with the historical prints, the cost of continuing proved prohibitive, especially as Fellows were entitled to a free copy of each set. Drawings by J. A. Repton of Norwich Cathedral purchased by the Society in 1806 were finally published in 1965.[16] Drawings of Tewkesbury Abbey commissioned from Frederick Nash about 1817 were eventually published in *Vetusta Monumenta* and no further sets were published. There was some criticism that the format was too large, the print too sharp and the production too extravagant.[17] It was left to another Fellow, John Britton, acknowledging his debt to Carter, to take up the challenge in his more affordable series of *Cathedral Antiquities* (1814–35).[18]

Bringing Truth to Light | 145

105

King Sebert and King Henry III
William Blake (1757–1827)
1778
Pen, watercolour and gold on paper,
31.5 × 12 cm
Society of Antiquaries of London
Selected references: Ayloffe 1780, plates xxix–xxxv; Butlin 1981; Binski 1995

In the summer of 1775, three monuments were revealed to the right and left of the high altar in Westminster Abbey when tapestries that had been screening them were temporarily removed. They commemorated Countess Aveline (d. 1272), Anne of Cleves (d. 1557) and King Sebert (fl. 637), the legendary Saxon founder of the Abbey. Shortly before the monuments were covered up again, Sir Joseph Ayloffe read a lengthy paper to the Society at four successive meetings from 12 March to 2 April 1778 about their history. He considered the paintings on Sebert's monument to be particularly important works of art and remarkable survivals from the reign of Edward I. Although he thought that the figures represented Sebert and Henry III, it is now thought that this would be an unlikely grouping, and that another Saxon king or an early bishop is more probable than Henry III.

The Society ordered that Ayloffe's paper be published in *Vetusta Monumenta* with illustrations, and, in July, the Society's engraver James Basire presented Council with nine finished coloured drawings. Although they are signed by Basire, following workshop practice, they have been attributed to William Blake on grounds of style and probability, as he is recorded as working for the Society on drawings of the tombs in Westminster Abbey, and he was apprenticed to Basire between 1772 and 1779. All the drawings were published in *Vetusta Monumenta* in 1780 with Ayloffe's account; and these two drawings were published together as a pair. BN

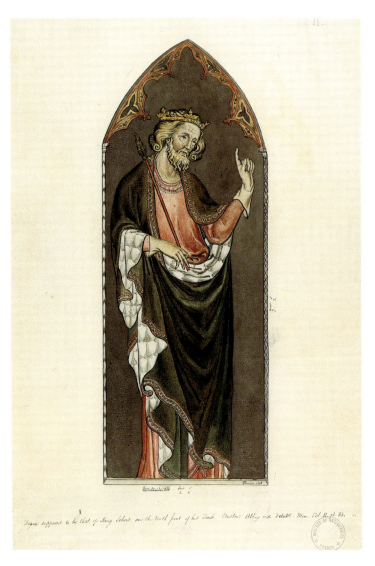

106

The Adoration of the Magi
Richard Smirke (1778–1815)
1800–02
Tempera and gold leaf on paper,
82.5 × 116.5 cm
Society of Antiquaries of London
Selected references: Scharf 1865, no. 69; Topham and Englefield 1795–1811; Howe 2001, pp. 259–303

St Stephen's Chapel in the Palace of Westminster was reconstructed in 1800 to create extra space for new Members of Parliament arising from the Act of Union with Ireland. Richard Smirke was commissioned by the Society to record the wall paintings discovered in the upper chapel, which in the Middle Ages had been reserved for the royal family and clergy. From tracings and reduced pencil drawings he was asked to produce highly finished coloured paintings to give an impression of what must have been one of the most richly decorated medieval buildings in Britain.

Smirke's drawings show the surviving remains uncovered on the left side of the high altar. They depict the Adoration of the Magi. On the top row, two kings followed by sword-bearing attendants bring gifts to the Virgin and Child. On the bottom row, looking towards the altar, St George on the far right is presenting Edward III and five of his sons in full armour. This mural was probably executed between 1355 and 1363 and would have been about 5 feet high by 6½ wide (1.5 by 2 metres). Smirke's four drawings have since been joined together; they were engraved in outline and published in 1811 as plate 16 in an additional volume of the Cathedral series on St Stephen's Chapel. All the wall paintings were obliterated in the building work, and almost all of the Palace of Westminster was destroyed by fire in 1834. BN

107

The Virtues Largesce and Debonereté
Charles Alfred Stothard (1786–1821)
1819
Watercolour with raised gilt detail,
37 × 12.8 cm; 37 × 12.6 cm
Society of Antiquaries of London
Selected references: Rokewode 1842, plates 26–39; Binski 1986; Reeve 2006, pp. 189–221

The Painted Chamber in the Palace at Westminster was regarded as one of the marvels of medieval Europe because of its magnificent decoration. Wall paintings were uncovered during refurbishment in 1819 and two of them depict Virtues in the character of armed females overcoming their opposite male Vices. *Largesse*, or Generosity, tramples on Covetousness while pouring coins into the Vice's mouth from a long purse. *Debonereté*, or Tranquillity, triumphs over Anger. The originals were painted facing each other on the splayed sides of the window opposite the King's state bed and would have been about three metres high by one wide. Historians have recently debated whether this work was carried out between 1263 and 1272 under the patronage of Henry III or later between 1292 and 1297 under Edward I, along with a series of Old Testament narratives. All the paintings were plastered over in 1819 and were completely destroyed in the fire of 1834 that burnt down the Palace.

The Society's Secretary, Henry Ellis, asked Charles Stothard to record the paintings as soon as they were found and his drawings were exhibited at a meeting in 1820. Publication was severely delayed by Stothard's untimely death in 1821. A detailed and perceptive description of the paintings was eventually read to the Society in 1842 by John Gage Rokewode, the Director, and shortly afterwards Henry Shaw, the best-known illuminator of the period, was commissioned to hand-colour several of the engravings. They were issued in the Society's series *Vetusta Monumenta* in 1842, with the two Virtues forming a pair as plate 38. BN

The triumph of Deboneretè or Meekness over Anger.
Vetusta Mon. Vol. VI. pl. xxxvm.

The triumph of Largesse or Bounty over Avarice.
Vetusta Mon. Vol. VI. pl. xxxviii.

108

The Burning of Westminster Palace in 1834
G. Drake for the Office of Woods
17 October 1834
Printed broadside with woodcut,
54 × 38.9 cm
Society of Antiquaries of London
Selected references: Lemon 1866,
no. 734; Port 1976, pp. 17–23

Over many years, the Society's artists had carefully recorded features of the medieval Palace of Westminster for publication, especially its outstanding wall paintings. In the nineteenth century the building was used for the Houses of Parliament and various law courts. When a new Court of Bankruptcy was required, a store that had housed wooden tallies previously used for accounting was ordered to be fitted up and the tallies burnt. On 16 October 1834, the clerk of the works decided that the stoves of the House of Lords would be 'a very safe and proper place to do it'. The furnaces overheated and the House of Lords caught fire, starting London's worse conflagration since the Great Fire of 1666. Westminster Hall was saved when the wind changed direction, but St Stephen's Chapel (cat. 106), the Painted Chamber (cat. 107) and the House of Lords were burned out.

The next day this news-sheet was published, describing the extent of the damage. The walls were still standing in many places and it would have been possible to patch up the buildings. However, the government, supported by the press, decided that the 'Mother of Parliaments' should have a new building worthy of a great nation. A competition for a design was ordered, and won by Charles Barry, assisted by Augustus Pugin (cat. 119). BN

DREADFUL FIRE!

And total destruction of both Houses of Parliament.

The Bayeux Tapestry
CATALOGUE NUMBERS 109–111

The Bayeux Tapestry is a unique representation of events surrounding William the Conqueror's victory over the Anglo-Saxon King, Harold II, at the Battle of Hastings in 1066. Although it is always described as a tapestry, the scenes were in fact embroidered on linen rather than woven. JS/EL

Selected references: Stothard 1821; Vetusta Monumenta 1821–3; Bridgeford 2004, pp. 35–6; Hill 2004; Musset 2005, pp. 216–17; Hicks 2006, pp. 124–5

109

(above)
'William the Conqueror at Hastings'
Engraved by James Basire (1769–1822), after Charles Alfred Stothard; hand-painted by Charles Alfred Stothard (1786–1821)
1816–19
Coloured engraving, 35 × 76 cm
Society of Antiquaries of London

110

(overleaf, left)
'William is told that Harold is near'
Engraved by James Basire (1769–1822) after Charles Alfred Stothard (1786–1821)
1819–22
Coloured engraving, 72 × 53 cm
Society of Antiquaries of London, 64J

111

(overleaf, right)
'William the Conqueror'
Charles Alfred Stothard (1786–1821)
1816–17
Hand-coloured plaster cast, 13.5 × 11 cm
Society of Antiquaries of London, LDSAL 109

In 1816 the Society's historical draughtsman Charles Stothard was commissioned to copy the entire Bayeux Tapestry. The same scene, where William the Conqueror receives intelligence of Harold and his army, is here represented in three different media. The drawings from his initial visit to France were engraved by James Basire. Stothard took these engravings with him on a later visit to Bayeux and hand-coloured them on site from the original work (cat. 109). These were published in *Vetusta Monumenta* between 1821 and 1823 (cat. 110) – the first time that a complete colour reproduction of the tapestry had been made available to the public. Stothard also published an article in *Archaeologia* that argued that the tapestry must have been made soon after 1066.

Stothard's work is also significant because it is the first record of the Bayeux Tapestry after it was damaged during the French Revolution and before repairs were carried out in the nineteenth century. By working with clues from surviving threads and colours he re-creates sections of missing embroidery and reveals scenes lost through damage.

During his three visits to France to complete the drawings, Stothard also made small plaster casts of the tapestry, one of which is shown here (cat. 111). His drawings are remarkably detailed but the casts provide a three-dimensional reproduction of the technique and texture of the embroidery, unaffected by interpretation. They were made by first making a wax impression of the linen and then pouring a thin layer of plaster of Paris onto it. The wax was removed once the plaster had set, and the cast was then painted to reflect the colours of the textile.

The later engraving (cat. 110) captures the fine detail of individual stitches with a close-up of William. The cast shows William's upper body.
JS/EL

A portion of the Tapestry of Bayeux, the size of the original. Pl. 17.

152 | Making History

112

The Field of Cloth of Gold
Engraved by James Basire
(c. 1730–1802), after a drawing by
Edward Edwards (1738–1806)
1771–73
Society of Antiquaries of London

(detail opposite; and right)
a) Engraved copperplate,
68.6 × 135.1 cm
Selected references: Ayloffe 1775B,
pp. 185–229; Evans 1956, pp. 160–1;
Anglo 1966, pp. 287–307

(below right)
b) Engraving, 56.5 × 115 cm
Restrike, 1990, by Charles Newington

One of the most spectacular events of the reign of Henry VIII was his meeting with the French king, François I, near Calais in June 1520. The occasion was depicted in two immense paintings, probably executed from c. 1550 to 1580 and now in the Royal Collection at Hampton Court. In the first, Henry VIII is shown departing from Dover, and, in its companion, known as *Le Champ de Drap d'Or*, better known as *The Field of Cloth of Gold*, the festivities that took place are shown in one composite view. Henry VIII appears three times and, in the foreground, fountains run with wine.

In 1770 Sir Joseph Ayloffe gave an account of this painting to the Society, and it was later agreed that it should be copied and published as the first in a series of historical prints. The drawing, by the painter Edward Edwards, although reduced, contained so much detail that innovative techniques had to be employed to fit the image on one sheet. The engraver, James Basire, made the largest single copperplate used up to then and the papermaker, James Whatman, invented special equipment to manufacture the largest sheet of handmade paper, known afterwards as 'Antiquarian' size (31 × 53 in.; 78.7 × 134.6 cm).

In all, 400 copies were printed of which some 230 were distributed to Fellows in 1775 and the rest offered for sale. The intricate, minutely detailed and finely executed copperplate is still in remarkably good condition and small quantities of restrikes have been occasionally taken since. BN

Bringing Truth to Light | 155

113

The Encampment of the British Forces near Portsmouth, 1545
Engraved by James Basire (c. 1730–1802) after the drawing by John (c. 1751–1790) and Charles (b. 1757) Sherwin
1778
Engraving, 55 × 177 cm
Society of Antiquaries of London
Selected references: Ayloffe 1775c, pp. 239–72; Hope 1919, pp. 54–6; Marsden 2003

In response to Henry VIII's capture of Boulogne in 1544, a French force of about 200 ships and 30,000 soldiers crossed the English Channel and entered the Solent in July 1545. Their intention was to invade the Isle of Wight and destroy the English fleet of about 80 ships. However, they made no progress in the 'Battle of the Solent' that followed and returned to France in August.

Although a victory for the English, this action is chiefly remembered today for the loss of one of Henry VIII's largest vessels, the *Mary Rose*. The events of 19 July were recorded on a large wall painting at Cowdray House in Sussex, the home of Sir Anthony Browne, the King's Master of Horse. The masts of the *Mary Rose* are shown with sailors standing on them just above the water, while Henry VIII can be seen riding along the shore. Part of the ship was raised in 1982 (cat. 152.5).

Sir Joseph Ayloffe read a paper to the Society on the wall paintings at Cowdray House in 1773 and, by 1775, the Sherwin brothers, who specialised in historic engravings, had made a watercolour copy. After much opposition because of the likely cost, it was eventually decided to publish the picture as the second in the series of historical prints and engrave it on two copperplates because the drawing was so large (six feet wide; about 1.8 metres). The print was published in 1778, and became the sole record of the scene after the interior of Cowdray House was destroyed by fire in 1793. BN

156 | Making History

FORCES NEAR PORTSMOUTH,
COMMENCEMENT OF THE ACTION BETWEEN THEM ON THE XIX.TH OF JULY MDXLV.
THE RIGHT HONOURABLE ANTHONY BROWNE LORD VISCOUNT MONTAGUE

Bringing Truth to Light

114

Coronation Procession of Edward VI
Samuel Hieronymous Grimm
(*c*. 1733–1794)
1785
Watercolour, 57.8 × 133.3 cm
Society of Antiquaries of London
Selected references: Ayloffe 1775c, pp. 239–72; Hope 1919, pp. 56–7; Clay 1941; Anglo 1969; Anglo 1998, pp. 452–7

Edward VI is shown processing from the Tower of London to the Palace of Westminster on 19 February 1547 before his coronation the following day. The young King can be seen under a golden canopy in the centre of the picture. His journey took about four hours while pageants and other entertainments were performed along the route. The Society has a detailed contemporary manuscript account of the event.

The Master of Horse, Sir Anthony Browne, had the scene painted as a large mural at Cowdray, his house in Sussex. Although none of the civic pageantry is depicted, the painting provides a unique record of the City, especially Cheapside with its goldsmiths' shops. The Society commissioned a copy from Samuel Hieronymous Grimm in 1785, and published the engraving in 1787 in their series of historical prints.

The original mural was destroyed when the interior of Cowdray House was consumed by fire in 1793, and the drawing is the only record of its appearance. Grimm has added codes, such as 'bl' for blue and 'r' for red, perhaps so that he would know which colours to add later. BN

115

Durham Cathedral, Section from East to West
Engraved by James Basire II (1769–1822)
after drawing by John Carter
(1748–1817)
1801
Engraving, 67.4 × 107 cm
Scale: *c.* 16 feet to 1 inch
(*c.* 4.9 metres to 2.5 cm)
Society of Antiquaries of London
Selected references: Carter 1801;
Crook 1995; Turner 2007

John Carter spent three months sketching and measuring Durham Cathedral in 1795. He was there when proposals were made to take down some of the old fabric and was incensed by what he regarded as unnecessary destruction. Soon afterwards the Chapter House was replaced by 'a modern chamber', but few other alterations were made after Carter's protests.

Although elected a Fellow in 1795, Carter was an outspoken critic of the architect and the church authorities at Durham. His opinions earned him many enemies; a few years later, he was refused entry to the Palace of Westminster to record the wall paintings recently discovered in St Stephen's Chapel. His persistent campaigning for the cause of preservation, linked with his careful observation and accurate drawings, made Carter a pioneer in the field of conservation.

The drawings of Durham Cathedral were completed by 1798, and the following year the Society's Council agreed to have them engraved by James Basire II; they were published in eleven plates with a commentary by Carter in 1801. His text was carefully scrutinised 'to avoid anything which can give offence or be considered of a personal nature'. His introduction stated that, after publishing two examples of Gothic architecture (Exeter Cathedral and Bath Abbey), the Society had selected Durham Cathedral 'as the most magnificent, as well as the most perfect building now remaining, constructed in the massive style adopted by the Norman conquerors of this Island'. The cross section (plate 5) was the largest and most expensive, at 200 guineas (about £5,000 today) for the cost of engraving. BN

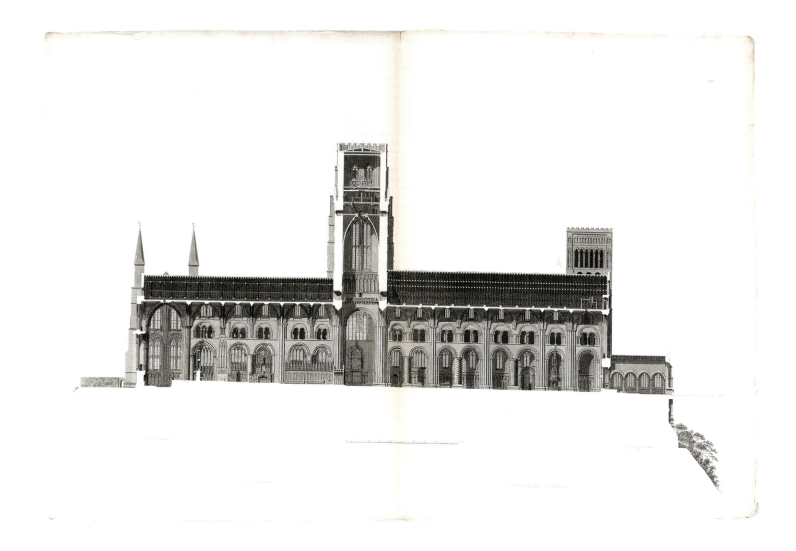

Section from East to West Wells Cathedral.

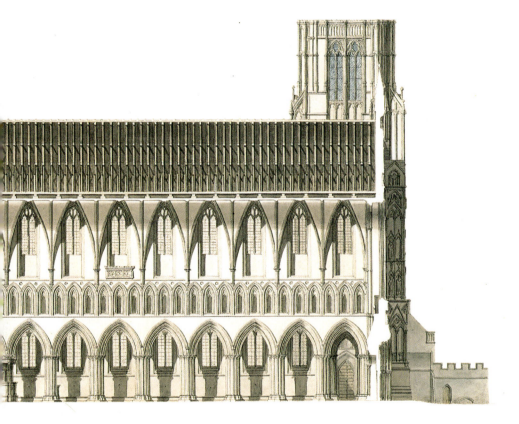

116

Wells Cathedral, Section from East to West
John Carter (1748–1817)
1807–08
Pen and black ink heightened by colour washes, 59.5 × 91 cm
Scale: *c.* 24 feet to 1 inch
Society of Antiquaries of London
Selected references: Rodwell and Leighton 2006

John Carter was commissioned by the Society to record Wells Cathedral in 1794 and spent five to six weeks there during that summer doing sketches and taking measurements. However, in succeeding years the Society was occupied in publishing expensive engravings of other cathedrals and it was not until 1806 that he was asked to make the finished drawings. The Society realised that no other artist could understand his notes and sketches, and he was paid in 1807 and 1808 to work up seven drawings. The first measured drawings of Wells Cathedral and its surroundings, they consist of a plan of the cathedral and its precincts, elevations and another section from north to south.

The drawings are so accurate that they are still used by Cathedral staff today. Prick-holes mark where a compass was put to inscribe roundels in the windows and dividers were used to space the nave arcades. This group was never engraved, probably because of the high cost. The drawings were first published as facsimiles from digital photographs in 2006 by the Somerset Record Society. BN

Antiquaries and the Arts

The period from the 1770s to the 1840s saw the rise of specialist fields in antiquarian research, which had a profound impact on contemporary cultural life. Antiquaries serviced the needs of contemporary artists and writers of imaginative literature, whose work was characterised by a new concern for accuracy of detail and precise reference to historical events and personages. During these same years – the Romantic era in the arts – historical and national themes in painting were growing in popularity, as were novels and poetry based upon history.

Certain historical eras, such as the Middle Ages, came to enjoy greater popularity and significance in the life of the nation. This was an age of revival in architecture and the decorative arts, particularly of the Gothic style, which was held to reflect the glories of Britain's ancient constitutional traditions and to symbolise the nation's essentially romantic notion of chivalry. The artistic output of William Morris and his circle reflected an attachment to this idealised medieval world.

til, at the laste, as e
Antony is shent, an
And al his folk togo

FLEETH ee
purpre sail,
for strokes
thikke as hail;

Antiquaries and the Arts

Stephen Calloway

In 1769 Joshua Reynolds (1723–1792), President of the newly founded Royal Academy of Arts, delivered the first of his celebrated annual lectures, or *Discourses*, to the students of the Royal Academy Schools.[1] Reynolds, who was also a Fellow of the Society of Antiquaries of London, had a highly developed sense of history. In the *Discourses* he codified for young British artists a set of values and assumptions about art that had long been established in France and Italy and which, passed down through the great European academies and artists' guilds, preserved intellectual and aesthetic ideals with origins in the Renaissance. Central to Reynolds's desire to cement a link between the works of the Old Masters and contemporary practitioners was his enunciation of a hierarchy of artistic endeavour. This placed landscape and portraiture – his own *métier* – above inferior genres such as still-life and animal painting, but enshrined as pre-eminent 'history painting': that is, the representation of noble, heroic or otherwise elevated subjects and 'striking' episodes from classical mythology, the scriptures, serious literature or historical texts.

Reynolds's aspirations for a British school of painting naturally led the Academy to encourage the depiction of British subjects. In the early Annual Exhibitions at the Academy's first home in Somerset House, pictures from national history, along with scenes drawn from the works of Shakespeare, Milton and other English writers, were well received. Outside the Academy's walls, enterprises such as Bowyer's History Gallery, a Milton Gallery and, most famously, Alderman Boydell's Shakespeare Gallery flourished as popular attractions.[2] Painters who, only a generation earlier, would have eked out an existence as jobbing portraitists or topographers now rushed to supply the demand for history pieces.

This rise in interest in historical and national themes in painting during the latter part of the century found its parallel in a great advance in antiquarian and historical studies, and in the growing popularity of historical writing. Two towering achievements of this movement were Gibbon's *Decline and Fall of the Roman Empire* (1776–88), and Hume's *History of Great Britain* (1754–62), which remained the standard accounts until well into the next century. A source for many representations of historic scenes can, however, be found in the earlier writings of Paul de Rapin-Thoryas, whose vivid descriptions of stirring events continued to have a broad appeal. Rapin's *Histoire de l'Angleterre* had been published in English between 1726 and 1731, but the monumental, seven-volume edition of 1743–47 is today the most highly prized for its inclusion of 'Vertue's Heads', the extensive series of historical portraits created by the indefatigable antiquary and engraver George Vertue.[3]

The decades from the 1770s to the 1840s were heroic years in scholarship, which saw the rise of many specialist fields of historical research. In a world still dominated by amateur scholars and gentleman antiquaries, the histories and classifications of architecture, painting, portraiture, the decorative arts, costume, coins and other artefacts – and, notably, the British aspects of these various disciplines – all made extraordinary advances. Many of the foundations of modern scholarship must be traced to pioneering studies published in these years. To name only two such books, both by eminent Fellows of the Society, Sir Samuel Rush Meyrick's *A Critical Enquiry into Antient Armour* (1824) and Thomas Rickman's *An Attempt to Discriminate the Styles of English Architecture* (1817) supplanted previous confused and erroneous accounts of their subjects and set frameworks for all subsequent research (Rickman gave us the terms still in use today to describe the successive periods of native Gothic: Early English, Decorated and Perpendicular). Such volumes not only provided information of lasting value to scholars, but also met a particular need of artists. Meyrick, in his laudatory introduction to his friend Henry Shaw's *Specimens of Ancient Furniture drawn from Existing Authorities* (1836), emphasised this point:

From the want of such a collection, artists of the highest repute have sometimes produced pictures, of which the details are so full of incongruities and anachronisms, as materially detract from the general merit of the piece ... extreme accuracy, even in the minutest detail, can alone produce that illusion which is requisite for the perfect success of a work of art.[4]

During these same years, from around 1770 to 1840 – the Romantic era in the arts – novels and poetry based on historic themes also enjoyed a great surge of popularity. At the beginning of the period, heralded by Horace Walpole's *The Castle of Otranto*, published anonymously in 1764, the Gothic novel tended to extravagance and broad-brush histrionic effects.[5] But with the advent of narrative poems and, later, the 'Waverley' novels of Sir Walter Scott a new concern for accuracy of detail and precise reference to historical events and personages became a defining characteristic of a major genre of imaginative literature.[6]

Scott was a formidably knowledgeable antiquary himself and a collector on a heroic scale, who did much to encourage the fashion for 'antiquarian interiors'. E. W. Cooke's picture *The Antiquary's Cell* (1835) (fig. 25) epitomises this taste, being both an accurate depiction of the artist's own room and an evocative illustration of Scott's description of the study of Jonathan Oldbuck, the eponymous central character of his novel *The Antiquary* (cat. 117). Scott was endowed with the great talent of making the places and characters of the past come to life. This drawing of real historical figures, events and places into the realm of the popular imagination by writers, artist and antiquaries seems also to have been the catalyst for two distinct but closely related trends. Personal relics of famous people became increasingly sought by collectors, written about and discussed, while simultaneously a new interest in visiting the locations associated with figures from the past arose. Castles and ruined abbeys, with their more generalised historical associations, had appealed, of course, to the picturesque tourist for many years. Now, a new breed of sentimental traveller sought out such numinous haunts as Rosamund's Bower at Woodstock or the tranquil garden of the poet George Herbert at Bemerton; those in search of a more urban and 'Gothick' sensation could visit the very site of executions at the Tower of London and thrill to the sight of the axe and the block.

As more and more novels, poems, pictures and prints with historical subject-matter appeared, some characters from fiction and actual historical figures became more popular than others, forming a canonical 'cast of characters' from the imagined past. From more distant eras colourful, chivalrous figures or great lovers stood out more than clerics, merchants or ordinary people. From later centuries, the characters about whom Shakespeare had written, such as Richard III, were especially favoured, while the cult of Elizabeth I – originally fashioned by herself and her poets and painters – was revived with a new, Romantic flavour by artists and antiquaries. Shakespeare himself also attained a cult

FIGURE 25
The Antiquary's Cell
Edward William Cooke
1835
Oil on panel
Victoria and Albert Museum, London,
Sheepshanks Gift, FA.42

Nostalgic pictures of picturesque but random collections like this were increasingly in demand. It has been suggested that the artist Edward Cooke was inspired by the description of Jonathan Oldbuck's study in Sir Walter Scott's novel *The Antiquary*, published in 1816 (cat. 117).

FIGURE 26
A Knight Enters the Lists at the 'Eglinton Tournament' of Archibald William Montgomery, 13th Earl of Eglinton
Edward Henry Corbould
1840
Oil on panel
Victoria and Albert Museum, London,
P.5-1981

This painting shows Lord Eglinton dressed in gold armour at the 'Eglinton Tournament' which he hosted on his Scottish estate in 1839.

status at this time, initiated mainly by the actor David Garrick's extravagant adulation, which placed Shakespeare's reputation far beyond that of any other literary personality. Figures from the more recent past, such as Cromwell and Charles I, Charles II and Nell Gwyn, or Bonnie Prince Charlie were also romanticised, but their stories were told in ways that reveal a more political edge to the reinterpretation and re-creation of the past.

As with individuals, certain historical eras, such as the Middle Ages, enjoyed greater popularity in art and literature, and attained greater significance in more general, philosophical or moral ways in the life of the nation. By the 1830s tales of romance and chivalry inspired an interest in costume and events of the period. The Eglinton Tournament of 1839 was a highly elaborate re-enactment with the guests dressing up in medieval-style costume, and taking part in processions and competitions (fig. 26). In what was rapidly becoming an age of revivals in architecture and the decorative arts, styles had meaning and a wider resonance. When, for example, in 1834 a disastrous fire destroyed almost all of the Old Palace of Westminster (cat. 108) except for the medieval Westminster Hall, it became necessary to contemplate the creation of a large new building to house Parliament. Debate raged concerning the appropriate style in which to build, Gothic or classical. Following a heated 'battle of the styles' over the design competition, the 'Goths' won. The choice of a late-medieval Gothic idiom, rather than a 'modern' and 'foreign' Neoclassicism, was held to reflect the glories of Britain's ancient constitutional traditions and to be symbolic of the nation's essentially Romantic chivalry.

The solution was, in reality, a clever stylistic compromise for the new palace was thoroughly modern in its bones. The overall conception and planning of the vast new complex with its up-to-date heating, ventilation and other services was the work of the suavely practised classicist Charles Barry (1795–1860), while every decorative detail – from crocketed pinnacles down to medievalising chairs and tables, encaustic floor-tiles, candelabra and door locks – was entrusted to the most able and learned of the Goths, Augustus Welby Pugin (1812–1852) (see cat. 119). By the 1840s, standing at the heart of the nation, the palace was the single most conspicuous monument of the Gothic-revival taste in architecture and a formidable statement of the power and confidence of the Establishment. Up and down the country, in new civic buildings and churches and in the houses of rich (and often newly rich) men, equally bold statements of self-confidence were being made in similar style (fig. 27).

The 1843–44 national competition for designs for mural decorations for the new palace predictably required artists to submit compositions, or 'cartoons', based on historical subjects. Some entries, especially by untried artists, were monumental but wooden, and revealed both hasty research and shaky technique. Others, by young painters such as Ford Madox Brown, looked forward to the highly worked, historicising style that dominated the art world of the 1850s. In their depictions of a supposedly golden age in which a beneficent feudal, aristocratic authority had given the nation stability, strength and social justice, popular artists such as William Powell Frith and Charles Robert Leslie tapped into the myth of 'Merry England' that made such scenes the most successful of pictorial genres in the principal London exhibitions in the middle years of the century.[7]

Antiquaries and the Arts | 167

The way in which Victorian painters created their images of the 'Olden Time' is significant. In the time-honoured academic tradition, artists still based their work on the study of the human figure and the rules of pictorial arrangement, but, having 'found their subjects' – in literature, history or popular legend – they proceeded to elaborate their compositions, piling on incidental detail from reference works or, more directly, from the dresses, armour and other props that had become an essential adjunct of the nineteenth-century artist's studio. Many painters interested themselves in the history of costume, though few seem to have been concerned over-much with strict chronology. Easy sources for these details were the standard books by Joseph Strutt, James Planché, Camille Bonnard and, in particular, the antiquary-artist F. W. Fairholt.[8]

An altogether more exacting method is to be seen in the work of Madox Brown (1821–1893). He trained on the Continent in the studio of Baron Wappers, a pedantic Antwerp painter of costume pieces, and brought back with him an obsession with painstaking research in preparation for picture-making. Brown entered the competition for cartoons for the new Palace of Westminster, submitting in 1844 a powerful evocation of *The Body of King Harold Brought to William the Conqueror*. For the next twenty years he worked tirelessly – though often with poor financial reward – at a series of historical subjects, most famously, *Chaucer at the Court of Edward III* (cat. 118), the original version of which he exhibited in 1851, the culmination of considerably more than one year's work.[9]

Brown's diary entries record with painful earnestness the elaborate process of creating these large pictures.[10] The preliminary work was exhausting, including the investigation of tomb sculptures in order to fix the features of his protagonists, and research into early furniture as well as costume.[11] This meticulous planning gave way to the hard and relatively mechanical grind of working up studies, not only for the principal figures but also for every minor detail that would form part of the completed canvas.

Most intriguing are his many references to searches for correct costume props. Unable, since so little survived, to secure actual examples of medieval dress from which to paint, Brown sought out pieces of old fabric, often spending far in excess of what he could prudently afford or reluctantly parting with one prized piece in order to secure another more immediately useful sample.[12] When sufficiently in funds, he employed a 'workwoman' to sew for him items such as gowns or medieval hoods which he copied from costume books. Such a desire for accuracy, which reached its highwater mark in these years, is in stark contrast to the practice of earlier painters, exemplified in the well-known dictum of Sir Joshua Reynolds that one aspiring to the Grand Manner should not 'debase his conceptions' by niggling with period costume: 'It is the inferior stile that marks the variety of stuffs. With [the historical painter] the cloathing is neither woollen, nor linen, nor silk, sattin, or velvet: it is drapery; it is nothing more.'[13] For Brown and others who cared about social themes in history, the difference between silk velvet and homespun, as signifiers of grandeur or poverty and insignificance, possessed not only a crucial artistic, but also a moral, implication.

Among the historians it was Thomas Babington Macaulay, writing in 1849, who was the first to move away from the stories of great men and narratives 'of battles and sieges, of the rise and fall of

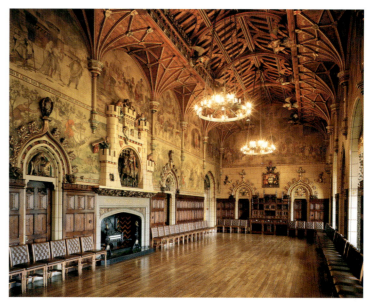

FIGURE 27
The Banqueting Hall (top) and the Winter Smoking Room (above) of Cardiff Castle
William Burges

From 1866, the 3rd Marquess of Bute commissioned the architect William Burges to transform the Norman castle at Cardiff into a Victorian fantasy of a medieval palace. The suite of rooms within the castle constitute one of the highest achievements of Victorian Gothic Revival design.

administrations, of intrigues in the palace' in favour of a new sort of social history, emphasising the experience of ordinary people and 'placing before the English of the nineteenth century a true picture of the life of their ancestors'.[14] The moral dimension of attitudes to the past continued to gain in importance as the pace of innovation in science and technology gathered speed. For a growing band of artists, writers and thinkers, the past now served as more than just a dressing-up box and an attractive alternative to undesirable aspects of the present. Rather than offering escape, the Middle Ages appeared to many to present a model for cultural renewal, design reform and even social innovation.

Rejecting the inevitability of the triumph of modern industrial culture, John Ruskin (1819–1900) wrote at immense length about the redemptive power of art and the need to return to the values of the past. His championing of the Pre-Raphaelite Brotherhood in the early 1850s, at the moment when these young revolutionary painters were most under attack by the art establishment, was of the greatest importance, even though in many respects his ideas and aims were at odds with those of the movement's key figures. Curiously, it was with Dante Gabriel Rossetti (1828–1882) and his wife and muse Lizzie Siddal (1829–1862) that Ruskin found himself personally most in sympathy. He was fascinated by the self-obsessed, gauche and Bohemian lifestyle of these strangely attractive people, content to ignore the fact that Rossetti, a poet-painter interested only in the realm of the imagination, cared little for his benefactor's social ideals and moral earnestness.

Rossetti was steeped in the romance of the past, but never scholarly or antiquarian in temperament. One of the very few instances in which he consciously adopted an accurate ancient form was in a jewel-casket (cat. 122) that he and Lizzie decorated shortly before her death in 1862. It was shaped like a medieval strong-box or perhaps based upon a recollection of the gabled shrine of St Ursula painted by Hans Memling in 1489, which Rossetti had seen at Bruges ten years before. The casket is a perfect expression of the taste of Rossetti's intimate circle at this time, a group that included the young William Morris and his friend Edward Burne-Jones, both of whom were recently graduated from the University of Oxford and shared a deeply felt attachment to an idealised, Ruskinian medieval world. The casket serves too as a reminder of the important role that Rossetti played in the founding and early work of Morris, Marshall, Faulkner & Co., the association of 'Art Workmen' established by Morris in order to further his aims of creating beautiful objects and furnishings. Later, Rossetti gave the casket to Morris's wife Jane, with whom he had become obsessed.

Following the death of Lizzie Siddal, Rossetti established himself in a romantic old house on Cheyne Walk in Chelsea. Surrounded by 'artistic' bric-a-brac, including seventeenth-century oak furniture bought from Wardour Street curio-dealers, Chinese hardwood chairs and tables, and a large collection of blue-and-white china, his interiors became hugely influential.[15] In 1871, Rossetti and Morris took a shared lease on the old Cotswold manor house of Kelmscott (now owned by the Society of Antiquaries). Both held highly romanticised attitudes to the past and for a while the idyll worked. Sadly, in spite of their initially close friendship, insurmountable differences of character and ideals – exacerbated by their competition for the affections of Jane Morris – led first to a cooling and ultimately to a complete break. Abandoning Kelmscott to Morris, who henceforth made the house the centre of his existence, Rossetti retreated to Cheyne Walk where, surrounded by his collections and his own brooding canvases, he spent his last years in deepening gloom and isolation.

By contrast, Morris, increasingly the public man, seemed ever more vigorous and more passionately devoted to active causes. He was a prime mover in the formation of the Society for the Protection of Ancient Buildings (SPAB) and active in assisting the South Kensington Museum, which later became the Victoria and Albert Museum, to acquire important examples of decorative arts. He also gave his energies and crucial funding to the nascent Socialist Movement. Despite all these associations with new organisations, he particularly valued the exceptional continuity of the Society of Antiquaries to which he was elected a Fellow.

In his remaining years Morris continued tirelessly to write and design, concentrating latterly on the sumptuous printed books that he issued from his Kelmscott Press (cats 125, 126). Although tireless, too, in his pursuit of beauty, he never collected for the sake of possession; his collections – Persian carpets, English oak, Indian metalwork and his fine early printed books and illuminated manuscripts – were gathered to enable him to understand the past and to serve as immediate models for his practice as a craftsman. His inspiration came from a love of natural forms and his deep knowledge of the past. For Morris, close in this respect to Ruskin, the two great instructors of mankind were Nature and History and every aspect of his thinking and teaching, for all its exuberance and optimism, had at its core some sense of regret for a lost, ancient, rural England of the antiquarian imagination.

Setting himself in opposition to all that he considered base, ugly and meretricious in modern civilisation, Morris believed in the transformative power of his ideal of the beauty of life and work in the Middle Ages. In that, for all his practicality, he remains a romantic. As he himself said: 'As for Romance, what does Romance mean? I have heard people miscalled for being romantic, but what romance means is the capacity for a true conception of history, a power of making the past part of the present.'[16] It is here that Morris the idealist and social reformer and Morris the maker of beautiful things come closest to Morris the passionate antiquary.

117

The Antiquary
Walter Scott (1771–1832)
1816
Printed book, 19 × 28 cm
Society of Antiquaries of London
Selected references: Van Riper 1993, p. 23; Hewitt 1995

The Romantic movement was characterised by a new appreciation of the medieval past, reflected in the arts, music and literature. In the late eighteenth and early nineteenth centuries, poetry and fiction with historical themes were much in vogue. Celebrated for his work in both these genres, Sir Walter Scott was a highly prolific writer and a central figure in literary and artistic circles in both London and Edinburgh. His narrative poems and, in particular, his 'Waverley' novels, an extensive series of tales set in the distant as well as more recent past, did much to foster popular interest in history. With their combination of accurate historical detail, vivid characterisation and exciting action, Scott's works became favourites with both amateur and professional artists and illustrators; many other writers borrowed from and adapted them in their own work. *The Antiquary*, one of the best-loved of the Waverley novels, according to the records of London art exhibitions of the time, inspired some 266 paintings by various artists over a 25-year period.

Scott himself was involved in historical studies, gaining a considerable reputation as an antiquary for his wide knowledge of Scottish buildings and artefacts, ancient poetry and traditions; he wrote the archaeological treatise *The Border Antiquities of England and Scotland*, which was published in 1814. A Fellow of the Society of Antiquaries of London, and Antiquary to the Royal Academy, he also dabbled in amateur archaeology and is said to have played some part in the excavation of a Roman fort while visiting the home of his fiancée in 1794. This incident may have inspired one of the key scenes in *The Antiquary*, in which the central character, Jonathan Oldbuck, is gently ridiculed for paying a high price for a barren field in which he had mistaken some fragment of recent masonry for the remains of a Roman *castrum*. ARP/BN/SC

118

(opposite)
Chaucer at the Court of Edward III
Ford Madox Brown (1821–1893)
1856–68
Oil on canvas, 123.2 × 99.1 cm
Tate Britain, London, N02063
Selected reference: Strong 1978

Ford Madox Brown's depiction of Chaucer reading his works at the court of Edward III was the first important work that he showed at the Royal Academy. Having originally intended it to be the central panel of a triptych symbolising the birth of the English language in the person of Chaucer, Brown never completed the projected wings, but returned to the main theme, beginning this second version in 1856, and continuing to work on it until the late 1860s. The earlier painting now belongs to the Art Gallery of New South Wales, Australia.

Brown set his scene at Edward III's court at the Palace of Sheen on the Black Prince's forty-fifth birthday. He tried to be as historically accurate as possible, using several antiquarian sources. The composition is based on a medieval miniature (Corpus Christi College, Cambridge, MS 61) that shows Chaucer reading *Troilus and Cressida* to the court of Richard II. The figures of the Black Prince and Edward III are probably taken from illustrations of tomb effigies in Charles Stothard's *Monumental Effigies* (1817–32), and the women's headdresses from Joseph Strutt's copies of medieval manuscripts published in the second edition of his *Complete View of the Dress and Habits of the People of England* (1842). Both Strutt's and Stothard's works were much used by artists at a time when historical realism was in vogue.

Brown was closely associated with the Pre-Raphaelite Brotherhood, one of whose founder members was Dante Gabriel Rossetti, who modelled for the figure of Chaucer. Brown was also a partner in the firm of Morris, Marshall, Faulkner and Co. from its establishment in 1861 until its dissolution in 1875, and he contributed many designs, especially for furniture and stained-glass windows. BN/SC

library ceiling

large bosses real size

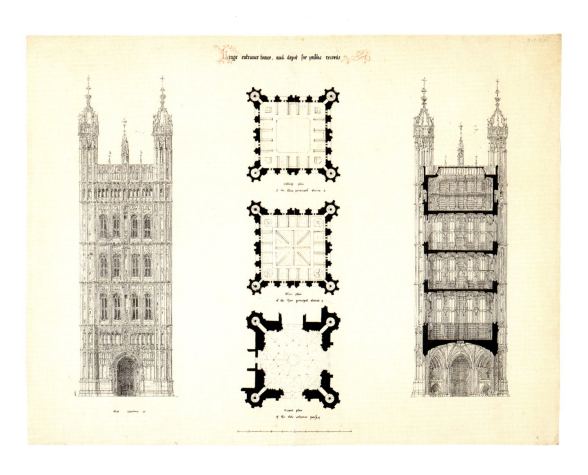

Gothic Revival Archictecture and A. W. N. Pugin
CATALOGUE NUMBERS 119–120

119

(opposite)
Design for the King's (later Victoria) Tower, Houses of Parliament, Westminster
A. W. N. Pugin (1812–1852)
1836–37
Black and red pen and black and yellow washes on paper, 44.5 × 60 cm
Society of Antiquaries of London, B-P. 2/19
Selected reference: Wedgwood 1992

120

Design for large bosses of the library ceiling for King Edward VI Grammar School, Birmingham
A. W. N. Pugin (1812–1852)
1835–36
Pen and grey, red and black washes on paper, 55 × 74 cm
Society of Antiquaries of London, B-P.1/4

From an early age Augustus Welby Pugin was fascinated by medieval architecture, and assisted his father Augustus Pugin, the architectural and topographical draughtsman. An important early influence on Pugin's style came from his study of the illustrations by Wenceslaus Hollar and others in the books of the seventeenth-century antiquary Sir William Dugdale (1605–1686). Pugin also followed the ideas of the antiquarian artist John Carter (1748–1817) in championing English Gothic. Pugin's historical studies and polemical books, such as *Contrasts* (1836), were to have a considerable impact on the course of Gothic Revival architecture, especially church building, for the rest of the nineteenth century.

These two drawings were made by Pugin at the beginning of his career for projects in which he assisted the architect Charles Barry. Barry had won the competition for the New Street buildings at the King Edward VI Grammar School in Birmingham in 1833, and two years later he commissioned Pugin to provide drawings for decorative details. Pugin's skill as a designer and draughtsman is shown in the lively drawing, made for a sculptor, of the large bosses in the library ceiling. The buildings were demolished in the last century.

Many of Barry and Pugin's ideas for the school were developed on a larger scale for the world's best-known Gothic Revival building, the new Palace of Westminster. Following the destruction by fire of the Old Palace in 1834, an architectural competition was held that stipulated that the design should be Gothic or Elizabethan, styles that were considered to be particularly British and to reflect the antiquity of Parliament. For his entry, Barry relied heavily upon Pugin for his knowledge of medieval detail and his facility to produce rapid designs. Between August 1836 and March 1837, Pugin prepared the large number of drawings needed to make a detailed estimate of costs. The King's Tower (now called the Victoria Tower) was intended to form the ceremonial entrance for the monarch and, with the experience of the 1834 conflagration in mind, to provide also a fire-proof repository for documents. The tower now holds the Parliamentary Archives.
BN/SC

121

Medieval-style settle
Designed by Philip Speakman Webb
(1831–1915)
c. 1860
Ebonised oak, with panels decorated with painted and gilded embossed leather, 209 × 194 × 56.5 cm
Society of Antiquaries of London, Kelmscott Manor 034
Selected references: Lethaby 1935; London 1996, p. 168; Kirk 2005

Philip Webb and William Morris met when both were apprenticed to the Gothic Revival architect George Edmund Street. They remained close friends and colleagues, and when Morris married he asked Webb to design his new home. Red House in Kent (now in the London Borough of Bexley) was a sophisticated, free interpretation of Gothic and later vernacular styles and, as a precursor of the Arts and Crafts Movement, greatly influenced the subsequent development of domestic architecture. Webb was also a founding partner of Morris, Marshall, Faulkner and Co., where he designed glass, metalwork and furniture, which played a key role in the formation of the early Morris style of interior decoration.

This settle was designed by Webb specifically for Red House, where Morris and his family lived between 1860 and 1865. Describing the dining room, May Morris, William's daughter, recorded that 'the black settle with gilt and painted leather panels … was placed by the hospitable fireplace'. It is now housed in the north hall at Kelmscott Manor.

Medieval inspiration is also evident in the design, the overhanging curved top being based on medieval ceremonial chairs. The painted pattern in the upper part of the canopy, presumably also designed by Webb, is identical to that found on panels of an upright 'cottage' piano that belonged to Ford Madox Brown (the piano is now at the William Morris Gallery in Walthamstow, London). Several versions of the settle were later made by Morris & Co., including some with gilded or silvered gesso decoration by Kate Faulkner and painted decoration by J. H. Dearle.

With Morris and Faulkner, Webb was also one of the founders of the Society for the Protection of Ancient Buildings (SPAB), which aims to prevent the destruction of the ancient fabric and character of buildings through over-zealous 'restoration'. JS/PC/SC/JC

122

Medieval-style jewel casket belonging to Jane Morris
Dante Gabriel Rossetti (1828–1882) and Elizabeth Siddal (1829–1862)
c. 1859
Wood bound with studded iron bands, 17.7 × 29.2 × 17.7 cm
Society of Antiquaries of London, Kelmscott Manor 202
Selected references: Harris 1984; Liverpool 2003, no. 169, pp. 227–8

This jewel casket has long been celebrated as a Pre-Raphaelite relic. It may have been designed by the architect Philip Webb, who worked for William Morris's firm. Made of painted wood with iron bands and typical of the earliest, rough, historicising productions of the firm, the casket follows the form of many surviving medieval caskets or strong-boxes. It may also bear some relation to the celebrated St Ursula Reliquary at Bruges; Dante Gabriel Rossetti had seen this famous late medieval object, painted by Hans Memling in the 1480s, about a decade earlier, during his journey through France and Belgium in 1849.

The panels of the jewel casket were painted by Rossetti and his wife Lizzie Siddal, and probably completed only shortly before her tragic death in 1862. Of the original fourteen panels, only seven on the front and sides retain their original painted decoration. Although they are contemporary with, and similar in style to, Rossetti's major series of watercolours on themes from legend, the scenes are also typical of Siddal's work in their small scale and the derivation of their subject-matter from medieval romance. At least one panel, that depicting two lovers, seems to have been taken specifically from a medieval manuscript, the image of the young couple being closely related to a miniature in a fifteenth-century volume of the poems of Christine de Pisan from the Harleian Collection in the British Library (MS Harley 4431).

The casket was possibly given by Dante Gabriel Rossetti to Jane Burden on her marriage to William Morris in 1859, or in the early 1870s at the time when Morris, Rossetti and Burden, with whom Rossetti was in love, all moved to Kelmscott Manor in Oxfordshire. In later years, Burden's daughter May Morris always referred to the box as her mother's 'jewel casket', but its precise origin and purpose remain obscure. JS/SC/JC/PC

123

Embroidered wall hanging of St Catherine
William Morris (1834–1896) and Jane Morris (1839–1914)
c. 1860
Embroidery in silk and wool thread on linen, applied to velvet, 180 × 136 cm
Society of Antiquaries of London, Kelmscott Manor 043
Selected references: Parry 1983; Dufty 1985, pp. 14–15, pl. 27; Parry 2005

Among the most important and novel aspects of the decoration of Morris's Red House, and later of Kelmscott Manor, was the use of embroidered textiles as hangings. The designs for them were mostly made by Morris himself, and many wall panels, bed curtains and other pieces were worked by Jane Morris, her sister Bessie and later the daughters of the Morrises. This early panel with a representation of St Catherine is one of a projected series of twelve, depicting women from legend, loosely based on Geoffrey Chaucer's poem *The Legend of Goode Wimmen*. The set was intended to hang around the walls of the drawing room at Red House but it was never finished; a number of the panels do, however, survive in various stages of completion.

With her accompanying tree, St Catherine is the most finished of the surviving figures. The embroidery is attached to a brown velvet curtain, having been used for many years by Morris's friend and colleague Edward Burne-Jones as a door curtain at his house, The Grange, in Fulham, London.

Morris took a particular interest in the styles and techniques of early textiles, and the medieval inspiration behind these embroideries is evident in both their traditional craftsmanship and the nature of the subject. St Catherine was a popular medieval saint; according to legend she was a scholarly noblewoman, condemned to death on the wheel for her defence of Christianity against the scholars of the Emperor Maxentius. When the wheel miraculously broke she was beheaded with a sword. She is typically represented with the attributes seen here: a wheel, a book and a sword. Morris's design for the figure was also adapted for stained glass by Morris, Marshall, Faulkner and Co.; an example (1865) can be seen in the church of All Saints, Middleton Cheney, Northamptonshire. JS/PC/SC/JC

124

The 'Acanthus and Vine' Tapestry
William Morris (1834–1896)
c. 1879
Woven wool, with some silk, on a cotton warp, 191 (max.) × 234 cm
Society of Antiquaries of London, Kelmscott Manor 032
Selected references: Parry 1983; London 1996, p. 286, H.155

The 'Acanthus and Vine', designed and woven by William Morris, was his first attempt at tapestry weaving. It depicts facing birds and swirling acanthus leaves in a mirror-image pattern. The design owes its inspiration to a type of sixteenth- and seventeenth-century French and Flemish verdure tapestry, probably first seen by Morris as a young boy at Queen Elizabeth's Hunting Lodge in Epping Forest. According to his diary, it took Morris 516 hours, 30 minutes to complete the tapestry between May and September 1879, working in his bedroom at his London home on the River Thames at Hammersmith.

Morris was influenced by medieval textile production; he began the project with a design and cartoon, and wove the tapestry using a traditional vertical loom. Although uneven tension and variation in the weave created some distortion, and Morris subsequently nicknamed the result 'cabbage and vine', it is an astonishing achievement for a first effort in the medium. His original design for the tapestry, the working cartoon and his notebook recording its progress are held at the Victoria and Albert Museum, London. JS/PC/SC/JC

The Kelmscott Press
CATALOGUE NUMBERS 125–126

125
(right)
News from Nowhere
William Morris (1834–1896)
1893
20.5 × 14 cm
Society of Antiquaries of London,
Kelmscott Manor

126
(opposite)
'The Legend of Goode Wimmen' from
The Works of Geoffrey Chaucer
William Morris (1834–1896)
1896
43.2 × 60 cm
Society of Antiquaries of London
Selected reference: London 1996

William Morris, an avid collector of medieval manuscripts and early printed books, loaned several of his illuminated manuscripts to the Society's exhibition on medieval art in 1896. Having previously experimented with calligraphy and also taken a serious interest in the printing and binding of his own writings, in his mid-fifties Morris decided to set up his own private press to produce books 'with a definite claim to beauty'. The Kelmscott Press, named after his country house in Oxfordshire, was established in 1891 near his London home at Hammersmith. He based his typefaces on those of the third quarter of the fifteenth century, taken from books in his own library, but made easier to read, and designed to harmonise in 'weight' or thickness of line with the woodcut initial letters, decorative borders and illustrations that he wanted to feature. His paper-maker was asked to supply a pure linen handmade paper similar to that used in his copy of a book written by Alexander de Ales and printed in Venice in 1475; this volume now belongs to the Society of Antiquaries. In the six years before his death, Morris published 66 titles, creating a kind of limited-edition book production that was much emulated in the Private Press movement of 1890–1914, but which also had a beneficial and lasting influence on later book design in terms of both style and quality of materials.

News from Nowhere, the best known of Morris's books, was first published in parts in the Socialist journal *The Commonweal* from January to October 1890. Commercial editions in book form appeared in America in 1890 and in England in 1891. Morris revised the text for the small Kelmscott Press edition that was dated 1892 but issued early in the following year. The 'Nowhere' of the title is an imagined England in 2102, an ideal pastoral society born out of revolution. The tale ends with the central character, based on Morris himself, arriving at Kelmscott Manor, the 'many-gabled' old house which he saw as the ideal home in complete harmony with its past. The frontispiece, engraved by W. H. Hooper after a drawing by Charles March Gere, shows the front entrance to the manor. This copy of the book was given by Morris to his daughter May in 1893. The house and its contents passed to the Society of Antiquaries in 1962.

The Works of Geoffrey Chaucer was the finest achievement of the Kelmscott Press, providing a complete edition of Chaucer's writings with type and decorations by Morris, and illustrations by his oldest and closest friend, Edward Burne-Jones. Morris and Burne-Jones were particularly fond of Chaucer, having first discovered his poetry while students at Oxford forty years earlier. They often took themes from Chaucer as the inspiration for their decorative schemes, for example basing embroideries, tiles and stained-glass designs on his *Legend of Goode Wimmen* (cat. 123). The great Kelmscott *Chaucer* was issued just a few months before Morris's death, the last major volume to be published by the press and a fitting culmination of all Morris's efforts to create 'the book beautiful'.
BN/SC

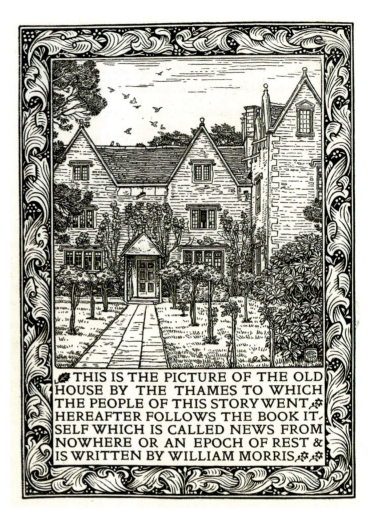

127

Ceramic tiles featuring 'The Legend of Goode Wimmen'
Edward Coley Burne-Jones (1833–1898)
1860s
Hand painted tin-glazed tiles,
26 × 13 cm (average per pair)
Society of Antiquaries of London, Kelmscott Manor 143
Selected references: Myers and Myers 1996, pp. 21–5, 78–9, pls 8, 9, fig. 122

One of the early specialities of William Morris's firm was the manufacture of hand-painted glazed tiles for use either in fireplaces or as decorative panels. Morris himself made a number of designs for tiles with floral or conventionalised ornament, while Edward Burne-Jones supplied the drawings for figure subjects drawn from literature and romance. The designs were mostly painted onto the tile blanks by the firm's women associates, such as Lucy and Kate Faulkner, before firing.

These tiles, designed by Burne-Jones, come from a series depicting heroines from Geoffrey Chaucer's *Legend of Goode Wimmen*, a poem recounting stories of virtuous women from classical antiquity who suffered or died through love. They were among the firm's most popular designs, being used in several commissions with varying tile sizes and different border treatments and also adapted for stained glass and embroidery.

The panel of Cleopatra, a design of 1861–62, was probably painted in the workshop. The other, labelled 'If Hope Were Not Heart Should Break', is more closely related to Burne-Jones's stained-glass designs of 1863–64 and to a second three-tile panel series of the *Legend*. It is painted with more skill than the Cleopatra and has Burne-Jones's initials on its lower half, suggesting that, as well as being the designer, he may have been its painter. The two panels here come from a set of seven on display at Kelmscott Manor. Other heroines featured include Dido, Lucretia and Philomela. JS/PC/SC/JC

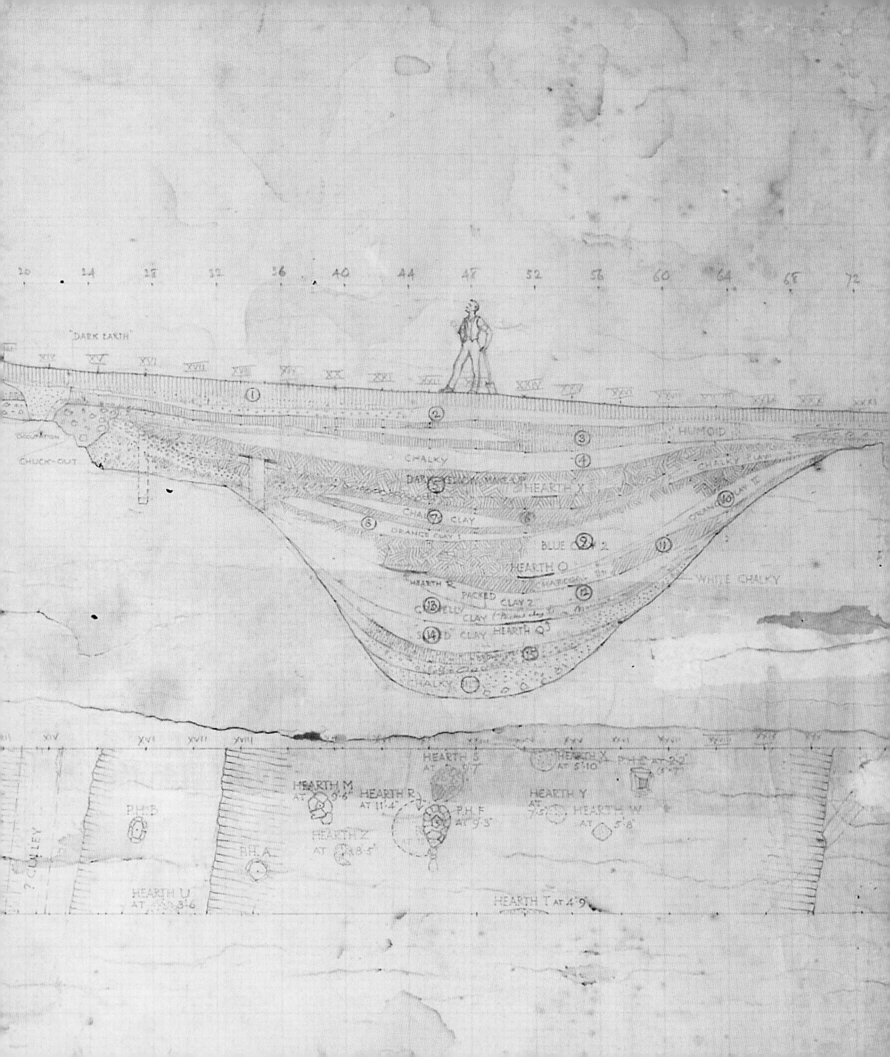

From Antiquaries to Archaeologists, 1850–2007

The Victorian age saw many dramatic changes to the way in which the past was studied and understood. Major discoveries, particularly in geology and natural history, demonstrated the depth of time and enabled the development of a system of relative dating. Stratigraphic principles exercised a profound effect on the study of human antiquity, revealing an earlier prehistory than had previously been envisaged. This, in turn, led to the forging of new methods and techniques for the study of antiquity, and the establishment of categories of classification that are still in use. These developments led to the creation of archaeology as the scientific discipline we know today.

From the middle of the nineteenth century, the large-scale development of urban areas and the destruction of ancient monuments and historic buildings sparked a renewed concern among antiquaries for the preservation of ancient fabric. Fellows of the Society of Antiquaries of London were at the forefront of the growing preservation movement in Britain: Charles Roach Smith, a London chemist, spent his spare time recording and rescuing artefacts from metropolitan sites that were about to be redeveloped. His Museum of London Antiquities became the foundation collection for the department of British Antiquity at the British Museum.

Fellows of the Society have always been concerned to communicate the results of their research more widely. From the studio-based *Animal Vegetable Mineral?* of the 1950s to the *Time Team* phenomenon at the turn of the millennium, the medium of television has proved a very effective vehicle for reaching new audiences for history and archaeology.

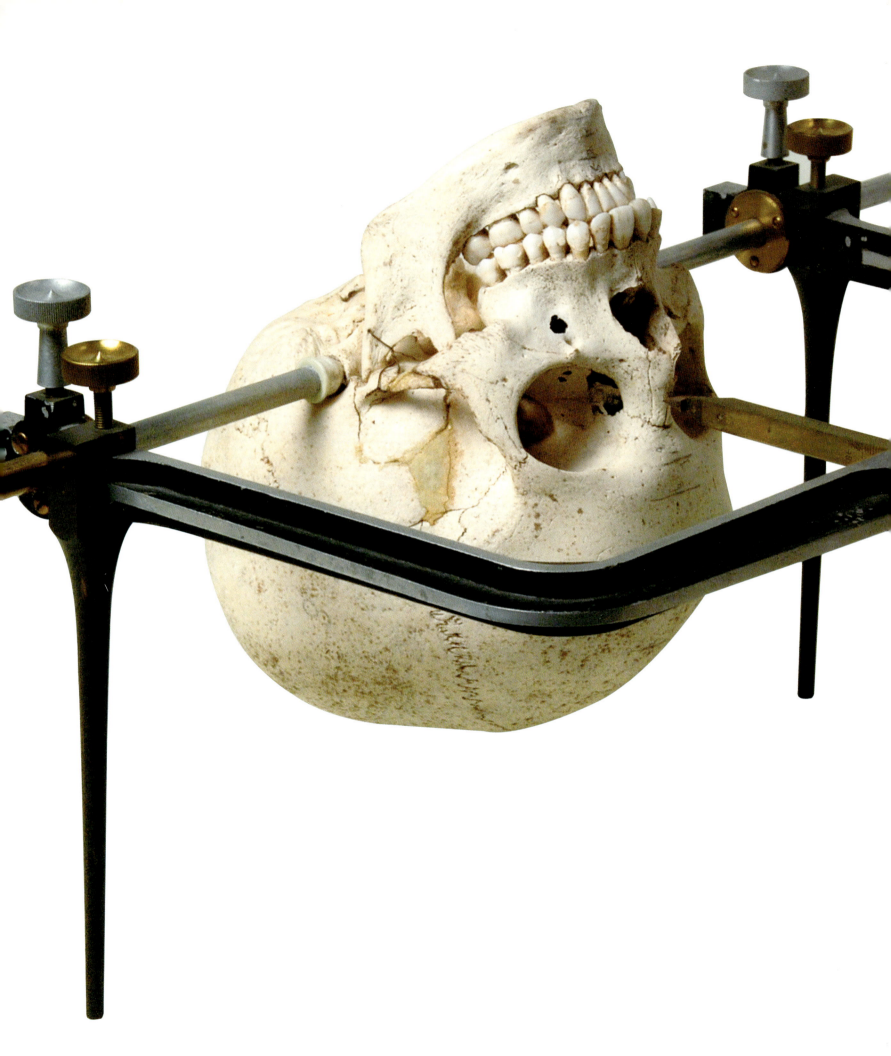

The Birth of Modern Archaeology

Christopher Evans

FIGURE 28
The 'New Prehistory'
John Evans
1860–73
Society of Antiquaries of London

The various Palaeolithic, Neolithic and Bronze Age implements shown here (plate XV from Evans 1860, figures 273–75 from Evans 1872, and plate 1 from London 1873), respectively paired from left to right, come from John Evans's artefact studies and Society exhibition catalogues of the 1870s.

One object, perhaps more than any other, stands out for the way it changed our perception of the past. This is the handaxe from Abbeville (cat. 130) that John Evans and Joseph Prestwich collected in 1859 on a formal visit to France,[1] as part of a Society delegation to adjudicate the finding of early flintwork with bones of extinct animals in gravels exposed by quarrying. On these turned the entire issue of 'deep time' and the span of human ancestry, and thereby the dismantling of the short biblical chronology and the divine-Creationist dogma. Duly observing that the flints did occur *in situ* along with animal remains, Evans and Prestwich travelled back to London to deliver their findings at a Society meeting; the artefacts themselves were on public display in the Society's rooms, placed then at Somerset House. It is interesting to note that, given the general reluctance of archaeologists to adopt the medium, the two verified their findings with a series of photographs that accompanied the paper they presented to the Society. The key point here is how an archaeological 'fact' could, at a time when there was not yet any absolute basis of scientific dating, be constructed and broadly accepted so as to have such momentous implications.

The question of how to demonstrate the secure stratigraphic association of findings of 'Early Man' was established at Brixham Cave, near Torquay in Devon, where flint tools had been found with extinct faunal remains.[2] However, it was not until the work of Lieutenant-General Pitt Rivers in the 1860s and 1870s that a formal sense of 'proof' was introduced. His background included the test demonstration of ordnance and work as a military prosecutor, so it is perhaps not surprising that he introduced the concept that archaeological evidence should be able to stand up in a court of law. Accordingly, he introduced modes of group-adjudication and cited named 'witnesses' to excavation findings.[3]

The main plank on which this concept of proof rested was the vertical stratigraphic section (and the relative situation of artefacts within it). This was a concept borrowed from the field of geology in which the principles of stratification had been established during the first half of the nineteenth century,[4] largely as a result of the work of William Smith (see cat. 132), whose geological map of England and Wales appeared in 1815. Also crucial was the development of the new prehistoric chronology; the Three Age system (Stone, Bronze and Iron) had been established in Denmark during the first decades of the century, and provided its basic framework. It was introduced to Britain from 1846 to 1847 by the Danish archaeologist Jens Worsaae.[5] The basis of this classification was, thereafter, firmly enshrined by John Evans in his acclaimed artefact studies of the 1860s to the 1880s (fig. 28)[6] and, too, by a series of period-specific exhibitions held by the Society in the early 1870s.[7]

In the debates surrounding the 'deep time' chronology, the Society provided a stamp of authority and an 'official' marking of change. However, due largely to its antiquarian Fellowship and its diversity of specialist interests, the Society never presented a radical platform. This is most apparent in the avowedly evolutionist 'New Prehistory' of the period 1850 to 1870/80 as embraced by the circle of John Lubbock.[8] Lubbock, a Member of Parliament, was influenced by his friend Charles Darwin's theories of evolution and natural selection, and viewed the development of prehistory in terms of a lengthy biological and cultural evolution, with the 'modern European' as the end product of the process. His book

Prehistoric Times (1865) did much to further the adoption of prehistoric chronology in Britain and was responsible for the categorisation of prehistory, dividing the Stone Age into the Palaeolithic and Neolithic eras, denoting the progression from old to new.

Although the 'New Prehistory' had many advocates among Fellows of the Society, its agenda was more vigorously advanced more within the newer, more anthropologically oriented societies of the day. During the debates leading to the introduction of the Ancient Monuments Protection Act of 1882,[9] the broader, more representative agenda of the Antiquaries was overshadowed by Lubbock's emphasis on pre-history, which drew adverse comment when it was observed that in a Christian nation no medieval (i.e. Christian) monuments were afforded protection under the Act.[10]

Throughout most of the nineteenth century, excavation remained essentially a matter of personal pursuit. Most serious practitioners of the time were Fellows of the Society, and they duly presented their results at its London meetings. They had something of the atmosphere of a *conversazione*. George Cruikshank's cartoon of 1812 (cat. 39) shows artefacts displayed, and excavation drawings unfurled, upon the enormous table that dominated the Society's meeting room.[11] It was effectively upon this great table that 'the past' was sorted, ordered and adjudicated. The face-to-face nature of this process meant that there was no clear need to illustrate these communications. The Antiquaries first acquired a magic lantern in 1890,[12] and the meeting room was arranged as a modern lecture space as late as 1929.

Early archaeological reports published in the Society's journals are sparsely illustrated and were little more than the letter-based chronicles that were read aloud at meetings. They are intimate accounts with little sense of posterity or future value. Only in the second half of the nineteenth century did the emphasis begin to change, with the production of weighty tomes devoted to artefact studies and personal campaigns of excavation, of which Pitt Rivers's *Cranborne Chase* series (1887–98) (fig. 29) and Canon Greenwell's *British Barrows* (1877) are prominent examples.[13]

Most excavation efforts during the nineteenth century generally focused either on cemeteries or upstanding barrows that were visible and readily identifiable. Such sites generally fulfilled the desire for rich and complete artefact assemblages, which met the purposes of both display and further typological study.[14] Whatever the impulse, prior to the latter decades of the century, settlement archaeology received relatively little attention.

Here we must be wary of being blinkered by (over-) national concerns for the later nineteenth century was also an era of discoveries overseas. Fieldwork by British antiquaries in Mesopotamia, Egypt, Greece and Troy was regularly featured in the *Illustrated London News*.[15] The discoveries of great Continental prehistoric sites such as Hallstatt and La Tène were nearer at hand. Perhaps most significant was the discovery from 1853 of the Swiss prehistoric lake villages with their wealth of well-preserved, organic artefacts. The 1866 English translation of these findings[16] proved highly influential for the development of archaeology in Britain and directly inspired Bulleid and Gray's 1892–1907 excavations of the waterlogged Iron Age settlement at Glastonbury.[17]

Mortimer Wheeler's 1934–37 Society-sponsored excavations at Maiden Castle, the great Iron Age hill fort at Dorchester, are justifiably highlighted here.[18] Encouraging visitors to come to the site and courting the press, Wheeler certainly intended the project to be the public flagship of its day, with the chequerboard of his hallmark 'box-grid' technique asserting the orderly and precise control of archaeological data (fig. 30).[19]

Maiden Castle was, nonetheless, only one of a series of groundbreaking excavations sponsored by the Society during the later nineteenth and earlier twentieth centuries. Since the 1850s, the Society had provided financial assistance for excavations by its Fellows.[20] The work of George E. Fox and William St John Hope at the Romano-British town of Silchester in Hampshire from 1890 to 1909 was a new departure in specialist collaboration.[21] Previously,

FIGURE 29
Wor Barrow, Handley Downs
1893–94
Salisbury and South Wiltshire Museum, Anthony Pitt Rivers Collection

One of the first Neolithic long barrows to be scientifically excavated. This photograph of Pitt Rivers's Cranborne Chase excavation shows one of his site models propped on the front edge of the mound.

excavations (including even those of Pitt Rivers) had been largely a matter of individual initiative involving a 'trained' director and his hired labourers, although separately authored human bone studies began to be included from the mid-nineteenth century. Under the auspices of the Society, the Silchester excavations benefited from the contributions of other Fellows with their expertise in scientific areas such as metallurgy, plant remains and animal bone studies. At Silchester the genesis of the interdisciplinary excavation projects that we know today took place.

The Geological Society had sponsored the Brixham Cave investigations (1858), and the British Association for the Advancement of Science those at Kent's Cavern, near Torquay (1865–80), but aside from these and occasional efforts by the Ministry of Works, the Society was, until the later 1930s, essentially the sole institution to fund excavations on any scale.

Its monopoly was, eventually, broken by the Prehistoric Society (founded in 1935), which sponsored the excavation of a large prehistoric settlement at Little Woodbury, thus echoing the declaration by the Peer Research Commission of 1930 (of the Society and the Congress of Archaeological Societies) that there needed to be an 'archaeology of the living' to balance the discipline's fixation with 'the dead'.[22]

Led by the renowned German practitioner Gerhard Bersu, then in Britain as a refugee from the Nazis, the excavation of the Iron Age settlement at Little Woodbury near Salisbury in Wiltshire used methods that were very much at odds with Wheeler's more limited box-trenching style. Through the use of large, open-area stripping techniques that were then standard in Germany, Bersu demonstrated that the inhabitants had lived in substantial post-built roundhouses (and not the subterranean pit-dwellings that until then had held sway in the conception of British prehistory[23]). This meant that the site provided, for the first time, a convincing picture of typical later prehistoric settlement, and it was celebrated as an example of the new 'functionalism'. (Although Glastonbury had earlier provided a model of how the 'bare skeleton' of the past could be fleshed out, its marsh-side location meant that it was a rare and 'special' instance of archaeological preservation.)

To this overview of the birth of the discipline must be added one final strand: Grahame Clark's investigations of early Fenland sites in the 1930s.[24] Reflecting Continental influences (in this case Scandinavian), Clark initiated Mesolithic ('Middle' Stone Age) studies in Britain and, through his collaboration with Harry Godwin at Peacock's Farm, near Mildenhall in Cambridgeshire, he introduced environmental sciences, such as pollen analysis, to archaeology. In the immediate post-war era, Clark, later Disney Professor of Archaeology at the University of Cambridge, expanded on this mode of overtly scientific, 'ecological' or 'economic archaeology' in his excavation of the Mesolithic lakeside site at Star Carr, near Scarborough in Yorkshire.[25]

It could be argued that by 1950, modern archaeology in Britain had been born. The choice of year is not accidental, it being the conventional datum by which radiocarbon dating sets 'the present'. Within the following decade, this basis of absolute dating was itself established, and it was at that time too earthmoving machinery first began to be regularly employed, an innovation that increasingly led to larger-scale excavations. When these last components were linked with stratigraphy, a framework of artefact chronology and the application of environmental sciences – in addition to a fuller realisation of interpretative possibilities – the critical ingredients of modern archaeology could be said to have been assembled.

Yet equally they could also be considered as only secondary outcomes. Perhaps the very moment of its conception was at that evening lecture in 1859 when the Abbeville handaxes were first presented. What ensued was the acceptance of the deep ancestry of humanity, and all that it implies.

FIGURE 30
Photograph of Mortimer Wheeler's Box Grid System at Maiden Castle
1934–37
Society of Antiquaries of London

The box grid system of excavation, a technique developed by Mortimer Wheeler after Pitt Rivers, retained baulks of earth between the excavation grid so that different layers could be correlated in vertical profiles across the site.

The Influence of Geology in the Early Nineteenth Century
CATALOGUE NUMBERS 128–132

In the eighteenth and nineteenth centuries, addressing the question of human antiquity was greatly hampered by the persistence of Bishop Ussher's chronology (cat. 2), which used biblical sources to set the date of the creation of the world at 4004 BC. However, the early decades of the nineteenth century saw an increase in geological explorations being undertaken in order to find new fossils, understand local geology and attempt to establish a new chronology for the earth. The development of the principles of stratigraphy together with the application of strict scientific method allowed the antiquity of the earth, and humans with it, to be demonstrated. SMC

128
(below left)
Pointed handaxe from Hoxne, Suffolk
Lower Palaeolithic, c. 400,000 BP
Worked flint, 19 × 8.7 × 4.2 cm
Society of Antiquaries of London,
LDSAL 58.1

129
(below right)
Drawing of pointed handaxe from Hoxne, Suffolk
Thomas Richard Underwood
(1772–1835)
1797
Watercolour on paper, 22.2 × 29.2 cm
Society of Antiquaries of London,
Primeval Antiquities, 21.4
Selected references: Frere 1800, pp. 204–5; Cook 2003, pp. 181–4

Some perceptive observations on the antiquity of humankind were already being made in the eighteenth century. In 1765 Charles Lyttelton, the Society's President, had commented that the numerous stone axes that had been discovered must have been made before the use of metals was known, and probably dated from the time of the first inhabitants of Britain. James Douglas had also argued in his *Dissertation on the Antiquity of the Earth* (1785) that animals and humans must have inhabited the world before Noah's flood.

In 1797 a collection of worked flint tools were discovered in a brickfield at Hoxne, Suffolk; they were identified as man-made by John Frere, a Norfolk landowner and antiquary. It was noted that many of them were to be found in stratified soil below a layer of sand and shells that must once have formed the bed or shore of the sea. Frere realised the importance of the flints as being 'evidently weapons of war, fabricated and used by people who had not the use of metals' and coming from 'a very remote period indeed'. He communicated this to the Society in a letter, later to be published in *Archaeologia* in 1800, and donated five of the flints. However, little was made of the finds at the time, and it was a further sixty years before the antiquity of humankind was more widely acknowledged.

Frere's letter was unique for the time in that it recorded the levels of the flints, found beneath and associated with extinct faunal remains. Although this was not the first reference to stone tools deriving from remote antiquity, it formed part of a growing consensus that they were not 'meteorites' or 'thunderbolts', a once popular interpretation.

The drawings were commissioned by the Society from the geologist and draughtsman Thomas Underwood, to illustrate Frere's letter. ARP/BN

130

Handaxe from Abbeville, France
Palaeolithic, *c.* 300,000 years old
Worked flint, 11.5 × 9.5 cm
Department of Palaeontology, Natural
History Museum, London, E.574
Selected references: Evans 1860,
pp. 280–307; Evans 1956, pp. 281–5;
Daniel 1981, pp. 48–55

Investigations in the early part of the nineteenth century at Kent's Cavern and Brixham Cave, both in Devon, uncovered worked stone tools in association with extinct faunal remains. Their discovery alongside the bones of ancient mammals in sealed layers of soil had led geologists to argue that they must have been deposited during Noah's flood. However, such diluvial theories began to be challenged as a new generation of geologists began to look closely at the stratigraphic layers in soil and rocks, recognising that these levels could not have been created in one event, but rather were the product of a long period of time.

In 1859, the geologist Joseph Prestwich was alerted to the work of the French geologist and antiquary Boucher de Perthes, who had also discovered stone tools in sealed layers in relation to extinct faunal remains at Abbeville in northern France. Prestwich and the antiquary John Evans visited the site to observe and collect samples. In their respective reports to the Royal Society and to the Antiquaries, they were both convinced by the findings of de Perthes, linking them to the work of Frere in 1797 and to finds from other sites in Britain, and reported back to the Society of Antiquaries and the Royal Society in London. The discovery of handaxes in undisturbed stratigraphy in the Somme Valley, when linked to finds that had already been made at Brixham and Hoxne, was one of the main forces of change in the perception of prehistory.
ARP

The Birth of Modern Archaeology | 189

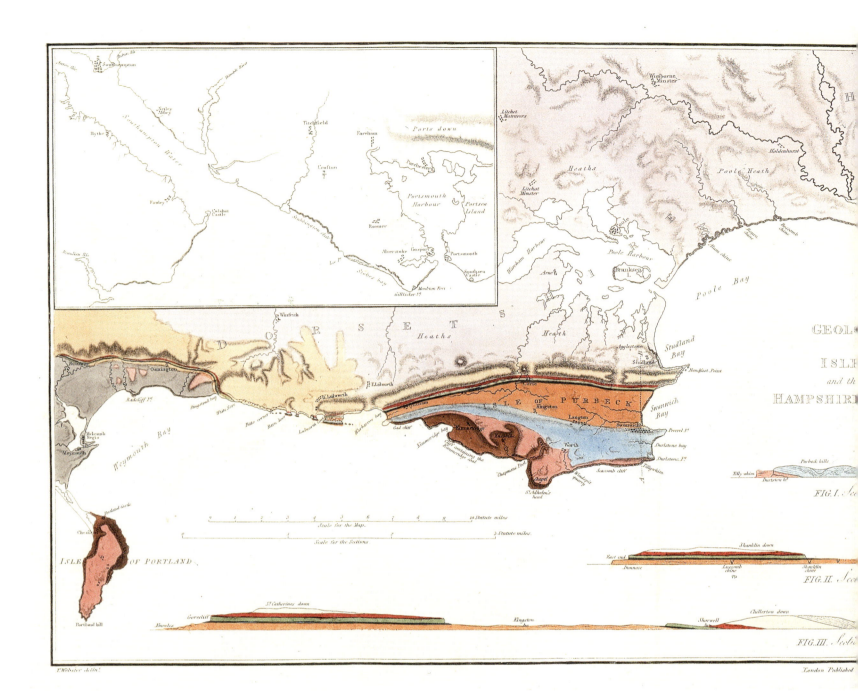

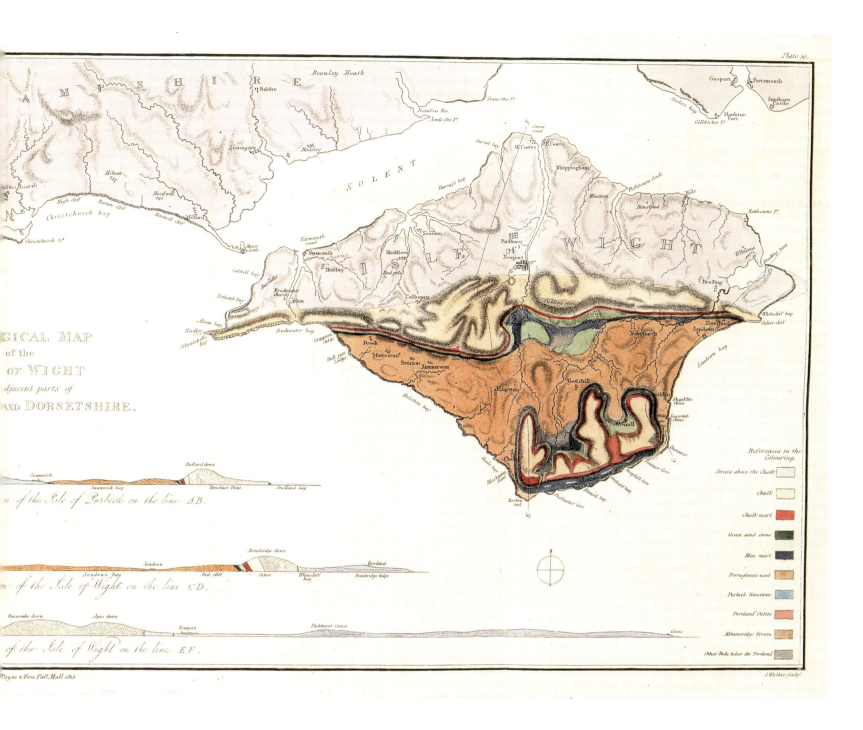

131

Geological Map and Sections of the Isle of Wight and the Adjacent Parts of Hampshire and Dorsetshire
Thomas Webster (1772–1844)
1816
Coloured engraving, 40 × 76 cm
Society of Antiquaries of London
Selected references: Boud 1975, pp. 73–96; Edwards 2004; Nurse 2004

Sir Henry Charles Englefield (c. 1752–1822), President of the Society in 1811, did not limit his interests to antiquities, but wrote widely on other scientific subjects, often cross-referencing these subjects in his work.

His chief topographical work, *A Description of the Picturesque Beauties, Antiquities and Geological Phaenomena of the Isle of Wight* (1816), was a culmination of his antiquarian and geological knowledge. Alongside his observations and sketches, he incorporated maps drawn by the geologist Thomas Webster, including the one shown here, which featured as plate L.

From 1811 to 1813 Webster worked on a commission for Englefield in the Isle of Wight, during which he made careful observations of the geology. The result was this first hand-coloured geological map of the Isle of Wight and parts of Hampshire and Dorset. The structural geology of the Hampshire Basin is shown in detail, permitting the elucidation of the Mesozoic (251–65 million years ago; more popularly known as the 'age of the dinosaurs') and Tertiary (65–1.8 million years ago; modern era) stratigraphy. Webster's map was published after William Smith's *Geological Map of Britain*, and led Smith to revise his ideas on the geological morphology of the area.

Englefield's volume emphasised the advances that could be made through the combination of knowledge derived from different disciplines. Hard scientific fact was employed in the development of stratigraphic theory, which was eventually to play an important role in establishing the age of the earth and, consequently, a chronology for human evolution. ARP

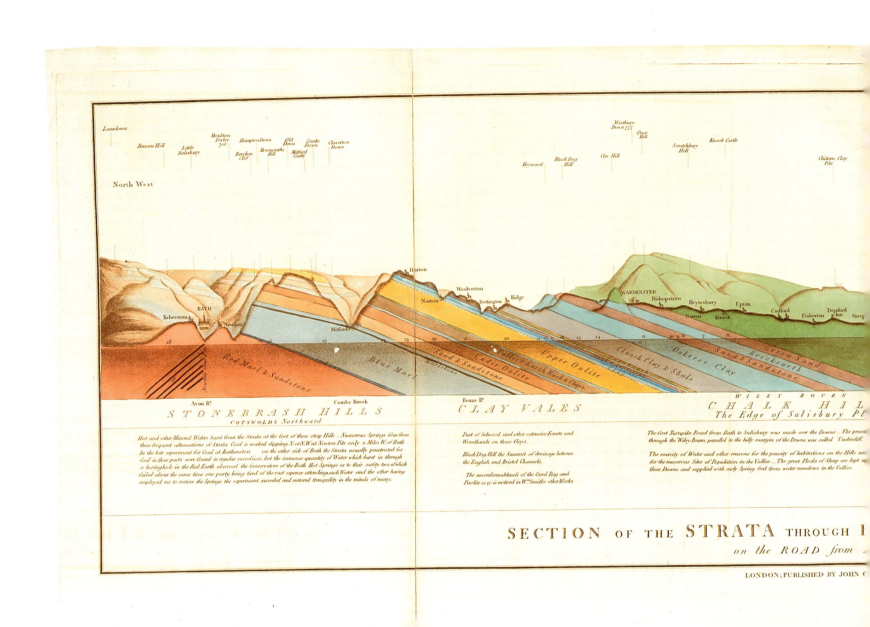

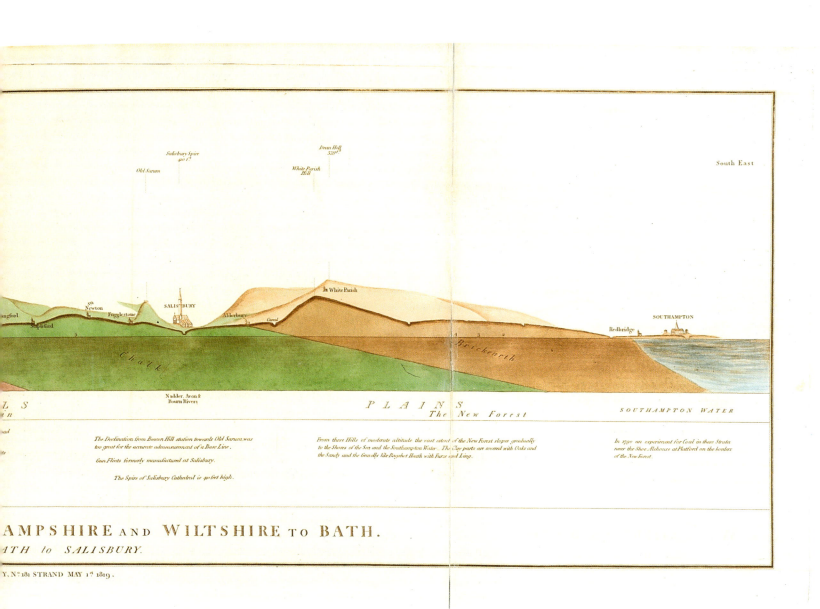

132

Section of the Strata through Hampshire and Wiltshire to Bath on the road from Bath to Salisbury
William Smith (1769–1839)
1817–19
Coloured engraving, 27.3 × 93.5 cm
Geological Society of London, LDGSL 1006/2
Selected references: Boud 1975, pp. 73–96; Torrens 1998, pp. 35–59

William Smith has been credited with pioneering geological cartography through his map of England and Wales in 1815, the first geological map to cover the area. Smith started out as a surveyor of coal mines in Bath, but was soon employed to work on the Somerset Coal Canal. While engaged on this project he recognised a pattern of sequences between the area in which he was working and Bath, realising that fossils could be used to identify and characterise strata. Smith's later employment as a mineral surveyor in different parts of the country helped him to build a general picture of the geological composition of England. By the early 1800s he was encouraged to publish these results.

Although the map was utilitarian in aim and purpose, Smith had not intended it to refute contemporary geological theory. Yet it provided Smith's contemporaries and future geologists with evidence to challenge the idea that geological layers were the result of Noah's flood.

Shown here is one of a series of geological cross-sections that Smith published. It demonstrates the composition of the underlying strata on a line surveyed from Bath to Salisbury. ARP/TS

Lieutenant-General Pitt Rivers and his Excavations at Cranborne Chase
CATALOGUE NUMBERS 133–135

Lieutenant-General Augustus Pitt Rivers (1827–1900) is credited with being one of the first to take a scientific approach to archaeology in Britain, helping to shake off the discipline's reputation as a gentleman's hobby. Born Augustus Henry Lane Fox, he adopted the additional surname Pitt Rivers in 1880 when he inherited his great-uncle's estate in south-west England. A large part of his adult life was spent as an officer in the British Army, during which he served on various overseas postings. He developed a keen interest in ethnology and archaeology, acquiring a diverse collection of material during his tours overseas, which later formed the basis of the Pitt Rivers Museum in Oxford.

Pitt Rivers stayed abreast of new ideas and applied them in his own studies. During the 1860s he became interested in Charles Darwin's work on natural selection, and incorporated theories of evolution into his own work. Initially he applied them to his collection as a method of classification, showing a natural progression from simple to more advanced materials.

Pitt Rivers became the first Inspector of Ancient Monuments in 1882 after the introduction of the Ancient Monuments Protection Act, which was championed by his friend and fellow antiquary John Lubbock. ARP/BN

133
(opposite)
Model of a pit at Handley Hill showing the position of a skeleton
Late nineteenth century
Painted mahogany, 24.4 (front), 26 (back) × 39 × 38.8 cm
Salisbury and South Wiltshire Museum, 2C.1.16

134
(below left)
Scale-model of Handley Hill barrow
Late nineteenth century
Painted mahogany, 7 (front), 9.2 (back) × 41 × 46.7 cm
Salisbury and South Wiltshire Museum, 2C.4.31
Selected references: Thompson 1977; Evans 2004

135
(below right)
Craniometer with skull
Late nineteenth century
Metal and human bone, 4.1 × 45.5 cm
Salisbury and South Wiltshire Museum
Selected references: Pitt Rivers 1898; Thompson 1977; Daniel 1981; Greene 2002

The estate of Rushmore in Cranborne Chase, which Pitt Rivers inherited in 1880, was rich in archaeological monuments. On his retirement from the Army Pitt Rivers turned his attention to the excavation of many of them, including Wor Barrow and Handley Hill. Introducing three dimensional grids and applying a highly methodical approach, reflecting his military training, he insisted that all artefacts were recorded. Pitt Rivers's interest in anthropometry (the measurement of the size and proportions of the human body) is evident in his later work at Cranborne Chase. He was one of the first to undertake detailed studies of human remains recovered during archaeological excavations. Like many of his contemporaries in the second half of the nineteenth century, he believed mistakenly that racial characteristics were reflected in skull shapes and sizes, and that measuring them would help to identify different groups of early inhabitants and invaders in Britain and Europe. His craniometer is an adaptation of a instrument developed in France by Alphonse Bertillon for the purpose of identifying criminals.

Pitt Rivers was also an innovator in using models to explain his work. He commissioned over 100, and they took up a central position in the museum he established at Farnham for his estate workers and their families. These scaled representations translated the data recorded on site into a precise area-dimensional image and illustrated the processes of excavation as well as the position of skeletons and artefacts within the excavated barrows and tombs. This concern to communicate the results of archaeology to local people was ahead of its time and helped to give the subject a broader appeal among the public. Occasionally, as can be seen in fig. 29, models showing the results of the previous season were displayed on site during excavation. ARP/BN

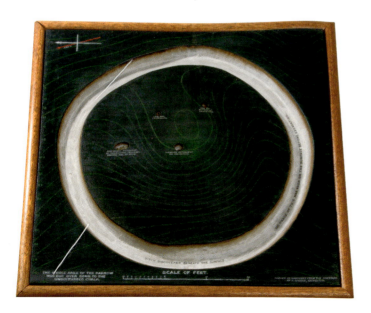

The Birth of Modern Archaeology | 195

Sir Mortimer Wheeler and the Maiden Castle excavations
CATALOGUE NUMBERS 136–139

Sir Mortimer Wheeler was one of the most influential archaeologists of the twentieth century. A diverse career saw him work widely on prehistoric and Roman sites in Britain and abroad; in 1944 he was appointed as Director-General of the Archaeological Survey of India. Wheeler was never afraid to use new ideas and techniques to advance the study of the past, and his influence is still felt today.

One of his chief aims was to make archaeology accessible to the public, and he also recognised the potential source of funding that widespread press coverage could bring. He was often criticised by his peers for associating with the press, but was successful in persuading the *Daily Mail* to sponsor and produce regular features on his excavations. In this way news of important discoveries was disseminated quickly, helping to capture the imagination of the public. Regular appearances on BBC TV programmes led to Wheeler becoming a celebrity.

As an archaeologist, he believed strongly in the principles established by Lieutenant-General Pitt Rivers in the previous century, which held precision recording of data at their core. Furthermore, Wheeler felt it important to train young archaeologists to advance the discipline; to this end, he co-founded the Institute of Archaeology in London in 1937, part of University College, London, and today one of the largest departments of archaeology in the world. In the 1930s, Wheeler's research interests focused on Iron Age and Roman Britain, and especially the period between the invasions of Julius Caesar and the Emperor Claudius in southern Britain. SMC/ARP

136

Huntly Strathearn Gordon's theodolite and tripod
Ex-HMF (His Majesty's Forces) Ordnance *c.* 1923
Wood and enamelled metal, stamped '↑'; leather case stamped 'CASE no. 6 DIRECTOR M.K.I. – W. OTTWAY Co. Ltd.– 1923'; metal detachable tripod support with wood legs, cased
*c.*16.5 cm³, legs 92 × 184 cm
Dorset Natural History and Archaeological Society at the Dorset County Museum, Dorchester, 2001.18.1 and 2
Selected references: Wheeler 1932, pp. 1–15; Gordon 1950; Gordon 1967; Hawkes 1982

137

Film of Maiden Castle excavations
Mortimer Wheeler (1890–1976)
c. 1934–36
16 mm black and white film
Institute of Archaeology, University College London
Selected references: Hawkes 1982; Sharples 1991

Following Wheeler's excavations of Roman sites at Lydney in Gloucestershire and St Albans in Hertfordshire, which had been significantly sponsored by the Society, in 1933 the Society's Research Committee decided to support excavation at Maiden Castle, the Iron Age hill fort in Dorset. It would be undertaken by the Fellows Charles Drew, of the Dorset Natural History and Archaeological Society, and Mortimer Wheeler and his wife Tessa, as a joint venture between the two societies. The Maiden Castle project became a template for future work as it set out clear research objectives: the investigation of the earthwork sequence, the identification of the 'associated cultures' and the recovery of a part of the 'town-plan'. Wheeler believed that he achieved the first two objectives, but not the third. However, he did find dramatic evidence of burials in the 'war cemetery', which he interpreted as evidence of a Roman siege.

Spectacular results were obtained with modest funding from the Society over three seasons from 1934 to 1936. More money was raised through publicity and public appeals. The first season of excavation was more than fully funded through a cycle of publicity, subscription and lectures. Wheeler also encouraged site tours to allow excavation to be seen as work in progress. The film illustrates Wheeler's encouragement of site visitors, with a group shown walking up the side of Maiden Castle. It is believed that he used the film as a visual aid in public lectures about the site, and to stimulate further interest in the subject. Small objects from the excavation that had 'no archaeological value' were sold after lengthy debate in committee. It is highly unlikely that such practices would be allowed today. PW/ARP/BN

138

(right top and detail opposite)
Maiden Castle Dorset, Contour and hachure plan at a scale of 1:1250
Huntly Strathearn Gordon
1934
Linen-backed paper with pencil annotations, 60.9 × 99 cm
Dorset Natural History and Archaeological Society at the Dorset County Museum, Dorchester, 1939.55.28.2.z10
Selected references: Gordon 1932; Wedlake 1934; Wheeler 1943; Gordon 1967; Hawkes 1982

139

(right bottom)
Maiden Castle Dorset: Section and Plan of Cutting 'A' Across Original Western Defences, scale of 1 inch to 4 feet (2.5 cm to 1.2 m)
Charles Drew and Mortimer Wheeler
1934
Pencil on graph paper, 57.2 × 97.5 cm
Dorset Natural History and Archaeological Society at the Dorset County Museum, Dorchester, 1939.55.28.2.A2
Selected references: Wedlake 1934; Wheeler 1943; Wedlake 1975A; Wedlake 1975B

The survey of Maiden Castle, undertaken by Huntly Gordon with his theodolite, was the first comprehensive survey of the large earthworks of the site. The theodolite (cat. 136) is celebrated by Wheeler in his foreword to Huntly Gordon's autobiographical account of his time as a field-gunner in Flanders from 1917 to 1918:

> *We stood, Huntly Gordon and I, upon a densely wooded hilltop in Normandy with an aged artillery 'director' (War Office disposals, £3) between us. It was August 1938, and we had known each other for several years. In vacation we would forgather, and he with this familiar instrument of World War I would survey for me whatever archaeological site was my peaceful battlefield for the moment.*

In 1931 Gordon, inspired by an article in *The Times* on Verulamium by Wheeler, visited the site and offered to survey the earthworks in Prae Wood in 'a desire to solve the riddle of the whereabouts of Cassivellaunus' stronghold'. This offer was 'warmly welcomed', the ex-Army theodolite purchased and the collaboration with the Wheelers begun. The instrument shown here was used in all Gordon's earthwork surveys, including those at Maiden Castle (cats 138, 139). In these surveys he developed the use of hachures, or arrows, to depict the slope and angle of archaeological structures and earthworks. Shown here is his Maiden Castle plan, annotated in pencil by Gordon from 1935 (cat. 138). The excavation foreman Bill Wedlake described the first events of the excavation in his diary.

> *Tuesday July 24th (1934) ... Drew gave the object of the excavations ... the 1st Cutting ... 95 ft by 10 ft [29 by 3 m] ... through the vallum and bottom of the opposed original bank ...*
> *Dr Wheeler with a wave ... these (garden forks) were dispensed with ... he would not have them on the site ... we were given precise instructions of what he expected from his staff ... the Wheeler system of excavation was put to the test.*

The heroic figure with a spade captures the moment in one of the first section drawings of modern excavation practice. PW/ARP

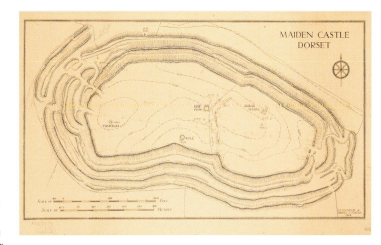

The Birth of Modern Archaeology | 199

Rescuing the Past

David Gaimster

In the 1960s and early 1970s Britain's heritage was under threat as it had never been since the Industrial Revolution. Historic town centres were redeveloped and the countryside was bulldozed to create thousands of miles of motorway. In response, a popular conservation movement emerged, county archaeologists were employed, and monuments records and professional excavation units were established, supported by active local voluntary groups and societies. The escalating rate of demolition of historic buildings prompted the foundation of the campaigning group SAVE Britain's Heritage in 1975. In many ways the destruction unleashed by politicians and planners in the 1960s led to the creation of modern protection regimes, the increasingly professionalised heritage sector and the energetic conservation lobby that we know today. These changes could not contrast more starkly with the previous phase of infrastructure development that took place in Britain's towns and countryside during the mid-nineteenth century.

Britain did not develop its first heritage protection legislation until the late nineteenth century. It took the form of the 1882 Ancient Monuments Protection Act and, in 1900, an amendment to the legislation offering limited protection for historic buildings. Both measures were due in no small part to the pressures applied by the Society of Antiquaries of London and, from 1885, its crusading Assistant Secretary, Sir William St John Hope.[1] Under St John Hope the Society led a series of protests against the desecration or demolition of important historic monuments, including, among

FIGURE 31
Charles Roach Smith's London Museum
1840s
Engraving
Guildhall Library, London

The interior of Charles Roach Smith's Museum of London Antiquities, London, at his pharmacy shop in Liverpool Street, London, as it appeared in the late 1840s.

ROMAN PAVEMENT FOUND IN THE POULTRY, NEAR THE MANSION HOUSE.—SEE PAGE 550.

FIGURE 32
'Bucklersbury Roman pavement' from the *Illustrated London News*, May 1869
London Library

About 33,000 people visited the exposed Roman mosaic pavement on Bucklersbury in the City of London over three days, before a section was removed for display in the fledgling Museum of Antiquities at the London Guildhall.

others, the City of London churches, the Old Jewry Wall in Leicester, and the Rolls Chapel in Chancery Lane, and against the 'restoration' of the royal tombs at Westminster, the west front of Peterborough Cathedral and of the Hospital of St Cross in Winchester.[2] Instrumental in the battle to prevent insensitive 'improvements' to medieval buildings, particularly churches, was the foundation of the Society for the Protection of Ancient Buildings in 1877, led by William Morris as its first Secretary. In 1894 Morris was elected a Fellow of the Society of Antiquaries as much in recognition of his conservation work as for his interest in late medieval material culture.

Popular consciousness regarding the destruction of the historic environment and legislation to protect it was mainly a late Victorian development. Only a generation or so before, when the first railways, sewage systems and commercial office buildings were carving vast tracts of destruction through the cores of Britain's historic cities, the rescue and record of monuments and artefacts under threat relied almost entirely on the efforts of a small number of amateur pioneers, often in the face of considerable institutional opposition. In London, one of the most important was Charles Roach Smith (1806–1890), Fellow of the Society from 1836, who amassed a collection of some 5,000 artefacts recovered from developments in the City from the mid-1830s to the mid-1850s. Roach Smith's collection, eventually acquired by the British Museum in 1856, formed the foundation of the first national collection of antiquities for England.[3]

An amateur numismatist and antiquary, Roach Smith had established a pharmacy business at Founders' Court, Lothbury, in 1834, just in time to see the greatest destruction to the historic fabric of the City of London since the Great Fire of 1666. The opening of his business coincided with excavations for the extension to the Bank of England in the same year. Within two years Roach Smith had begun writing his diary (cat. 142), in which he recorded the impact on London's historic fabric of the wave of road building, railway cutting, bridge widening, tunnel sinking, sewer trenching and the construction of commercial buildings with deep basements that characterised this Victorian age of steam, speed and sanitary improvement. Given a free hand, the railway companies, it was said in 1846, would have taken 'a sponge and sponged out the whole of the City, leaving St Paul's standing in the midst'.[4]

Roach Smith's diary is full of notes and drawings of the artefacts bought from workmen throughout the City. Although he acknowledged that his museum was 'formed itself out of a series of accidents', Roach Smith was conscious of acting with 'self-imposed stewardship'. The purpose of his endeavours was the accumulation of 'materials to illustrate the early history of the metropolis'.[5] His aims were threefold: first, an understanding of how London began and grew; second, the foundation of a City museum in which evidence of the past could be housed and exhibited; and, third, the preservation of ancient monuments in the City.[6] In these he was obstructed, both by the City Corporation, which was offended by his public lambasting of its complacent attitude in the press, and by the development of a trade in freshly discovered antiquities.

Much of Roach Smith's collection was purchased from workmen in stiff competition from unscrupulous dealers who allegedly preferred to see artefacts deliberately smashed rather than let them fall into the hands of others and so potentially lower the market value of such finds.[7] Roach Smith's work in London represents the first sustained campaign of urban site recording in Britain, and it enabled him to conjecture the topography of the Roman city, its defences and monumental buildings, together with the probability of a Roman bridge over the Thames. His *Illustrations of Roman London* (1859) remained the principal work on the subject for half a century.[8]

Roach Smith devoted considerable time to observing dredging works along the Thames foreshore, an area rich in historic artefacts discarded into the city's main sewer by generations of Londoners: 'It was, for me, an exciting recreation to be on the barge when the machinery for raising the gravel was at work upon a fertile spot, and to help pick out the coins as they were poured out in the gravel upon the deck.'[9] The state of preservation in the deep mud was excellent and many of Roach Smith's finest discoveries derive from the City waterfront. Coins aside, these finds included Late Bronze Age swords, spears and a shield; medieval lead pilgrim badges; and 'a very curious collection of medieval leatherwork probably unrivalled by any other private museum'.[10]

By 1853 ill health, financial problems and the impending termination of the lease for his pharmacy business prompted Roach Smith to consider selling his collection (fig. 31). With the publication of his *Catalogue of the Museum of London Antiquities* in 1854, came the support of his fellow antiquaries that it should be preserved for the nation. Having been disappointed by the lack of interest shown by the City Corporation (which was influenced, ironically, by financial uncertainty caused by an impending Bill before Parliament to make the establishment of free libraries and museums a charge on the rates),[11] Roach Smith offered his collection to the British Museum for £3,000. Provoking an outcry in the press, the museum refused to purchase it as it then maintained a policy of mainly acquiring only classical or ancient Near Eastern antiquities, particularly those with artistic merit. Such inflexibility also led the British Museum's Trustees to refuse the extensive Faussett collection of Anglo-Saxon grave goods (cats 123, 223–25) in the same year, 1854.[12]

Rejected by both institutions, Roach Smith's collection was in danger of being broken up at auction. He was widely praised 'for having effected more than any other man, or than the British Museum has ever attempted in illustration of British History in the Roman and Anglo Saxon periods'.[13] Petitions signed by over 250 antiquaries were prepared for submission to the Lords of the Treasury and to the House of Commons. The Treasury responded favourably to the application from the British Museum's Trustees for special funds and in March 1856 sanctioned the purchase of the collection for a sum not exceeding £2,000. The acquisition effectively changed the collecting policy of the British Museum and laid the foundation in 1860 of an entirely new department dedicated to British and Medieval Antiquities and Ethnography under the keepership of A. W. Franks.

The antiquities collections of the Society of Antiquaries of Scotland passed into government hands in 1851 to form the new National Museum of Antiquities of Scotland in Edinburgh. However, a move to transfer the museum collection of the Society of Antiquaries of London to the British Museum in 1901, in the interests of creating more library space, was heavily defeated at the Society's Anniversary Meeting,[14] and the collection today forms one of its most important learning resources, particularly with respect to the history of collecting in Britain. Nevertheless, the Society discontinued its default collecting role in deference to the role of the new antiquities department at the British Museum, and oncentrated instead on acquiring documentary or representative artefacts.[15]

For the mid-nineteenth century, it was a considerable achievement for Charles Roach Smith to record and collect important archaeological remains. Unfortunately, his example was not emulated in the years after 1856 and no one individual was capable of recording or preserving the volume of archaeological finds made in London during the latter half of the century when the rebuilding and expansion of the metropolis accelerated at an even greater rate. Any survey of the development of archaeological method in the Victorian age must, therefore, take Roach Smith's work into account. Although it was not necessarily driven by specific research questions, the practice of rescue archaeology had been born. Within a generation, crowds of onlookers would swarm to view the magnificent Roman mosaic pavement discovered between Bucklersbury and Poultry in May 1869 (fig. 32).[16] The *Illustrated London News* reported 33,000 visitors in the three days before the mosaic was lifted. The City Fathers could no longer ignore the force of public interest in the preservation of the past. Soon afterwards, the Guildhall Library was rebuilt with a Museum Room in the basement, and part of the Bucklersbury pavement was set into the wall of the new exhibition room.[17]

By the close of the nineteenth century, public museums and private cultural institutions had developed facilities capable of recording, and preserving, albeit in a rudimentary way, even the most fragile of archaeological discoveries. A case in point comes from the opening in March 1890 of the tomb of Archbishop Hubert Walter of Canterbury, who was buried at Canterbury Cathedral in 1205. William St John Hope, Assistant Secretary of the Society, recorded the event and presented his findings at the Society in May that year.[18] Rather than reinterring the contents – including the embroidered silk vestments, the mitre, stole and buskins (stockings) and fragments of the dalmatic and chasuble – with the body, they were deposited in the Cathedral Archives. Conscious of the particularly fragile state of the textiles and their potential deterioration, the Society ordered the contents of the tomb to be recorded as full-sized colour illustrations, and published the results as the first part of a new volume of *Vetusta Monumenta* in 1893 (cat. 148).[19]

Charles Roach Smith's 'Museum of London Antiquities'
CATALOGUE NUMBERS 140–146

The figure who stands out among mid-nineteenth-century antiquaries is Charles Roach Smith, who created the first reference collection of Roman and medieval antiquities by rescuing artefacts from sewage-main and railway excavations, river dredging and office construction works over a twenty-year period of intensive metropolitan development. The 5,000 or so items in his 'Museum of London Antiquities' were intended to illustrate 'the institutions, the habits, the customs, and the arts of our forefathers'. The eventual acquisition of the collection in 1856 by the British Museum laid the foundation of the Museum's first department dedicated to British antiquity. Cats 140–146 are all a cross-section from Roach Smith's collection of artefacts from the City of London. DG

140

Portrait medal of the London antiquary Charles Roach Smith (1806–1890)
1890
Bronze, diameter 5.8 cm
Society of Antiquaries of London, LDSAL 475
Selected reference: Hobley 1975, fig. 2

This medal was presented by fellow British antiquaries a few days before Roach Smith's death in 1890, 'in recognition of lifelong services to archaeology', with a testimonial by Dr John Evans, President of the Society of Antiquaries of London. Subscriptions over and above the cost of the medal and testimonial realised a cheque for 100 guineas. DG

141

Roman coins from the bed of the Thames, City of London
First and second centuries AD
Copper and brass
British Museum, London, C & M, 1935,0404.7, 9, 14, 25, 32, 48, 53, 56, 60
Selected reference: Hobley 1975, p. 332

In 1883 the Numismatic Society presented Charles Roach Smith with the first medal conferred by its council for his work on Roman coins in Britain. Shown here is a selection of these, of different material and denomination, from the reigns of:

Claudius AD 41–54
Nero AD 54–68
Vespasian AD 69–79
Titus AD 79–81
Domitian AD 81–96
Nerva AD 96–98
Trajan AD 98–117
Hadrian AD 117–138

DG

204 | Making History

142

Charles Roach Smith's 'Diary', vol. 2
1836
Leather-bound paper manuscript,
20 × 17 × 4 cm (book closed)
British Museum, London, PEE,
notebook no. 44, pp. 74–5
Selected reference: Gaimster 1997,
p. 24

Roach Smith kept a diary in which he recorded finds made in the City of London between 1836 and 1842. The entry for August 1836 records the discovery in East Cheap of a Rhenish salt-glazed stoneware jug of the late sixteenth century applied with relief medallions depicting biblical scenes. The jug was found together with a 'number of small crucifixes'. DG

143

Medieval mail collar found in the City of London
Second half of the fifteenth century
Steel, 27 × 66 cm
British Museum, London PEE 1856,
7-1, 2244
Selected reference: Laking 1920

Designed to protect the neck, the collar still retains part of its fastener at one corner. DG

Rescuing the Past | 205

144

Pilgrim badge of Thomas Becket found in the City of London
Fifteenth century
Pewter and lead alloy, height 8.5 cm
British Museum, London,
PEE 1856,7-1,2030
Selected reference: Spencer 2000

One of the more common late medieval pilgrim badges, this example is cast in the form of the martyr Thomas Becket's mitred bust. The badges represented the appearance of the head-reliquary, which was made to hold the crown of St Thomas's skull. This reliquary was exhibited to pilgrims in a chapel close to the saint's shrine and formed part of the conducted tour of Canterbury Cathedral made by medieval pilgrims. DG

145

Armour defence for upper right arm found in the City of London
Mid-fourteenth century
Leather, 29 × 24 cm
British Museum, London, PEE 1856, 7-1, 1665
Selected reference: Norman 1974–76

This is a rare survival of pressed-leather armour dating from the high Middle Ages, whose purpose was to protect the upper right arm (the 'sword arm'). The 'crossbar' would have covered the outside of the arm above the elbow and the shank would have curved round to protect the biceps. Leather armour was extremely popular in the fourteenth century but is mainly known from inventories and tomb effigies. This complete armour defence must have been preserved in anaerobic ground conditions. In the pre-Industrial age leather was a versatile medium for intricate moulded and tooled decoration. The decoration, pressed in relief, depicts grotesque birds and beasts amid foliage. DG

206 | Making History

146

Medieval earthenware jug found in
Cannon Street, City of London
Mid-thirteenth century
Lead-glazed earthenware with copper
and iron staining, height 29.2 cm
British Museum, London, PEE 1856,
7-1, 1566
Selected reference: Nenk 1997, fig. 2

The demand for jugs in a fine white
earthenware body with complex
polychrome-glazed relief decoration,
such as those from northern France,
led to the establishment of an industry
producing replica wares, at Kingston
upon Thames, during the thirteenth
century. The stamped decoration,
applied in relief, features lozenges with
fabulous beasts. This jug is one of the
finest and most complete survivals of
its type. DG

Grave Goods from the Tomb of Hubert Walter, Archbishop of Canterbury, opened in 1890
CATALOGUE NUMBERS 147–151

Hubert Walter, one of the greatest statesmen of twelfth-century England, influenced both religious and secular life as Archbishop of Canterbury (1193–1205) and chief minister to Richard I, with whom he went on crusade. Walter died on 13 July 1205 and was buried the following day at Canterbury Cathedral.

In 1881, Scott Robertson, one of the Cathedral Canons, suggested that the tomb in the Trinity Chapel, previously thought to have been that of an earlier archbishop, might be that of Hubert Walter. To establish who was buried there, the tomb was opened in March 1890 and some of its contents, including the chalice, paten and mitre, were exhibited at a meeting in the Society's rooms at Burlington House the following month. As doubts still remained as to the identity of the relics, the Society's Assistant Secretary, William St John Hope, visited Canterbury. He showed, from careful measurements and rubbings, that the magnificent Purbeck marble tomb and the stone coffin were made for the place they now occupied, and from documentary evidence, that they must be those made for Hubert Walter. Recent research has supported the identification by Robertson and Hope.

An exceptionally fine collection of over forty pieces of textile, including silk vestments worn by the archbishop, as well as his cedar-wood crozier, ring, silver-gilt chalice and paten were found. St John Hope dated the contents to the twelfth century and recognised them as rare survivals from a period in which few English examples are known. The mitre (cat. 149) is one of the earliest of a type designed with a central horn that was introduced into England in the late twelfth century. The outer inscription on the paten (cat. 151) draws parallels between Christ's Passion and the sacrament of the Eucharist, in part translating as 'the chalice [represents] the tomb and the paten the stone'; it is not recorded on any other paten. Eight pieces of varying lengths of the stole (cat. 147), which is embroidered with coloured silks now faded to shades of brown and green, have survived. Cruciform, swastika and labyrinth designs can be seen, and it has been suggested that the embroidery represents Islamic inscriptions.

Although the linen vestments had perished, the silk fabrics applied to them were found in a remarkable state of preservation. They had been kept in dry conditions in the coffin, and have been well cared for since their removal; they have recently been cleaned and remounted. They remain extremely fragile, however, especially the sandals (more correctly described as slippers), which contain some of the finest embroidery, and the amice apparel (one of the vestments); the buskins (stockings) are the only pair surviving in England. The silk for the vestments was probably imported from the Near East, Byzantium or Spain, but the garments themselves are likely to have been embroidered in England.

In order to provide full-size colour illustrations of these and the rest of the contents, which could be studied by others, the Society published them in its large-format series *Vetusta Monumenta* with St John Hope's description (cat. 148). William Griggs, the pioneer and leading exponent of colour photo-lithography in Britain, was employed to print the reproductions. The painstaking process involved separating the colours by means of several photographic negatives, painting out areas and superimposing transparent tints exactly over a key printed in a suitable colour. Although they lack the contrast obtained by later printing methods, the results are remarkable for their time. The reproductions were produced at a lower cost and with greater accuracy than previous methods that required drawing and colouring by hand, but they still required two years to complete. ARP/BN

Selected references: Hope 1893; Stratford et al. 1982, pp. 71–93; London 1984, no. 324; Annesley and Whitehead 2006, pp. 31–4

147

(opposite)
Stole
Late twelfth century
Eight pieces of embroidered silk, 5.2 cm wide, attached to a canvas board
Canterbury Cathedral Archives, Dean and Chapter of Canterbury

148

Illustration of sandals, buskin
and amice apparel
William Griggs (1832–1911)
1893
Photo-chromolithograph from
Vetusta Monumenta 1893, vol. 7,
pl. 4, 52.22 × 75.8 cm
Society of Antiquaries of London

210 | Making History

149

Mitre
Late twelfth century
Unpatterned silk, 24.5 × 29.5 cm
with lappets 39 cm long
Canterbury Cathedral Archives,
Dean and Chapter of Canterbury

Rescuing the Past | 211

150

Chalice
Mid-twelfth century
Silver-gilt and engraved,
height 14.2 cm
Dean and Chapter of Canterbury

151

Paten
Mid-twelfth century
Silver-gilt and engraved,
diameter 14 cm
Dean and Chapter of Canterbury

Radio Times April 18, 1968
EIGHTPENCE—LONDON AND SOUTH-EAST

Radio Times

APRIL 20–26

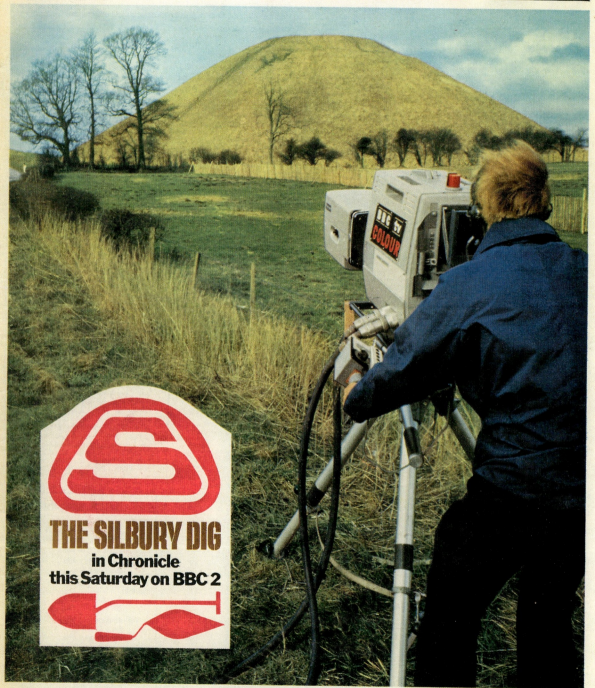

THE SILBURY DIG in Chronicle this Saturday on BBC 2

CHAMPION HOUSE: special feature in colour

Communicating the Past: From the Earth to the Airwaves

Carenza Lewis

FIGURE 33
(opposite)
The front cover of the *Radio Times*, 20–26 April 1968

Silbury Hill, constructed around 4500 BC, is the largest man-made prehistoric mound in Europe. From 1968 to 1969 the BBC funded a programme of excavation led by Richard Atkinson, which was broadcast in four *Chronicle* programmes.

Archaeology has long been of interest to an audience wider than those directly involved in it, and has been disseminated to the public via contemporary media. However, the arrival of broadcast media, particularly television, in the second half of the twentieth century has allowed a new and wider audience to engage with the past. This situation has, in general, benefited both sides: for the media, archaeological stories can be a valuable resource, while, for archaeology, public enthusiasm underpins financial support for research, rescue, preservation and presentation. As costs have risen, so has the need to keep the public engaged, using all possible avenues of communication. Crucial to this exchange of information has been the role of interpreters – those individuals or teams, seen or unseen by the viewer, who decide what is to be seen by viewers and how it is to be presented to them – who bring the archaeological 'story' from the earth to the airwaves.

Although the earliest moving images of archaeology for public consumption appeared in the cinema,[1] the most direct ancestor of televised archaeological programmes was actually the radio. In 1946, *The Archaeologist*, presented by Glyn Daniel of the University of Cambridge, became the first 'magazine' programme, featuring archaeologists discussing new discoveries and ideas, to be regularly broadcast into ordinary homes.

Within a few years archaeology, along with increasing numbers of the public, had made the transition to television, with the first broadcast of *Animal, Vegetable, Mineral?* in 1952. This series (1952–59; cat. 152.1), produced by the 'father' of archaeology on television, Paul Johnstone and his young assistant David Attenborough, made perfect use of the already well-honed communication skills of Glyn Daniel and Mortimer Wheeler, who, once a fortnight for seven years, speculated and expounded on the identity of a succession of 'mystery' objects from museums across Britain. Unexpectedly, given its educated subject-matter and tone, *Animal, Vegetable, Mineral?* was 'an instant and spectacular success'.[2] This was in no small measure due to the charm, wit, passion and knowledge of its presenters, whose appeal was such that Wheeler and Daniel were successively elected 'Television Personality of the Year' for 1954 and 1955 respectively.

The 'instant and spectacular' success of *Animal Vegetable, Mineral?* promptly led to the commissioning of another series by Johnstone, using the same faces to present archaeology in a rather different way. *Buried Treasure* (1954–58) adopted a similar format to *The Archaeologist* and took Daniel and Wheeler across the world, visiting sites ranging from Neolithic Orkney to Mohenjo-daro, Etruscan Italy and Zimbabwe. Perhaps one of the most memorable moments was Wheeler's disgusted tasting in 1954 of a meal based on the stomach contents of the then recently discovered Tollund Man (an Iron Age body found in a bog in Denmark), his last meal before his violent death two thousand years ago.[3] Both *Animal, Vegetable, Mineral?* and *Buried Treasure* tapped into the public interest in the mystery and romance of the past that was also reflected in wider fictional broadcasting, which increased with the arrival of ITV in the mid-1950s.[4] However, by the early 1960s a shift away from historical genres towards more contemporary subjects was beginning to become apparent, reflecting wider social changes. Both *Animal, Vegetable, Mineral?* and *Buried Treasure* had ceased by 1959 and, for half a decade, archaeology lost its regular slot in the television schedules.

The arrival of BBC2 in 1964, of which shortly afterwards David Attenborough became the controller, provided new slots for factual broadcasting and led to the establishment of the world's first permanent history and archaeology unit. In 1966, the first of a new historical and archaeological series was aired. Each *Chronicle* (1966–91) programme covered a specific archaeological or historical subject, presented by its leading expert.[5] *Chronicle*, led by Johnstone, survived and almost immediately began to push at the boundaries of broadcasting. The introduction of 'portable' cameras allowed filming on location but initially with severe limitations of picture and sound. The early live televising of excavations required huge and complex equipment, large crews and vehicles. Between 1967 and 1969 archaeological excavations tunnelling into the centre of the vast Neolithic mound of Silbury Hill in Wiltshire, which were commissioned by the BBC, were broadcast live, constituting an early, albeit rather extenuated, version of the 'fly-on-the-wall' documentary.[6] The appeal of such an excavation propelled the monument onto the front page of the *Radio Times* in April 1968 (fig. 33).[7]

The success of *Chronicle*, which ran for a remarkable 25 years, was in no small measure due to the skills of such luminaries as Glyn Daniel, Magnus Magnusson, Colin Renfrew, Richard Atkinson, Barry Cunliffe, Eric Thompson and many others, who were able to make complex archaeological evidence and ideas compelling to the viewer. The *Chronicle* years also coincided with an expansion of archaeological activity, both within academia (as new universities and new archaeological departments were founded as part of a general expansion of higher education) and beyond (as post-war reconstruction followed by commercial and infrastructure expansion in the 1960s and 1970s provided opportunities for excavation). Combined, they provided a wealth of material for broadcast. Similarly successful were a succession of fine historical documentaries in the late 1960s and early 1970s presented by the author.[8]

Other programmes from the same era presented archaeological subject-matter in rather different ways: in 1971 a sub-discipline of archaeology based on experimental testing of reconstructed artefacts and structures provided the inspiration for a *Chronicle* spin-off the BBC2 documentary *The Ra Expedition*, which followed the attempts by Thor Heyerdahl to cross the Atlantic on a reconstructed Egyptian papyrus boat from the time of the Pharaohs. An even more innovative approach to broadcasting, also based on experimental archaeology, came in 1978 when *Living in the Past* (BBC2) followed the attempts of a group of fifteen adults and children to survive for a year using only the technology of the Iron Age. This memorable series anticipated, by more than twenty years, reality-TV formats such as *The 1900 House* (BBC2, 1999) and *Surviving the Iron Age* (BBC1, 2001).[9]

Early in the following decade, more conventional documentary series such as *Vikings!* (BBC2, 1980), written and presented by Magnus Magnusson, became major successes for the BBC. Other successes capitalised on new discoveries such as that of the largely intact remains of Henry VIII's flagship, the *Mary Rose*, in the waters of the Solent repeatedly made the news headlines. In October 1982 the raising of the ship from the seabed provided *Chronicle* viewers with a total of sixteen hours broadcasting over three days, including nail-biting live transmissions of the lift itself that kept viewers hooked and delivered an aggregate audience approaching four million.[10]

The early 1980s also saw the appearance of a number of new documentary series, including *Timewatch* (BBC2), first broadcast in 1981 as a bright new show to complement *Chronicle*. With its tone firmly on investigation, *Timewatch*, which still regularly includes subjects of primarily archaeological content, has become 'the new longest-lasting TV history series in the world'.[11] Two other series of the early 1980s focused more exclusively on archaeology and, crucially, brought in younger, less conventional presenters, endearing the subject to the newly arrived Channel 4. In 1981, thirty-three-year-old Michael Wood presented *In Search of the Dark Ages* (BBC2), while in 1984 Catherine Hills, a young lecturer in archaeology at the University of Cambridge, became the first female presenter/writer of an archaeological series (*Blood of the British*, Channel 4). Both series managed to combine serious content with popular appeal through dynamic presentation.

Despite this apparently rosy outlook, by the mid-1980s, television's enthusiasm for regular archaeological programming was beginning to wane. This was in part a consequence of developments elsewhere in British archaeology, as new technology and a growing awareness of the finite nature of archaeological evidence both increased the cost and reduced the scale of excavation. *Chronicle* and *Timewatch* featured fewer archaeological subjects and interested viewers were restricted to a sparse diet only occasionally supplemented by archaeological programmes within other series such as *Horizon*.[12] In 1990 a new series called *Down to Earth* (Channel 4), presented by Catherine Hills and Roberta Gilchrist, another young female academic, briefly revitalised archaeological broadcasting by reporting on new discoveries in a magazine-style format, but was discontinued after three years. With the final decommissioning of *Chronicle*, archaeology lost a regular slot on the nation's television screens.

This situation changed, rather unexpectedly, in 1994 with the broadcast of a new, small four-part series called *Time Team* (Channel 4) (cat. 152.7). It brought together the talents of the archaeologist Mick Aston, of the University of Bristol, and the producer Tim Taylor, who had first worked together on the minor 1991 series *Time Signs* (Channel 4).[13] *Time Team* rethought how archaeology was presented to the viewer and in the process hugely increased and widened the appeal of archaeology to the general public.[14] The series combined elements of BBC1's *Challenge Anneka* (1989–95) and *Antiques Roadshow* (1979–ongoing) with the subject-matter and learning of *Chronicle* and *Down to Earth*, while abandoning most of the generally accepted rules for successful archaeological programme-making.[15] The series was presented by Tony Robinson, a well-known actor with no pretence at erudition,[16] and the sites were 'ordinary' places – back gardens, arable fields, village greens – rather than the ancient monuments or historic sites conventionally considered capable of delivering satisfactory viewing figures. *Time Team* commissioned its own three-day archaeological projects on these sites and allowed the viewer to watch each stage of the hunt for answers to crucial archaeological questions, including not only discoveries, but also deliberations, disagreements, dead-ends and mistakes.

By 1999 the series had expanded to thirteen programmes (supplemented by further documentaries and live broadcasts), with the excavations directed weekly by Mick Aston, supported by the archaeologists Phil Harding and Carenza Lewis and a large team of different archaeological specialists. They in turn were helped in their task by cutting-edge technology, which enables archaeological data-gathering and data-processing to be conducted at a speed, and in on-site locations, that would have been unimaginable a generation before, while computer graphics allowed entities, ranging from tiny artefacts to entire landscapes, to be vividly and dynamically reconstructed for the viewer from the fragmentary evidence recovered by the archaeologists. However, despite its effective exploitation of technology and its engaging 'challenge' format, the success of *Time Team*, like all its forebears, still relies ultimately on the communication and narrative skills of its presenters and editors.

Time Team is now widely known beyond the niche of archaeological broadcasting, and recognised as 'one of Channel 4's most durable, if unlikely, hits',[17] and its format was promptly reproduced by other time-limited challenge programmes involving activities as diverse as gardening[18] and home-decorating.[19] The success of *Time Team* also rapidly led to the appearance of numerous other series based on active archaeological investigation, mostly themed around specific specialisms within, or associated with, archaeology. One of the earliest was *Meet the Ancestors* (later *Ancestors*, BBC2), which ran for seven years from 1996. Presented by the archaeologist Julian Richards, this series focused specifically on the investigation of human remains with the graphic reconstruction of the face of the subject usually acting as the programme's ultimate dénouement. *House Detectives* (later *House Detectives at Large*, BBC2, 1999–2002) ran for three years, investigating the architectural, historical and archaeological investigation of standing buildings and propelled its presenter Dan Cruickshank to further archaeologically related series. *Secrets of the Dead* (Channel 4), with an investigative, quasi-forensic angle, started in 1999 and is still running. Other series extended over a shorter run of one or two seasons: *History Hunters* (Channel 4, 1998–99) focused on family history; *Two Men in a Trench* (BBC2, 2002–04) on historic battlefields; *Time Fliers* (BBC2, 2002) on aerial archaeology; *Buried Treasure* (BBC2, 2003) on metal-detecting; while *Extreme Archaeology* (Channel 4, 2004) exploited the 'dangerous-sports' appeal of investigating isolated archaeological remains.

In a very different style, the early years of the twenty-first century, with interest in the past sparked by the turn of the millennium, have seen the successful return of the major historical documentary presented by the author, a genre long out of fashion but confidently revived by Simon Schama's *A History of Britain* (BBC2, 2000–02) and David Starkey's *Monarchy* (Channel 4, from 2004 and ongoing). In particular, Francis Pryor's *Britain BC* (Channel 4, 2003) and *Britain AD* (Channel 4, 2005) put archaeology firmly at their centre. These examples are all high-quality visionary productions spanning many centuries, broadcast over more than one series as a succession of conjoined essays, and they offer the viewer an elegant counterpoint to the site-specific, action-centred investigations of *Time Team* and its fellows.

During the same period, another new departure in archaeological and heritage-related television reflected developments elsewhere in the media that used new communications technology to encourage the public to become more directly, and personally, involved with the subject of the broadcast. The year 2003, in particular, saw the broadcast of two 'interactive' programme runs: *Restoration* (BBC2) asked viewers to choose which neglected historic building the BBC should save from ruin,[20] while *Time Team's Big Dig* (Channel 4) invited members of the public to copy the on-screen experts and excavate for themselves on their own property, using instruction packs supplied by the programme-makers. Both BBC and Channel 4 now have websites to allow the viewer to take their interest in archaeology and heritage beyond the living room.

Archaeology currently seems to hold a strong position on television, as the wide variety of programmes on the subject show. However, in a fast-developing world, this state of affairs cannot be taken for granted. The future of archaeology on the small screen will, as in the past, be determined by developments in media technology, and by the energy and imagination of those determined to use it to bring archaeology to the wider public. The recent proliferation of new satellite and digital television channels has increased the capacity for historical and archaeological programming, with channels such as the History Channel dedicated entirely to the genre. However, in diffusing the audience it has also reduced viewing figures which has affected revenue and consequently limited spending on new programme-making, often with negative effects on quality, range and innovation. Internet-disseminated content increases capacity for 'niche' viewing of subjects such as archaeology. As in the past, it must be surmised that today's cutting-edge technology may become tomorrow's mass media. Broadcast archaeology in the past has always relied heavily on its editors and presenters to convey the complexities of archaeological evidence in a cogent, intelligible and engaging way; new forms of dissemination can and do cut out these mediators. The challenge now is to ensure that archaeological stories will continue to engage future audiences accessing screen-based information and entertainment in new ways.

Archaeology on Television from 1952 to 2007. Clips compiled and edited by David Groundwater, Sarah McCarthy, Alex Patterson.
CATALOGUE NUMBERS 152.1–152.8

Interest in archaeology on television has grown enormously since the pioneering enthusiasm of the BBC in 1952. By 2006, a further 25 channels were making archaeology programmes on many subjects in a multiplicity of styles and techniques. One factor has remained constant throughout: the force of the presenters' personalities and their desire to communicate.

When archaeology first made its mark on television with *Animal, Vegetable, Mineral?* in 1952 (cat. 152.1), the content was studio-bound and static. The introduction of portable cameras permitted filming on location, but initially there were severe limitations of picture and sound to contend with. In 1964 the launch of BBC2 led to the world's first permanent history and archaeology television unit; *Chronicle*, the channel's groundbreaking programme, was to provide many of the seminal moments in archaeology on British television (cat. 152.5). The early live televising of excavations, such as *Chronicle*'s dig at Silbury Hill in 1968–69 (cat. 152.3), required huge and complex equipment and large crews and vehicles, in stark contrast to today, when similar exercises can be carried out by a handful of people.

The first sixteen years of broadcasting were in black and white. The advent of colour in 1968 immediately extended the scope and appeal of archaeology on television (cat. 152.4). More recently, the transition from film to digital recording and editing has broadened yet further the flexibility of production, which has had profound consequences on the style of programmes.

The continuing success of archaeology on television has been sustained, as ever, by the ability of its communicators to inspire and enthuse, not merely with material artefacts but also, in Sir Mortimer Wheeler's famous phrase, by 'digging up people'. The Society's Fellowship has always been at the forefront of both. RS

Selected references: Johnstone 1957; Sutcliffe 1978; Hawkes 1982; Aston 2000; Attenborough 2002; Piccini and Kulik 2007

152.1

Animal, Vegetable, Mineral?
BBC Television
1952–59
In this popular, studio-based quiz programme, archaeologists, art historians and natural-history experts were asked to identify objects from museum and university collections. Here, Sir Mortimer Wheeler discusses an Iron Age carved head. SMC/ARP

152.2

Buried Treasure
BBC Television
1954–58
The popularity of *Animal, Vegetable, Mineral?* led the BBC to commission Paul Johnstone to produce *Buried Treasure*. Here, in one of a series of archaeology experiments undertaken by Johnstone with Richard Atkinson, the puzzle of how the sixty stones of the Stonehenge circle were conveyed from the Prescelly Hills in Pembrokeshire, a distance of two hundred miles, is explored. ARP/SMC

152.3

'Silbury Hill', from *Chronicle*
BBC2
1968–69
Following the launch of BBC2 in 1964 came the first dedicated television archaeology unit, responsible for one of the longest-running programmes on British television: *Chronicle*, which was broadcast from 1966 to 1991. In another TV first, the BBC sponsored Richard Atkinson's two-year excavation of Silbury Hill in Wiltshire, and produced a complete series of live broadcasts and edited documentaries. SMC/ARP

152.4

'Bath Waters', from *Chronicle*
BBC2
1980
This film of the excavation of the Roman Baths at Bath, which ran between 1969 and 1975, led by Barry Cunliffe, reveals not only the advantages of broadcasting in colour but also many advances in camera equipment, which now permitted a recording of the actual moment of discovery. SMC/ARP

152.5

'Raising the Rose', from *Chronicle*
BBC2
11 October 1982
Chronicle's live transmission of the raising of the *Mary Rose* was seen by millions worldwide. After 437 years beneath the Solent, and fifteen years of underwater archaeological investigations, the remains of Henry VIII's flagship were lifted and taken to Portsmouth Dockyard. SMC/ARP

152.6

Living in the Past
BBC2
23 February – 11 May 1978
In what seems as much a prototype for twenty-first-century reality television as an examination of Britain's distant past, fifteen adult and children volunteers sustained themselves for a year in a re-creation of an Iron Age settlement, equipped only with tools, crops and livestock that were available in Britain in the second century BC. SMC/ARP

152.7

Time Team
Channel 4
1994–ongoing
One of the longest-running British television programmes on archaeology, *Time Team* is characterised by a three-part format, which reflects the three-day duration of each of its excavations, an overtly discursive format, and the employment of a range of modern and traditional techniques, through which the 'team' explains the process of archaeology. Here, the team discusses a Roman settlement and a Bronze Age barrow at Cranborne Chase, Dorset, in 2004. SMC/ARP

152.8

Meet the Ancestors
BBC2
1998–2005
Presented by Julian Richards, *Meet the Ancestors* took excavated human remains into the laboratory and, through the application of scientific techniques used for forensic purposes, brought the viewer face to face with people from the past. The series illustrated the wealth of information that the science of archaeology can uncover, including where our ancestors came from and how they may have looked. ARP/SMC

152.1

152.6

152.2

152.4

152.5

152.7

152.3

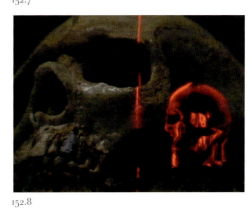

152.8

Communicating the Past: From the Earth to the Airwaves | 219

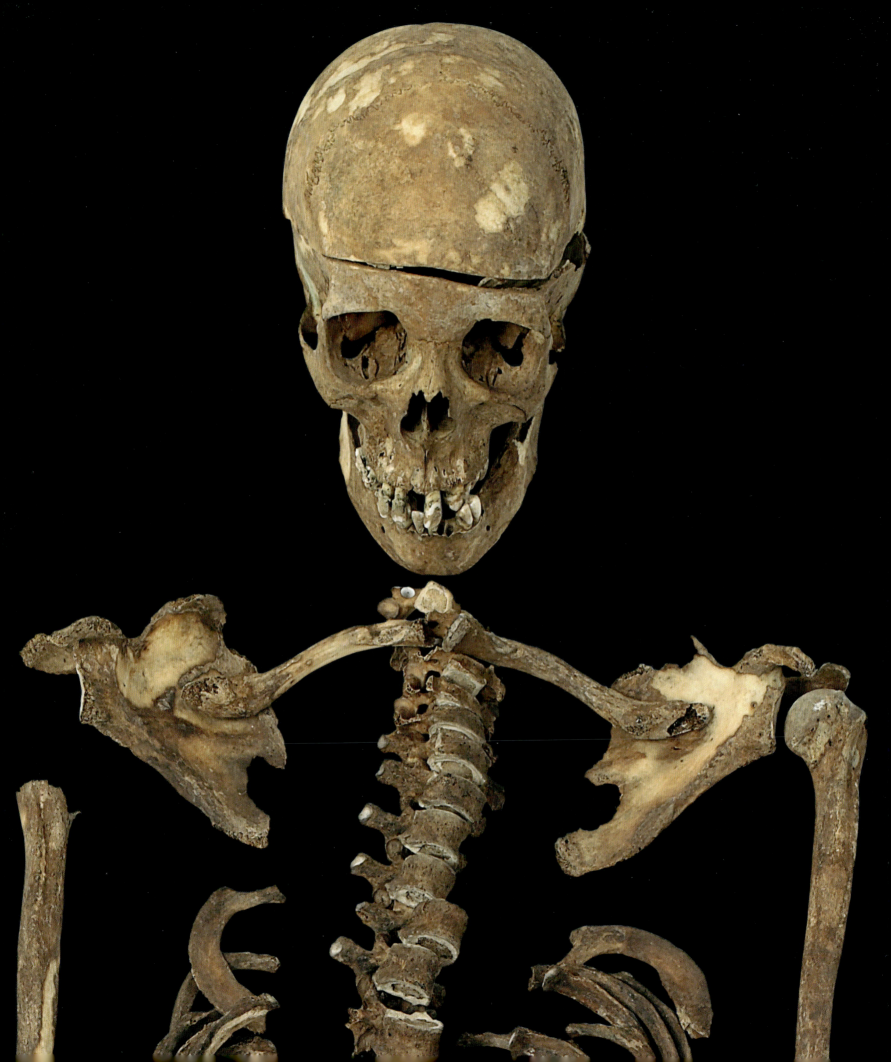

Face to Face with the Past

Bill White

When the Society of Antiquaries of London was founded in 1707, if a skeleton was found, the most that antiquaries could do was to estimate its owner's gender and stature. Although grave goods generally found their way into private collections, bones tended to be discarded. This remained broadly the pattern until the mid-twentieth century.

Then, about fifty years ago, human skeletons began to be recognised as repositories of data about the life of the deceased, as rich in information as the artefacts buried with them. Direct studies of the bones could contribute knowledge complementary to the findings of environmental archaeology and documentation. The discipline of the study of human skeletal remains has gone by a number of names since then, notably physical anthropology, human osteology, biological anthropology, osteoarchaeology and, most recently, human bioarchaeology. Irrespective of the variety of terms, the specialist involved is a biologist who, by analysing a large sample of human remains from a cemetery, seeks to understand more about human life in a time or place in the past so that general conclusions can be drawn about an ancient population. This may be contrasted with the findings of forensic anthropology, whose aim is to provide as much information as possible about an individual death. There is, in fact, no dichotomy between the two, as both approaches use the same range of accumulated, standardised techniques to arrive at their result.

The bioarchaeologist treats each skeleton in a systematic manner, observing the condition of preservation of the bone, the state of integrity of the skeleton, estimating the age and sex, and, where possible, measuring bones to establish the stature and physique of the person. Not all diseases afflict an individual for long enough to leave traces on bones, although a number of pathological conditions do leave skeletal evidence. However, it is extremely unusual to be able to deduce cause of death from bones alone. Most people die through organ failure, damage to other soft tissue or a severe infection, but these conditions act too quickly to become registered upon bones. Severe interpersonal violence is sometimes evident in the bone, such as a fracture caused by a blunt instrument, or a cut from a sharp weapon. At the Museum of London, since 2003, over 10,000 human skeletons have been recorded in an electronic database, from which information on an individual skeleton (or groups of skeletons) can be downloaded online. This programme is at the cutting edge of skeletal data management.

Further information can be obtained from stable isotope analysis of bones and teeth, which may provide evidence of diet. As well as revealing whether the diet was vegetarian or contained meat, the isotopic analysis is now capable of showing whether the diet protein came from a grazing animal or from fish, and if the latter, whether its habitat was marine or freshwater. Analysis of tooth enamel can detect specific patterns of isotopes characteristic of the geographical locality of the subject's childhood (the time when dental enamel was developing). Ancient DNA can also now be extracted from teeth and bones, and this can be analysed alongside the chemical isotopes in the same tissues, adding information about geographical origins and migration patterns. Finally, forensic investigation techniques based on laser scans of the skull now permit the reconstruction of the face of the deceased.

153

Female skeleton from St Bride's Lower
Churchyard, Farringdon Street, London
Eighteenth or nineteenth centuries
(excavated 1990)
Museum of London
Previously unpublished

This skeleton of a middle-aged woman was excavated by the Museum of London Archaeological Service (MoLAS) from the eighteenth- and nineteenth-century Lower Churchyard of St Bride's, London. A battery of criteria for establishing the skeleton's sex were applied to the skull and pelvis, and all indicated that its owner was female. The Museum of London took advantage of recent research that allows estimation of age at death to be based on lifetime degenerative processes that have been shown to advance at a known rate. Thus, for this woman, examination of the condition of the auricular (rear) surface of the *Ilium* (pelvis) and changes in the *Symphysis* pubis (pubic bone) and the sternal ends of the ribs all pointed to an age between 36 and 45 years.

Regression equations involving measured leg bones show that she was 1.471 m tall (4 feet 7 inches), whereas the average height for a woman from St Bride's was 1.604 m (5 feet 3 inches). Many of her teeth were affected by dental caries and she had suffered a chronic lung disease, which is indicated by lesions on the visceral surface of the ribs. A rare neoplastic (cancerous) disease probably caused the wearing away of the sphenoid bone inside the skull. The top of the skull was sawn off as part of an autopsy performed before burial, a post-mortem examination perhaps intended to identify her terminal illness. BW

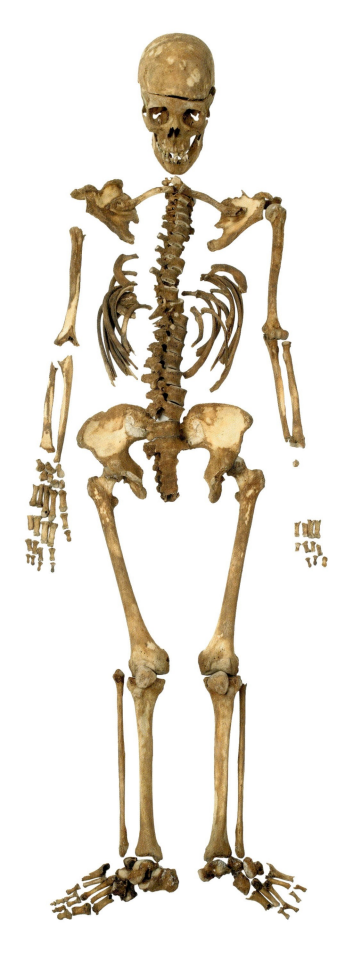

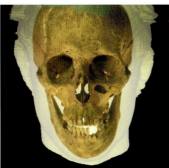
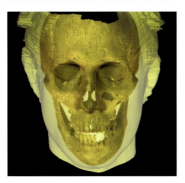
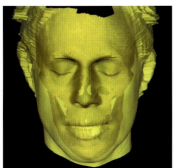
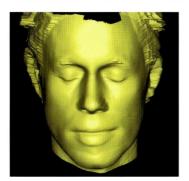

154

Facial reconstruction based on the skull of Richard Brandon
Rendered by Dr Robin Richards, University College Hospital, London
1998
Computer animation
Museum of London
Previously unpublished

A need often arises to provide an accurate facial appearance to identify the skeleton of a missing person. Traditionally, this was done by building up layers of modelling clay upon the skull or, preferably, upon a cast of the skull, and building up the 'skin' to the known average thickness required. Eyes, hair and paint were added to provide a realistic 'portrait' of the deceased, and the methods involved art as much as science.

A technique has now been developed that uses laser scans of thousands of faces to create a database. This has found particular use in craniofacial units within hospital surgery schools. Computer scans of faces are used in conjunction with scans of repaired skulls to assist in the surgical restoration of the faces of accident victims. If these techniques are applied to a scanned unknown skull from archaeology, a search of the database produces a composite face that gives a best fit to the skull. This technique is very rapid compared with the traditional method, no casting or other handling of the skull being required.

The computer animation shows the process of reconstructing the face of Richard Brandon, the seventeenth-century hangman who executed King Charles I in Whitehall on 30 January 1649. Brandon apparently did not long survive his royal victim, dying on 20 June later that year. It is believed that Brandon's body was later exhumed as an act of revenge for his regicide; however, the exact details surrounding these events are not known. Brandon's skull eventually found its way into the possession of a private collector, and in the early twentieth century was donated to the London Museum (Kensington Palace), along with a collection of 'Cromwelliana'. BW

Stonehenge

'Every age has the Stonehenge it deserves – or desires'
Jacquetta Hawkes, 1967

Stonehenge is arguably the most recognised ancient site in Britain. Even before the first antiquaries, it excited the curiosity of travellers and chroniclers, and featured in popular myths and legends. It has long been a central subject of study for antiquaries; indeed, our current understanding of Stonehenge has been informed by fieldwork and excavations by Fellows of the Society of Antiquaries of London over the last three hundred years.

The mystery surrounding Stonehenge has proved irresistible to artists, and many of Britain's most famous practitioners have attempted to 'capture' its essence. The artistic representations of the last three hundred years contrast with those produced using modern survey methods. No less aesthetic, these high-resolution digital images illustrate our continuing fascination with this iconic monument and demonstrate that however much is revealed about the past, questions will always remain.

Huius tempore p[er] xl dies co[n]stantinopoli terremot[us] fact[us] est, terra fluctuante. Qui d[icitu]r cora ô[mn]ib[us] e[st] in aera d[i]u stitit et admonuit ut facti[s] letanii[s] os canent. S[an]c[tu]s d[eu]s s[an]c[tu]s [fortis] s[an]c[tu]s [et] i[m]mortalis miserere nobis. michyl nientes. Quo facto cessa[vit] terremot[us]. Hoc pauli[n]us nolane ciuitatis ep[iscopu]s p[ro] filio... du[m] se t[ra]didit [et] africa[m] deductu[s] s[un]t. b[ea]t[us] [Gregorius] h[oc] di[c]it dialo[gorum] l[ibro] 3°. c[apitulo] 1°.

Iste zenon i[m]p[er]auit annis xvij.

Huius te[m]pore passa e[st] s[an]c[t]a Theodora virgo.

Stonehenge

Aurelia[nus] Ambrosi[us] ann[is]

H[uius] anno chorea gigantiu[m] de hiberma non vi s[ed] arte merlini est deuecta ap[u]d Stonehenge iuxta amisbery.

Huius [et] tempore facta est invenc[i]o crypte s[an]c[t]i Michaelis in monte tu[m]ba.

Tempore Helasij pape inventu[m] est corp[us] b[eati] Barnabe ap[osto]li [et] cu[m] eo eu[an]g[e]liu[m] q[uo]d p[ro]p[r]ia manu s[cri]pserat hebra[i]ce matheus.

Iste Anastasi[us] i[m]p[er]at ann[is] xxvj.

[right column fragments]

h[uius] tempore expellendu[m] Hillaru[m]...
s[an]c[tu]s [fortis]
alm[us] appo...
te[m]pore s[an]c[tu]s...
ci[vi]tat[is]...
de q[u]o s[cri]b[itu]r

Aurelia[n]us Ambrosi[us]

Iste an[nus]...
brosi[us]...
ann[is]...
xx...

Gyse...

Stonehenge

Mike Pitts

'You ask me', wrote Henry of Huntingdon, Archdeacon of Lincoln, 'why I began my narrative of past events in our native land [only] from the time of Julius Caesar.'[1] Travelling to Rome in January 1139, Henry had stayed at the Abbey of Le Bec, Normandy, where he encountered every author's greatest nightmare. He had just written a history of the English people, with, one imagines, a reasonable expectation of it becoming very well known, and there in front of him was a more expansive and engaging version written by a fellow countryman, Geoffrey of Monmouth.

Henry's text contained nothing about Britain before Rome: 'Such is the destructive oblivion that in the course of the ages obscures and extinguishes the glory of mortals.' Geoffrey, however, had plenty to say about more ancient times. If Henry gave us the first, brief, written reference to Stonehenge,[2] it was Geoffrey who answered the questions that baffled Henry and have challenged every observer since.

Henry knew when he was beaten. He addressed an addendum to an imaginary reader, summarising Geoffrey's new insights as if he believed every one. Geoffrey's *Historia Regum Britanniae* became one of northern Europe's most successful early books. Others retold the story, as down the centuries it fed into Arthurian romances, Spenser's *Faerie Queene*, Shakespeare's *King Lear* and more.[3] Of all the renderings and cribs, the one most precious for Stonehenge and ideas about our remote past is the British Library manuscript (cat. 155). Scribed and magnificently illustrated in England two centuries after Henry's stay at Le Bec, it contains Geoffrey's complete explanation of Stonehenge.[4]

Over 650 years later, in 1995, another book was launched, to the quiet clinking of teacups at the Society of Antiquaries of London. Called *Stonehenge in its Landscape: Twentieth-Century Excavations*,[5] it was a compilation of everything revealed about Stonehenge from excavations in the twentieth century. Little of the work described had been previously published. A major achievement for its many authors, English Heritage and its contractors Wessex Archaeology, the book was greeted by archaeologists with appalled delight: they would have to revisit almost every detail they thought they knew about the monument.

It would be hard to find two more different texts than Geoffrey of Monmouth's and *Stonehenge in its Landscape*, the one written by a medieval cleric, the other by a paid team of specialists led by three women. How did we get from Merlin to English Heritage? The Society of Antiquaries and its Fellows have been key players in the transformation, and the history of thinking on Stonehenge is a microcosm of our growing awareness of ancient history and its place in our lives. It is a fascinating and important story.

Stonehenge today, after the repositioning or straightening of 23 megaliths between 1901 and 1964, does not seem very different from the ruin as it was first depicted in a recognisable form. A 'trilithon', one of five individually lintelled pairs of tall uprights that once stood in an arc at the centre of the site, is missing from the portrayals by Turner and Constable (cats 166 and 168): it fell in 1797 and was repositioned in 1958. We may imagine, however, that the Stonehenge Geoffrey saw – if he did actually go there – was the Stonehenge we see now. So the monument and the questions asked about it have not changed. What have, profoundly, are the answers we give to those questions, the wider context in which we see Stonehenge, and the way we engage with its physical presence.

Geoffrey tackled all the Ws. What is Stonehenge? A ring of large stones with medicinal powers. Who built it? Merlin, for the British king Aurelius Ambrosius. In what way? Aurelius's soldiers tried cables, ropes and ladders, but only Merlin's magic could do it. Why? As a memorial to 460 British leaders slain by the Saxon king Hengist; Aurelius, Uther Pendragon (Arthur's father) and Constantine were later buried there. When? Around AD 485. Where did the stones come from? A mountain in Ireland. Where are they now? Near Amesbury, not far from Salisbury. The most interesting of these questions is 'when'. Henry of Huntingdon knew that there was a pre-Roman Britain, but time had destroyed the evidence. Geoffrey was less reticent: he filled the gap by extending history back in the only way he could imagine – he invented literature.

The first advance was to ditch the myth and focus on real history. Debate about whether Stonehenge was Roman, Danish or British, however, was doomed, and it took the great Stonehenge antiquarian investigators – John Aubrey visiting in the 1660s and William Stukeley in the 1720s – to ignore the books and look at the remains. Stukeley argued that the burial mounds in the area (round barrows, of which there are well over 400 close to Stonehenge and many others beyond – an exceptional concentration) were of the same age as the stones. In the early nineteenth century William Cunnington and Richard Colt Hoare 'opened' over 200 of them, and found artefacts – copper daggers, gold jewellery and strange pots – that spoke further of a lost culture. The idea was growing that whole epochs of British 'history' preceded the first text.[6]

By the mid-nineteenth century it was accepted that three successive ages – the Stone Age, the Bronze Age and the Iron Age – had preceded Roman civilisation. The politician and amateur scientist John Lubbock argued from the evidence of Colt Hoare's excavations that the barrows and Stonehenge both dated from the Bronze Age.[7] Surveying Stonehenge in 1877, Flinders Petrie (1853–1942), shortly to embark on his career as an Egyptologist, broke down the construction of the monument itself into four stages (cat. 170).[8] In 1901 William Gowland (1842–1922), directing the first and best scientific excavation at Stonehenge, said it was late Neolithic or early Bronze Age, and older than the barrows (cats 171, 172).[9] Extensive excavations at the site in the 1920s by William Hawley revealed much about structures now missing.[10] He strengthened the phasing anticipated by Petrie, which was later clarified by two of Britain's first university archaeologists, Stuart Piggott (1910–1996) and Richard Atkinson (1920–1994).[11]

So thus we arrive, in outline at least, at the position taken by the English Heritage team in 1995, the key addition being absolute dates offered by radiocarbon analysis. We now know that Stonehenge was an active ritual site for 1,400 years from 3000 BC.

It is easy to look back and find a direct route from Geoffrey's flounderings to modern understanding, but good judgements have always been matched by false. Caesar's ancient Druids were wrongly but inextricably attached to Stonehenge by Aubrey and Stukeley (cat. 160). John Britton (1771–1857), a contemporary of Cunnington and Colt Hoare, said Stonehenge was Roman. Gowland said Stonehenge was built all at once, while for most of the last century archaeologists believed that it was contemporary with the barrows.

Yet the comparison between the *Historia Regum Britanniae* and *Stonehenge in its Landscape* is instructive. The good but fictional read of the former has ceded to the directory-like mass of information in the latter, with nine appendices, sixty-nine tables and over three hundred technical illustrations. To the specialist it is priceless; to most it must be impenetrable.

Let us pause to consider this new knowledge. It presents a Stonehenge that we can now understand as representative of one of the most remarkable eras of Britain's, indeed Europe's past, and it has moved on again in recent years – we are enjoying a time of spectacular discoveries and frenzied new research. Excavation is at the heart of this, and the most important excavations at Stonehenge were conducted by the Society of Antiquaries over 80 years ago.

After centuries as a curious encumbrance in a large farming estate (fig. 35), Stonehenge finally had been recognised as an asset in its own right when the Antrobus family auctioned it off in 1915. Three years later the buyer, Cecil Chubb, had passed it on to the nation, who, in the form of the Office of Works, decided to continue Gowland's 1901 project of tidying fences, making the site safe and investigating its history. The latter task was entrusted to the Society, which appointed Lieutenant-Colonel William Hawley (1851–1941) as its excavation director.

Hawley's work at Stonehenge was criticised after his death. Atkinson called it a 'melancholy chapter' that bequeathed a 'most lamentable legacy of doubt and frustration'.[12] It was, says Christopher Chippindale, 'a disaster … managed on absurdly inadequate resources', that went 'badly wrong'.[13]

Any archaeologist today might wish that no one had ever excavated at Stonehenge, imagining an untouched site ripe for new investigations with the latest ideas and technologies. It is archaeology's tragedy that excavation, which alone can provide the evidence for unwritten stories – for almost everything that has ever happened in the long history of humankind – is necessarily subjective and destructive; nothing can ever be re-excavated, only reconsidered. The Society's excavations, entirely typical of Hawley's time, were inadequate for the site. Yet it is only because of them, continuing over eight years from 1919 to 1926, that we recognise the length and complexity of Stonehenge's ancient history. Though half of the subterranean monument was opened up then, and more has been swept away before and since (the record of Atkinson's excavations is no better than Hawley's), deposits that will answer new questions still remain; new excavation will bring its own destruction, but it must happen.

This is not the place for a description of Stonehenge archaeology,[14] but rather for recounting some significant recent changes in perception. Our growing understanding of the monument's chronology is perhaps the most fundamental modern development. For the 1995 study, English Heritage funded a major radiocarbon-dating programme (for which most of the samples came from Hawley's trenches), both innovative in itself in its use of statistical analysis, and revolutionary for Stonehenge.[15]

Radiocarbon told us for how long Stonehenge was an active ritual or religious site. We now know that its history spans profound changes in contemporary societies. The 1,400 years that separate the first encircling ditch and bank cut out of the chalk from the last ring of empty pits that surround the megaliths, perhaps then already starting to fall down, represent 50 or 60 generations, as many as separate us from the kingly Anglo-Saxon ship burials at Sutton Hoo in Suffolk. We still know distressingly little about how people lived

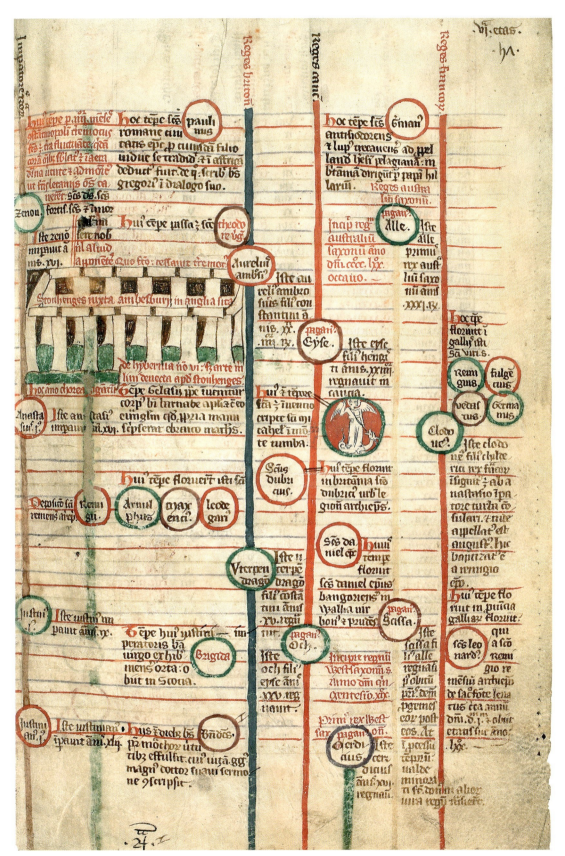

FIGURE 34
'Stonhenges' in a Scala Mundi
Fourteenth century
Illumination on vellum
Parker Library, Corpus Christi College, Cambridge, MS.194, fol. 57r

Squeezed into a spreadsheet of historical events (many in fact mythical), Stonehenge makes one of three known medieval pictorial appearances in this *Scala Mundi*.

Stonehenge | 229

– their houses, their clothes, details of their diet and health – but during this time we can see major changes in the way people disposed of their dead (and by inference in beliefs and rituals), and in styles of pottery and stone tools. The first metals appear, copper and gold, as rare personal weapons and ornaments. The whole phenomenon of 'henges', massive banks excavated from an interior ditch that enclose a wide variety of apparently ritual structures built with timber and stone, comes and goes.

No informed observer would now offer a single 'explanation' for Stonehenge, which began as a circular enclosed space, accumulated an assortment of ancient bones and buried infant animals, hosted little-understood timber constructions and the country's largest prehistoric cremation cemetery, and witnessed a succession of megalithic arrangements whose full patterns are still to be understood: its life was too long and complex. The oldest stone on the site is unlikely to have meant the same to the people who saw it erected as it did to those who later placed the most recent. Alongside this change in understanding, we now take a greater, and less judgmental interest in Stonehenge's continuing history to the present day. What later prehistoric people did at, or thought of, the site, or medieval visitors, eighteenth-century antiquaries or modern Druids or tourists, all these and more attract our interest.

By contrast, Stonehenge was not an ancient place where everything happened very slowly. What most of us think of as 'Stonehenge' – the unique silhouette of lintelled megaliths – did not take 1,400 years to build. Ironically, we still do not know when that happened. Options range between around 2600 and 2300 BC – only new excavation will resolve that question (by contrast, the excavation of the ditch circle, the first structure on the site, is dated to within 80 years around 2970 BC). However, the design and likely working practices behind the carved and engineered megaliths imply that construction took a few years, perhaps as much as a single generation, but, most of us would guess, little more.

Whichever date we come to favour for this moment, this unique coming together of labour, organisation and vision in religious architecture, it is now clear that Stonehenge was not built by the people who lie buried beneath the round barrows, most of whom we would call 'early Bronze Age', but in the 'late Neolithic' or 'Chalcolithic' period. To put it simply: Stonehenge is Stone Age.

This is profoundly significant. It means that the carved megaliths are broadly contemporary with what in plan at least appear to be similar structures revealed by excavation and ground survey. Sometimes, as was discovered by geophysical survey in 1997 at Stanton Drew in Somerset, where nine concentric rings of four or five hundred closely spaced posts formed circles 62 to 301 feet (19 to 92 metres) across, these wooden 'henges' are larger than Stonehenge; Woodhenge and nearby structures closer to Stonehenge, are of comparable scale. Here, then, is a tradition that spawned Stonehenge, in an indigenous feat of imagination that merged the spectacle and engineering of the great timber henges with the craft and geological know-how of tiny stone tools.

Discoveries made since the 1995 English Heritage publication are adding detail to this Late Stone Age world. Across the River Avon to the east, excavations accompanying the expansion of Amesbury have chanced upon another ritual circle, a simple ring of pits, and, most famously, three graves. The first to be found held the remains of a man, dubbed the 'Amesbury archer', with around

FIGURE 35
The Wiltshire Champion Coursing Meeting at Stonehenge from the *Illustrated London News*, 11 November 1865
Engraving after a sketch by G. B. Goddard
Society of Antiquaries of London

In this scene of hare coursing with greyhounds, Stonehenge legitimises Wiltshire worthies much as it did monarchs in medieval chronologies.

FIGURE 36
Stonehenge, Midsummer Day
Mike Pitts
2006

Usually conserved like the baize on a snooker table, on Midsummer Day Stonehenge's turf is democratised. The stones continue to find a contemporary role.

100 artefacts, including copper knives, gold ornaments and five 'Beaker' pots (distinctive mug-like vessels found across much of Europe and variously and controversially associated with migrating people, powergames or cults): not only was the sheer size of this grave group unprecedented, but Beaker graves are normally distinguished by just one of these finely decorated pots. Nearby was a younger man, with similar gold ornaments and an unusual variation in his foot bones found also in his neighbour, suggesting a close relationship. The third grave contained the jumbled remains of at least seven individuals, some of them children, and a variety of further Beaker pots.

Analysis of the Amesbury archer's teeth indicated he was born not in Wessex, but in central Europe – he is Britain's first proven prehistoric immigrant. Similar study points to several possible birth locations beyond southern England for men in the mass grave, though reports that they brought Stonehenge bluestones (a range of distinctive rocks) from Wales were driven by publicity, not science.

Meanwhile on the Stonehenge side of the river, excavations that are part of a large, continuing university-based research project are uncovering further surprises at the long-known earthwork henge at Durrington Walls. Houses have been found whose floor deposits, scientifically analysed, promise unique insights into the times. The site is now seen as intimately linked to Stonehenge in rituals of feasting, celebration and disposal of the dead.

This work is largely unpublished and has yet to make its full impact. Yet the recent academic emphasis on exclusively local, indigenous development has been thrown into doubt; after years of promoting ideas of egalitarian, simple societies, archaeologists are beginning to return to old talk about chiefs and high priests.

And yet, still, one returns to Geoffrey of Monmouth, not for enlightenment, but for a sense of wonder without which our engagement with Stonehenge can never be complete. The assembly of images in this chapter allows us a rare opportunity[16] to absorb the interaction of the two strands of observation and theory that drive representation and thought, like long ribbons in the wind that sometimes entwine, sometimes flicker alone, while off-stage a single unseen hand holds both.

Geoffrey's tale, depending neither on Stonehenge nor attempts to shape it, is pure myth, though remarkably we already see an apparent field depiction in the later medieval sketch now in Douai (cat. 156; compare fig. 34). Lucas de Heere's sixteenth-century illustrations, and others related, aim for pure representation (cat. 157). Daniel Loggan's observations (c. 1684–85) are so good that they bear detailed comparison with the monument today (cat. 158), while Petrie claimed precision for his plan (1877), which far exceeds the scale of the print (cat. 170): we still use his numbering scheme. He would undoubtedly have been delighted at the extreme and genuine precision that digital technology can now deliver (cat. 179).

Even in an apparently objective reconstruction, however, William Stukeley (cat. 160) cannot hide his sense of excitement and awe at Stonehenge, which he mapped for us in precious detail in perceptive drawings of the stones and surrounding landscape. By contrast, Inigo Jones's restoration, with the faces on the stones impossibly straightened and the addition of an imaginary trilithon in pursuit of a Roman design, kills it dead (cat. 159).

It is, appropriately, to one of our greatest artists that we turn for the most genuine re-invention of the monument. Turner's watercolour (cat. 166) transforms the megaliths into an idea, a potent, sublime vision, whose light and colours owe little to Wiltshire.

Alan Sorrell, too, imitating grand Romantic history painting, captured an overwhelming sense of time and place, a dark vision of ancient Britain (cats 175, 176, 177, 178) while working closely with conservative archaeologists, who ensured his holes in the ground were correct. This was no mean feat: comparison with the bizarre reconstruction of Meyrick and Smith, who, like Sorrell, consulted contemporary specialists for verisimilitude, shows how far that approach can fail (cat. 164).

Of course, the visionary has a stronger grip on the public imagination than the academic. Despite today's far larger population, we can be sure that fewer people have read English Heritage's *Stonehenge in its Landscape* than knew Geoffrey's *Historia Regum Britanniae* in medieval Europe. Indeed, more copies of Geoffrey's work were in circulation. Even ignoring the numerous spin-offs, it is today the third most common surviving medieval history, with 217 copies known; at least 1,000 were written.[17] English Heritage printed 840 copies of *Stonehenge*.[18]

Conversely, huge numbers of people now visit the stones (fig. 36). Since the publication of *Stonehenge in its Landscape* in 1995, well over the equivalent of Britain's population in Geoffrey's time have paid to enter. Stonehenge retains its power. Somewhere, perhaps, in the spaces between the pictures and the objects in this section, lies a monument true to both us and the past.

155

'With Merlin's aid Stonehenge is built'
Wace, Canon of Bayeux
(c. 1115–c. 1183)
1338–42
Illumination on vellum, 21 × 24 cm
British Library, London, Egerton
MS 3028, folio 30
Selected references: Southampton 1987; Chippindale 2004; Darvill 2006; Heck 2006A, pp. 253–60

One of the earliest depictions of Stonehenge is a miniature in a manuscript now in the British Library, recently dated to 1338–42. The manuscript contains a shortened version in French of the chronicle written by Wace in the twelfth century and known as the *Roman de Brut*. It gives the legendary origins of the British people going back to the followers of Brutus of Troy, and was based on the writings of Geoffrey of Monmouth.

According to Geoffrey, the British king, Aurelius Ambrosius, sought a memorial to 460 British leaders slain by the Saxon Hengist. The Welsh wizard Merlin told him to 'send for the Giant's Round [from the medieval Latin name for Stonehenge] which is on Mount Killaraus in Ireland … The stones are enormous … Many years ago the Giants transported them from the remotest confines of Africa and set them up in Ireland … they used to pour water over them and to run this water into baths in which their sick were cured' (a healing association with Stonehenge that Timothy Darvill, Professor of Archaeology at Bournemouth University, has recently revived). In the miniature, one of some twenty illustrating the story, the prominent Merlin is shown taking down the stones in Ireland before re-erecting them in Wiltshire (as the French art historian Christian Heck has argued, contrary to the traditional view that the illustration shows Stonehenge itself). A kneeling man tries unsuccessfully to lift a stone, while a third looks on in astonishment.

The legend would date Stonehenge to the fifth century AD, but it has been suggested that the idea that the stones came from Ireland could represent a distant folk memory of the prehistoric journey made by the bluestones from Wales to Salisbury Plain. However, the illustration shows sarsen stones, not bluestones. BN/MP

156

(opposite)
'Stonehenge' from a *Scala Mundi*
c. 1440–41
Miniature on vellum, 39.5 × 53 cm
Bibliothèque Municipale, Douai,
MS. 803, fol. 55r
Selected references: Heck 2006A, pp. 253–60; Heck 2006B, pp. 10–15

This sketch of Stonehenge, recently discovered in Douai in France and dated to c. 1440–41, is the earliest to show what seems to be field observation of the megaliths. It is unclear whether the former circle has been represented as four trilithons, or the three trilithons likely then to have been standing have been turned into four. Notable is the depiction of lintels penetrated by tenons on the uprights: though wrong in detail, this is the first known recognition of Stonehenge's unique construction-jointing. The modern spelling of the name is recorded for the first time.

The drawing comes within the text of a *Scala Mundi* ('ladder of the world'), which gives a Christian view of world history from the Fall of Adam. Many manuscript copies circulated in the medieval period, of which over 400 have survived. The section on Stonehenge takes the same story, based on Geoffrey of Monmouth, as the manuscript in the British Library (cat. 155). The drawing is placed between AD 480 and 486 in the chronicle. Translated from the Latin, the text reads: 'That year the giants' round was transported from Ireland by Merlin not by force but by art to Stonehenge near Amesbury.'

An earlier *Scala Mundi* of c. 1338–42 at Corpus Christi College, Cambridge, depicts Stonehenge as a rectangle (fig. 34). The Douai sketch therefore falls between the symbolic representations of the fourteenth century and the larger-scale, more detailed views of the late sixteenth century. The manuscript is thought to have originated in England, reaching Douai through one of the groups of English Catholic refugees who settled there after the Reformation. BN/MP

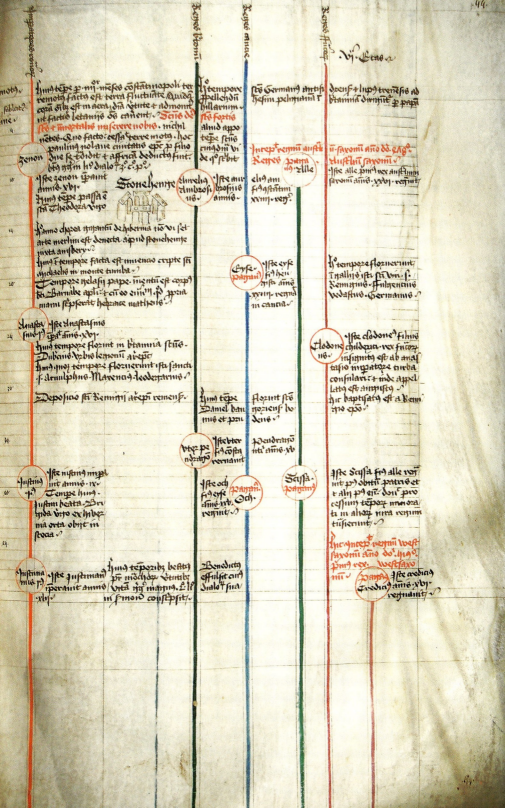

157

'View of Stonehenge' from *Corte Beschryuinghe van Engheland, Schotland, ende Irland*
Lucas de Heere (1534–1584)
c. 1572
Pen and wash on paper, 32 × 42 cm
British Library, London, Add MS 28330, fol. 36
Selected references: Bakker 1979; Chippindale 2004, pp. 33–6

The first detailed representations of Stonehenge were made in the reign of Elizabeth I, and include, apart from the one shown here, an engraving by an unidentified 'R. F.', and a watercolour by the herald and writer William Smith (1588). Their strong similarities encouraged Chippindale to suggest that they were derived from a lost common original, which style and documentary sources would indicate to have been the work of the Flemish artist Joris Hoefnagel (1542–*c.* 1601), who may have accompanied his compatriot Lucas de Heere to Stonehenge from 1568 to 1569.

Between 1573 and 1575 de Heere wrote a guidebook to England, its history and costumes, of which this single manuscript copy survives. He describes the monument as having 'three ranks of stones … as I myself have drawn them on the spot'. Nearby was an earthen rampart made by the Romans, and many mounds under which are found the bones of giants. His drawing shows Stonehenge from the north-west, in an imaginary perspective, with two round barrows in the foreground. The view is recognisable, despite some errors, and the ditch is shown closer to the stones than in reality.

The 1575 engraving by 'R. F.' shows two apparent stones outside the main circle on the left, possibly the Heel and Slaughter Stones, and a castle on the horizon, probably the result of a confusion over the Latin word *castrum* applied by antiquaries to the ancient hill fort near Amesbury; men dig a barrow in the foreground. The print was frequently copied, with increasing remoteness from real life. BN/MP

158

A Prospect of Stone-Henge from the West and
A Prospect of Stone-Henge from the South
Daniel Loggan (*c.* 1635–1692)
c. 1684–85
Engraving, two prints on one sheet,
43.6 × 61.5 cm
Society of Antiquaries of London,
Coleraine Collection, VII, fol. 16
Selected references: Latham and
Matthews 1976, vol. 9, p. 229;
Chippindale 2004

Daniel Loggan's meticulous and detailed representation of Stonehenge from two viewpoints was frequently reissued from the late seventeenth to the second half of the eighteenth century. The arms and dedication to William Prince (1663–1703), Secretary to the Duchess of York, suggest a date of *c.* 1684–85 for the original engraving. Loggan clearly shows the ditch and the Heel Stone, as well as the leaning trilithon known as Stone 56, which was put upright in 1901 (cat. 171), but, like de Heere, he has portrayed the ditch and peripheral stones closer to the central monument than they really are. His text sets out different views on the origins of the monument. He claimed that 'modern Historians and Antiquaries have more accurately deciphered the matter' and, following Charleton's views published in 1663, said it was probable that the Danes were responsible.

Loggan noted that the 'Gigantik pile … creates astonishment in all sorts of spectators' and shows visitors arriving by coach and on horseback. In the seventeenth century the stone circle was increasingly becoming an attraction, and in 1680 the owner was granted the right to hold an annual fair there. Two notable royal visitors were James I and Charles II; Samuel Pepys recorded an expensive outing from Salisbury in his diary for 11 June 1668:

> *Thence to the inn; and there not being able to hire coach-horses, and not willing to use our own, we got saddle horses, very dear … to Stonehenge, over the Plain and some great hills, even to frighten us. Come thither, and find them as prodigious as any tales I ever heard of them, and worth going the journey to see. God knows what their use was! … Gave the shepherd-woman, for leading our horses, 4 d.*

BN

Stonehenge | 235

159

Depiction of Stonehenge restored from *The most notable Antiquity of Great Britain, vulgarly called Stone-Heng*
Inigo Jones (1573–1652) and John Webb (1611–1672)
1655
Engraving from Jones and Webb 1655, pl. NUM V, 26.8 × 35 cm
Society of Antiquaries of London
Selected references: Tait 1978, pp. 154–9; Chippindale 2004

This is the first book on Stonehenge and possibly the first in any language on a single prehistoric monument. Jones, Surveyor of the King's Works, was strongly influenced by the buildings of classical antiquity that he had seen in Rome; he saw his mission as bringing back to Britain the monumental architecture of the Romans. He was commanded by James I to find out 'what possibly I could discover' about Stonehenge and started work in 1620. He was the first to survey the stones, make a plan and suggest their use as a temple. He concluded that Stonehenge, since it was a structure of 'elegancy and proportion', had been erected, not by the native Britons but by the Romans – as a temple to the god of the sky, Coelus. Jones reconstructed the plan as if it were a Roman theatre – adding stones that were never there to create a central circle, and ignoring the fact that the uprights are not columns and do not follow classical proportions.

His notes were written up posthumously by his pupil Webb, as an architectural treatise published in 1655. His fiercest critic, Walter Charleton, argued instead that Stonehenge was built in the shape of a crown by the Danes in the ninth century as an ancient place of coronation. This rival treatise, published in 1663, reflected the restoration of the monarchy a few years earlier. Neither Jones nor Charleton believed that anyone before the Romans was capable of such a construction.
BN/MP

A peep into the Sanctum Sanctorum 6 June 1724.

160

'Peep into the Sancta Sanctorum' from *Stonehenge, a Temple restor'd to the British Druids*
William Stukeley (1687–1765)
1724, published 1740
Engraving
34.4 × 44.5 cm
Society of Antiquaries of London
Selected references: Stukeley 1740; Piggott 1985; Haycock 2002; Chippindale 2004; Burl 2006; Darvill 2006

William Stukeley popularised the theory that Stonehenge was a temple built by the Druids probably around 480 BC. He was following the ideas of the Wiltshire antiquary John Aubrey (1626–1697), who realised that Avebury and Stonehenge were constructed before written history, and that only careful observation, recording and comparisons would throw light on their origins. Aubrey suggested that the stone circles found in many parts of Britain were the work of the native British and were probably the temples of the Druids, who, according to classical writers, were their priests. Aubrey's notes have been published in full only in recent years, but copies circulated among antiquaries, and were known to Stukeley.

Stukeley had been inspired by seeing Loggan's prints (cat. 158) to make a 'groundplot' and an 'exact Model of that most noble and splendid piece of Antiquity'. He spent every summer between 1721 and 1724, while Secretary of the Society of Antiquaries, working at Avebury and Stonehenge. At the latter he discovered early features in the surrounding landscape, notably the Avenue and the Cursus, recognised that the stones came from different sources and coined the word 'trilithon' to describe the large sarsen stones with lintels in the great horseshoe.

Stukeley's theories on the Druids and their origins, which he published in 1740, were highly influential until the middle of the nineteenth century, until recently obscuring the value of his detailed fieldwork. BN

Stonehenge | 237

161

Stonehenge during a Thunderstorm
Thomas Girtin (1775–1802)
1794
Watercolour over indications in graphite, touched with reed pen,
10.5 × 14.8 cm
Ashmolean Museum, Oxford, WA1916.8
Selected references: Girtin and Loshak 1954; Smiles 1994

There is no evidence that Girtin ever visited Stonehenge, and this drawing is presumed to be a result of working up a drawing by another artist, possibly the antiquary James Moore. Recognising Girtin's artistic power, Moore began collaborating with him in 1793. He employed him initially to take relatively pedestrian sketches by himself or other artists and turn them into more accomplished pictures.

The watercolour captures the experience tourists enjoyed, as expressed by William Gilpin in his *Observations on the Western Parts of England* (1798):

Stonehenge, at a distance, appeared only as a diminutive object. Standing on so vast an area as Salisbury Plain, it was lost in the immensity around it. As we approached, it gained more respect … but when we arrived on the spot, it appeared astonishing beyond conception … it is not the elegance of the work, *but the* grandeur of the idea *that strikes us.*

Girtin's compressed image likewise brings the spectator close in to the monument and animates it with a bolt of lightning and a vivid contrast of light and shade. In doing so, rather than detailing its physical structure, he captures the emotional impact of Stonehenge. The balance between antiquarian exactitude and the Sublime here tilts decisively in favour of the latter. ss

162

(left)
Stonehenge before 3 January 1797 from the west
The Revd Thomas Rackett (1755–1840)
Late eighteenth century
Pencil and watercolour on paper, 18.3 × 31.8 cm
Society of Antiquaries of London, RP Wilts 12

163

(bottom left)
Stonehenge from the south-west, the Trilithons lately fallen
W. J. Beechey (dates unknown)
1797
Pencil and watercolour on paper, 18.6 × 31.6 cm
Society of Antiquaries of London, RP Wilts 12
Selected references: Maton 1800; Chippindale 2004

On 3 January 1797, the large south-west trilithon fell outwards, the first stone whose collapse is recorded. The sound was heard by people working in nearby fields, and the *Gentleman's Magazine* for January 1797 reported the event. The fall was variously attributed to a sudden thaw after a period of deep snow, burrowing rabbits and sheltering gypsies. The central horseshoe was thus reduced to two standing trilithons until this trilithon was re-erected in 1958.

Among those who visited the scene was the 23-year-old William Maton (1774–1835), a Fellow of the Linnean Society, future physician to Queen Charlotte and the author of the first geological map published of any part of England. He was travelling in the region collecting material on natural history and antiquities. Maton estimated the weight of the fallen stones to have been about 70 tons, and was surprised to find that they had been set no more than three feet six inches (about 1 metre) in the ground. His report was read to a meeting of the Society of Antiquaries in June 1797 and by November he had obtained two drawings to illustrate the scene before and after the fall. The earlier drawing was provided by his travelling companion, the Revd Thomas Rackett. William Maton was elected a Fellow the same year and his paper with illustrations was published in the next issue of *Archaeologia*. BN

164

Grand Conventional Festival of the Britons
Charles Hamilton Smith (1776–1859),
pl. XI of Sir Samuel Rush Meyrick's
Costume of the Original Inhabitants of the British Islands
1815
Hand-coloured aquatint, 41.5 × 67 cm
Society of Antiquaries of London
Selected references: Smiles 1994; Moser 1998; Chippindale 2004

Samuel Meyrick (1783–1848) and Charles Smith produced the first substantial costume book to attempt to depict the dress and customs of the ancient Britons, *Costume of the Original Inhabitants of the British Islands*. They were the first to use archaeological evidence to help create visual images of an imagined prehistoric past. By referring to learned journals such as *Archaeologia* and depicting genuine artefacts and monuments, they made their images appear in a historical context, making them seem more authentic.

This reconstruction of Stonehenge provides the setting for an imaginary festival of Ancient Britons. The subject was derived from William Stukeley's interpretation of the site as a temple for Druidic ceremonies with Old Testament origins. The image of the serpent and the procession of the Ark of the Covenant come from Stukeley, the costumes from medieval sources.

The publication was an expensive one using hand-coloured aquatints by a leading British engraver, Robert Havell. However, Meyrick and Smith were able to appeal to a new audience with antiquarian interests, who accepted images of prehistoric landscapes as a feature of contemporary Romantic art. BN

165

John Britton's *Celtic Cabinet*
c. 1824
Mahogany and pine, 128 × 91 × 75 cm
Wiltshire Heritage Museum, Devizes
Selected references: Chippindale 1985, pp. 121–38; Chippindale 1986, pp. 874–5

This 'Celtic Cabinet', whose form evokes one of the trilithons at Stonehenge, was designed to hold an antiquary's 'drawings, sketches, manuscripts, books and prints, illustrative of the Celtic, or Druidic monuments of the world'. A plaster model depicting Stonehenge as it was in the early nineteenth century stands on top of the cabinet, inside a case of pale yellow, orange, red and clear panes of glass through which the model could be viewed in different colours of light.

The first of the three drawers beneath holds a companion model of Stonehenge, the second a plaster model of Avebury as it was. The bottom drawer is now empty but at the time of the second owner, the topographer and antiquary John Britton (1771–1857), it held drawings and prints. The models were made in *c.* 1820 by Henry Browne, a 'Lecturer on Ancient and Modern History', and the first guardian of Stonehenge. From 1807 he made and sold models of Stonehenge, and his customers included the antiquaries Sir Richard Colt Hoare and the Revd Edward Duke, as well as the Ashmolean Museum in Oxford.

The cabinet was designed to be viewed from the front only. Of the five watercolours mounted horizontally in the topmost level, the largest, central work is not original. The other four depict from left to right: *Trethevy Portal Dolmen, St Clears, Cornwall* by Samuel Prout or John Britton; *Kits Coty House, Aylesford, Kent* by T. R. Underwood; *Chun Quoit, St Just, Cornwall* by Samuel Prout or John Britton; and *Maen y Bardd, near Rowen, Gwynedd* by an unknown artist. Reading from left to right and top to bottom, the six panels on the cupboards depict: *Double Cromlech, Plas Newydd, Anglesey* (1824) by John Sell Cotman; *Druidical Circle near Winterbourne, Dorset* (1824) by John Sell Cotman; *A Bird's Eye View of Stonehenge* after W. H. Hyett; *A Bird's Eye View of Avebury* by an unknown artist; *The Druid's Circle at Penmaenmawr, Gwynedd* after G. Shepherd; and *Stonehenge S. E.* by G. Cattermole.

Crafted from mahogany and pine, with the front, top and sides veneered in pollarded elm and bird's eye maple, the cabinet was made by an unidentified furniture maker for George Watson Taylor, presumably for his house, Erlestoke Park near Devizes, which his family had purchased in 1820. By 1843 John Britton had acquired the cabinet, at which time it was the centrepiece of his octagonal 'cabinet room' on the first floor of his house in Burton Street, St Pancras, and was already being referred to as the 'Celtic Cabinet'. In 1853, for the reasonable price of 100 guineas, Britton sold it to the Wiltshire Archaeological and Natural History Society, as the first acquisition for the newly formed Devizes Museum. PR

166

Stonehenge
Joseph Mallord William Turner
(1775–1851)
c. 1827
Watercolour on paper, 27.9 × 40.4 cm
Salisbury and South Wiltshire Museum, Wilton, no. 811
Selected references: Ruskin 1906, vol. 21; Shanes 1990; Forrester 1996

Turner made this watercolour as part of the commission from the publisher Charles Heath for *Picturesque Views in England and Wales*, a topographical publication issued between 1827 and 1838.

Turner had already made just over a dozen pencil sketches of the monument: some around 1799 (in his *Studies for Pictures* sketchbook) and others in 1811 (in the *Devonshire Coast No. 1* and *Stonehenge* sketchbooks). He produced a watercolour treatment of Stonehenge at sunset (c. 1811–13) and had intended to include an engraving of Stonehenge at daybreak in his landscape treatise the *Liber Studiorum*, which remained unissued, however, when the *Liber* ceased publication in 1819.

The scene painted here is Turner's most dramatic treatment of Stonehenge, showing a shepherd and some of his flock struck down by lightning, and his dog howling at the sky. John Ruskin surmised that Turner wished to make a point about God's vengeance on the false religion of Druidism, but it is more reasonable to suppose that Turner was reflecting the traditional associations of Stonehenge with the Sublime. Characteristically, he distorts and manipulates the monument's architectural features for effect as they compete with one of his most grandly conceived storm scenes.

The watercolour was engraved by Robert Wallis, and published in 1829. ss

167

Stonehenge
Richard Tongue (fl. 1835–1838)
c. 1837
Oil on canvas, 150 × 211 cm
British Museum, London
Selected references: Michell 1982, pp. 50–1; Evans 1994, p. 205, fig. 3; Evans 2000

The artist Richard Tongue of Bath, unlike many of his peers, specialised in reproducing ancient monuments. He advertised himself as a 'painter and modeller of megaliths' and examples of both have survived. Other prehistoric sites to inspire him include the Welsh burial chambers of Plas Newydd and Pentre Ifan (cat. 89), and the Tolmen, a natural phenomenon in Cornwall, then believed to be Druidic (cat. 90).

Stonehenge was presented to the British Museum by Tongue in 1837 with his painting of Plas Newydd, and a second, of the Tolmen, since lost. They indicate his attention to the atmospheric presentation of sites; each shows a different time of day, with Stonehenge representing noon. They were clearly intended to be displayed together and in order, with *Stonehenge* flanked either side by 'morning' and 'evening'. Emphasis was given to the central *Stonehenge* by its size, a third larger than the others, reflecting its superiority among Britain's ancient monuments. Tongue wrote to the British Museum in 1838 to complain that the paintings were not displayed above his models as he had intended.
JS/CE/PTC

168

Stonehenge
John Constable (1776–1837)
c. 1835
Watercolour, 38.7 × 59.7 cm
Victoria and Albert Museum, London.
Bequeathed by Isabel Constable,
daughter of the artist
Selected references: Hawes 1975;
Reynolds 1984; Smiles 1994

Constable exhibited this watercolour at the Royal Academy in 1836, accompanied by the following caption: 'The mysterious monument of Stonehenge, standing remote on a bare and boundless heath, as much unconnected with the events of past ages as it is with the uses of the present, carries you back beyond all historical record into the obscurity of a totally unknown period.'

Although Constable visited Stonehenge only once, on 15 July 1820, he was well informed about it. His patron, John Fisher, Bishop of Salisbury, was a friend of Sir Richard Colt Hoare, and Constable had visited Stourhead in 1811 at the time Colt Hoare was finishing his *History of Ancient Wiltshire*. By 1830 Constable was also acquainted with the topographer and antiquary John Britton and had a copy of Britton's *Wiltshire* (1814) in his library, providing him with a digest of the current theories on Stonehenge and its origins. In 1834 Constable wrote to Britton about treating Stonehenge 'poetically' to combat 'its literal representation as a "stone quarry" ' in the hands of antiquarian topographers. Allusions to time, decay and eternity may be read in the contrast between human and animal life, the stones, the storm and the rainbow. ss

244 | Making History

Stonehenge | 245

169

Stonehenge from the East
John William Inchbold (1830–1888)
1866–69
Oil on canvas, 85.1 × 181.6 cm
Society of Antiquaries of London,
Scharf Add.83
Selected references: Society of
Antiquaries of London 1916; Leeds
1993, pp. 60–1, no. 31

Inchbold was never a popular artist with the Royal Academy nor with the general public, but he enjoyed the admiration and friendship of a distinguished group of poets and connoisseurs, Alfred Lord Tennyson, John Ruskin and Algernon Charles Swinburne among them. He painted in the Pre-Raphaelite style and often chose rugged aspects of nature or the works of primitive people as his subjects. In describing this treatment of Stonehenge in a letter to the art critic and biographer W. M. Rossetti (brother of Dante Gabriel) on 10 May 1869 he says:

It is (as you also, I believe, know) literal as to state of this strange weird ruin at present. I have tried to secure architectural grandeur and natural sublimity, especially that religiousness by the introduction of the sun setting in the very centre of the altar-like portal; whilst the clouds are meant to suggest what is at once fiery and spiritual, the forms being (as often in nature) scarcely draped in cloudy matter. At the base is a barrow of the big past about which the ever lasting flowers are opening seed-petals to the wind.

The painting was presented to the Society by Sir Charles Holroyd, Director of the National Gallery, in June 1916. JS/PT-C

170

Plan of Stonehenge
William Matthew Flinders Petrie
(1853–1942)
1877
Pen and ink, 56 × 57.5 cm
Society of Antiquaries of London
Selected references: Petrie 1880;
Drower 1985; Cleal et al. 1995

In 1874, the young would-be archaeologist Flinders Petrie began a survey of English ancient monuments at Stonehenge with his father. Unhappy with the result, the son dragged the father back in 1877 and over six days completed one of the most detailed and precise plans ever made of the stones, using a surveying chain of his own design. He returned again with a ladder to measure the lintels, and, in 1880, to record the midsummer sunrise. In the same year Petrie began his survey of the pyramids at Giza. Petrie's final result was an accurate plan of Stonehenge with a numbering system he devised for the layout of all the Stonehenge stones, which is still in use today.

By estimating the date at which the midsummer sun would have appeared directly over the Heel Stone, Petrie proposed that Stonehenge was built in AD 730 (by a similar and equally flawed process, in 1906 the astronomer Sir Norman Lockyer came up with 1680 BC). Petrie said the circular ditch around the stones, to which little attention had previously been paid, was likely to have been the first structure to be built, followed by the Avenue earthwork, the sarsen stones and finally the bluestones. While we now know this to be only partly correct, the idea of a succession of phases (published with the plan in 1880) is fundamental to modern understanding of the site. ARP/MP

Stonehenge | 247

William Gowland's Excavation
CATALOGUE NUMBERS 171–172

171

(above)
Gowland raising leaning stones at Stonehenge
1901
Black-and-white photograph
Society of Antiquaries of London

172

(right)
Stone maul excavated at Stonehenge
Neolithic period
Sandstone, 13 × 19.5 × 21 cm
Society of Antiquaries of London,
LDSAL 866
Selected references: Gowland 1897;
Gowland 1902; Cleal et al. 1995,
pp. 9–12; Chippindale 2004, pp. 167–9;

On New Year's Eve 1899 three stones at Stonehenge collapsed. The Society of Antiquaries wrote to the owner, Sir Edward Antrobus, soon afterwards, offering to help in any future works, as he came under public pressure to make the monument safe. Antrobus proposed an advisory committee, which the Society chaired and which appointed Professor William Gowland (1842–1922), a mining engineer known as the father of Japanese archaeology, to undertake archaeological supervision.

Several restorations were planned, but only one implemented: the straightening of Stone 56, the tallest on site, which was leaning dangerously. Wrapped in a timber cradle, the stone was slowly winched upright a few inches at a time as cement was poured into the base. It was finally re-erected on 19 September 1901 in front of a large crowd.

Gowland opened a trench measuring 17 by 13 feet (about 5 by 4 metres) around the stone to record the archaeology, insisting that all material should be sieved. The work was distinguished not only by its high quality, but also Gowland's prompt and detailed publication of the results: they remain exceptional for Stonehenge to this day. He showed how the sarsens were set into the ground, and he proposed a construction date with which we would now agree: 'antecedent to the full development of the use of bronze if not to the neolithic age itself'. From the many small stone fragments he found, he argued that the megaliths were dressed on site: up to football-sized stones of a very hard type of sarsen were mauls used for that purpose. Heavy pounding reduced the mauls (such as this example donated to the Society with Gowland's bequest in 1925) to their rounded shapes, and the smooth faces and depressions on the megaliths may be signs of their use. ARP/JS/MP

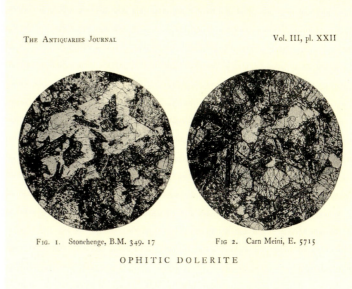

173

(above left)
Aerial photograph of Stonehenge
Philip Henry Sharpe
1906
Black and white photograph, 29 × 36 cm
Society of Antiquaries of London
Selected references: Capper 1907,
pp. 571–72; Chippindale 2004; Barber
2006, pp. 18–23

The year 2006 marked the centenary of the first aerial photograph of a British archaeological site: Stonehenge, shot from an Army reconnaissance balloon based at Bulford Camp on Salisbury Plain. The balloon section's officer in charge of photography was 2nd Lieutenant Philip Henry Sharpe, whose role was to test the military potential of photography from the air; Stonehenge was doubtless an easily identifiable target with which to experiment.

The balloon would have been tethered according to standard military procedure, connected to a winch a short distance south-west of the monument and allowed to drift over the site. The precise day the photographs were taken is not known (three prints survive), but parching in the grass suggests late September. Two images were displayed to the Society on 6 December by the commanding officer, Colonel John Edward Capper RE and were published the following year in *Archaeologia*.

Archaeological air photography, now an important, routine research and record procedure around the world, was inspired less by these Stonehenge shots than observations made from aircraft during and after the First World War. It was realised that archaeological sites that were scarcely visible on the ground could be more readily seen from the air. Influential among these discoveries was a continuation of the Stonehenge Avenue earthwork down to the River Avon, noticed in 1923 by O. G. S. Crawford, who became an influential figure in the field; and the discovery of nearby Woodhenge by Squadron-Leader Gilbert Insall in 1925. ARP/MP

174

(above right)
'Source of stones for Stonehenge determined' from *Antiquaries Journal*, 3
1923
Plate XXII in Thomas 1923
17 × 41 cm
Society of Antiquaries of London
Selected references: Thomas 1923, pp. 239–60, pls 21–22; Darvill and Wainwright 2005; Darvill 2006, pp. 136–41

Neither the larger Stonehenge stones (a hard sandstone known as sarsen) nor the smaller (mostly a range of igneous rocks known colloquially as bluestones) are today found on Salisbury Plain, perhaps the inspiration for the medieval idea of the monument's Irish origin. Surface boulders 18 miles (30 kilometres) to the north on the Marlborough Downs have, since at least the time of Pepys in 1665, been thought the likely source for the sarsens (though this has yet to be scientifically tested).

The first formal bluestone studies were conducted by the geologist N. S. Maskelyne in the 1870s, but it was not until 1920 that their origin, previously sought over much of highland Britain and even in Brittany, was traced by H. H. Thomas, petrographer to the Geological Society of London, to the Preseli Mountains in Pembrokeshire.

Thomas was confident that human labour could alone account for the bluestones at Stonehenge, and modern research supports him: but some find the idea that glaciers brought them from Wales (proposed by, among others, the geologist J. W. Judd, examining fragments from Gowland's excavations in 1901 [cats 171, 172]) hard to relinquish. The three main types of bluestone identified by Thomas – dolerite (occasionally spotted), rhyolite and volcanic ash – have since been traced specifically to outcrops on Carn Menyn. Geoffrey Wainwright and Timothy Darvill, current Fellows of the Society, are conducting an intensive survey of the Preseli landscape in search of quarries and abandoned megaliths.

Photographs of thin sections were published in the *Antiquaries Journal* with Thomas's article, showing the similarity between the dolerites and schists found at Stonehenge and 'Prescelly'. ARP/MP

Archaeological Reconstruction Drawings by Alan Sorrell (1904–1974)
CATALOGUE NUMBERS 175–178

Alan Sorrell was best known for his archaeological and historical reconstructions. Popular with archaeologists, with whom he worked closely to produce accurate interpretations of excavations, he placed sites in their contemporary landscapes, bringing them to life with people and incident. His first such work was for Southend Council in the 1930s. He continued for 40 years, depicting all eras of British history. ARP/MP/DG

175

(top)
Stonehenge: Transport of the Sarsens
c. 1958
Pen and ink on paper, 16.5 × 47.5 cm
The family of the late Alan Sorrell

176

(above left)
Stonehenge: Raising the Sarsens
c. 1958
Pen and ink on paper, 18.7 × 23.7 cm
The family of the late Alan Sorrell

177

(above right)
Stonehenge: The Final Stage
c. 1958
Pen and ink on paper, 195 × 237 mm
The family of the late Alan Sorrell

178

Sketchbook drawing for the raising of a large sarsen megalith
c. 1950s
Pen and ink on paper, 25 × 40.5 cm
The family of the late Alan Sorrell
Selected references: Atkinson 1959; Green and Sorrell 1971; Sorrell 1981; Pitts 2005, pp. 16–19

In the 1950s Alan Sorrell drew a significant set of Stonehenge studies that illustrated the monument's phases of construction as they were then understood. Commissioned first by the Ministry of Works in 1956, Sorrell was in continual consultation with Richard Atkinson (1920–1994), who co-directed major excavations at Stonehenge intermittently between 1950 and 1964. This marked an important step in confirming Sorrell's reputation as an archaeological reconstruction artist.

An initial painting of the final phase of Stonehenge was produced in 1957 for the Ministry of Works, and a further two commissions followed – one from *Life* magazine and the other from the Ministry – which brought to life Atkinson's idea of three phases of Stonehenge construction in quick succession. His sketches and diagrams were used alongside text by Atkinson in an official guide to Stonehenge and Avebury published in 1959. In later years, he illustrated school and popular history books, giving his work a broad appeal. ARP/MP/DG

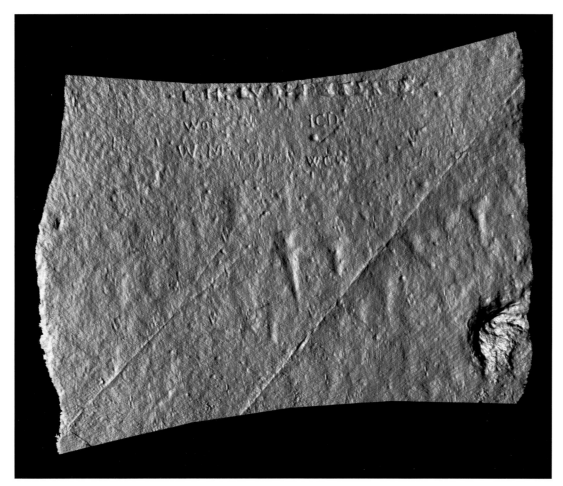

179

Aspects of Stonehenge revealed through LIDAR, high-resolution photography and laser scanning
Wessex Archaeology, Archaeoptics Ltd, and Spheroview
2003
Selected reference: Goskar et al. 2003, pp. 8–13

Rock 'art' (often no more than seemingly abstract dimples and grooves that can be difficult to date) is a feature of many prehistoric landscapes. The geology of southern England provides little opportunity for such art, but, while photographing some early graffiti on one of the Stonehenge trilithons in 1953, Richard Atkinson spotted a carved dagger. Subsequent searches revealed many carved axe blades, which, like the dagger, are broadly in an Early Bronze Age style. Despite various attempts with rubbings, latex moulds and stereoscopic photography, no full survey of these carvings has yet been carried out. A solution may lie in laser technology, which, in a trial by Wessex Archaeology and Archaeoptics Ltd in 2003, revealed axes invisible to the naked eye. Through the innovative use of software, a virtual light source was directed from multiple angles, and revealed the lost carvings, seen on the surface as shadows (left). Aside from showing up historic graffiti, detailed laser recording of the stones is also valuable in helping to understand the rate and extent of their erosion.

The image (trimmed to the left) shows a partial laser scan of stone 53. The left and right boundaries represent the edge(s) of the stone. Due to the convex and uneven shape of the stone and the fixed position of the scanner, the upper and lower limits of the scan data are not straight. The writing seen at the top of the image is eighteenth-century graffiti, which reads: 'IOH [Johan] LUD; [Ludvic] DEFERRE'.

The Environment Agency has recently surveyed the landscape surrounding Stonehenge from the air using LIDAR (airborne laser scanning). The high level of detail reveals aspects of historic land use that would otherwise have remained hidden (opposite top).

Stonehenge's iconic status makes it an extremely popular tourist attraction. Due to conservation concerns, access to the interior of the monument is highly restricted. However, through the use of a specialised SpheroCamHDR scanning camera, which produces high-resolution panoramic images, such as that produced by Spheroview (opposite bottom), it is possible for everyone to experience what it would be like to stand in the middle of Stonehenge.
SMC/ARP/MP/TG

Endnotes

Mists of Time
PAGES 17–35

Selected references: McKisack 1971; Ferguson 1979; Carley 1989; Ferguson 1993; Parry 1995; Woolf 2003.

Earliest Antiquaries
PAGES 37–49

Selected references: Douglas 1939; Fox 1956; Hunter 1975; Piggott 1976; Sharpe 1979; Mendyk 1989; Piggott 1989; Parry 1995; Woolf 2003.

Founders and Fellows
PAGES 53–67

1 Sweet 2004, pp. 81–7; MacGregor 2007; Evans 1956, pp. 33–60.
2 Clark 2000.
3 Haycock 2002; Piggott 1985; Sweet 2004, pp. 128–32.
4 Levine 1986, p. 21.
5 Pugh 1982, pp. 347–55; MacGregor 2007.
6 Sweet 2004, pp. 93–8.
7 Society of Antiquaries Minute Book, viii, pp. 103–6; Bodleian MS Eng Misc e 124, fol. 116; Sweet 2004, p. 302.
8 Sweet 2004, pp. 105–6.
9 Sweet 2004, pp. 31–3, 100.
10 Hingley 2007.
11 Ebbatson 1999; Levine 1986.
12 Torrens 1998.
13 Hingley 2007.

Collecting for Britain
PAGES 69–91

1 Nurse 2007.
2 Evans 1956, p. 43.
3 Lewis 2007. The drawings of portable antiquities were digitised between 2004 and 2006 and can be seen on the Society's website (www.sal.org.uk); the topographical collections are described in Barley 1974.
4 The household book of Edward IV (MS 211) given by Lyttelton was published by the Society in 1790; the *Winton Domesday* (MS 154) was published by the Record Commission in 1816; the inventory of Henry VIII (MS 129) had to wait until 1998.
5 Willetts 2000; the entries are also available on the National Archives A2A website.
6 Scharf 1865. The Society now possesses about 90 oil paintings, and a new catalogue is in preparation.
7 Pearce 2007.
8 Way 1847; de Cardi 1988. De Cardi's expansion of Way's catalogue comprised over 1,000 entries.
9 Stanhope 1861–64, 23 April 1863, pp. 256–7.
10 Lemon 1866.

Opening the Tomb
PAGES 95–107

1 Dodson 2004.
2 Christopher Scalia, 'The Grave Scholarship of Antiquaries', in *Literature Compass*, 2, part 1, RO, 166, 2005, pp. 1–13 (online journal).

Lost and Found
PAGES 109–121

1 Meaney 1964, pp. 121–2.
2 Rashleigh 1789, p. 187.
3 Gough 1787, pp. 116–19.
4 Anon. 1800, p. 410, pl. 27.
5 Evans 1956, p. 41.
6 Evans 1956, p. 182.
7 Wilson and Blunt 1961, pp. 75–122.
8 Franks 1880, pp. 251–66.
9 Graham-Campbell 2004, pp. 358–71.
10 Evans 1956, p. 270.

The Art of Recording
PAGES 123–141

1 Article VI: 'The Director shall Superintend and regulate all the Drawings, Prints, Plates and books of the Society and all their works of Printing, drawings or Engraving.' Evans, 1956, pp. 58–60.
2 SAL MS 268, p. 2. This is Stukeley's comment in his copy of the minutes and was inserted some time after 1726.
3 Gough 1768, p. xxix.
4 Nurse 2007, pp. 199–225.
5 The Bayeux Tapestry plates, engraved by Basire from 1819 to 1822, were reproduced in *Vetusta Monumenta* (1821–23). For information on, and illustrations of, Stothard's copies of wall paintings in the Painted Chamber at Westminster, see Binski, 1986, pp. 24–30.
6 Carter 1803, I, pp. 106–7.
7 Douglas 1793, p. 25.
8 Evans 1994, pp. 200–8.
9 Gilpin 1768, pp. 126–7. See also John Nichols's comment: 'Mr Vertue would have had more admirers as an engraver, if his style had been more spirited. But the Antiquary and the Historian, who prefer truth to elegance of design, and correctness to bold execution, have properly appreciated his works…', *Literary Anecdotes*, vol. 2, p. 254. Both references are cited in Myrone, 2007, pp. 99–121.
10 Gough 1786, p. 9.
11 Stothard 1817–32, p. 5.
12 In 1795 Moore also bought Turner's *Transept of Tintern Abbey, Monmouthshire* (c. 1794) from the Royal Academy exhibition but appears to have had no further contact with him. For Moore's patronage see Bell, 1917, pp. 47–83.
13 Woodbridge, 1970.
14 See Burnley, 1982.
15 Letter to Dawson Turner, 3 September 1841.
16 Kitson 1937, and Oppé 1942, pp. 163–6 and 169–71.
17 Pidgley 1972, pp. 780–6.

Bringing Truth to Light
PAGES 143–161

1 King 1784, p. 5, quoted by Sweet 2004, p. 101.
2 Sweet 2007 and Sweet 2004.
3 Evans 1956, p. 62, note 7.
4 For the Society's engravers and Stukeley's views see Myrone 2007. See also Myrone 1999.
5 Peltz 2004.
6 Stukeley 1724, preface: 'It is evident how proper engravings are to preserve the memory of things and how much better an idea they convey to the mind than written descriptions.' See also Evans 1956, p. 117, and Bruce-Mitford 1951, pp. 21–20.
7 For example, *Vetusta Monumenta*, vol. 1, plates 33, 42 and 48. See also Lolla 1999.
8 See especially *Vetusta Monumenta*, vol. 6, plate 43, for Margaret Stokes's copy of a page from the *Book of Kells*. See also fig. 30
9 BL Add MS 35615, fol. 45, letter to Lord Hardwicke, 25 September 1778.
10 BL Add MS 35608, fol. 370, letter to Lord Hardwicke, 12 June 1769; see also Sweet 2004, pp. 96–8.
11 Nurse 1989.
12 Sweet 2007.
13 Chambers 1791, p. 24. He claimed it would 'preserve the remembrance of an extraordinary style of building now fast sinking into oblivion, and, at the same time, publish to the world the riches of Britain in the splendour of her ancient structures'.
14 Crook 1995, p. 23; Carter 1803.
15 SAL Council Minutes, 10 May 1799, contains their progress report on the series and proposals for its future. For Wells see Rodwell and Leighton 2006.
16 Repton 1965 includes 'A note on the Cathedral Series' by the editor.
17 Evans 1956, p. 214; Crook 1995, p. 23.
18 Sweet 2004, p. 266; Britton 1850, part 2, pp. 72–85.

Antiquaries and the Arts
PAGES 165–181

1 Since their delivery between 1769 and 1790, Reynolds's *Discourses* have been printed many times. The standard edition is Reynolds 1959.
2 Robert Bowyer's History Gallery was established to commission pictures to be engraved for an illustrated edition of Hume's *History of England* (1754–62). After some success, the gallery closed in 1806. See Strong 1978, p. 13.
3 Rapin-Thoryas 1743–47. The plates drawn by George Vertue were engraved by himself, Charles Grignion and Hubert François Gravelot.
4 Meyrick and Shaw 1836, p. 2.
5 [Walpole] 1764. In the first edition, Walpole claimed that the novel was 'translated by William Marshall, Gent. from the original Italian of Onuphrio Muralto, Canon of St Nicholas, Otranto', a black-letter text printed in Naples in 1529. In the second edition of 1765 he abandoned this antiquarian *jeu d'esprit* and acknowledged authorship.
6 Scott's popular poems include *The Lay of the Last Minstrel* (1805) and *Marmion* (1808). *Waverley*, the first of the novels, appeared anonymously in 1814, followed by Waverly, the first of the novels appeared anonymously in 1814, followed by Guy Mannering (1815) and the Antiquary 1816.
7 William Powell Frith's most celebrated picture in this style was *Coming of Age in the Olden Time* (1848). He introduced many accurate costume details from books and, as he described in his memoirs, cobbled the architectural setting together from various illustrations in Joseph Nash's popular architectural volume, *The Mansions of England in the Olden Time*, London, 1839–49.
8 Strutt 1796–99; Planché 1834 (1847, 1874); Bonnard 1829–30; Fairholt 1846 (1860).
9 Brown exhibited the first version of Chaucer (Art Gallery of New South Wales, Sydney) at the Royal Academy of Arts, London, in 1851 to considerable acclaim; the second, smaller version (Tate, London) was painted between 1856 and 1868. The model for the figure of the poet was Dante Gabriel Rossetti.
10 Brown 1981.
11 For the figures of Edward III and the Black Prince, Brown consulted the illustrations of their tombs in Westminster and Canterbury in Stothard 1817–33, and Blore 1826.
12 See, for example, Brown 1981, p. 11: '27th Oct. 1847. Went out to seek for velvet and brocades, got some velvet to suit & an old yellow satin dress. Saw some fine old brocade told the Jew to bring it me to my study to bargain some old cloath against it' [*sic*].
13 Reynolds 1959: Discourse IV, 1771, p. 62.
14 Macaulay, 1849–61, vol. 1, p. 3.
15 Le Gallienne 1926, p. 12.
16 Quoted in Morris 1936, vol. 1, p. 148.

The Birth of Modern Archaeology
PAGES 185–199

1 Evans 1860, pp. 208–307; Evans 1956, pp. 281–5.
2 See, for example, Gruber 1965, pp. 373–402, and van Riper 1993. Falconer, 1863, pp. 459–60.
3 Pitt Rivers 1867, pp. lxxiv, lxxx and lxxxi; 1875, pp. 376–88, and 1883, p. 436; see also Bowden 1991, pp. 20–1, and Evans 2006, p. 966.

4 See, for example, Gruber 1965, pp. 373–402, and van Riper 1993.
5 See, for example, Evans 1956, pp. 280–1, and Levine 1986, p. 91.
6 Evans 1872 and 1881.
7 London 1873, and London 1874.
8 For example, Lubbock 1867, pp. 190–209; see also Chapman 1989, pp. 23–42, and Stocking 1987, pp. 150–6.
9 Chippindale 1983, pp. 1–55; Murray 1989, pp. 55–67.
10 Thompson 1977, p. 60.
11 Evans 2007.
12 Evans 1956, p. 364.
13 Greenwell 1877; Pitt Rivers 1887, 1892
14 Evans 2007.
15 See Bacon 1976.
16 Keller 1866.
17 Bulleid and St Gray 1911–17.
18 Wheeler 1943.
19 Lucas 2001, pp. 36–43.
20 Evans 1956, pp. 274, 306.
21 For example, George Fox and William St John Hope in *Archaeologia*, 54 and 57, 1895 and 1901, respectively; see also, for an overview, Boon 1974.
22 Evans 1989, p. 438.
23 Evans 1989, pp. 436–50.
24 Clark *et al.* 1935, pp. 283–319; see also Smith 1997, pp. 11–30.
25 Clark 1954.

Rescuing the Past
PAGES 201–213

1 Evans 1956 pp. 333, 365–6. See also Turner 2007.
2 Evans 1956, pp. 333–6, 369–70.
3 Hobley 1975; Kidd 1977.
4 Inwood 1998, p. 548.
5 Smith 1848–80, vol. 1, p. 4. Quoted in MacGregor 1998, p. 143.
6 Marsden 1996, p. 14.
7 Kidd 1977, pp. 112–13.
8 Merrifield 1965, p. 4; Sloane 2004, p. 10; Rhodes 2006.
9 Smith, *Retrospections*, vol. 2, p. 206; quoted in Kidd 1977, p. 115.
10 Letter by Augustus Wollaston Franks to Edward Hawkins, Keeper of the British Museum's Department of Antiquities, 5 March 1856. Quoted by Kidd 1977, p. 116.
11 Kidd 1977, p. 129.
12 MacGregor 1998, pp. 127–34.
13 *The Atlas*, 16 June 1855. Quoted in Kidd 1977, p. 129.
14 Evans 1956, pp. 362–63.
15 See, in this volume, Bernard Nurse, 'Collecting for Britain', pp. 68–91.
16 Anon. 1869, p. 550.
17 Merrifield 1965, p. 5.
18 Hope, second series, 1889–91, pp. 150 and 320–1.
19 Hope 1893.

Communicating the Past:
From the Earth to the Airwaves
PAGES 215–219

1 Membury 2002, pp. 9–13.
2 *The Times*, 17 March 1976, obituary of AVM3 series producer, Paul Johnstone.
3 Glob 1965.
4 For example, *Clementina* (BBC, 1954); *Adventures of Robin Hood* (ITV, 1955–60); *Adventures of Sir Lancelot* (ITV, 1956–57); *Buccaneers* (ITV, 1956–57); and *Sir Francis Drake* (ITV, 1961–62).
5 Norman 1983, p. 27.
6 Atkinson 1978.
7 See http://www.tvradiobits.co.uk/radiotimes/radiotimes68.htm.
8 For example, Kenneth Clark's *Civilisation* (BBC2, 1969); Alistair Cooke's *America* (BBC2, 1972–73); Jacob Bronowski's *Ascent of Man* (BBC2, 1973); and Jeremy Isaacs's *The World at War* (1973–74).

9 *Big Brother* (Channel 4, from 2000 and ongoing) is perhaps the best-known and longest-running of these, reminiscent of *Living in the Past* not least in its exploitation of public enthusiasm for witnessing scantily clad participants engaged in personal conflict.
10 Norman 1983, pp. 27–8.
11 See http://www3.open.ac.uk/media/fullstory.aspx?id=9376.
12 For example, the programme on Easter Island, broadcast in 1988.
13 Taylor 1998, pp. 8–18.
14 Holtorf 2006, pp. 39–43.
15 Norman 1983, pp. 28–32; Ascherson 2004, pp. 145–56.
16 Robinson was then already familiar to millions in a historical context from his portrayal of the dimly insightful and much-abused servant Baldrick in *Blackadder* (BBC1, 1983–89).
17 Evans 2006, p. 828.
18 For example, *Ground Force* (BBC2, later BBC1, 1997–2005).
19 For example, *Changing Rooms* (BBC2, later BBC1, 1996–2004).
20 See http://www.bbc.co.uk/history/programmes/restoration.

Stonehenge
PAGES 227–253

1 Greenway 1996, p. 559.
2 Greenway 1996, p. 23; he called it 'Stanenges'.
3 Chippindale 2004, pp. 24–7.
4 Thorpe 1966; Heck 2006 and 2006B.
5 Cleal et al. 1995.
6 Chippindale 2004.
7 Lubbock 1865.
8 Petrie 1880.
9 Gowland 1902.
10 Cleal et al. 1995, pp. 12–15.
11 Piggott 1956; Atkinson 1979; Pitts 2001.
12 Atkinson 1979, p. 196.
13 Chippindale 2004, p. 183.
14 See Darvill 2006 and Pitts 2001 for introductions.
15 Cleal et al. 1995, pp. 511–35.
16 The major precedent is *Visions of Stonehenge 1350–1987* with 112 works (Southampton City Art Gallery, September–October 1987, curated by Elizabeth Goodall and Barbara Milner, catalogue by Christopher Chippindale); *All About Stonehenge* (Wiltshire Heritage Museum, Devizes, July–August 2007) included some 40 Stonehenge depictions from the museum's own collection.
17 Crick 1991, p. 9 and personal communication.
18 Personal communication, Robin Taylor, English Heritage publishing manager; the book is now available by print on demand, one copy at a time.

Bibliography

Anglo 1961
Sydney Anglo, 'Archives of the English Tournament: Score Cheques and Lists', *Journal of the Society of Archivists*, 2, 1961, pp. 153–62

Anglo 1966
Sydney Anglo, 'The Hampton Court Painting of "The Field of Cloth of Gold" Considered as an Historical Document', *Antiquaries Journal*, 46, 1966, pp. 287–307

Anglo 1969
Sydney Anglo, *Spectacle, Pageantry and Early Tudor Policy*, Oxford, 1969

Anglo 1998
Sydney Anglo, 'The Coronation of Edward VI and Society of Antiquaries Manuscript 123', *Antiquaries Journal*, 78, 1998, pp. 452–57

Annable and Simpson 1964
F. K. Annable and D. D. A. Simpson, *Guide Catalogue of the Neolithic and Bronze Age Collections in Devizes Museum*, Devizes, 1964

Annesley and Whitehead 2006
Cressida Annesley and Peter Whitehead, 'The Vestments of a Medieval Archbishop', *Canterbury Cathedral Chronicle*, 2006, pp. 31–34

Anon. 1794
Anon., 'Spur Found in Towton Field Near York', *Archaeologia*, 11, 2nd edition, 1794, p. 433, Appendix, plate 20

Anon. 1800
Anon., 'Ancient Bronze Aeolipyle Found at Basingstoke', *Archaeologia*, 13, 1800, p. 410, plate 20

Anon. 1810
Anon., 'Presents to the Society', *Archaeologia*, 16, 1810, p. 372

Anon. 1869
Anon., 'Roman London', *Illustrated London News*, 1869, p. 550

Ascherson 2004
Neal Ascherson, 'Archaeology and the British Media', in Nick Merriman (ed.), *Public Archaeology*, London, 2004, pp. 145–58

Ashdown-Hill 2004
John Ashdown-Hill, 'The Bosworth Cross', *Transactions of the Leicestershire Archaeological and Historical Society*, 78, 2004, pp. 83–93

Aston 2000
Mick Aston, *Mick's Archaeology*, Stroud, 2000

Atkinson 1959
R. J. C. Atkinson, *Stonehenge and Avebury and Neighbouring Monuments: An Illustrated Guide*, London, 1959

Atkinson 1978
R. J. C. Atkinson, 'Silbury Hill' in Ray Sutcliffe (ed.) *Chronicle*, 1978, pp. 161–73

Atkinson 1979
R. J. C. Atkinson, *Stonehenge: Archaeology and Interpretation*, 3rd edition, Harmondsworth, 1979

Attenborough 2002
David Attenborough, *Life on Air: Memoirs of a Broadcaster*, London, 2002

Ayloffe 1775A
Joseph Ayloffe, 'An Account of the Body of King Edward the First, as it appeared on opening his tomb in the year 1774', *Archaeologia*, 3, 1775, pp. 376–413

Ayloffe 1775B
Joseph Ayloffe, 'An Historical Description of an Ancient Picture in Windsor Castle', *Archaeologia*, 3, 1775, pp. 185–229

Ayloffe 1775C
Joseph Ayloffe, 'An Account of Some Ancient English Historical Paintings at Cowdry, in Sussex', *Archaeologia*, 3, 1775, pp. 239–72

Ayloffe 1780
Joseph Ayloffe, 'An Account of Some Ancient Monuments in Westminster Abbey', *Vetusta Monumenta*, 2, 1780

Bacon 1976
Edward Bacon (ed.), *The Great Archaeologists: The Modern World's Discovery of Ancient Civilisations as Originally Reported in the Pages of 'The Illustrated London News' from 1842 to the Present Day*, London, 1976

Badham 2006
Sally Badham, '"Beautiful Remains of Antiquity": The Medieval Monuments of the Former Priory Church at Ingham, Norfolk. Part 1: The Lost Brasses', *Church Monuments*, 21, 2006, pp. 7–33

Badham 2007 forthcoming
Sally Badham, '"Beautiful Remains of Antiquity": The Medieval Monuments of the Former Priory Church at Ingham, Norfolk. Part 2: The High Tombs', *Church Monuments*, 22, 2007 forthcoming

Badham and Fiske 2002
Sally Badham and Ron Fiske, 'John Sell Cotman's Sepulchral Brasses of Norfolk and Suffolk', *Transactions of the Monumental Brass Society*, 16, 2002, pp. 500–45

Bagford 1715
John Bagford, 'A Letter to the Publisher', in Thomas Hearne (ed.), *Lelandi antiquarii de rebus Britanniciis collectanea*, Oxford, 1715, p. lxiii–lxv

Bakker 1979
J. A. Bakker, 'Lucas de Heere's Stonehenge', *Antiquity*, 53, 1979, pp. 107–11

Bann 1994
Stephen Bann, *Under the Sign: John Bargrave as Collector, Traveler, and Witness*, Ann Arbor, 1994

Barber 2003
Martyn Barber, *Bronze and the Bronze Age: Metalwork and Society in Britain c. 2500–800 BC*, Stroud, 2003

Barber 2006
Martyn Barber, 'Palaeolithic Contrivance over Stonehenge', *British Archaeology*, 89, 2006, pp. 18–23

Barbour 2003
Reid Barbour, *John Selden*, Toronto, 2003

Baring-Gould 1914
Sakine Baring-Gould, *The Lives of the Saints*, vol. 13 (November part 1), Edinburg 1914

Barley 1974
Maurice Willmore Barley, *A Guide to British Topographical Collections*, London, 1974

Beck and Shennan 1991
Curt Beck and Stephen Shennan, *Amber in Prehistoric Britain*, Oxbow Monographs, 8, Oxford, 1991

Belcher 1888
W. D Belcher, *Kentish Brasses*, London, 1888

Bell 1917
C. F. Bell, 'Fresh Light on Some Water-Colour Painters of the Old British School, Derived from the Collection and Papers of James Moore, F.S.A.', *Walpole Society Journal*, 5, 1917, pp. 47–83

Bennett 1999
Jim Bennett, 'John Dee and His *Holy Table*', *The Ashmolean*, 37, 1999, pp. 4–5

Bertram 1971
Jerome Bertram, *Brasses and Brass Rubbing in England*, Newton Abbot, 1971

Biddle 1976
Martin Biddle (ed.), *Winchester in the Early Middle Ages: An Edition and Discussion of the Winton Domesday*, Oxford, 1976

Binski 1986
Paul Binski, *The Painted Chamber at Westminster*, Society of Antiquaries of London Occasional Paper, New Series 9, London, 1986

Binski 1995
Paul Binski, *Westminster Abbey and the Plantagenets: Kingship and the Representation of Power 1200–1400*, New Haven and London, 1995

Birley 1964
Eric Birley, 'The Orton Scar Find and Thomas Reveley of Kendal', *Transactions of the Cumberland and Westmorland Antiquarian and Archaeological Society*, 64 (new series), 1964, pp. 81–89

Blackstone 1759
William Blackstone, *The Great Charter and Charter of the Forest: With Other Authentic Instruments: to which is prefixed an introductory discourse, containing the history of the charters*, Oxford, 1759

Blore 1826
Edward Blore, *The Monumental Remains of Noble and Eminent Persons, Comprising the Sepulchral Antiquities of Great Britain*, London, 1826

Bonnard 1829–30
Camille Bonnard, *Costumes des XIIIe, XIVe et XVe Siècles, Extraits des Monumens les plus Authentiques de Peinture et de Sculpture, avec un Texte Historique et Descriptif*, Paris, 1829–30

Boon 1974
George C. Boon, *Silchester, the Roman Town of Calleva*, Newton Abbot, 1974

Boud 1975
R. C. Boud, 'The Early Developments of British Geological Maps', *Imago Mundi*, 27, 1975, pp. 73–96

Bowden 1991
Mark C. B. Bowden, *Pitt-Rivers: The Life and Archaeological Work of Lieutenant-General Augustus Henry Lane Fox Pitt-Rivers, DCL, FRS, FSA*, Cambridge, 1991

Brailsford 1958
John William Brailsford, *Guide to the Antiquities of Roman Britain*, 2nd edition, London, 1958

Brand 1789
John Brand, 'The History and Antiquities of the Town and the County of the Town of Newcastle-upon-Tyne [...]', London, 1789

Bridgeford 2004
Andrew Bridgeford, *1066: The Hidden History of the Bayeux Tapestry*, London, 2004

Britton 1850
John Britton, *The Autobiography of John Britton*, London, 1850

Brown 1981
Ford Madox Brown, *The Diary of Ford Madox Brown*, Virginia Surtees (ed.), New Haven and London, 1981

Brown and Harriss 1999
J. E. T. Brown and G. L. Harriss, *The Scroll Considerans (Magdalen MS 248) Giving the Descent from Adam to Henry VI*, Magdalen Occasional Paper, 5, Oxford, 1999

Bruce 1875
John Collingwood Bruce, *Lapidarium Septentrionale: or, A Description of the Monuments of Roman Rule in the North of England*, London, 1875

Bruce-Mitford 1951
Rupert Bruce-Mitford, *The Society of Antiquaries of London, Notes on Its History and Possessions*, London, 1951

Bruce-Mitford and Raven 2005
Rupert Bruce-Mitford and Sheila Raven, *A Corpus of Late Celtic Hanging-Bowls with an Account of the Bowls Found in Scandinavia*, Oxford, 2005

Bullied and Gray 1911–17
Arthur Bullied and Harold St George Gray, *The Glastonbury Lake Village: A Full Description of the Excavations and the Relics Discovered, 1892–1907*, Glastonbury, 1911–17

Burl 2006
Aubrey Burl, *Stonehenge: A New History of the World's Greatest Stone Circle*, London, 2006

Burnley 1982
Turner and Dr Whitaker, Stanley Warburton and Susan Bourne (eds), exh. cat., Towneley Hall Art Gallery, Burnley, 1982

Bury 1949
Adrian Bury (ed.), *Rowlandson Drawings*, London, 1949

Butlin 1981
Martin Butlin, *The Paintings and Drawings of William Blake*, 2 vols, New Haven and London, 1981

Capper 1907
J. E. Capper, 'Photographs of Stonehenge as Seen from a War Balloon', *Archaeologia*, 60, 1907, pp. 571–72

Carley 1989
James P. Carley, 'John Leland and the Foundations of the Royal Library: The Westminster Inventory of 1542', *Bulletin of the Society for Renaissance Studies*, 7, 1989, pp. 13–22

Carter 1801
John Carter, *Some Account of the Cathedral Church of Durham: Illustrative of the Plans, Elevations, and Sections, of that Building*, London, 1801

Carter 1803
John Carter, 'Publication of Cathedrals by the Antiquarian Society', *Gentleman's Magazine*, 73 (1), 1803, pp. 106–07

Caudron 1975
Simone Caudron, 'Les Châsses de Reliquaires de Thomas Becket Emaillées à Limoges: Leur Géographie Historique', in Raymonde Foreville (ed.), *Thomas Becket: Actes du Colloque International de Sédières, 19–24 août 1973*, Paris, 1975

Chambers 1791
William Chambers, *Treatise on the Decorative Part of Civil Architecture*, London, 1791

Chandler 1993
John Chandler (ed.), *John Leland's Itinerary: Travels in Tudor England*, Stroud, 1993

Chapman 1989
William Chapman, 'The Organisational Context in the History of Archaeology: Pitt-Rivers and Other British Archaeologists in the 1860s', *Antiquaries Journal*, 59, 1989, pp. 23–42

Chippindale 1983
Christopher Chippindale, 'The Making of the First Ancient Monuments Act, 1882, and Its Administration under General Pitt-Rivers', *Journal of the British Archaeological Association*, 136, 1983, pp. 1–55

Chippindale 1985
Christopher Chippindale, 'John Britton's *Celtic Cabinet* in Devizes Museum and Its Context', *Antiquaries Journal*, 65, 1985, pp. 121–38

Chippindale 1986
Christopher Chippindale, 'Antiquarians and Druids. John Britton's *Celtic Cabinet*.', *Country Life*, September 1986, pp. 874–75

Chippindale 2004
Christopher Chippindale, *Stonehenge Complete*, 3rd edition, London, 2004

Clark 1954
Grahame Clark, *Excavations at Star Carr: An Early Mesolithic Site at Seamer near Scarborough, Yorkshire*, Cambridge, 1954

Clark 2000
Peter Clark, *British Clubs and Societies, 1580–1800: The Origins of an Associational World*, Oxford, 2000

Clark et al. 1935
J. G. D. Clark et al., 'Report on Excavations at Peacock's Farm, Shippea Hill, Cambridgeshire', *Antiquaries Journal*, 15, 1935, pp. 283–319

Clarke 1982
Giles Clarke, 'The Roman Villa at Woodchester', *Britannia*, 13, 1982, pp. 197–228

Clay 1941
Rotha Mary Clay, *Samuel Hieronymus Grimm of Burgdorf in Switzerland*, London, 1941

Cleal et al. 1995
Rosamund Cleal et al., *Stonehenge in Its Landscape: Twentieth-Century Excavations*, English Heritage Archaeological Report, 10, London, 1995

Coles 1962
John M. Coles, 'European Bronze Age Shields', *Proceedings of the Prehistoric Society*, 28 (new series), 1962, pp. 156–90

Coles et al. 1999
J. M. Coles et al., 'A Later Bronze Age Shield from South Cadbury, Somerset, England', *Antiquity*, 73, 1999, pp. 33–48

Colvin 1982
Howard M. Colvin (ed.), *The History of the King's Works*, 4 (part 2; 1485–1660), London, 1982

Comerford 1881
James W. Comerford, 'Exhibited and Presented … a Bronze Figure from a Crucifix', *Proceedings of the Society of Antiquaries of London*, 8 (2nd series), 1881, p. 541

Cook 2003
Jill Cook, 'The Discovery of British Antiquity', in K. Sloan and A. Burnett (eds), *Enlightenment: Discovering the World in the Eighteenth Century*, London, 2003, pp. 178–91

Combe 1814–16
William Combe, *English Dance of Death*, London 1814–16

Cormack 1975
Malcolm Cormack, *J. M. W. Turner RA (1775–1851): A Catalogue of Drawings and Watercolours in the Fitzwilliam Museum*, Cambridge, Cambridge, 1975

Cotman 1819
John Sell Cotman, *Engravings of the Most Remarkable of the Sepulchral Brasses in Norfolk*, 1st edition, London, 1819

Crick 1991
Julia C. Crick, *The 'Historia Regum Britannicae' of Geoffrey of Monmouth 4: Dissemination and Reception in the Middle Ages*, Cambridge, 1991

Crook 1995
J. Mordaunt Crook, *John Carter and the Mind of the Gothic Revival*, Society of Antiquaries of London Occasional Paper, New Series 17, London, 1995

Cross 1961
Frank Leslie Cross, *The Oxford Dictionary of the Christian Church*, 3rd edition, Oxford, 1961

Cruikshank 1812
George Cruikshank, *The Scourge*, 3, 1812

Cunnington 1806
William Cunnington, 'Account of Tumuli Opened in Wiltshire: in Three Letters From Mr William Cunnington to Aylmer Bourke Lambert', *Archaeologia*, 15, 1806, pp. 122–29

Daniel 1981
Glyn Daniel, *A Short History of Archaeology*, London, 1981

Darvill 2006
Timothy Darvill, *Stonehenge: The Biography of a Landscape*, Stroud, 2006

Darvill and Wainwright 2005
Timothy Darvill and Geoffrey Wainwright, 'Beyond Stonehenge: Carn Menyn and the Bluestones', *British Archaeology*, 83, 2005, pp. 28–31

Davis 1977
Godfrey Rupert Carless Davis, *Magna Carta*, London, 1977

de Cardi 1988
Beatrice de Cardi, 'Miscellaneous Collections in the Possession of the Society of Antiquaries of London', *Antiquaries Journal*, 68, 1988, pp. 287–90

Deacon 1968
Richard Deacon, *John Dee: Scientist, Geographer, Astrologer and Secret Agent to Elizabeth I*, London, 1968

Dee 1659
John Dee, *A True and Faithful Relation of what Passed for Many Years Between Dr John Dee and Some Spirits*, Méric Casaubon (ed.), London, 1659

Ditchfield 1889–91
Peter H. Ditchfield, *The Quarterly Journal of the Berks Archaeological and Architectural Society*, 1, 1889–91

Dodson 2004
Aidan Dodson, *The Royal Tombs of Great Britain: An Illustrated History*, London, 2004

Dolman 2003
Brett Dolman, '"Everything Curious": Samuel Hieronymous Grimm and Sir Richard Kaye', *Electronic British Library Journal*, London, 2003, http://www.bl.uk/collections/eblj/2003/pdfarticles/article2.pdf, Article 2

Douglas 1793
James Douglas, *Nenia Britannica: or, A Sepulchral History of Great Britain; From the Earliest Period to Its General Conversion to Christianity*, London, 1793

Douglas 1939
David Douglas, *English Scholars*, London, 1939

Drower 1985
Margaret Drower, *Flinders Petrie: A Life in Archaeology*, London, 1985

Dufty 1985
Arthur Richard Dufty, *Morris Embroideries: The Prototypes*, London, 1985

Ebbatson 1999
Linda Ebbatson, *Condition of the Emergence and Existence of Archaeology in the Nineteenth Century: The Royal Archaeological Institute*, Durham, University of Durham PhD thesis, 1999, unpublished

Edwards 1992
B. J. N. Edwards, *The Ribchester Hoard*, Preston, 1992

Edwards 2004
N. Edwards, 'Webster, Thomas (1772–1844)', *Oxford Dictionary of National Biography*, Oxford, 2004, http://www.oxforddnb.com/view/article/28945

Emanuel 2000
Raphael Ralph Emanuel, 'The Society of Antiquaries' Sabbath Lamp', *Antiquaries Journal*, 80, 2000, pp. 309–15

Evans 1860
John Evans, 'On the Occurrence of Flint Implements in Undisturbed Beds of Gravel, Sand, and Clay: Read June 2, 1859', *Archaeologia*, 38, 1860, pp. 280–307

Evans 1872
John Evans, *The Ancient Stone Implements, Weapons and Ornaments of Great Britain*, London, 1872

Evans 1881
John Evans, *The Ancient Bronze Implements, Weapons, and Ornaments of Great Britain and Ireland*, London, 1881

Evans 1889–91
John Evans, 'Anniversary Address 23 April 1891', *Proceedings of the Society of Antiquaries of London*, 13 (2nd Series), 1889–91, pp. 320–21

Evans 1956
Joan Evans, *A History of the Society of Antiquaries*, Oxford, 1956

Evans 1994
Christopher Evans, 'Natural Wonders and National Monuments: A Meditation Upon the Fate of The Tolmen', *Antiquity*, 68, 1994, pp. 200–08

Evans 1989
Christopher Evans, 'Archaeology and Modern Times: Berou's Woodbury 1938/39', *Antiquity*, 63, 1989, pp. 436–50

Evans 2000
Christopher Evans, 'Megalithic Follies: Soane's "Druidic Remains" and the Display of Monuments', *Journal of Material Culture*, 5 (3), 2000, pp. 347–66

Evans 2004
Christopher Evans, 'Modelling Monuments and Excavations', in S. de Chadarevian and N. Hopwood (eds), *Models: The Third Dimension of Science*, Stanford, 2004, pp. 109–37

Evans 2006
Christopher Evans, 'Engineering the Past: Pitt-Rivers, Nemo and The Needle', *Antiquity*, 80, 2006, pp. 960–69

Evans 2006
Jeff Evans, *The Penguin TV Companion*, 3rd edition, London, 2006

Evans 2007
Christopher Evans, '"Delineating Objects": Nineteenth-Century Antiquarian Culture and the Project of Archaeology', in Susan Pearce (ed.), *Visions of Antiquity: The Society of Antiquaries of London 1707–2007*, London, 2007, pp. 267–305

Fairholt 1846
Frederick William Fairholt, *Costume in England: A History of Dress From the Earliest Period Until the Close of the Eighteenth Century*, London, 1846

Falconer 1863
M. Falconer, 'Primeval Man: What led to the question', *Athenaeum*, 41, 1863, pp. 459–60

Falk 1949
Bernard Falk, *Thomas Rowlandson: His Life and Art. A Documentary Record … with … Illustrations*, London, 1949

Farington 1978
Joseph Farington, *The Diary of Joseph Farington*, 4, Kenneth Garlick, Angus Macintyre and Kathryn Cave (eds), New Haven and London, 1978

Ferguson 1979
Arthur B. Ferguson, *Clio Unbound: Perception of the Social and Cultural Past in Renaissance England*, Durham NC, 1979

Ferguson 1993
Arthur B. Ferguson, *Utter Antiquity: Perceptions of Prehistory in Renaissance England*, Duke University Press, 1993

Fiske 2000
R. Fiske, 'Heraldry in an Indecorous Age', *The Norfolk Standard*, 1 (9), 2000, pp. 133–34

Forrester 1996
Gillian Forrester, *Turner's "Drawing Book": The Liber Studiorum*, London, 1996

Fox 1956
Levi Fox (ed.), *English Historical Scholarship in the Sixteenth and Seventeenth Centuries: A Record of the Papers Delivered at a Conference Arranged by the Dugdale Society to Commemorate the Tercentenary of the Publication of Dugdale's 'Antiquities of Warwickshire'*, London and New York, 1956

Fox and Hope 1895
George Edward Fox and William H. St John Hope, 'Excavations on the Site of the Roman City of Silchester, Hants, in 1893', *Archaeologia*, 54, 1895, pp. 199–238

Fox and Hope 1901
George Edward Fox and William H. St John Hope, 'Excavations on the Site of the Roman City of Silchester, Hants, in 1899', *Archaeologia*, 57 (1), 1901, pp. 87–112

Franks 1880
Augustus Wollaston Franks, 'Notes on a Sword Found in Cotterdale, Yorkshire, Exhibited by Lord Wharncliffe, and on Other Examples of the Same Kind', *Archaeologia*, 45, 1880, pp. 251–66

Freeman 2004
Michael Freeman, *Victorians and the Prehistoric: Tracks to a Lost World*, New Haven and London, 2004

French 1972
Peter J. French, *John Dee: The World of an Elizabethan Magus*, London, 1972

Frere 1800
John Frere, 'Account of Flint Weapons Discovered at Hoxne in Suffolk', *Archaeologia*, 13, 1800, pp. 204–05

Gage 1965
John Gage, 'Turner and the Picturesque', *Burlington Magazine*, 107 (742), 1965, pp. 16–25

Gaimster 1997
David Gaimster, *German Stoneware 1200–1900: Archaeology and Cultural History*, London, 1997

Gascoigne 1994
John Gascoigne, *Joseph Banks and the English Enlightenment: Useful Knowledge and Polite Culture*, Cambridge, 1994

Gatch 1986
Milton McCormick Gatch, 'John Bagford, Bookseller and Antiquary', *The British Library Journal*, 12 (2), 1986, pp. 150–171

George 1949
Marie Dorothy George, *Catalogue of Prints and Drawings in the British Museum*, 9, no. 11952, 1949

Gilpin 1768
William Gilpin, *An Essay Upon Prints: Containing Remarks upon the Principles of Picturesque Beauty, the Different Kinds of Prints, and the Characters of the Most Noted Masters; Illustrated by Criticisms Upon Particular Pieces; to Which Are Added, Some Cautions That May be Useful in Collecting Prints*, London, 1768

Girtin and Loshak 1954
Thomas Girtin and David Loshak, *The Art of Thomas Girtin*, London, 1954

Glob 1965
P. R. Glob, *The Bog People: Iron Age Man Preserved*, New York, 1965 (English translation in 1969, Faber & Faber, London)

Gordon 1932
Huntly S. Gordon, *Prae Wood and Verulamium, St Alban's, 1930–1932, Personal Notes and Correspondence*, Dorset County Museum Accession 2001.18. 3, Dorchester, 1932

Gordon 1950
Huntly S. Gordon, *The Survey of an Archaeological Site, 9th May 1950, With Annotations by HSG, Prepared for a Field Trip for London Transport to St Albans, May 1950*, Dorset County Museum Accession 2001.18.6., Dorchester, 1950

Gordon 1967
Huntly S. Gordon, *The Unreturning Army: A Field Gunner in Flanders, 1917–1918*, London, 1967

Goskar et al. 2003
Thomas Goskar et al., 'The Stonehenge Laser Show', *British Archaeology*, 73, 2003

Gough 1768
Richard Gough, *Anecdotes of British Topography; or, An Historical Account of What has been Done for Illustrating the Topographical Antiquities of Great Britain and Ireland*, London, 1768

Gough 1779
Richard Gough, 'Introduction: Containing an Historical Account of the Origin and Establishment of the Society of Antiquaries', *Archaeologia*, 1, 2nd edition, 1779, p. i–xliii

Gough 1786
Richard Gough, *Sepulchral Monuments in Great Britain: Applied to Illustrate the History of Families, Manners, Habits and Arts, at the Different Periods from the Norman Conquest to the Seventeenth Century*, vol. 1, part 1, as p. 105, London, 1786

Gough 1787
Richard Gough, 'Account of the Discoveries in Digging a Sewer in Lombard-Street and Birchin-Lane, 1786. In a Letter to Mr Gough, Communicated by Him', *Archaeologia*, 8, 1787, pp. 116–26

Gough 1796
Richard Gough, *Sepulchral Monuments in Great Britain: Applied to Illustrate the History of Families, Manners, Habits and Arts, at the Different Periods from the Norman Conquest to the Seventeenth Century*, vol. 2, part I, as p. 107, London, 1796

Gowland 1897
William Gowland, 'The Dolmens and Burial Mounds in Japan', *Archaeologia*, 55, 1897, pp. 439–524

Gowland 1902
William Gowland, 'Recent Excavations at Stonehenge', *Archaeologia*, 58, 1902, pp. 37–105

Graham-Campbell 1974
James Graham-Campbell, 'A Viking Hoard from Ireland', *Antiquaries Journal*, 54, 1974, pp. 269–72

Graham-Campbell 1975
James Graham-Campbell, 'Bossed Penannular Brooches: A Review of Recent Research', *Medieval Archaeology*, 19, 1975, pp. 33–47

Graham-Campbell 1980
James Graham-Campbell, *Viking Artefacts: A Select Catalogue*, London, 1980

Graham-Campbell 1992
James Graham-Campbell, *Viking Treasure from the North West: The Cuerdale Hoard in Its Context*, Liverpool, 1992

Graham-Campbell 2004
James Graham-Campbell, 'On the Witham Bowl', *Antiquaries Journal*, 84, 2004, pp. 358–71

Gravett 2003
Christopher Gravett, *Towton 1461: England's Bloodiest Battle*, Oxford, 2003

Green and Sorrell 1971
Barbara Green and Alan Sorrell, *Prehistoric Britain*, London, 1971

Greene 2002
Kevin Greene, *Archaeology: An Introduction*, 4th edition, London, 2002

Greenway 1996
Diana E. Greenway (ed.), *Historia Anglorum: The History of the English People by Henry of Huntingdon, 1084?–1155*, Oxford, 1996

Greenwell 1877
William Greenwell, *British Barrows: A Record of the Examination of Sepulchral Mounds in Various Parts of England*, Oxford, 1877

Grose 1792
Francis Grose, *The Olio: Being a Collection of Essays, Dialogues, Letters, Biographical Sketches, Anecdotes, Pieces of Poetry, Parodies, Bon Mots, Epigrams, Epitaphs, &c., Chiefly Original*, London, 1792

Gruber 1965
J. W. Gruber, 'Brixham Cave and the Antiquity of Man', in Melford E. Spiro (ed.), *Context and Meaning in Cultural Anthropology: In Honor of A. Irving Hallowell*, London, 1965, pp. 373–402

Hamper 1827
William Hamper (ed.), *The Life, Diary and Correspondence of Sir William Dugdale*, London, 1827

Harmsen 2000
Theodor Harmsen, *Antiquarianism in the Augustan Age: Thomas Hearne 1678–1735*, Oxford, 2000

Harmsen 2004
Theodor Harmsen, 'Bagford, John (1650/51–1716)', *Oxford Dictionary of National Biography*, Oxford, 2004, http://www.oxforddnb.com/view/article/1030

Harris 1984
Jennifer Harris, 'Jane Morris's Jewel Casket', *Antique Collector*, 12, 1984, pp. 68–71

Hawes 1975
Louis Hawes, *Constable's Stonehenge*, London, 1975

Hawkes 1982
Jacquetta Hawkes, *Mortimer Wheeler: Adventurer in Archaeology*, London, 1982

Hawkes 1990
Sonia Chadwick Hawkes, 'Bryan Faussett and the Faussett Collection: An Assessment', in Edmund Southworth (ed.), *Anglo Saxon Cemeteries: A Reappraisal*, Stroud, 1990, pp. 1–24

Hay 1977
Denys Hay, *Annalists and Historians: Western Historiography from the Eighth to the Eighteenth Centuries*, London, 1977

Haycock 2002
David Boyd Haycock, *William Stukeley: Science, Religion and Archaeology in Eighteenth-Century England*, Woodbridge, 2002

Haycock 2004
David Boyd Haycock, 'Stukeley, William (1687–1765)', *Oxford Dictionary of National Biography*, Oxford, 2004, http://www.oxforddnb.com/view/article/26743

Hayward 1996
Maria Hayward, 'Luxury or Magnificence? Dress at the Court of Henry VIII', *Costume*, 30, 1996, pp. 37–46

Hayward 2007
Maria Hayward, *Dress at the Court of Henry VIII*, Leeds, 2007

Hearne 1773
Thomas Hearne, *A Collection of Curious Discourses Written by Eminent Antiquaries Upon Several Heads in our English Antiquities*, London, 1773

Heck 2006A
Christian Heck, 'Histoire Mythique et Archéologie au Quinzième Siècle: Une Représentation Inédite de Stonehenge', in J. F. Hamburger and A. S. Korteweg (eds), *Circumdederunt Me Amici Multi: A Tribute to James Marrow from His Friends*, Belgium, 2006, pp. 253–60

Heck 2006B
Christian Heck, 'A New Medieval View of Stonehenge', *British Archaeology*, 92, 2006, pp. 10–15

Helgerson 1992
Richard Helgerson, *Forms of Nationhood: The Elizabethan Writing of England*, Chicago and London, 1992

Henderson 1967
Philip Henderson, *William Morris: His Life, Work and Friends*, London, 1967

Hepburn 1986
Frederick Hepburn, *Portraits of the Later Plantagenets*, Woodbridge, 1986

Hewitt 1995
D. Hewitt, 'Essay on the Text', in D. Hewitt (ed.), *The Edinburgh Edition of the Waverly Novels: Walter Scott: The Antiquary*, Edinburgh, 1995

Hibbs 1985
James Hibbs, 'Little Master Stonehenge: A Study of the Megalithic Monument from Le Mont de la Ville, Saint Helier', *Annual Bulletin Société Jersiaise*, 24 (part 1), 1985, pp. 49–74

Hicks 2006
Carola Hicks, *The Bayeux Tapestry: The Life Story of a Masterpiece*, London, 2006

Hill 2004
David Hill, 'The Bayeux Tapestry: The Establishment of a Text', in Pierre Bouet, Brian Levy and Francois Neveux (eds), *The Bayeux Tapestry: Embroidering the Facts of History*, Caen, 2004, pp. 383–401

Hingley 2007
Richard Hingley, 'The Society, Its Council, the Membership and Publications from 1820 to 1850', in Susan Pearce (ed.), *Visions of Antiquity: The Society of Antiquaries of London 1707–2007*, London, 2007, pp. 173–97

Hinton 2005
David Alban Hinton, *Gold and Gilt, Pots and Pins: Possessions and People in Medieval Britain*, Oxford and New York, 2005

Hoare 1812
Sir Richard Colt Hoare, *The Ancient History of Wiltshire*, 2 vols, London, 1812–19

Hobley 1975
B. Hobley, 'Charles Roach Smith (1807–1890): Pioneer Rescue Archaeologist', *London Archaeologist*, 2 (13), 1975, pp. 328–33

Hodgson 1913
John Crawford Hodgson, 'History of the Society, 1813–1913', *Archaeologia Aeliana*, 10 (3rd series), 1913, pp. 1–5

Holt 1969
James Clarke Holt, *Magna Carta*, Cambridge, 1969

Holtorf 2006
Cornelius Holtorf, *Archaeology Is a Brand! The Meaning of Archaeology in Contemporary Culture*, Oxford, 2006

Hope 1889–91
William H. St John Hope, 'Thursday 1 May 1890, William H. St John Hope Read a Paper Descriptive of the Contents of the Archbishops Tomb', *Proceedings of the Society of Antiquaries of London*, 13 (2nd series), 1889–91, p. 150

Hope 1893
William H. St John Hope, 'On the Tomb of an Archbishop Recently Opened in the Cathedral Church of Canterbury', *Vetusta Monumenta*, 7 (part 1), 1893

Hope 1919
William H. St John Hope, *Cowdray and Easthourne Priory in the County of Sussex*, London, 1919

Hourihane 2005
Colum Hourihane, *The Processional Cross in Late Medieval England: The 'Dallye Cross'*, Reports of the Research Committee of the Society of Antiquaries of London, 71, London, 2005

Howe 2001
Emily Howe, 'Divine Kingship and Dynastic Display: The Altar Wall Murals of St Stephen's Chapel, Westminster', *Antiquaries Journal*, 81, 2001, pp. 259–303

Hudson 1981
Kenneth Hudson, *A Social History of Archaeology: The British Experience*, London, 1981

Hunter 1975
Michael Hunter, *John Aubrey and the Realm of Learning*, London, 1975

Ibbetson 2004
David Ibbetson, 'Doddridge, Sir John (1555–1628)', *Oxford Dictionary of National Biography*, Oxford, 2004

Inwood 1998
Stephen Inwood, *A History of London*, London, 1998

Jackson and Craddock 1995
R. P. Jackson and P. T. Craddock, 'The Ribchester Hoard: A Descriptive and Technical Study', in Barry Raftery (ed.), *Sites and Sights of the Iron Age: Essays on Fieldwork and Museum Research Presented to Ian Mathieson Stead*, Oxford, 1995, pp. 75–102

Jessup 1975
Ronald Jessup, *Man of Many Talents: An Informal Biography of James Douglas 1753–1819*, London, 1975

Jury 2007
Louise Jury, 'Paintings Show Royal Ring that was Lost to History', *The Independent*, 19 March 2007, p. 22

Johnson 1966
Robert C. Johnson, 'The Lotteries of the Virginia Company 1612–21', *Virginia Magazine of History and Biography*, 74, 1966, pp. 259–92

Johnstone 1957
Paul Johnstone, *Buried Treasure*, London, 1957

Keller 1866
Ferdinand Keller, *The Lake Dwellings of Switzerland*, 1st edition, John Edward Lee (ed.), London, 1866

Kempe 1830
Alfred John Kempe, 'Description of Some Ancient Paintings on Panel in Baston House, Kent', *Gentleman's Magazine*, 100 (2), 1830, pp. 497–502

Kendrick 1950
Thomas Downing Kendrick, *British Antiquity*, London, 1950

Keynes 1996
Simon Keynes, 'The Reconstruction of a Burnt Cottonian Manuscript: The Case of Cotton MS. Otho A.1', *British Library Journal*, 22 (2), 1996, pp. 126–29

Kidd 1977
Dafydd Kidd, 'Charles Roach Smith and His Museum of London Antiquities', *British Museum Yearbook*, 2, 1977, pp. 105–36

King 1784
Edward King, *A Speech Delivered by E. King, Esq., President of the Society of Antiquaries of London*, London, 1784

Kirk 2005
Shelia Kirk, *Philip Webb: Pioneer of Arts and Crafts Architecture*, Chichester, 2005

Kitson 1937
Sydney Kitson, *The Life of John Sell Cotman*, London, 1937

Knox 2003
Tim Knox, 'The Vyne Ramesses: "Egyptian Monstrosities" in British country house collections', *Apollo*, 494, 2003, pp. 32–38

Lack et al. 1993
William Lack et al., *The Monumental Brasses of Berkshire*, London, 1993

Laking 1920
G. F. Laking, *A Record of European Armour and Arms through Seven Centuries*, vol. 2, London, 1920, cat. 524

Lankester 2004
Philip Lankester, 'Charles Stothard's Drawings for "The Monumental Effigies of Great Britain"', *Church Monuments Society Newsletter*, 20 (1), 2004, pp. 6–9

Latham and Matthews 1976
Robert Latham and William Matthews (eds), *The Diary of Samuel Pepys*, vol. 9, Berkeley, 1976

Le Gallienne 1926
Richard Le Gallienne, *The Romantic Nineties*, London, 1926

Leeds 1993
John William Inchbold: Pre-Raphaelite Landscape Artist, Christopher Newell (ed.), exh. cat., City Art Gallery, Leeds, 1993

Lemon 1866
Robert Lemon, *Catalogue of a Collection of Printed Broadsides in the Possession of the Society of Antiquaries of London*, London, 1866

Lethaby 1935
William Richard Lethaby, *Philip Webb and His Work*, London, 1935

Levine 1986
Philippa Levine, *The Amateur and the Professional: Antiquarians, Historians and Archaeologists in Victorian England, 1838–1886*, Cambridge, 1986

Lewis 2007 forthcoming
Elizabeth Lewis, 'Drawings of Antiquities in the Society's Albums, c. 1750–1860', *Antiquaries Journal*, 87, 2007 forthcoming

Limoges 1999
Valérie et Thomas Becket: de l'influence des Princes Plantagenêt dans l'Oeuvre de Limoges, Bernadette Barrière, Jean-Loup Lemaître, Geneviève François, Simone Caudron and Véronique Notin (eds), exh. cat., Musée municipal de l'Evêché/Musée de l'Email, Limoges, 1999

Liverpool 2003
Dante Gabriel Rossetti, Julian Treuherz, Elisabeth Prettejohn and Edwin Becker (eds), exh. cat., Walker Art Gallery, Liverpool, 2003

Llandudno 1984
Turner in Wales, Andrew Wilton (ed.), exh. cat., Mostyn Art Gallery, Llandudno, 1984

Lolla 1999
Maria Grazia Lolla, 'Ceci n'est pas un Monument: *Vetusta Monumenta* and Antiquarian Aesthetics', in Martin Myrone and Lucy Peltz (eds), *Producing the Past: Aspects of Antiquarian Culture and Practice 1700–1850*, Aldershot, 1999, pp. 15–34

London 1873
Exhibition of Bronze Implements and Weapons, exh. cat., Society of Antiquaries of London, 1873

London 1874
Exhibition of Palaeolithic and Neolithic Implements and Weapons, exh. cat., Society of Antiquaries of London, 1874

London 1934
Commemorative Catalogue of the Exhibition of British Art, exh. cat., Royal Academy of Arts, London, 1934

London 1976
William Caxton: An Exhibition to Commemorate the Quincentenary of the Introduction of Printing into England, Janet Backhouse, Mirjam Foot and John Barr (eds), exh. cat., British Library, London, 1976

London 1977
Richard III, Pamela Tudor-Craig (ed.), exh. cat., National Portrait Gallery, London, 1977

London 1984
English Romanesque Art 1066–1200, G. Zarnecki, J. Holt and T. Holland (eds), exh. cat., Hayward Gallery, London, 1984

London 1987A
The Age of Chivalry: Art in Plantagenet England, 1200–1400, Jonathan Alexander and Paul Binski (eds), exh. cat., Royal Academy of Arts, London, 1987

London 1987B
Manners and Morals: Hogarth and British Painting 1700–1760, Elizabeth Einberg (ed.), exh. cat, Tate Gallery, London, 1987

London 1991
The Making of England: Anglo-Saxon Art and Culture: AD 600–900, Leslie Webster and Janet Backhouse (eds), exh. cat., British Museum, London, 1991

London 1996
William Morris, Linda Parry (ed.), exh. cat., Victoria and Albert Museum, London, 1996

London 2002
Thomas Girtin: The Art of Watercolour, Greg Smith (ed.), exh. cat., Tate Britain, London, 2002

London 2003A
Elizabeth, Susan Doran (ed.), exh. cat., National Maritime Museum, 2003

London 2003B
Gothic: Art for England, 1400–1547, Richard Marks and Paul Williamson (eds), exh. cat., Victoria and Albert Museum, London, 2003

London 2007
Lost Faces: Identity and Discovery in Tudor Royal Portraiture, David Starkey and Bendor Grosvenor (eds), London, 2007

Lubbock 1865
John Lubbock, *Pre-historic Times: As Illustrated by Ancient Remains, and the Manners and Customs of Modern Savages*, London, 1865

Lubbock 1867
John Lubbock, 'Address Delivered to the Section of "Primeval Antiquities" at the London Meeting of the Archaeological Institute, July 1866', *Archaeological Journal*, 23, 1867, pp. 190–209

Lucas 2001
Gavin Lucas, *Critical Approaches to Fieldwork: Contemporary and Historical Archaeological Practice*, London, 2001

Lyons 1917–18
George Babington Croft Lyons, 'Address, Thursday 6 June 1918', *Proceedings of the Society of Antiquaries of London*, 30 (2nd series), 1917–18, p. 224

Lysons 1792–96
Daniel Lysons, *The Environs of London: Being an Historical Account of the Towns, Villages, and Hamlets, within Twelve Miles of that Capital: Interspersed with Biographical Anecdotes*, London, 1792–96

Lysons 1797
Samuel Lysons, *An Account of Roman Antiquities Discovered at Woodchester in the County of Gloucester*, London, 1797

Macaulay 1849–61
Thomas Babington Macaulay, *The History of England from the Accession of James II*, 1, New York, 1849–61

MacGregor 1994
Arthur MacGregor (ed.), *Sir Hans Sloane, Collector, Scientist, Antiquary, Founding Father of the British Museum*, London, 1994

MacGregor 1998
Arthur MacGregor, 'Antiquity Inventoried: Museums and "National Antiquities" in the Mid-Nineteenth Century', in Vanessa Brand (ed.), *The Study of the Past in the Victorian Age*, Oxbow Monographs, Oxford, 1998, pp. 125–37

MacGregor 2007
Arthur MacGregor, 'Forming an Identity: The Early Society and Its Context, 1707–51', in Susan Pearce (ed.), *Visions of Antiquity: The Society of Antiquaries of London 1707–2007*, London, 2007, pp. 45–73

MacGregor and Impey 1985
Arthur MacGregor and Oliver Impey, *The Origins of Museums: The Cabinet of Curiosities in Sixteenth and Seventeenth-Century Europe*, Oxford, 1985

Maclagan 1956
Michael Maclagan, 'Genealogy and Heraldry in the Sixteenth and Seventeenth Centuries', in Levi Fox (ed.), *English Historical Scholarship in the Sixteenth and Seventeenth Centuries: A Record of the Papers Delivered at a Conference Arranged by the Dugdale Society to Commemorate the Tercentenary of the Publication of Dugdale's 'Antiquities of Warwickshire'*, London and New York, 1956, pp. 31–48

Manchester 1975
Thomas Girtin, Francis Hawcroft (ed.), exh. cat., Whitworth Art Gallery, Manchester, and Victoria and Albert Museum, London, 1975

Mantell 1847
Gideon Algernon Mantell, *Geological Excursions Round the Isle of Wight, and Along the Adjacent Coast of Dorsetshire, Illustrative of the Most Interesting Geological Phenomena and Organic Remains*, London, 1847

Mantell 1850
Gideon Algernon Mantell, 'On the Remains of Man and Works of Art Imbedded in Rocks and Strata', *Archaeological Journal*, 7, 1850, pp. 327–46

Marsden 1996
Peter Marsden, 'The Beginnings of Archaeology in the City of London', in Joanna Bird, Mark Hassall and Harvey Sheldon (eds), *Interpreting Roman London: Papers in Memory of Hugh Chapman*, Oxford, 1996, pp. 11–18

Marsden 1999
Barry Marsden, *The Early Barrow Diggers*, Stroud, 1999

Marsden 2003
Peter Marsden, *Sealed by Time: The Loss and Recovery of the Mary Rose*, Portsmouth, 2003

Matheson 1998
Lister Matheson, *The Prose Brut: The Development of a Middle English Chronicle*, Tempe, Arizona, 1998

Maton 1800
William George Maton, 'Account of the Fall of Some of the Stones of Stonehenge', *Archaeologia*, 13, 1800, pp. 103–6

McFarlane and Lundberg 2005
Donald A. McFarlane and Joyce Lundberg, 'The Nineteenth-Century Excavation of Kent's Cavern, England', *Journal of Cave and Karst Studies*, 67 (1), 2005, pp. 39–47

McKisack 1971
May McKisack, *Medieval History in the Tudor Age*, Oxford, 1971

Meaney 1964
Audrey Meaney, *A Gazetteer of Early Anglo Saxon Burial Sites*, London, 1964

Membury 2002
S. Membury, 'The Celluloid Archaeologist: An X-rated Exposé', in Miles Russell (ed.), *Digging Holes in Popular Culture*, Oxford, 2002, pp. 8–18

Mendyk 1989
Stan A. E. Mendyk, *'Speculum Britanniae': Regional Study, Antiquarianism and Science in Britain to 1700*, London and Toronto, 1989

Merrifield 1965
Ralph Merrifield, *The Roman City of London*, London, 1965

Meyrick and Shaw 1836
Samuel Rush Meyrick and Henry Shaw, *Specimens of Ancient Furniture Drawn from Existing Authorities by Henry Shaw*, London, 1836

Meyrick and Smith 1815
Samuel Rush Meyrick and Charles Hamilton Smith, *The Costume of the Original Inhabitants of the British Islands: From the Earliest Periods to the Sixth Century: To which is added, that of the Gothic Nations on the Western Coasts of the Baltic, the Ancestors of the Anglo-Saxons and Anglo-Danes*, London, 1815

Michell 1982
John Michell, *Megalithomania: Artists, Antiquarians and Archaeologists at the Old Stone Monuments*, London, 1982

Molesworth 1787
Richard Molesworth, 'Description of the Druid Temple Lately Discovered on the Top of the Hill Near St Hillary in Jersey', *Archaeologia*, 8, 1787, pp. 384–85

Morgan 1982
Nigel J. Morgan, *Early Gothic Manuscripts*, 1, New York, 1982

Morley 1924
Henry T. Morley, *Monumental Brasses of Berkshire (Fourteenth to Seventeenth Centuries): Illustrated and Described*, Reading, 1924

Morris 1936
May Morris, *William Morris, Artist, Writer, Socialist*, 1, Oxford, 1936

Morris 1986
Susan Morris, *Thomas Girtin: 1775–1802*, New Haven and London, 1986

Moser 1998
Stephanie Moser, *Ancestral Images: The Iconography of Human Origins*, Stroud, 1998

Murray 1989
Tim Murray, 'The History, Philosophy and Sociology of Archaeology: The Case of the Ancient Monuments Protection Act (1882)', in Valerie Pinsky and Alison Wylie (eds), *Critical Traditions in Contemporary Archaeology: Essays in the Philosophy, History and Socio-Politics of Archaeology*, Cambridge, 1989, pp. 55–67

Musset 2005
Lucien Musset, *The Bayeux Tapestry*, Woodbridge, 2005

Myers and Myers 1996
Richard Myers and Hilary Myers, *William Morris Tiles*, Shepton Beauchamp, Somerset, 1996

Myrone 1999
Martin Myrone, 'Graphic Antiquarianism in Eighteenth-Century Britain', in Martin Myrone and Lucy Peltz (eds), *Producing the Past: Aspects of Antiquarian Culture and Practice, 1700–1850*, Aldershot, 1999, pp. 35–54

Myrone 2007
Martin Myrone, 'The Society and the Graphic Arts, 1717–1842', in Susan Pearce (ed.), *Visions of Antiquity: The Society of Antiquaries of London 1707–2007*, London, 2007, pp. 99–121

Nash 1839–49
Joseph Nash, *Mansions of England in the Olden Times*, London, 1839–49

Neal 1981
David Neal, *Roman Mosaics in Britain: An Introduction to their Schemes and a Catalogue of Paintings*, Gloucester, 1981

Needham 1979
Stuart Needham, 'Two Recent British Shield Finds and their Continental Parallels', *Proceedings of the Prehistoric Society*, New Series, 45, 1979

Nenk 1997
B. Nenk, 'Highly Decorated Pottery in Medieval England', in I. Freestone and David Gaimster (eds), *Pottery in the Making. World Ceramic Traditions*, London, 1997, pp. 92–97

Nichols 1811
John Nichols, *The History and Antiquities of the County of Leicester*, 4 (part 2), 1811, p. 557

Nicolson and Hawkyard 1995
Nigel Nicolson and Alasdair Hawkyard, *The Counties of Britain: A Tudor Atlas by John Speed*, London, 1995

Norman 1974–76
A. V. B. Norman, 'Notes on a Newly Discovered Piece of Fourteenth-Century Armour', *Journal of the Arms and Armour Society*, 8, 1974–76, pp. 229–33

Norman 1983
B. Norman, 'Archaeology and Television', *Archaeological Review from Cambridge*, 2.1, 1983, pp. 27–32

Nurse 1989
Bernard Nurse, *Eighteenth-Century Engravings for the Society of Antiquaries of London*, London, 1989

Nurse 2000
Bernard Nurse, 'George Cruikshank's *The Antiquarian Society*, 1812, and Sir Henry Charles Englefield', *Antiquaries Journal*, 80, 2000, pp. 316–20

Nurse 2001
Bernard Nurse, *A Note on 'The Barrow Diggers' by James Douglas, c. 1787*, London, 2001, unpublished

Nurse 2004
Bernard Nurse, 'Englefield, Sir Henry Charles, Seventh Baron (c. 1752–1822)', *Oxford Dictionary of National Biography*, Oxford, 2004, http://www.oxforddnb.com/view/article/8812

Nurse 2007
Bernard Nurse, 'The Development of the Library', in Susan Pearce (ed.), *Visions of Antiquity: The Society of Antiquaries of London 1707–2007*, London, 2007, pp. 199–225

Oppé 1923
Adolph Paul Oppé, *Thomas Rowlandson: His Drawings and Water-colours*, London, 1923

Oppé 1942
Adolph Paul Oppé, 'Cotman and His Public', *Burlington Magazine*, 81 (472), 1942, pp. 163–71

Parry 1983
Linda Parry, *William Morris Textiles*, London, 1983

Parry 1995
Graham Parry, *The Trophies of Time: English Antiquarians of the Seventeenth Century*, Oxford, 1995

Parry 2005
Linda Parry, *Textiles of the Arts and Crafts Movement*, London, 2005

Pearce 2007
Susan Pearce, 'Antiquaries and the Interpretation of Ancient Objects 1770–1820', in Susan Pearce (ed.), *Visions of Antiquity: The Society of Antiquaries of London 1707–2007*, London, 2007, pp. 147–71

Peltz 2004
Lucy Peltz, 'Basire, Isaac (1704–1768)', *The Oxford Dictionary of National Biography*, Oxford, 2004, http://www.oxforddnb.com/view/article/1619

Peltz and Myrone 1999
Lucy Peltz and Martin Myrone, 'Introduction: "Mine are the Subjects Rejected by the Historian": Antiquarianism, History and the Making of Modern Culture', in Martin Myrone and Lucy Peltz (eds), *Producing the Past: Aspects of Antiquarian Culture and Practice, 1700–1850*, Aldershot, 1999, pp. 115–34

Petrie 1880
William Flinders Petrie, *Stonehenge: Plans, Description and Theories*, London, 1880

Pfungst 1911–12
Henry Pfungst, 'Vote of Thanks to Pfungst for Present of an Original Drawing by Rowlandson Representing "The Reception of a New Member in the Society of Antiquaries" in 1782', *Proceedings of the Society of Antiquaries of London*, 24 (2nd series), 1911–12

Piccini and Kulik 2007
Angela Piccini and Kard Kulik, *British Archaeology*, 94, 2007

Pidgley 1972
Michael Pidgley, 'Cornelius Varley, Cotman, and the Graphic Telescope', *Burlington Magazine*, 114 (836), 1972, pp. 780–86

Piggott 1950
Stuart Piggott, 'Swords and Scabbards of the British Early Iron Age', *Proceedings of the Prehistoric Society*, 16, 1950, pp. 1–28

Piggott 1951
Stuart Piggott, 'The Society's Lamp', *Antiquaries Journal*, vol. 31, 1951

Piggott 1956
Stuart Piggott, 'Stonehenge', *Wiltshire Archaeological and Natural History Magazine*, 56, 1956, pp. 232–37

Piggott 1976
Stuart Piggott, *Ruins in a Landscape: Essays in Antiquarianism*, Edinburgh, 1976

Piggott 1978
Stuart Piggott, *Antiquity Depicted: Aspects of Archaeological Illustration*, London, 1978

Piggott 1985
Stuart Piggott, *William Stukeley: An Eighteenth-Century Antiquary*, 2nd edition, London, 1985

Piggott 1989
Stuart Piggott, *Ancient Britons and the Antiquarian Imagination: Ideas from the Renaissance to the Regency*, London, 1989

Pitt Rivers 1867
Augustus Henry Lane-Fox Pitt Rivers, 'A Description of Certain Piles Found near London Wall and Southwark, Possibly the Remains of Pile Buildings', *Anthropological Review*, 5, 1867, pp. lxxi–lxxxiii

Pitt Rivers 1875
Augustus Henry Lane-Fox Pitt Rivers, 'Excavations of Cissbury Camp, Sussex', *The Journal of the Anthropological Institute of Great Britain and Ireland*, 5, 1875, pp. 357–90

Pitt Rivers 1883
Augustus Henry Lane-Fox Pitt Rivers, 'Excavations at Caesar's Camp, near Folkestone, Conducted in 1878', *Archaeologia*, 47, 1883, pp. 429–65

Pitt Rivers 1887
Augustus Henry Lane-Fox Pitt Rivers, *Excavations in Cranborne Chase*, 1, London, 1887

Pitt Rivers 1892
Augustus Henry Lane-Fox Pitt Rivers, *Excavations in Cranborne Chase*, 3, London, 1892

Pitt Rivers 1898
Augustus Henry Lane-Fox Pitt Rivers, *Excavations in Cranborne Chase, near Rushmore, on the Borders of Dorset and Wilts*, 4, London, 1898

Pitts 2001
Mike Pitts, *Hengeworld*, 2nd edition, London, 2001

Pitts 2005
Mike Pitts, 'Hysteria, Gloom and Foreboding', *British Archaeology*, 83, 2005, pp. 16–19

Planché 1834
James Robinson Planché, *History of British Costume*, London, 1834

Port 1976
Michael H. Port (ed.), *The Houses of Parliament*, New Haven and London, 1976

Pryor 2003
Francis Pryor, *Britain BC: Life in Britain and Ireland Before the Romans*, London, 2003

Pugh 1982
R. B. Pugh, 'Our First Charter', *Antiquaries Journal*, 62, 1982, pp. 347–55

Ramsay 2004
Nigel Ramsay, 'Faussett, Bryan (1720–1776)', *Oxford Dictionary of National Biography*, Oxford, 2004, http://www.oxforddnb.com/view/article/9214

Rapin-Thoryas 1743–47
Paul de Rapin-Thoryas, *History of England*, 7 vols, London, 1743–47

Rashleigh 1789
Philip Rashleigh, 'Account of Antiquities Discovered in Cornwall, 1774', *Archaeologia*, 9, 1789, pp. 187–88

Rashleigh 1808
Philip Rashleigh, 'Further Account of Antiquities Discovered in Cornwall', *Archaeologia*, 11, 1808, pp. 83–84

Reeve 2006
Matthew Reeve, 'The Painted Chamber at Westminster, Edward I and the Crusade', *Viator*, 37, 2006, pp. 189–221

Repton 1965
John Adey Repton, *Norwich Cathedral at the End of the Eighteenth Century, with Descriptive Notes by William Wilkins*, Stephen Rowland Pierce (ed.), Farnborough, 1965

Reveley 1852
Thomas Reveley, 'Letter from Thomas Reveley, Esq. … to Capt. W. H. Smyth … Presenting to the Society a Torque', *Archaeologia*, 34, 1852

Reynolds 1959
Joshua Reynolds, *Discourses on Art*, Robert R. Wark (ed.), San Marino, 1959

Reynolds 1984
Graham Reynolds, *The Later Paintings and Drawings of John Constable*, London and New Haven, 1984

Rhodes 2006
Michael Rhodes, 'Smith, Charles Roach (1806–1890)', *Oxford Dictionary of National Biography*, Oxford, 2006, http://www.oxforddnb.com/view/article/25789

Richards 1999
Julian Richards, *Meet the Ancestors: Unearthing the Evidence which Brings us Face to Face with the Past*, London, 1999

Richmond 1950
Ian Richmond, 'Stukeley's Lamp, the Badge of the Society of Antiquaries', *Antiquaries Journal*, 30, 1950, pp. 22–27

Rodwell and Leighton 2006
Warwick Rodwell and Gerard Leighton (eds), *Architectural Records of Wells by John Carter, F. S. A., 1784–1808*, Taunton, 2006

Rogers 1867
J. J. Rogers, 'Saxon Silver Ornaments and Coins Found at Trewhiddle, St Austell', *Journal of the Royal Institution of Cornwall*, 8, 1867, pp. 292–305

Rokewode 1842
John Gage Rokewode, 'A Memoir on the Painted Chamber in the Palace of Westminster', *Vetusta Monumenta*, VI, 1842, plates 26–39

Ruskin 1906
John Ruskin, *Works*, vol. 21, E. T. Cook and A. Wedderburn (eds), London, 1906

Scalia 2005
Christopher Scalia, 'The Grave Scholarship of the Antiquaries', *Literature Compass 2*, (2005), pp. 1–13, RO 166

Scharf 1865
George Scharf, *A Catalogue of the Pictures Belonging to the Society of Antiquaries, Somerset House*, London, 1865

Scoones 1999
Francesca Scoones, 'Dr William Stukeley's House at Grantham', *The Georgian Group Journal*, IX, 1999, pp. 158–65

Shanes 1990
Eric Shanes, *Turner's England*, London, 1990

Sharpe 1979
Kevin Sharpe, *Sir Robert Cotton 1586–1631: History and Politics in Early Modern England*, Oxford, 1979

Sharples 1991
Niall M. Sharples, *English Heritage Book of Maiden Castle*, London, 1991

Sloane 2004
Barney Sloane, 'Archaeology in London: Annual Round-Up and News for 1855/6', *Transactions of the London and Middlesex Archaeological Society*, 55, 2004, pp. 9–17

Smiles 1994
Sam Smiles, *The Image of Antiquity: Ancient Britain and the Romantic Imagination*, New Haven and London, 1994

Smiles 2000
Sam Smiles, *Eye Witness: Artist and Visual Documentation in Britain 1770–1830*, Aldershot, 2000

Smiles 2007
Sam Smiles, 'Art and Antiquity in the Long Nineteenth Century', in Susan Pearce (ed.), *Visions of Antiquity: The Society of Antiquaries of London 1707–2007*, London, 2007, pp. 123–45

Smith 1848
Charles Roach Smith, *Collectanea Antiqua: Etchings and Notices of Ancient Remains, Illustrative of the Habits, Customs and History of Past Ages*, 7, London, 1848

Smith 1856
Charles Roach Smith, *Inventorium Sepulchrale: An Account of some Antiquities Dug Up at Gilton, Kingston, Sibertswold, Barfriston, Beakesbourne, Chartham, and Crundale, in the County of Kent, from AD 1757 to AD 1773 / By the Rev. Bryan Faussett … Edited, from the Original Manuscript in the Possession of Joseph Mayer, Esq., with Notes and Introduction, by Charles Roach Smith*, London, 1856

Smith 1907–10
Lucy Toulmin Smith (ed.), *The Itinerary of John Leland in or about the years 1535–1543*, 5 vols, London, 1907–10 (reprinted 1964)

Smith 1997
Pamela Smith, 'Grahame Clark's New Archaeology: The Fenland Research Committee and Cambridge Prehistory in the 1930s', *Antiquity*, 71, 1997, pp. 11–30

Society of Antiquaries of London 1740
Society of Antiquaries of London, *Minutes*, vol. 3, 1740, 6 March, 8 May, unpublished

Society of Antiquaries of London 1740
Society of Antiquaries of London, *Minutes*, vol. 4, 1740, 25 September, unpublished

Society of Antiquaries of London 1755
Society of Antiquaries of London, *Minutes*, vol. 7, 1755, 27 February, unpublished

Society of Antiquaries of London 1773
Society of Antiquaries of London, *Minutes*, vol. 13, 1773, 4 November, pp. 127–28, unpublished

Society of Antiquaries 1787
Society of Antiquaries of London, *Minutes*, vol. 22, 1787, 8 March, unpublished

Society of Antiquaries 1788
Society of Antiquaries of London, *Minutes*, vol. 22, 1788, 8 March, unpublished

Society of Antiquaries of London 1790
Society of Antiquaries of London, *Minutes*, vol. 23, 1790, 4 March, unpublished

Society of Antiquaries of London 1791
Society of Antiquaries of London, *Minutes*, vol. 24, 1791, 17 November, unpublished

Society of Antiquaries of London 1792
Society of Antiquaries of London, *Minutes*, vol. 24, 1792, 8 November, unpublished

Society of Antiquaries of London 1801
Society of Antiquaries of London, *Minutes*, vol. 28, 1801, 8 June, unpublished

Society of Antiquaries of London 1808
Society of Antiquaries of London, *Minutes*, vol. 31, 1808, 11 June, unpublished

Society of Antiquaries 1830
Society of Antiquaries of London, *Minutes*, vol. 36, 1830, 4 March and 1 April, unpublished

Society of Antiquaries of London 1851
Society of Antiquaries of London, *Minutes*, vol. 40, 1851, 22 May, unpublished

Society of Antiquaries of London 1870
Society of Antiquaries of London, *Minutes*, vol. 43, 1870, 24 February, unpublished

Society of Antiquaries 1880
Society of Antiquaries of London, *Proceedings*, second series, vol. 8, 1880, 17 June

Society of Antiquaries of London 1916
Society of Antiquaries of London, *Minutes*, vol. 49, 1916, 29 June, unpublished

Society of Antiquaries of London 2004
Society of Antiquaries of London, *Royal Charters and Statutes of the Society of Antiquaries of London*, London, 2004, unpublished

Society of Antiquaries of Newcastle upon Tyne 1816
Society of Antiquaries of Newcastle upon Tyne, *Archaeologia Aeliana*, 1, 1816, p. 8

Sorrell 1981
Mark Sorrell (ed.), *Alan Sorrell: Reconstructing the Past*, London, 1981

Sorrenson 1996
Richard Sorrenson, 'Towards a History of the Royal Society in the Eighteenth Century', *Notes and Records of the Royal Society of London*, 50, 1996, pp. 29–46

Sotheby's 1994
Sotheby's, 'Description of lot 23: "The Antiquary" by Thomas Rowlandson', London, 10 November 1994

Southampton 1987
Visions of Stonehenge, 1350–1987, exh. cat., City Art Gallery, Southampton, 1987

Spencer 2000
Brian Spencer, 'Medieval Pilgrim Badges Found at Canterbury, England', in D. Kicken, A. M. Koldeweij and J. R. ter Molen (eds), *Gevonden Voorwerpen: Lost and Found: Essays on Medieval Archaeology for H. J. E. van Beuningen*, Rotterdam, 2000, pp. 316–27

Stanhope 1861–64
Lord Arthur Philip Stanhope, 'Anniversary Address, 23 April 1863', *Proceedings of the Society of Antiquaries of London*, 2 (2nd series), 1861–64, pp. 256–57

Starkey 1998
David Starkey (ed.), *The Inventory of King Henry VIII (Society of Antiquaries MS 129 and British Library MS Harley 1419): The Transcript*, London, 1998

Starkey 1999
David Starkey, 'Henry VI's Old Blue Gown', *The Court Historian*, 4, 1999, pp. 1–28

Starkey et al. in prep.
David Starkey et al., *The Inventory of King Henry VIII*, 2–4, Belgium, in preparation

Stead and Lang 2006
Ian Mathieson Stead and Janet Lang (eds), *British Iron Age Swords and Scabbards with a Report on the Technology of Some of the Swords*, London, 2006

Stephenson and Dixon 2003
Ian P. Stephenson and Karen R. Dixon, *Roman Cavalry Equipment*, Stroud, 2003

Stocking 1987
George W. Stocking, *Victorian Anthropology*, New York, 1987

Stothard 1817–32
Charles Alfred Stothard, *The Monumental Effigies of Great Britain*, London, 1817–32

Stothard 1821
Charles Alfred Stothard, 'Some Observations on the Bayeux Tapestry in a Letter Addressed to Samuel Lysons', *Archaeologia*, 19, 1821, pp. 184–91

Stratford et al. 1982
N. Stratford et al., 'Archbishop Walter's Tomb and Its Furnishings' *Medieval Art and Architecture at Canterbury Before 1220*, British Archaeological Association Conference Transactions for 1979, Leeds, 1982, pp. 71–93

Strong 1969
Roy Strong, *Tudor and Jacobean Portraits*, 2 vols, London, 1969

Strong 1978
Roy Strong, *And When Did You Last See Your Father? The Victorian Painter and British History*, London, 1978

Strong 1995–98
Roy Strong, *The Tudor and Stuart Monarchy: Pageantry, Painting, Iconography*, Woodbridge, 1995–98

Strutt 1796–99
Joseph Strutt, *A Complete View of the Dress and Habits of the People of England: From the Establishment of the Saxons in Britain to the Present Time*, 2, London, 1796–99

Stukeley 1724
William Stukeley, *Itinerarium Curiosum*, London, 1724

Stukeley 1740
William Stukeley, *Stonehenge, a Temple Restor'd to the British Druids*, London, 1740

Sturdy and Henig 1983
David Sturdy and Martin Henig, *The Gentle Traveller: John Bargrave, Canon of Canterbury and His Collection*, Abingdon, 1983

Sutcliffe 1978
Ray Sutcliffe (ed.), *Chronicle: Essays from Ten Years of Television Archaeology*, London, 1978

Sutton et al. 2005
Anne F. Sutton et al., *The Royal Funerals of the House of York at Windsor*, London, 2005

Swann 2001
Marjorie Swann, *Curiosities and Texts: The Culture of Collecting in Early Modern England*, Philadelphia, 2001

Sweet 2001
Rosemary Sweet, 'Antiquaries and Antiquities in Eighteenth-Century England', *Eighteenth-Century Studies*, 34, 2001, pp. 181–206

Sweet 2004
Rosemary Sweet, *Antiquaries: The Discovery of the Past in Eighteenth-Century Britain*, London, 2004

Sweet 2007
Rosemary Sweet, 'The Incorporated Society and Its Public Role', in Susan Pearce (ed.), *Visions of Antiquity: The Society of Antiquaries of London 1707–2007*, London, 2007, pp. 75–97

Sympson 1739–41
Thomas Sympson, 'Extract of Letters from Mr T. Sympson, to Browne Willis … Concerning the Remains of a Roman Hypocaustum or Sweating-Room, Discovered Underground at Lincoln, Anno 1739', *Royal Society Philosophical Transactions*, 41, 1739–41, pp. 855–60

Tait 1978
A. A. Tait, 'Inigo Jones's Stone-heng', *Burlington Magazine*, 120, no. 900, 1978, pp. 155–9

Taylor 1998
Tim Taylor, *Behind the Scenes at Time Team*, London, 1998

Taylor 2005
Joan J. Taylor, 'The Work of the Wessex Master Goldsmith: Its Implications', *Wiltshire Archaeological and Natural History Magazine*, 98, 2005, pp. 316–26

Thomas 1923
H. H. Thomas, 'The Source of the Stones of Stonehenge', *Antiquaries Journal*, 3, 1923, pp. 239–60

Thompson 1977
Michael W. Thompson, *General Pitt Rivers: Evolution and Archaeology in the Nineteenth Century*, Bradford-upon-Avon, 1977

Thorpe 1966
Lewis Thorpe (ed.), *Geoffrey of Monmouth: The History of the Kings of Britain*, Harmondsworth, 1966

Topham and Englefield 1795–1811
J. Topham and H. Englefield, *Some Account of the Collegiate Chapel of St Stephen, Westminster; Issued with 14 Additional Plates*, London, 1795–1811

Torrens 1998
H. S. Torrens, 'Geology and the Natural Sciences: Some Contributions to Archaeology in Britain 1780–1850', in Vanessa Brand (ed.), *The Study of the Past in the Victorian Age*, Oxbow Monograph, Oxford, 1998, pp. 35–59

Trevor-Roper 1987
Hugh Trevor-Roper, 'James Ussher', *Catholics, Anglicans and Puritans: Seventeenth-Century Essays*, London, 1987, pp. 120–65

Tudor-Craig 2004
Pamela Tudor-Craig, 'Kerrich, Thomas (1748–1828)', *Oxford Dictionary of National Biography*, Oxford, 2004, http://www.oxforddnb.com/view/article/15471

Tudor-Craig et al. 2004
Pamela Tudor-Craig et al. (eds), *Old St Paul's: The Society of Antiquaries Diptych*, London, 2004

Turner 2007
Rick Turner, 'Fabric, Form and Function: The Society and "The Restoration Question"', in Susan Pearce (ed.), *Visions of Antiquity: The Society of Antiquaries of London 1707–2007*, London, 2007, pp. 307–27

Ucko et al. 1991
Peter J. Ucko et al. (eds), *Avebury Reconsidered, from the 1660s to the 1990s*, London, 1991

Van Riper 1993
A. Bowdoin Van Riper, *Men Among the Mammoths: Victorian Science and the Discovery of Human Prehistory*, Chicago and London, 1993

Vertue 1929–30
George Vertue, 'Autobiography', *Walpole Society Journal, 18 Vertue Note Books*, vol. 1, 1929–30

Vetusta Monumenta 1724
Society of Antiquaries of London, *Vetusta Monumenta*, 1, 1724

Vetusta Monumenta 1740
Society of Antiquaries of London, *Vetusta Monumenta*, 1, 1740

Vetusta Monumenta 1768
Society of Antiquaries of London, *Vetusta Monumenta*, 2, 1768

Vetusta Monumenta 1789
Society of Antiquaries of London, *Vetusta Monumenta*, 2, 1789

Vetusta Monumenta 1790
Society of Antiquaries of London, *Vetusta Monumenta*, 3, 1790

Vetusta Monumenta 1796
Society of Antiquaries of London, *Vetusta Monumenta*, 3, 1796

Vetusta Monumenta 1815
Society of Antiquaries of London, *Vetusta Monumenta*, 4, 1815

Vetusta Monumenta 1819
Society of Antiquaries of London, *Vetusta Monumenta*, 5, 1819

Vetusta Monumenta 1821–23
Society of Antiquaries of London, *Vetusta Monumenta*, 6, 1821–23

Wagner 1987
Anthony Wagner, *Heralds of England: A History of the Office and College of Arms*, London, 1987

[Walpole 1764]
[Horace Walpole], *The Castle of Otranto*, London, 1764

Wark 1975
R. R. Wark, *Drawings by Thomas Rowlandson in the Huntington Collection*, San Marino, 1975

Way 1847
Albert Way, *A Catalogue of Antiquities, Coins, Pictures and Miscellaneous Curiosities in the Society's Possession*, London, 1847

Way 1858
Albert Way, 'The Signet-Ring and Silver Bell of Mary, Queen of Scots', *Archaeological Journal*, 15, 1858, pp. 253–66

Wayment 1981
Hilary Wayment, 'The East Window of St Margaret's Westminster', *Antiquaries Journal*, 61, 1981, pp. 292–301

Wedgwood 1992
Alexandra Wedgwood, 'New Houses of Parliament', in Celina Fox (ed.), *London: World City, 1800–1840*, London, 1992, p. 609

Wedgwood 2004
Alexandra Wedgwood, 'Pugin, Augustus Welby Northmore (1812–1852)', *Oxford Dictionary of National Biography*, Oxford, 2004, http://www.oxforddnb.com/view/article/22869

Wedlake 1934
W. J. Wedlake, *Diary 1934*, Dorset County Museum, Accession 2004.77.18.1, Dorchester, 1934

Wedlake 1975A
W. J. Wedlake, *Maiden Castle, Hand-Written Reminiscence, Lecture Manuscript*, Dorset County Museum, Accession 2004.77.16.1, Dorchester, 1975

Wedlake 1975B
W. J. Wedlake, *The Excavation of Maiden Castle, Dorset, 1934–1937, Reminiscence, Typed Lecture Manuscript*, Dorset County Museum, Accession 2004.77.16.2., Dorchester, 1975

Wheeler 1932
Robert Eric Mortimer Wheeler, 'A Prehistoric Metropolis: The First Verulamium', *Antiquity*, 6, 1932, pp. 1–15

Wheeler 1943
Robert Eric Mortimer Wheeler, *Maiden Castle, Dorset, Report of the Research Committee of the Society of Antiquaries of London XII*, Oxford, 1943

Whitelock 1955
Dorothy Whitelock (ed.), *English Historical Documents c. 500–1042*, 1st edition, London, 1955

Whittingham 1973
Selby Whittingham, *Constable and Turner at Salisbury*, Salisbury, 1973

Willetts 2000
Pamela J. Willetts, *Catalogue of Manuscripts in the Society of Antiquaries of London*, Woodbridge, 2000

Wilson 1964
David M. Wilson, *Anglo-Saxon Ornamental Metalwork, 700–1100, in the British Museum*, London, 1964

Wilson 1968
P. A. Wilson, 'The Cult of St Martin in the British Isles with Particular Reference to Canterbury and Candida Casa', *Innes Review*, 19, 1968, pp. 129–43

Wilson and Blunt 1961
David M. Wilson and Christopher E. Blunt, 'The Trewhiddle Hoard', *Archaeologia*, 98, 1961, pp. 75–122

Wilton 1979
Andrew Wilton, *The Life and Work of J. M. W. Turner*, London, 1979

Wood 2004
Jason Wood (ed.), *Conservation Plan for Lincoln's Roman Monuments*, 2, Lincoln, 2004

Woodbridge 1970
Kenneth Woodbridge, *Landscape and Antiquity: Aspects of English Culture at Stourhead, 1718–1838*, London, 1970

Woodcock 2004
Thomas Woodcock, 'Le Neve, Peter (1661–1729)', *Oxford Dictionary of National Biography*, Oxford, 2004, http://www.oxforddnb.com/view/article/16440

Woolf 2003
Daniel Woolf, *The Social Circulation of the Past: English Historical Culture 1500–1730*, Oxford, 2003

Wright 1997
C. J. Wright (ed.), *Sir Robert Cotton as Collector*, London, 1997

Wright and Wright 1966
C. E. Wright and R. C. Wright (eds), *The Diary of Humfrey Wanley, 1715–1726*, two vols, London, 1966

Wyon 1887
Alfred B. Wyon, *The Great Seals of England*, London, 1887

Lenders to the Exhibition

Cambridge
Fitzwilliam Museum

Canterbury
The Dean and Chapter of Canterbury Cathedral

Derrick Chivers

Devizes
Wiltshire Heritage Museum

Dorchester
The Dorset Natural History and Archaeological Society at the Dorset County Museum

Douai
Bibliothèque Municipale

Liverpool
National Museums Liverpool (World Museum Liverpool)

London
British Library
British Museum
Paul Childs/Spheroview
The College of Arms
Geological Society
Institute of Archaeology, University College London
Museum of London
National Portrait Gallery
Natural History Museum
The Royal Society
Society of Antiquaries of London
Tate Britain
University College Hospital
Victoria and Albert Museum

Oxford
Ashmolean Museum
Museum of the History of Science

Salisbury
Salisbury and South Wiltshire Museum

The family of the late Alan Sorrell

Wessex Archaeology and Archaeoptrics Ltd

and others who wish to remain anonymous

Photographic Acknowledgements

All works of art are reproduced by kind permission of the owners. Specific acknowledgements are as follows:

© BBC, cats 152.1–6/8; fig. 33
Cardiff: © The City and County of Cardiff, fig. 27
Cambridge: © The Master and Fellows of Corpus Christi College, Cambridge, fig. 34
Cambridge: © Fitzwilliam Museum, cat. 100
Canterbury: © Dean and Chapter of Canterbury/Roy Fox, cats 7, 8, 9, 10, 11, 12, 147, 149, 150, 151
Courtesy of 'Time Team', Channel 4 TV © Videotext Communications Ltd, cat. 152.7
Devizes: © Wiltshire Heritage Museum/Richard Pearce, cats 63, 64, 65, 66, 67, 165
Dorchester: © The Dorset Natural History and Archaeological Society at the Dorset County Museum/Jonathan Gooding, cats 136, 138, 139
Douai: © D. Lefebvre et Bibliothèque municipale de Douai, cat. 156
Liverpool: © National Museums Liverpool (World Museum Liverpool), cats 56, 57, 58, 59, 61
London: © British Library Board. All rights reserved, G.2931/TP: cat. 15, Add. 71474/f.164: cat. 20, Harley Mss. 7055/f.1: cat. 26, G.6863/pl.10: cat. 60, Add 15541/f.88: cat. 73, Add. 15541/f.79: cat. 93, Eg.Ms.3028/f.30: cat. 155, Add. 28330/f.36: cat. 157; fig. 1
London: © Copyright The Trustees of The British Museum, cats 43, 75, 77, 79, 103, 128, 142, 143, 144, 145, 146, 167, fig. 2, fig. 12/Stephen Dodd, cats 14, 141.1–9
London: © John Chase/Museum of London, cat. 153
London: © The College of Arms, cat. 28
London: courtesy of the Geological Society of London, cat. 132
London: © Guildhall Library, fig. 31
London: © Institute of Archaeology, UCL/Stills by Stuart Laidlaw, cat. 137
London: © Kings College, fig. 24
London: © London Library/John Hammond, fig. 32
London: © Natural History Museum, cat. 130
London: National Portrait Gallery, cat. 18
London: © Robin Richards/Museum of London, cat. 154
London: © The Royal Society/Roy Fox, cat. 25
London: © Society of Antiquaries of London, cats 116, 169, 212; figs 20, 28/Geremy Butler, cats 24, 30, 37, 38, 45, 51, 62, 105, 106, 107; fig. 7/Glyn Goodrick, cat. 76/John Hammond, cats 1, 2, 3, 5, 6, 13, 16, 17, 19, 21,22, 23, 27, 29, 31, 32, 33, 34, 35, 36, 39, 40, 41, 42, 44, 46, 53, 54, 55, 68, 69, 70, 71, 72, 74, 78, 80, 81, 82, 83, 84, 85, 86, 87, 88, 89, 90, 91, 92, 97, 98.1–2, 99, 101, 104, 108, 109, 110, 111, 112, 113, 114, 115, 117, 119, 120, 121, 122, 123, 125, 126, 127, 129, 131, 140, 148, 158, 159, 160, 162, 164, 170, 171, 172, 173, 175, 176, 177, 178; figs 3, 4, 5, 8, 9, 10, 11, 13, 14, 15, 16, 17, 18, 19, 21, 22, 23, 36/Chris Titmus, cats 47.1–2, 48, 49, 50, 52/Howard Wilson, cat. 124
London: Spheroview/Paul Childs, cat. 179
London: © Tate, 2007, cat. 118
London: © V&A Images/Victoria and Albert Museum, cats 102, 168; figs 25, 26
© Mike Pitts, fig. 37
Oxford: Ashmolean Museum, cats 94, 95, 161
Oxford: © Bodleian Library, fig. 6
Oxford: By permission of the Museum of the History of Science, University of Oxford. MHS inv. 15449/Keiko Ikeuchi, cat. 4
Salisbury: © By kind permission of Salisbury & South Wiltshire Museum, cats 96, 166; courtesy of Anthony Pitt Rivers, fig. 29/David Cousins, cats 133, 134, 135
Salisbury: Wessex Archaeology, Archaeoptrics Ltd., cat. 179

Index

All references are to page numbers; those in bold type indicate catalogue plates, and those in italic type indicate essay illustrations.

Abbeville handaxe 185, 187, **189**
Abell, William 21
Aberdeen, Lord 55, 67
Adam and Eve 21, 24
Aeolipile (hearth-blower) *111*
Alban, Roger 21
Albert, Prince Consort 64
Ales, Alexander de 178
altars, Roman 109, **113**
Amesbury, Wiltshire 231, 234
Ancient Britons 17, 37, 39, 63, 95
Ancient Monuments Protection Act (1882) 186, 195, 201
Anglo-Saxons 19, 37, 94, 95, 98, 100, 109
   silver hanging bowl **120**
   Trewhiddle hoard 109, 110, *111*, **116–17**
Animal, Vegetable, Mineral? (television series) 183, 215, 218, **219**
Anne of Cleves 146
Anthony, Derrick
   Elizabeth I, second Great Seal **136**
anthropology, physical 221
Antiquaries Journal 249
Antiquaries Roll 70, 77
'Antiquitas Rediviva' 38, 45, 46
Antrobus, Sir Edward 248
Antrobus family 228
Archaeological Institute *111*
The Archaeologist (radio programme) 215
archaeology
   barrows 95–9
   development of 38–9, 183–7, 195
   forensic archaeology 97, 218, 221
   on radio and television 215–19
   stratigraphy *111*, 185
Archaeoptics Ltd 253
Aristotle 31
armour **205**, **206**
Arthur, King 24, 227
Arthur, Prince 87
Arts and Crafts Movement 174
Ashmolean Museum, Oxford 30, 99, 241
Aston, Mick 216–17, 218, **219**
Athelstan, King 80
Atkinson, Richard 215, 216, 218, **219**, 228, 251, 253
Attenborough, David 215–16
Aubrey, John 38, 39, 49, 63, 228, 237
   Monumenta Britannica 39, *39*
Aurelius Ambrosius 228, 232
Avebury 39, *39*, **49**, 53, **63**, 237, 241
Aveline, Countess 146
Ayloffe, Sir Joseph 105, 144, 146, 155, 156
Ayrshire 109, 112

Babington, Thomas 110
Bacon, Sir Francis 18, 30
badge, pilgrim **206**
Bagford, John 33, 51, 53, 54, 56, **59**
Baker, Henry 70
Banks, Sir Joseph 97
Banner of 'St Martin and the Beggar' **79**
Bargrave, John 18
   Cabinet of Curiosities **30–1**
Barraud, Mark and Francis
   The Wiltshire Champion Coursing Meeting at Stonehenge 230
barrows 95–6, *96*, 98, 101, 102, 186, *186*, 218, **219**, 228, 230
Barry, Charles 149, 167, 173
Basingstoke Canal 109, *111*
Basire, James I 64, 105, 114, 137, 143, 144, 146
   Durham Cathedral, Section from East to West **159**
   The Encampment of the British Forces near Portsmouth **156–7**
   The Field of Cloth of Gold 144, **154–5**
Basire, James II 143, 159
   'William is told that Harold is near' *150*, **152**
   William the Conqueror at Hastings **150–1**
Bateman, Thomas 96
   Ten Years' Diggings in Celtic and Saxon Grave Hills 96
   Vestiges of the Antiquities of Derbyshire 96

Bath Abbey 145, 159
Bayeux Tapestry 123, 144, **150–3**
BBC 196, 215–16, 217, 218, **219**
Beaker culture 231
Becket, St Thomas
   pilgrim badge **206**
   St Thomas Becket Casket 71, **76–7**
Beechey, W. J.
   Stonehenge from the south-west, the Trilithons lately fallen **239**
Beith, Ayrshire 112
Bentham, James
   History of the Conventual and Cathedral Church of Ely 133
Benwell, Northumberland 109, *109*, 113
Bersu, Gerhard 187
Bertillon, Alphonse 195
Bible 15, 17, 21, 22, 75
bioarchaeology 221
Blackstone, William 73
Blake, William 69, 143, 144
   King Sebert and King Henry III **146**
   The Opening of the Tomb of Edward I **105**
Blomefield, Francis 59
Blood of the British (television programme) 216
Bodleian Library, Oxford 34
Boleyn, Anne 90
Bolton, Edmund
   Petition to King James I for a Royal Academy 37, **48**, 69
bones 96, 221, **222**
Bonnard, Camille 168
Book of Kells 143
Borlase, William 123
Bosworth, Battle of (1485) 119
Bosworth cross **119**
Bothwell, Earl of 121
Boucher de Perthes, Jacques 189
Brand, Revd John 118
Brander, Gustavus 90
Brandon, Richard **223**
Branson, Elizabeth 80
brass rubbings **138–9**
British Archaeological Association 55, 111
British Association for the Advancement of Science 187
   'The British History' 17
British Museum 59, 71, 98, 110, 124, 183, 202, 203, 204, 243
Britton, John 228
   Cathedral Antiquities 145
   'Celtic Cabinet' **241**
   Wiltshire 244
Brixham Cave, Devon 185, 187, 189
Bronze Age 185, 203
   dating of Stonehenge 228, 253
   grave goods 96, **102–3**
   palstave *124*
   shields 109, **112**, *125*
Brown, Ford Madox 167, 174
   The Body of King Harold Brought to William the Conqueror 168
   Chaucer at the Court of Edward III 168, **170–1**
Browne, Sir Anthony 156, 158
Browne, Henry 241
Browne, Thomas
   Hydriotaphia, Urne-Buriall 19, **35**
   Brut d'Angleterre 23
Brutus of Troy 17, 17, 21, 23, 24, 26, 232
Buckingham, Duke of 48
Bucklersbury Roman pavement, London 202, 203
Bulleid 186
Burges, William
   The Banqueting Hall of Cardiff Castle 168
Burghley, Lord 37, 40
Buried Treasure (radio programme) 215
Buried Treasure (television series) 217, 218, **219**
Burlington House, London 61, 67, 71
Burne-Jones, Edward 169, 176, 178
   ceramic tiles featuring 'The Legend of Goode Wimmen' **180–1**
Burrell, Sir William 132
Burton, William 34

cabinets of curiosities 18, **30–1**
Caesar, Julius 17, 102, 196, 228
Camden, William 15, 24, 28, 38–9, **40–1**, 45, 49

Britannia 18, 26, 37, 39, **40**, 130
Remains Concerning Britain 40
Canterbury Cathedral 203, 206, **208–13**
Capper, Colonel John Edward 249
Cardiff Castle *168*
Carter, John 54, 69, 123, 124, 145, 173
   A Bronze Age Shield from Capel Curig, Conwy 125
   Durham Cathedral, Section from East to West **159**
   'John Carter Exhibiting his Drawings of Durham Cathedral …' *145*
   Wells Cathedral, Section from East to West **160–1**
Catherine, St **176**
Catherine of Aragon 87, 140
Cattermole, G. 241
Caxton, William 23
ceramics, medieval **207**
chain-mail collar **205**
chalice, from Archbishop Walter's tomb 209, **212**
Chambers, Sir William 145
Chandler, Daniel 140
   Stained-glass Window from New Hall, Essex **140–1**
Channel 4 216–17, 218, **219**
Charles I, King 38, 97, 167, 223
Charles II, King 21, 49, 167, 235
Charles, Nicholas 45
Charleton, Walter 39, 235, 236
   Chorea Gigantum **49**
   Plan of Avebury **49**
Charlie, Bonnie Prince 167
Chatterton, Thomas 65
Chaucer, Geoffrey **170–1**
   'The Legend of Goode Wimmen' 176, **178–81**
Chippindale, Christopher 228, 234
Christine de Pisan 175
Chronicle (television series) 216, 218, **219**
Chubb, Cecil 228
churches 97
Civil War 17, 38, 44, 46
Clark, Grahame 187
Claudius, Emperor 196
coins, Roman **204**
Coleraine, Lord 54
College of Antiquaries 15
College of Arms 59, 77
Collins, Richard
   William Stukeley **62**, 70
Colt Hoare, Sir Richard 95–6, 99, 102, 103, 125, 228, 241
   History of Ancient Wiltshire 95–6, 135, 244
Combe, William 97, 104
Constable, John
   Stonehenge 227, **244–5**
Constantine, Cornwall 128–9
Conway, General 126
Conyers, John 33
Cooke, Edward William
   The Antiquary's Cell 166, *166*
Corbould, Edward Henry
   A Knight Enters the Lists at the 'Eglinton Tournament' … *167*
Cosway, Richard 69
Cotman, John Sell 138, 241
   Drawing of a Brass at Ketteringham, Norfolk, Commemorating Thomas Hevnyngham Esq. and His Wife, Anne Yerde **139**
   Engravings of the Most Remarkable of the Sepulchral Brasses in Norfolk 138
   Miscellaneous Etchings 125
Cotterdale, Yorkshire 113
Cotton, Sir Robert 24, 38–9, 40, 48, 49, 59
Covel, Dr John 56
Cowdray House, Sussex 132, 144, 156, 158
Cranborne Chase, Dorset 195, 218, **219**
craniometer **195**
Crawford, O. G. S. 249
Crocker, Philip 103
   Bronze Age Barrow at Upton Lovell 96
Cromwell, Oliver 69, 167
cross, Bosworth **119**
Cruickshank, Dan 217
Cruikshank, George
   The Antiquarian Society **67**, 186
Cunliffe, Barry 216, 218, **219**
Cunnington, William 95, 96, 102, 103, 228

264 | Making History

Daily Mail 196
Daniel, Glyn 215, 216
Darnley, Lord 121
Darvill, Timothy 232, 249
Darwin, Charles 185, 195
Dayes, Edward 125
de Lacy family 137
Dearle, J. H. 174
Dee, John 17
 Holy Table **24–5**
Derbyshire 96
Dering, Sir Edward 38, 45
 Church Notes and Drawings relating to Kent **46–7**
Dethick, Sir William 45
Devizes Museum 241
DNA 221
Dodderidge, Sir John 37, **49**
Dodsworth, Roger 38
Domesday Book 54, **72**
Donne, John 42, **44**
Douai 232
Douce, Francis 121
Douglas, Revd James 95, 109, 123
 The Barrow Diggers **101**
 Dissertation on the Antiquity of the Earth 188
 Nenia Britannica 95, *95*, 98, **99**, 100, 124
Douglas, John, Dean of Windsor 106
Down to Earth (television programme) 216
Drake, G.
 The Burning of Westminster Palace in 1834 **149**
Drapers Company 79
Drayton, Michael
 Poly-Olbion 18, **26–7**
Drew, Charles 197
 Section and plan … at Maiden Castle **199**
Druids 26, 32, 228, 237, 240, 242
Dugdale, Sir William 37, 38, 46, 173
 The Antiquities of Warwickshire 33, **37**, 38
 Baronage of England 45
 Book of Arms **45**
 Book of Monuments **44**, 45
 Book of Seals 45
 The History of St Paul's Cathedral 44
 Monasticon Anglicanum 38, *38*
Duke, Revd Edward 241
Durham Cathedral 145, *145*, 159
Durrington Walls 231

earthenware jug **207**
Edward, Black Prince 170
Edward I, King 61, 97, 104, **105**, 148
Edward III, King 147, **170–1**
Edward IV, King 70, **84**, 85, 97, 118
Edward VI, King 90, **106**, 132, 144, **158**
Edward VII, King 64
Edward the Confessor, St *123*, 143
Edwards, Edward
 The Field of Cloth of Gold **154–5**
Eglinton Tournament 167, *167*
Eleanor, Queen 61
Elizabeth I, Queen 40, 49, 89, 166–7
 seal **136**
Elizabeth of York 70
Ellis, Sir Henry 70, 148
Eltham Palace 80
Ely Cathedral **133**, 135
embroidery
 Bayeux Tapestry 123, 144, **150–3**
 from Archbishop Walter's tomb **208**, 209
 wall hanging **176**
Emlyn, Henry
 The Tomb of Edward VI at St George's Chapel, Windsor **106**
Enclosure Acts 109
Englefield, Sir Henry 67, 125, 145, 191
 A Description of the Picturesque Beauties, Antiquities and Geological Phenomena of the Isle of Wight 191
English Heritage 227, 228, 231
Environment Agency 253
Ethnological Society 129
Evans, John 185, 189, 204
 The 'New Prehistory' 185
Eworth, Hans
 Mary I **88–9**
Exeter Cathedral 145, 159
Extreme Archaeology (television series) 217

facial reconstruction 217, 218, 221, **223**
Fairholt, F. W. 168
 Meeting of the Society of Antiquaries of London at Somerset House **55**
Farley, Henry 42
Faulkner, Kate 174, 181
Faulkner, Lucy 181
Faussett, Revd Bryan 95, 98, 99, 109, 203
 Field diaries *95*, **100**
 Inventorium Sepulchrale 95
Faussett, Henry 98
Fenland 187
Ferris, Dr 112
Field of Cloth of Gold (1520) **77**, 144, **154–5**
Fisher, John, Bishop of Salisbury 244
flint tools *185*
 Abbeville handaxe 185, 187, **189**
 Gray's Inn Axe 18, **33**, 59
 Hoxne handaxes **188**
Fogge, Sir John 46
Folkes, Martin *53*, 54
forensic archaeology 97, 218, 221
Fox 186–7
France 165, 185, 207
François I, King of France 77, 155
Franks, Sir Augustus Wollaston 110, 113, 203
Frere, John 188
Frith, William Powell 167
Fry, Edmund 109
furniture
 Medieval-style settle **174**

Garrick, David 167
genealogies **20–1**
Gentleman's Magazine 80, 239
Geoffrey of Monmouth 17, 23, 24, 26, 232
 Historia Regum Britanniae 227, 228, 231
Geological Society of London 55, 187
geology 183, 185, **188–93**
George II, King 54, 64
George III, King 64, 67, 70, 130, 144
George IV, King 64
George V, King 64
Gere, Charles March 178
Germany 187
Gheeraerts, Marcus the Younger
 William Camden **40–1**
Gibbons, Edward
 Decline and Fall of the Roman Empire 165
Gibson, Edmund 39
Gibson, Thomas
 George Vertue **60**, 70
Gilchrist, Roberta 216
Gilpin, William 124
 Observations on the River Wye 134
 Observations on the Western Parts of England 238
Gipkyn, John
 Diptych of *Old St Paul's* **42–3**, 70
Girtin, Thomas 69, 93, 125, 135
 A Bronze Age Palstave and a Roman Bow Brooch **124**
 Ely Cathedral from the South-East **133**
 Stonehenge during a Thunderstorm **238**
Glastonbury 186, 187
Godwin, Harry 187
'Golden Barrow', Upton Lovell **102–3**
Gordon, Huntly Strathearn
 survey of Maiden Castle **198–9**
 theodolite and tripod **196**
Gothic style 163, 167, 173, 174
Gough, Richard 54, 97, 105, 107, 123, 124, 145
 Sepulchral Monuments in Great Britain **97**, *97*, 107, 124
Gowland, William 228, **248**
Grand Tour 54, 109
grave goods 221
 bishops and archbishops 97, *97*, 107, **208–13**
 Kingston Barrow **98**, 99, 100
 royal burials 97
Gravesend, Bishop Richard of *97*, **107**, 132
Gray 186
Gray's Inn Axe 18, **33**, 59
Greenwell, Canon
 British Barrows 186
Griggs, William 209
Grimm, Samuel Hieronymous 124
 Coronation Procession of Edward VI **158**

The Embarkation of Henry VIII at Dover 144, *144*
The Entrance to the Prison Chamber at Lincoln Cathedral **132**
Skeleton of Bishop Gravesend in Lincoln Cathedral **107**
Grosseteste, Bishop 97
Guildhall Library, London 203
Gwyn, Nell 167

Hadrian's Wall 38, 109, 113
Halesowen Abbey 73
Hallstatt 186
Hamilton, Sir William 70–1, 77
Hampshire Basin 191
handaxes *see* flint tools
Handley Hill, Wiltshire **194–5**
Harding, Phil 217, 218, **219**
Hardwicke, Philip Yorke, 2nd Earl of 144
Hare Island, Ireland 121
Harold II, King 150
Hastings, Battle of (1066) **150–3**
Hatton, Sir Christopher 38, 44, 46
 Book of Arms **45**
Havell, Robert 240
Hawkes, Jacquetta 225
Hawley, William 228
Hearne, Thomas 34
Heath, Charles 242
Heck, Christian 232
Heere, Lucas de
 View of Stonehenge 231, **234**
Hengist 232
Henry, Bishop of Blois 72
Henry II, King 77
Henry III, King 73, **146**, 148
Henry V, King 70
Henry VI, King 21, 84, **86**
Henry VII, King 70, 80, **87**, 119
Henry VIII, King 19, 34, 67, 70, 77, 89, **90–1**, 140, 144, *144*, 155, 156, 216, 218
Henry of Huntingdon 227, 228
heraldry 45, 70
Herbert, George 166
heritage protection 201–3
Hevnyngham, Thomas 139
Heyerdahl, Thor 216
Higden, Ranulph
 Polychronicon 23
Hill, Thomas
 Humfrey Wanley **56–7**, 70
Hilliard, Nicholas
 Elizabeth I, second Great Seal **136**
Hills, Catherine 216
History Channel 217
History Hunters (television series) 217
history painting 165, 167–9
Hoefnagel, Joris 234
Holbein, Hans 89, 91, 104
Hole, William 26
Holland, Philemon 40
Hollar, Wenceslaus 44, 173
 The Ruins of Osney Abbey 38
 William Dugdale 37
Hollis, Thomas 78
Holroys, Sir Charles 246
Hondius, Jodocus 28
Hooper, W. H. 178
Hope, William St John 144, 186–7, 201–2, 203, 209
Horizon (television series) 216
House Detectives (television series) 217
Howard, Hugh 59
Hoxne, Suffolk 71, **188**, 189
Hugh, Little Saint 107
Hume, David
 History of Great Britain 165
Hyett, W. H. 241

Illustrated London News 186, **202**, 203, 230
In Search of the Dark Ages (television programme) 216
Inchbold, John William
 Stonehenge from the East **246**
Industrial Revolution 93
Ingham, Sir Oliver de 139
Innocent III, Pope 73
Insall, Squadron-Leader Gilbert 249
Institute of Archaeology 196

Inventory of Henry VIII 70, **90**
Iron Age 185, 196, 228
 Glastonbury settlement 186
 Little Woodbury 187
 Maiden Castle 197
 sword and scabbard 110, **113**
 television recreation of 216, 218, **219**
Isle of Wight **190–1**
Italy 17–18, 54, 165
ITV 215

Jackson, Canon 80
James I, King *17*, 21, 37, 39, 42, 48, 78, 235, 236
Japhet 17
Jekyll, Joseph 70, 77
Jersey 126
John, King 73, 97
Johnstone, Paul 215, 216, 218, **219**
Jones, Inigo 39, 49
 Depiction of Stonehenge restored from *The most notable Antiquity of Great Britain, vulgarly called Stone-Heng* 231, **236**
Joseph of Arimathea 19
jousting cheque for a contest at the Field of Cloth of Gold **76–7**
Judd, J. W. 249

Kaye, Sir Richard 97, 107, 132
Kelly, Edward 24
Kelmscott Manor, Oxfordshire 169, 174, 175, 176, 178, 181
Kelmscott Press 169, **178–9**
Kempe, Alfred John 80
Kent 46, 95, 99, 101, 109
Kent's Cavern, Devon 187, 189
Kerrich, Revd Thomas *69*, 70, 91
 Collection of Royal Portraits **84–9**
Ketteringham, Norfolk 139
King, Edward 64, 143
King Edward VI Grammar School, Birmingham **173**
Kingston Barrow **98**, 99, 100
Kingston upon Thames 207
Kneller, Sir Godfrey 60
Knight, Dr Samuel 91
Kyngston, Felix
 Virginia Company Lottery 71, **78**

La Tène 186
Lambert, Aylmer 103
Lamp of Knowledge **61**, 70
Lansdowne, Marquess of 121
laser scanning, Stonehenge 253
Le Neve, Peter *53*, 54, **58–9**
leather armour **206**
Lee, James 49
Legge, Heneage 113
legislation, heritage protection 201–3
Leland, John 19, 24
 The Laboryouse Journey & Serche … for Englandes Antiquities 34
Leslie, Charles Robert 167
Lethieullier, Smart 75
Lewis, Carenza 217, 218, **219**
Lewis chessmen 110
Lincoln, Henry de Lacy, Earl of
 seal of **136**
Lincoln Cathedral 97, 107, 127, **132**
Lind, James 106
Lindesey, Robert de 75
Lindsey Psalter 69, **74–5**
Little Woodbury, Wiltshire 187
Living in the Past (television series) 216, 218, **219**
Lockyer, Sir Norman 247
Loggan, Daniel
 A Prospect of Stone-Henge … 231, **235**, 237
Lomberdale House, Derbyshire 96
London, archaeology 202–3, **204–7**
Lubbock, John 185–6, 195, 228
 Prehistoric Times 186
Lysons, Samuel
 The Excavation of Woodchester Roman Villa **130**
 The Great Pavement (the 'Orpheus Mosaic') at Woodchester Roman Villa **130–1**
Lyte, Thomas
 'King James I Enthroned' *16*
Lyttelton, Charles 69, 73, 75, 188

Macaulay, Thomas Babington 168–9
Magna Carta 69, **73**
Magnusson, Magnus 216
Maiden Castle, Dorset 186, *187*, **196–9**
Mansfield, 3rd Earl of 111, 121
Markland, John 71
Martin, St **79**
Mary, Queen of Scots 111
  Drawing of the ring of Mary, Queen of Scots **121**
Mary I, Queen 70, **88–9**, 140
Mary Rose 156, 216, 218, **219**
Maskelyne, N. S. 249
Maton, William 239
mauls, from Stonehenge **248**
Mayer, Joseph 98, 100
Meet the Ancestors (television series) 217, 218, **219**
Melville, H. S.
  Meeting of the Society of Antiquaries of London at Somerset House **55**
Memling, Hans 169
  St Ursula Reliquary 175
memorials, church 97
Merlin 228, 232
The Merton Head 71, *71*
Meyrick, Sir Samuel Rush
  Costume of the Original Inhabitants of the British Islands 231, **240**
  A Critical Enquiry into Antient Armour 165
  Specimens of Ancient Furniture drawn from Existing Authorities 166
Miles, William
  A Description of the Deverel Barrow 96
Milles, Dr Jeremiah 65
Milton, John 69, 165
Ministry of Works 251
mitre, from Archbishop Walter's tomb 209, **211**
Mitre Tavern, London 110
model of a passage-grave from Jersey **126**
Mold Cape 110
Mont St Helier 126
Moore, James 133, 134, 238
  Monastic Remains and Ancient Castles in England and Wales 124–5, 133
More, Thomas 86
Morris, Jane 169, 175, 176
Morris, Marshall, Faulkner & Co. 169, 170, 174, 176
Morris, May 174, 175
Morris, William 15, 169, 174, 175, 181, 202
  'Acanthus and Vine' Tapestry **177**
  embroidered wall hanging of St Catherine **176**
  News from Nowhere **178**
  The Works of Geoffrey Chaucer **178–9**
Museum of London 201, 221
'Museum of London Antiquities' 183, 203, **204**
Museum of London Archaeological Service (MoLAS) 222

Nash, Frederick 145
National Museum of Antiquities of Scotland 203
Neoclassicism 167
New Hall, Essex **140–1**
'New Prehistory' 185–6
Newton, Sir Isaac 53, 62
Nichols, John 119
The 1900 House (television programme) 216
Noah's flood 15, 17, 21, 33, 188, 189, 192
Nonsuch Palace 28
Norfolk, Duke of 67
Normandy, Dukes of 21
Norwich School 139
novels, historical 166, 170
Novum Inventorium Sepulchrale 98
Numismatic Society 204

Office of Works 228
Old Testament 22, 75
Ortelius, Abraham 24, 37, 40
Orton Scar, Westmorland 110, **118**
Osney Abbey, Oxfordshire *38*
Ouvry, Frederick 111
Oxford, Robert Harley, 1st Earl of 53, 56, 59, 90

Park Place, Henley-on-Thames 126
Parker, Matthew 37
Parkyns, George Isham 133
Parr, Catherine 90
paten, from Archbishop Walter's tomb 209, **213**
Peacock's Farm, Cambridgeshire 187
Peer Research Commission 187
Pentre Ifan, Pembrokeshire 128–9
Pepys, Samuel 235
Petrie, Sir William Matthew Flinders 228, 231
  Plan of Stonehenge **247**
Philip II, King of Spain 89
Phoenicians 17, 32
physical anthropology 221
Piggott, Stuart 228
pilgrim badge **206**
Pitt, Thomas 73
Pitt Rivers, Lieutenant-General Augustus 185, *186*, 187, 195, 196
  Cranborne Chase 186
Pitt Rivers Museum, Oxford 195
Pitts, Mike
  Stonehenge, Midsummer Day 230
Planché, James 168
Plas Newydd, Llangollen 129
Pococke, Dr Richard 66, 111
Portsmouth 144
Pownall, Governor 111
Pre-Raphaelite Brotherhood 169, 170, 175, 246
Prehistoric Society 187
Prestwich, Joseph 185, 189
Prince, William 235
prints
  Cathedral Series 143, 145
  historical prints 143, 144, 154–8
  print collection 69
  Vetusta Monumenta 143–6, 148
Prout, Samuel 241
Pryor, Francis
  Britain AD (television documentary) 217
  Britain BC (television documentary) 217
Pugin, A. C. 104, 173
Pugin, Augustus Welby 149, 167
  Contrasts 173
  design for the King's (later Victoria) Tower, Houses of Parliament, Westminster **172–3**
  design for large bosses of the library ceiling for King Edward VI Grammar School, Birmingham **173**
Pycroft, James Wallis 79
Pygot, Robert
  Four Scenes from the Life of St Etheldreda, Abbess of Ely in the Seventh Century 69

The Ra Expedition (television programme) 216
Rackett, Revd Thomas
  Stonehenge before 3 January 1797 from the west **239**
radio programmes 215
Radio Times *214*, 216
Rapin-Thoryas, Paul de
  Histoire de l'Angleterre 165
Rashleigh, John 116
Rashleigh, Philip 109, 116
Rashleigh family 110
Rawlinson, Richard 24
Red House, Bexley 174, 176
Renaissance 22, 165
Renfrew, Colin 216
Repton, J. A. 145
Restoration 39
Restoration (television series) 217
Reveley, Thomas 118
Reynolds, Sir Joshua 168
  Discourses 165
The Ribchester Helmet 93, 110, **114–15**
Richard I, King 209
Richard II, King 170
Richard III, King 70, **84**, 85, 87, 111, 119, 166
Richard III with a Broken Sword **85**
Richards, Julian 217, 218, **219**
Richardson, Jonathan
  Martin Folkes 53
Richmond, Duke of 66
Richmond Palace 28

Rickman, Thomas
  An Attempt to Discriminate the Styles of English Architecture 165–6
Riddell, Robert 111
Roach Smith, Charles 54, 109, 111, 183, *201*, 202–3
  Catalogue of the Museum of London Antiquities 203, **204**
  diary **205**
  Illustrations of Roman London 203
  Inventorium Sepulchrale 100
  portrait medal of **204**
Robertson, Scott 209
Robin's Coffee House, Chancery Lane 69
Robinson, Tony 216, 218, **219**
rock 'art', Stonehenge 253
Rokewode, John Gage 148
Roll Chronicle **20–1**
Romans 17–18, 196
  altars 109, **113**
  Bucklersbury Roman pavement, London 202, 203
  coins **204**
  hypocausts 17
  Ribchester Helmet 93, 110, **114–15**
  Woodchester Roman Villa **130–1**
Romantic movement 95, 97, 166, 169, 170
Rossetti, Dante Gabriel 169, 170
  medieval-style casket belonging to Jane Morris 169, **175**
Rossetti, W. M. 246
Rothley Temple 110
Rous, John 86
Rowlandson, Thomas
  An Antiquarian **66**
  Death and the Antiquaries 97, **104**, 105
  The Reception of a New Member in the Society of Antiquaries **65**, 66
Rowley, Thomas 65
Roy, William
  The Military Antiquities of the Romans in Great Britain 143
Royal Academy of Arts 51, 54, 144
Royal Academy Schools 165
Royal Society 51, 53, 54–5, 123, 189
  foundation of 18
  John Aubrey and 39, 49
  Philosophical Transactions 59, 127
Ruddock, John 79
Rundel and Bridge 121
Ruskin, John 137, 169, 242, 246

St Bride's, London 222
St George's Chapel, Windsor 106
St Mary's, Ashford 46
St Paul's Cathedral, London **42–3**, 44, 70
St Thomas Becket Casket 71, **76–7**
Salisbury Cathedral 125, **135**
Sammes, Aylett 17
  Britannia Antiqua Illustrata **32**
SAVE Britain's Heritage 201
Saxton, Christopher 28
  'Hertfordshire' from *An Atlas of England and Wales* 19
scabbard, Iron Age **113**
Scala Mundi 229, **232–3**
Schama, Simon
  A History of Britain 217
Scharf, George 70
Schnebbelie, Jacob 111, 123, 124, 125, 133
  Drawing of the Anglo-Saxon hoard from Trewhiddle, Cornwall **116–17**
  Waltham Cross from the Swans Inn Looking towards London **61**
Scott, Sir Walter 166
  The Antiquary 166, **170**
  The Border Antiquities of England and Scotland 170
The Scourge 67
seals **136–7**
Sebert, King 146
Secrets of the Dead (television series) 217
Sedgwick, William 45
  'The Tomb of John Donne' **44**
Selden, John 26, 38, 48
Seven Kings **80–1**
Seymour, Jane 90
Shafto, Robert 109
  Sketch of Bathhouse at Benwell 109, *109*

Shakespeare, William 165, 166–7, 227
Shannon, River 121
Sharpe, Philip Henry
  aerial photograph of Stonehenge **249**
Shaw, Henry 148, 166
Sheffield City Museum 96
Shepherd, G. 241
Sherwin, John and Charles
  The Encampment of the British Forces near Portsmouth **156–7**
shields, Bronze Age 125, **112**
Shirley, Sir Thomas 38, 45, 46
Siddal, Elizabeth (Lizzie) 169
  medieval-style casket belonging to Jane Morris **175**
Sidney, Sir Philip 37, 40
Silbury Hill, Wiltshire *214*, 216, 218, **219**
Silchester, Hampshire 187
silver, Anglo-Saxon **120**
skeletons 96, 221, **222**
skull
  craniometer **195**
  facial reconstruction 217, 218, 221, **223**
Sloane, Sir Hans 33, 59, 61
Smirke, Richard 69, 145
  The Adoration of the Magi **147**
  Drawing of a Viking gold armlet from Ireland **121**
Smirke, Robert 69
  The Excavation of Woodchester Roman Villa **130**
  The Great Pavement (the 'Orpheus Mosaic') at Woodchester Roman Villa **130–1**
Smith, Charles Hamilton
  Grand Conventional Festival of the Britons 231, **240**
Smith, William 185, 234
  Geological Map of Britain 191
  Section of the Strata through Hampshire and Wiltshire to Bath … **192–3**
Soane, Sir John 66
Society of Antiquaries of London
  accommodation 54–5
  antiquities collection 203
  Archaeologia 54, 55, 84, 102, 103, 110, 111, 116, 143
  ballot box **64**
  Cathedral Series 143, 145, 159–61
  draughtsmen 123–5
  establishment of 51, 53–4, 56
  Fellows 54, 55, 64
  heritage protection 201–3
  historical prints 54, 143, 144, 154–8
  incorporation 54
  Lamp of Knowledge **61**, 70, 143
  library 71
  manuscripts 69–70
  meetings 55, **56**, **67**
  membership 53–4, 55, **65**
  Minute Book 110, *110*, 111
  pictures and antiquities 70–1
  prints and drawings 69
  Proceedings 55
  Register of Admissions **64**
  The Royal Charter 54, **64**, 69
  and Stonehenge 228
  Vetusta Monumenta 54, 55, 61, 110, 121, 143–6, *143*, 148, 150, 203, 209
Society of Antiquaries of Newcastle upon Tyne 113
Society of Dilettanti 145
Society for the Protection of Ancient Buildings (SPAB) 169, 174, 202
Somerset House, London 54, *55*, 67, 70, 144
Somme Valley 189
Sorrell, Alan 231
  sketchbook drawing for the raising of a large sarsen megalith **251**
  Stonehenge: The Final Stage **250**
  Stonehenge: Raising the Sarsens **250**
  Stonehenge: Transport of the Sarsens **250**
South Kensington Museum 169
Speed, John 18
  Theatre of the Empire of Great Britain **28–9**
Spelman, Sir Henry 38, 48
Spenser, Edmund
  Faerie Queene 227
Spheroview 253
spur, medieval **118**

stained-glass windows **140–1**
Stanhope, Philip, Lord 31, 71
Stanton Drew, Somerset 230
Stapleton family 138
Star Carr, Yorkshire 187
Starkey, David
   Monarchy 217
Stokes, Margaret *143*, 144
stole, from Archbishop Walter's tomb **208**, 209
Stone, Nicholas 44
Stone Age 185, 186, 187, 228, 230–1
Stonehenge 17, 32, 39, 49, 53, 129, 218, **219** *230*, 225–31, **232–53**
   Stonehenge in its Landscape 227, 228, 231
   Stonehenge from a Scala Mundi **232–3**
   'Stonehenges' in a *Scala Mundi* 229, 232
Storie, Baillie John 112
Stothard, Charles 69, 80, 124, 144
   Drawings of ... the Effigy Commemorating Sir Oliver de Ingham ... **139**
   Monumental Effigies of Great Britain 123, 139, 170
   The Virtues Largesce and Deboneretè **148**
   'William the Conqueror' 150, **153**
   'William the Conqueror at Hastings' **150–1**
   'William is told that Harold is near' 150, **152**
Stothard, Robert T.
   drawing of an Anglo-Saxon silver hanging bowl **120**
Stow, John 24, 28, 34
   Survey of London 37
Street, George Edmund 174
Strutt, Joseph 168
   Complete View of the Dress and Habits of the People of England 170
Stukeley, William 53, 54, 61, **62**, 70, 77, 95, 110, 123, 143, 228, 231, 240
   Ground Plot of Avebury **63**
   'Peep into the Sancta Sanctorum' from *Stonehenge, a Temple restor'd to the British Druids* **237**
   Roman Antiquitys 110
Surviving the Iron Age (television programme) 216
Swinburne, Algernon Charles 246
sword, Iron Age **113**
Sympson, Thomas 127

Tacitus 17
Talbot, Revd Thomas Sugden
   rubbing of a lost brass at Ingham commemorating Ela Brews **138**
Talman, John 51, 53, 54, 56, 61, 69, 123, 143
   Shrine of St Edward the Confessor 123, 143
tapestry weaving **177**
Taylor, George Watson 241
Taylor, Tim 216
television programmes 183, 196, 215–19
Tennyson, Alfred, Lord 246
Tewkesbury Abbey 145
textiles
   Bayeux Tapestry 123, 144, **150–3**
   from Archbishop Walter's tomb **208**, 209
   tapestry **177**
   wall hanging **176**
Thames foreshore 203
theodolites **196**, 199
Thomas, H. H. 249
Thomas, John, Dean of Westminster 105
Thompson, Eric 216
Thurnham, John 96
tiles **180–1**
Time Fliers (television series) 217
Time Team (television series) 183, 216–17, 218, **219**
Time Team's Big Dig (television series) 217
The Times 199
Timewatch (television series) 216
Tintern Abbey, Monmouthshire **134**
Tollund Man 215
Tongue, Richard 124
   Chamber Tomb of Pentre Ifan near Newport, Pembrokeshire **128–9**
   Stonehenge 243
   The Tolmen at Constantine, Cornwall **128–9**
Topham, John 72, 90
torque, Viking **118**
Tower of London 166

Townley, Charles 114
Towton, Battle of (1461) 118
Tradescant, John 30
Trevisa, John de 23
Trewhiddle hoard 109, 110, 111, **116–17**
Troy 17, 19
Turner, Dawson 138
Turner, J. M. W. 93, 125, 136
   The Interior of Salisbury Cathedral, looking towards the North Transept **135**
   Stonehenge 227, 231, **242**
   Studies of Seals from Whalley Abbey **137**
   Tintern Abbey, the Transept **134**
Turnpike Commission 61
Two Men in a Trench (television series) 217

Underwood, Thomas Richard 123, 241
   drawing of pointed handaxe from Hoxne, Suffolk **188**
   drawing of the Ribchester helmet **114–15**
Upton Lovell, Wiltshire 102
Ussher, James, Archbishop of Armagh, 17, 38, 188
   The Annals of the World **22**, 38

Vallancey, Charles
   Collectanea de Rebus Hibernicis 121
Varley, Cornelius 125
Vergil, Polydore 23
   Anglica Historia 17
Vertue, George 54, 56, **60**, 69, 70, 124, 140, 143
   Excavation of a Hypocaust at Lincoln 17
   John Bagford **59**
   Peter Le Neve, Norroy King of Arms **58–9**
   Shrine of St Edward the Confessor 123
   'Vertue's Heads' 165
Vewicke, Maynard 87
Victoria and Albert Museum 169
Vikings 110, **118**, 121
Vikings! (television programme) 216
Virginia Company 71, **78**

Wace, Canon of Bayeux
   Roman de Brut 227, **232**
Wainwright, Geoffrey 249
Wales 231, 249
Wallis, Robert 242
Wallis, Rosa 144
Walpole, Horace
   The Castle of Otranto 166
Walter, Hubert, Archbishop of Canterbury 97, 144, 203, **208–13**
Waltham, John Olmius, 1st Lord 140
Waltham Cross 54, **61**
Wanley, Humfrey 51, 53, 54, **56–7**, 59, 69, 70
Wappers, Baron 168
Wars of the Roses 85, 87, 118, 119
Way, Albert 71
Webb, John
   Depiction of Stonehenge restored from *The most notable Antiquity of Great Britain, vulgarly called Stone-Heng* **236**
Webb, Philip 175
   medieval-style settle **174**
Webster, Thomas
   Geological Map and Sections of the Isle of Wight and the Adjacent Parts of Hampshire and Dorsetshire **190–1**
Wedlake, Bill 199
Weever, John 38
Wells Cathedral 145, **160–1**
Wessex 95, 96
Wessex Archaeology 227, 253
'Wessex master goldsmith' 103
Westminster, Palace of 93
   fire 149, 167
   House of Lords 149
   Painted Chamber 123, 144, 148, 149
   rebuilding 149, 167, 168, 173
   St Stephen's Chapel 145, 147, 149, 159
Westminster Abbey 104, 105, 144, 146
Whalley Abbey, Lancashire 137
Wharncliffe, Lord 110, 113
Whatman, James 155
Wheeler, Sir Mortimer 186, 187, *187*, 196–7, 215, 218, **219**
   Maiden Castle Dorset: Section and Plan ... **199**

Whitaker, Revd Thomas Dunham 137
   History of ... Whalley 125
White, Gilbert 132
White, John
   A Pictish Warrior 18
William IV, King 64
William the Conqueror, King 72, 150
Willis, Browne 127
Wiltshire 95–6, 102
Wiltshire Archaeological Museum, Devizes 96
Windham, Sir Joseph 145
Winton Domesday 70, **72**, 90
Witham bowl 93, 111, **120**
Wood, Anthony 38
Wood, Michael 216
Woodchester Roman Villa, Gloucestershire **130–1**
Woodhenge, Wiltshire 230, 249
Woodstock, Oxfordshire 166
Woolls, Charles
   The Barrow Diggers 96
Wor Barrow, Handley Downs *186*, 195
Worde, Wynkyn de
   The Cronycle of Englonde and the Descrypcyon of Englonde 17, **23**
World Museum Liverpool 95
Worsaae, Jens 185

Benefactors of the Royal Academy of Arts

ROYAL ACADEMY TRUST
Major Benefactors
The Trustees of the Royal Academy Trust are grateful to all its donors for their continued loyalty and generosity. They would like to extend their thanks to all those who have made a significant commitment, past and present, to the galleries, the exhibitions, the conservation of the Permanent Collection, the Library collections, the Royal Academy Schools, the education programme and other specific appeals.

HM The Queen
The 29th May 1961 Charitable Trust
Barclays Bank
BAT Industries plc
The late Tom Bendhem
The late Brenda M Benwell-Lejeune
John Frye Bourne
British Telecom
John and Susan Burns
Mr Raymond M Burton CBE
Sir Trevor Chinn CVO and Lady Chinn
The Trustees of the Clore Foundation
The John S Cohen Foundation
Sir Harry and Lady Djangoly
The Dulverton Trust
Alfred Dunhill Limited
The John Ellerman Foundation
The Eranda Foundation
Ernst & Young
Esso UK plc
The Foundation for Sports and the Arts
Friends of the Royal Academy
Jacqueline and Michael Gee
Glaxo Holdings plc
Diane and Guilford Glazer
Mr and Mrs Jack Goldhill
Maurice and Laurence Goldman
Mr and Mrs Jocelin Harris
The Philip and Pauline Harris Charitable Trust
The Charles Hayward Foundation
Heritage Lottery Fund
IBM United Kingdom Limited
The Idlewild Trust
The JP Jacobs Charitable Trust
Lord and Lady Jacobs
The Japan Foundation
Gabrielle Jungels-Winkler Foundation
Mr and Mrs Donald Kahn
The Kresge Foundation
The Samuel H Kress Foundation
The Kirby Laing Foundation
The Lankelly Foundation
The late Mr John S Latsis
The Leverhulme Trust
Lex Service plc
The Linbury Trust
Sir Sydney Lipworth QC and Lady Lipworth
John Lyons Charity
John Madejski OBE DL
Her Majesty's Government
The Manifold Trust
Marks and Spencer
Ronald and Rita McAulay
McKinsey and Company Inc
The Mercers' Company
The Monument Trust
The Henry Moore Foundation
The Moorgate Trust Fund
Mr and Mrs Minoru Mori
Robin Heller Moss
Museums and Galleries Improvement Fund
National Westminster Bank
Stavros S Niarchos
The Peacock Trust
The Pennycress Trust
PF Charitable Trust
The Pidem Fund
The Pilgrim Trust
The Edith and Ferdinand Porjes Trust
John Porter Charitable Trust
The Porter Foundation
Rio Tinto plc
John A Roberts FRIBA
Virginia Robertson
The Ronson Foundation
The Rose Foundation

Rothmans International plc
Dame Jillian Sackler DBE
Jillian and Arthur M Sackler
Mrs Jean Sainsbury
The Saison Foundation
The Basil Samuel Charitable Trust
Mrs Coral Samuel CBE
Sea Containers Ltd
Shell UK Limited
Miss Dasha Shenkman
William and Maureen Shenkman
The Archie Sherman Charitable Trust
Sir Hugh Sykes DL
Sir Anthony and Lady Tennant
Ware and Edythe Travelstead
The Trusthouse Charitable Foundation
The Douglas Turner Trust
Unilever plc
The Weldon UK Charitable Trust
The Welton Foundation
The Weston Family
The Malcolm Hewitt Wiener Foundation
The Maurice Wohl Charitable Foundation
The Wolfson Foundation
and others who wish to remain anonymous

PATRONS
In recent years the Royal Academy has established several Patrons Groups to encourage the regular and committed support of individuals who believe in the Royal Academy's mission to promote the widest possible understanding and enjoyment of the visual arts. The Royal Academy is delighted to thank all its Patrons for generously supporting the following areas over the past year: exhibitions, education, the RA Schools, the Permanent Collection and Library, Anglo-American initiatives and for assisting in the general upkeep of the Academy, with donations of £1,250 and more.

Secretary's Circle
The Lillian Jean Kaplan Foundation
Mrs Coral Samuel CBE

Platinum Patrons
James Alexandre
Konrad O Bernheimer
Mr and Mrs William Brake
Mr and Mrs John Coombe
Mr and Mrs Patrick Doherty
Giuseppe Eskenazi
Mrs Helena Frost
Mr and Mrs Jack Goldhill
Mr D B Gottesman
Richard Green
Johnny van Haeften
Mrs Marina Hobson MBE
Lady Kaye
Salomon Lilian
Mr and Mrs Eyck van Otterloo
Simon and Virginia Robertson
Dame Jillian Sackler DBE
Mr and Mrs David Shalit
Richard and Victoria Sharp

Gold Patrons
The 29th May 1961 Charitable Trust
Miss B A Battersby
William and Judith Bollinger
Alain and Marie Boublil
Ivor Braka
Dr Christopher Brown
Mr Raymond M Burton CBE
CHK Charities Limited
Lawton Wehle Fitt
The Flow Foundation
Foster and Partners
Jacqueline and Michael Gee
David and Maggi Gordon
Lady Gosling
Sir Ronald Grierson
Charles and Kaaren Hale
Mrs Sue Hammerson
Michael and Morven Heller
Sir Joseph Hotung

Mrs Gabrielle Jungels-Winkler
Mr and Mrs Donald P Kahn
The Kirby Laing Foundation
Mrs Aboudi Kosta
The Leche Trust
The Leverhulme Trust
Sir Sydney Lipworth QC and Lady Lipworth
Mr and Mrs Ronald Lubner
John Lyon's Charity
John Madejski
Material World Charitable Foundation
The Paul Mellon Centre for Studies in British Art
Professor and Mrs Anthony Mellows
Mr and Mrs Tom Montague Meyer (Fleur Cowles)
JP Morgan Fleming Foundation
Elaine and David Nordby
Pidem Fund
Mrs Jenny Halpern Prince
The Rayne Foundation
Mr John A Roberts FRIBA
Richard and Veronica Simmons
Mrs Roama L Spears
The Steel Charitable Trust
David Tang
Sir Anthony and Lady Tennant
Jane and Anthony Weldon

Silver Patrons
Mr and Mrs Gerald Acher
Mrs Denise Adeane
Mrs Manucher Azmudeh
Mrs Gary Brass
The Peter Boizot Foundation
Mrs Elie Brihi
Mr and Mrs Charles H Brown
Mr and Mrs P G H Cadbury
The Late Lynn Chadwick CBE RA
Sir Charles and Lady Chadwyck-Healey
Sir Trevor and Lady Chinn
John C L Cox CBE
Stephen and Marion Cox
The de Laszlo Foundation
Benita and Gerald Fogel
Mr and Mrs Eric Franck
Jacqueline and Jonathan Gestetner
Patricia and John Glasswell
Alastair and Sarah Ross Goobey
The Headley Trust
Mr and Mrs Alan Hobart
Mr and Mrs Jon Hunt
Mr and Mrs Fred Johnston
Mr and Mrs S Kahan
Mr and Mrs Joseph Karaviotis
Mr and Mrs Nathan Kirsh
The Kobler Trust
Sir Christopher and Lady Lewinton
Mr Jonathon E Lyons
Fiona Mactaggart MP
The Lord Marks of Broughton
R C Martin
Mr Donald A Moore
The Mulberry Trust
Mr and Mrs D J Peacock
David Pike
Professor Richard Portes CBE
The Audrey Sacher Charitable Trust
Mr and Mrs Kevin Senior
Sally and Clive Sherling
Mr and Mrs Andrew Shrager
Mrs Elyane Stilling
Sir James and Lady Spooner
John Tackaberry and Kate Jones
Group Captain James Tait

Bronze Patrons
Agnew's
Steve and Jan Ahearne
Mrs Mira-Lisa Ahlstrom
Mr Derrill Allatt
Mr Peter Allinson
ALM London
Mr Paul Arditti
Artvest TM Limited
Edgar Astaire
The Atlas Fund
Aurelius Charitable Trust

Mrs Leslie Bacon
Jane Barker
Mrs Yvonne Barlow
Mrs Jill Barrington
Stephen Barry Charitable Settlement
James M Bartos
The Duke of Beaufort
Wendy Becker Payton
Mrs Frederick Bienstock
Elizabeth V Blackadder OBE RSA RA
Mark and Lucy Blair
Sir Victor and Lady Blank
Mr and Mrs Michael Bradley
Jeremy Brown
Mrs Alan Campbell-Johnson
Mr F A A Carnwath CBE
Jean and Eric Cass
The Chapman Charitable Trust
Mr and Mrs George Coelho
Denise Cohen Charitable Trust
David J and Jennifer A Cooke
Mr and Mrs Sidney Corob
Thomas Corrigan OBE
Julian Darley and Helga Sands
The Countess of Dartmouth
Mr Keith Day and Mr Peter Sheppard
Peter and Kate De Haan
The Bellinger Donnay Charitable Trust
Dr Anne Dornhorst
Lord Douro
Sir Philip Dowson PPRA and Lady Dowson
John Drummond FCSD HON DES RCA
Mr and Mrs Maurice Dwek
Dr and Mrs D Dymond
Miss Jayne Edwardes
Lord and Lady Egremont
Mary Fedden RA
Bryan Ferry
Mrs Donatella Flick
Mr and Mrs Edwin H Fox
Mr Monty Freedman
Arnold Fulton
The David Gill Memorial Fund
Michael Godbee
Mrs Alexia Goethe
Nicholas and Judith Goodison
Piers and Rosie Gough
David and Lesley Haynes
Robin Heller Moss
Mr and Mrs Robert A Hefner III
Mr and Mrs Christoph Henkel
Mr and Mrs Jonathan Hindle
Anne Holmes-Drewry
Mrs Sue Howes and Mr Greg Dyke
Mrs Pauline Hyde
Simone Hyman
S Isern-Feliu
Sir Martin and Lady Jacomb
Mrs Ian Jay
Harold and Valerie Joels
Fiona Johnstone
Joseph Strong Frazer Trust
Dr Elisabeth Kehoe
Mr D H Killick
Mr and Mrs James Kirkman
Norman A Kurland and Deborah A David
Joan H Lavender
Mr George Lengvari and Mrs Inez Lengvari
Lady Lever
Mrs Rosemarie Lieberman
Miss R Lomax-Simpson
The Marquess of Lothian
Mr and Mrs Mark Loveday
Mr and Mrs Henry Lumley
Sally and Donald Main
Mr and Mrs Eskandar Maleki
Mr and Mrs Michael (RA) and José Manser
Mr Marcus Margulies
Mr David Marks and Ms Nada Chelhot
Marsh Christian Trust
Mr and Mrs Stephen Mather
Miss Jane McAusland
Christopher and Clare McCann
Gillian McIntosh
Andrew and Judith McKinna
Mr Zvi Meitar
Lakshman Menon and Darren Rickards
The Mercers' Company

The Millichope Foundation
James Moores
Mr and Mrs Alan Morgan
Mr and Mrs Carl Anton Muller
Dr Ann Naylor
North Street Trust
Mrs Elin Odfjell
Mr and Mrs Simon Oliver
Mr Michael Palin
Mr and Mrs Vincenzo Palladino
John H Pattisson
The Pennycress Trust
Mr and Mrs A Perloff
Mr Philip Perry
R John Mullis
Eve and Godfrey Pilkington
Mr and Mrs Anthony Pitt-Rivers
Kathleen Murray and William Plapinger
John Porter Charitable Trust
Miss Victoria Provis
John and Anne Raisman
Lord and Lady Ramsbotham
Jane and Graham Reddish
Mr and Mrs Ian Rosenberg
Lady (Robert) Sainsbury
H M Sassoon Charitable Trust
The Schneer Foundation Inc
Carol Sellars
Mr and Mrs Marcus Setchell
Dr and Mrs Agustin Sevilla
Dr Lewis Sevitt
The Countess of Shaftesbury
Mrs Stella Shawzin
Alan and Marianna Simpson
Mr and Mrs Mark Franklin Slaughter
Brian D Smith
Mr and Mrs David T Smith
The Spencer Charitable Trust
The Peter Storrs Trust
Summers Art Gallery (Mrs J K M Bentley)
Mrs D Susman
The Swan Trust
Sir Hugh Sykes DL
Mrs Mark Tapley
Lord and Lady Taylor
Tiffany & Co
Miss M L Ulfane
Mrs Catherine Vlasto
Edna and Willard Weiss
Anthony and Rachel Williams
Manuela and Iwan Wirth
The Rt Hon Lord and Lady Young
    of Graffham
Mr and Mrs Michael Zilkha
and others who wish to remain anonymous

BENJAMIN WEST GROUP DONORS
Chairman
Lady Judge

Gold Patrons
Lady J Lloyd Adamson
Mrs Deborah L Brice
Lady Judge
Sir Paul Judge

Silver Patrons
Ms Ruth Anderson
Mrs Adrian Bowden
Mr and Mrs Paul Collins
Brian and Susan Dickie
Dr Yvonne von Egidy-Winkler and
    Mr Peter Philip Winkler
Nigel Little: Canaccordadams
Lady Rebecca Purves
Frank and Anne Sixt
Frederick and Kathryn Uhde
Mr and Mrs John D Winter

Bronze Patrons
Michael and Barbara Anderson
Mrs Alan Artus
Mr Oren Beeri and Mrs Michal Berkner
Tom and Diane Berger
Robert and Michele Bowman
Wendy Brooks and Tim Medland
Mrs J Morgan Callagy

Mr Joseph A Field
Cyril and Christine Freedman
Madeleine Hodgkin
Alistair Johnston and Christina Nijman
Mrs Richard Kaufman
Sarah H Ketterer
Mr and Mrs H A Lamotte
Charles G Lubar
Neil Osborn and Holly Smith
Mike and Martha Pedersen
Mr and Mrs K M Rubie
Carole Turner Record
Mr and Mrs Philip Renaud
Mr and Mrs Justus Roele
Sylvia Scheuer
Mr and Mrs Thomas Schoch
Ms Tara Stack
Carl Stewart
John and Sheila Stoller
Mrs Betty Thayer
Mr and Mrs Julian Treger
Michael and Yvonne Uva
Mary Wolridge
Sir Robert Worcester
and others who wish to remain anonymous

SCHOOLS PATRONS GROUP
Chairman
John Entwistle OBE DL

Gold Patrons
The Brown Foundation, Inc, Houston
The Ernest Cook Trust
D'Oyly Carte Charitable Trust
The Gilbert & Eileen Edgar Foundation
The Eranda Foundation
Mr and Mrs Jack Goldhill
The David Lean Foundation
The Leverhulme Trust
Paul and Alison Myners
Newby Trust Limited
Edith and Ferdinand Porjes Charitable Trust
Paul Smith and Pauline Denyer-Smith
Oliver Stanley Charitable Trust
The Starr Foundation
Sir Siegmund Warburg's Voluntary Settlement
The Harold Hyam Wingate Foundation

Silver Patrons
Lord and Lady Aldington
The Celia Walker Art Foundation
Mr and Mrs Ian Ferguson
Philip Marsden Family Trust
The Radcliffe Trust
The Stanley Picker Trust

Bronze Patrons
Mrs Elizabeth Alston
Lee Bakirgian Family Trust
Mark and Lucy Blair
The Charlotte Bonham-Carter Charitable Trust
The Selina Chenevière Foundation
May Cristea Award
The Delfont Foundation
John Entwistle OBE DL
Mr and Mrs John A Gardiner
Professor and Mrs Ken Howard RA
The Lark Trust
Mr Colin Lees-Millais FRICS
Mrs Diana Morgenthau
Pickett
Peter Rice Esq
Anthony and Sally Salz
Mr and Mrs Robert Lee Sterling, Jr
Roger Taylor
Mr and Mrs Denis Tinsley
Mr Ray Treen
The Worshipful Company of Painter-Stainers
and others who wish to remain anonymous

CONTEMPORARY PATRONS GROUP
Chairman
Susie Allen

Mrs Alan Artus
Susan and John Burns

Dr Elaine C Buck
Debbie Carslaw
Dania Debs-Sakka
Chris and Angie Drake
Mr John Eldridge
Lawton Wehle Fitt
Melanie C Gerlis
Marcia and Michael Green
Mrs Robin Hambro
Miss Pauline Karpidas
Mrs Mireille Masri
Sharon Maurice
Marion and Guy Naggar
Angela Nikolakopoulou
Libby Paskin and Daniel Goldring
Maria N Peacock
Ramzy and Maya Rasamny
Mr Andres Recoder and Mrs Isabelle Schiavi
John Tackaberry and Kate Jones
Britt Tidelius
Mr and Mrs John D Winter
Mary Wolridge
and others who wish to remain anonymous

AMERICAN ASSOCIATES OF THE ROYAL
ACADEMY TRUST
Burlington House Trust
Mr and Mrs James C Slaughter

Benjamin West Society
Mrs Walter H Annenberg OBE
Mr Francis Finlay
Mrs Nancy B Negley

Benefactors
Ms Susan L Baker and Mr Michael R Lynch
Mrs Deborah Loeb Brice
Mrs Edmond J Safra
The Honorable John C Whitehead
Mr and Mrs Frederick B Whittemore

Sponsors
Mrs Russell B Aitken
Ms Britt Allcroft
Mr and Mrs Stephen D Bechtel Jr
Mrs Katherine D Findlay
Mrs Henry J Heinz II
Mr David Hockney RA
Mr Arthur L Loeb
Mr Hamish Maxwell
Mrs Lucy F McGrath
Ms Diane A Nixon
Mr Arthur O Sulzberger and Ms Allison
    S Cowles
Mr and Mrs Vernon Taylor Jr

Patrons
Ms Helen Harting Abell
Mr and Mrs Steven Ausnit
Mr and Mrs E William Aylward
Mr Donald A Best
Mrs Edgar H Brenner
Mr and Mrs Henry W Breyer III
Mrs Mildred C Brinn
Mr Douglas F Bushnell and Ms Betty Johnson
Mrs Mary Sharp Cronson
Mrs Catherine G Curran
Anne S Davidson
Ms Zita Davisson
Mr and Mrs Beverley C Duer
Mrs June Dyson
Mr Jonathan D Farkas
Mr and Mrs John L Fiorilla
Mr and Mrs Lawrence S Friedland
Mr and Mrs Eugene Goldberg
Dr Bruce C Horten
The Honorable and Mrs W Eugene Johnston
Mr William W Karatz
Mr and Mrs Gary A Kraut
The Honorable and Mrs Philip Lader
Mrs Katherine K Lawrence
Mr and Mrs Daniel Leab
Mrs Helen Little
Ms Marcia V Mayo
Ms Barbara T Missett
The Honorable and Mrs Willliam A Nitze
Mr and Mrs Chips C Page

Mrs R L Peterson
Mr and Mrs Jeffrey Pettit
The Honorable and Mrs Leon B Polsky
Lady Renwick
Mr and Mrs Peter M Sacerdote
Mrs Louisa Stude Sarofim
Mrs Frances G Scaife
Ms Jan B Scholes
Mr and Mrs Stanley De Forest Scott
Mr and Mrs Albert H Small
Mr and Mrs Morton I Sosland
Mrs Frederick M Stafford
Mr and Mrs Stephen Stamas
Ms Joan N Stern
Ms Brenda Neubauer Straus
Ms Elizabeth F Stribling and Mr Guy Robinson
Mr Martin J Sullivan
Ms Britt Tidelius
Mr and Mrs Lewis Townsend
Mr and Mrs George White
Dr and Mrs Robert D Wickham
Mr Robert W Wilson

Corporate and Foundation Support
AIG
American Express
The Brown Foundation
General Atlantic
General Motors
GlaxoSmithKline
The Horace W Goldsmith Foundation
Henry Luce Foundation
Sony

CORPORATE MEMBERS OF THE ROYAL
ACADEMY OF ARTS
Launched in 1988, the Royal Academy's
Corporate Membership Scheme has proved
highly successful. Corporate Membership offers
benefits for staff, clients and community
partners and access to the Academy's facilities
and resources. The outstanding support we
receive from companies via the scheme is vital
to the continuing success of the Academy and
we thank all Members for their valuable support
and continued enthusiasm.

Premier Level Members
CB Richard Ellis
Deutsche Bank AG
Ernst & Young LLP
GlaxoSmithKline plc
Goldman Sachs International
Hay Group
HSBC plc
Intercontinental London Park Lane
King Sturge
LECG Ltd
Morgan Stanley
Northern Trust Corporation
Rio Tinto plc
Schroders plc
Smith and Williamson
Sotheby's
Standard Chartered

Corporate Members
All Nippon Airways
Arcadia Group plc
A. T. Kearney
Bank of America
Bear, Stearns International Ltd
Bibendum Wine Limited
BNP Paribas
The Boston Consulting Group
Bovis Lend Lease Limited
British American Business Inc.
British American Tobacco
The British Land Company plc
Calyon
Cantor Fitzgerald
Capital International Limited
Christie's
Citigroup
Clifford Chance
Concordia Advisors
Curzon Partnership LLP

Diageo plc
Doll
F & C Asset Management plc
Gallery 88
GAM
H & M
Heidrick & Struggles
Insight Investment
ITV plc
John Lewis Partnership
JPMorgan
KPMG
Lazard
Lehman Brothers
Linklaters
London College of Fashion
L'Oréal UK
Man Group plc
Mizuho International plc
Momart Limited
The National Magazine Company Ltd
Nedrailways
Norton Rose
Novo Nordisk
Osborne Samuel LLP
Pentland Group plc
The Royal Bank of Scotland
The Royal Society of Chemistry
Russell Reynolds
SG
Slaughter & May
Thinc Destini
Timothy Sammons
Troika
Trowers & Hamlins
Unilever UK Limited
Veredus Executive Resourcing
Weil, Gotschal & Manges

SPONSORS OF PAST EXHIBITIONS
The President and Council of the Royal
Academy would like to thank the following
sponsors and benefactors for their generous
support of major exhibitions during the last
ten years:

2007
239th Summer Exhibition
  Insight Investment
Impressionists by the Sea
  Farrow & Ball
Premiums and RA Schools Show
  Mizuho International plc
RA Outreach Programme
  Deutsche Bank AG
The Unknown Monet
  Bank of America

2006
238th Summer Exhibition
  Insight Investment
Chola: Sacred Bronzes of Southern India
  Travel Partner: Cox & Kings
Premiums and RA Schools Show
  Mizuho International plc
RA Outreach Programme
  Deutsche Bank AG
Rodin
  Ernst & Young

2005
China: The Three Emperors, 1662–1795
  Goldman Sachs International
Impressionism Abroad: Boston and French Painting
  Fidelity Foundation
Matisse, His Art and His Textiles:
  The Fabric of Dreams
  Farrow & Ball
Premiums and RA Schools Show
  The Guardian
  Mizuho International plc
Turks: A Journey of a Thousand Years, 600–1600
  Akkök Group of Companies
  Aygaz
  Corus
  Garanti Bank
  Lassa Tyres

2004
236th Summer Exhibition
  A. T. Kearney
Ancient Art to Post-Impressionism: Masterpieces
from the Ny Carlsberg Glyptotek, Copenhagen
  Carlsberg UK Ltd
  Danske Bank
  Novo Nordisk
The Art of Philip Guston (1913–1980)
  American Associates of the Royal
    Academy Trust
The Art of William Nicholson
  RA Exhibition Patrons Group
Vuillard: From Post-Impressionist to Modern Master
  RA Exhibition Patrons Group

2003
235th Summer Exhibition
  A. T. Kearney
Ernst Ludwig Kirchner: The Dresden and Berlin Years
  RA Exhibition Patrons Group
Giorgio Armani: A Retrospective
  American Express
  Mercedes-Benz
Illuminating the Renaissance: The Triumph of Flemish
Manuscript Painting in Europe
  American Associates of the Royal
    Academy Trust
  Virginia and Simon Robertson
Masterpieces from Dresden
  ABN AMRO
  Classic FM
Premiums and RA Schools Show
  Walker Morris
Pre-Raphaelite and Other Masters:
  The Andrew Lloyd Webber Collection
  Christie's
  Classic FM
  UBS Wealth Management

2002
234th Summer Exhibition
  A. T. Kearney
Aztecs
  British American Tobacco
  Mexico Tourism Board
  Pemex
  Virginia and Simon Robertson
Masters of Colour: Derain to Kandinsky.
Masterpieces from The Merzbacher Collection
  Classic FM
Premiums and RA Schools Show
  Debenhams Retail plc
*RA Outreach Programme**
  Yakult UK Ltd
Return of the Buddha: The Qingzhou Discoveries
  RA Exhibition Patrons Group

2001
233rd Summer Exhibition
  A. T. Kearney
Botticelli's Dante: The Drawings for Dante's
  Divine Comedy
  RA Exhibition Patrons Group
The Dawn of the Floating World (1650–1765).
  Early Ukiyo-e Treasures from the Museum of
  Fine Arts, Boston
  Fidelity Foundation
Forty Years in Print: The Curwen Studio
  and Royal Academicians
  Game International Limited
Frank Auerbach, Paintings and Drawings 1954–2001
  International Asset Management
Ingres to Matisse: Masterpieces of French Painting
  Barclays
Paris: Capital of the Arts 1900–1968
  BBC Radio 3
  Merrill Lynch
Premiums and RA Schools Show
  Debenhams Retail plc
*RA Outreach Programme**
  Yakult UK Ltd
Rembrandt's Women
  Reed Elsevier plc

2000
1900: Art at the Crossroads
  Cantor Fitzgerald
  The Daily Telegraph
232nd Summer Exhibition
  A. T. Kearney
Apocalypse: Beauty and Horror in Contemporary Art
  Eyestorm
  The Independent
  Time Out
Chardin 1699–1779
  RA Exhibition Patrons Group
The Genius of Rome 1592–1623
  Credit Suisse First Boston
Premiums and RA Schools Show
  Debenhams Retail plc
*RA Outreach Programme**
  Yakult UK Ltd
The Scottish Colourists 1900–1930
  Chase Fleming Asset Management

1999
231st Summer Exhibition
  A. T. Kearney
John Hoyland
  Donald and Jeanne Kahn
John Soane, Architect: Master of Space and Light
  Country Life
  Ibstock Building Products Ltd
Kandinsky
  RA Exhibition Patrons Group
Life? or Theatre? The Work of Charlotte Salomon
  The Jacqueline and Michael Gee
    Charitable Trust
Monet in the Twentieth Century
  Ernst & Young
Premiums
  Debenhams Retail plc
  The Royal Bank of Scotland
RA Schools Show
  Debenhams Retail plc
*RA Outreach Programme**
  Yakult UK Ltd
Van Dyck 1599–1641
  Reed Elsevier plc

1998
230th Summer Exhibition
  Diageo plc
Chagall: Love and the Stage
  RA Exhibition Patrons Group
Picasso: Painter and Sculptor in Clay
  Goldman Sachs International
Premiums and RA Schools Show
  The Royal Bank of Scotland
*RA Outreach Programme**
  Yakult UK Ltd
Tadao Ando: Master of Minimalism
  The Drue Heinz Trust

* Recipients of a Pairing Scheme Award,
managed by Arts + Business. Arts + Business
is funded by the Arts Council of England and
the Department for Culture, Media and Sport

OTHER SPONSORS
Sponsors of events, publications and other
items in the past five years:
Carlisle Group plc
Country Life
Derwent Valley Holdings plc
Dresdner Kleinwort Wasserstein
Foster and Partners
Goldman Sachs International
Gome International
Gucci Group
Rob van Helden
IBJ International plc
John Doyle Construction
Martin Krajewski
Marks & Spencer
Michael Hopkins & Partners
Morgan Stanley Dean Witter
Prada
Radisson Edwardian Hotels
Richard and Ruth Rogers
Strutt & Parker